CONTENTS

GENERAL INTRODUCTION

The Ancient Christian Texts series (hereafter ACT) presents the full text of ancient Christian commentaries on Scripture that have remained so unnoticed that they have not yet been translated into English.

The patristic period (A.D. 95-750) is the time of the fathers of the church, when the exegesis of Scripture texts was in its primitive formation. This period spans from Clement of Rome to John of Damascus, embracing seven centuries of biblical interpretation, from the end of the New Testament to the mid-eighth century, including the Venerable Bede.

This series extends but does not reduplicate texts of the Ancient Christian Commentary on Scripture (ACCS). It presents full-length translations of texts that appear only as brief extracts in the ACCS. The ACCS began years ago, authorizing full-length translations of key patristic texts on Scripture in order to provide fresh sources of valuable commentary that previously was not available in English. It is from these translations that the ACT Series has emerged.

A multiyear project such as this requires a well-defined objective. The task is straightforward: *to introduce full-length translations of key texts of early Christian teaching homilies and commentaries on a particular book of Scripture.* These are seminal documents that have decisively shaped the entire subsequent history of biblical exegesis, but in our time have been largely ignored.

To carry out this mission each volume of the ACT series has four aspirations:

1. To show the approach of one of the early Christian writers in dealing with the problems of understanding, reading and conveying the meaning of a particular book of Scripture.

2. To make more fully available the whole argument of the ancient Christian interpreter of Scripture to all who wish to think with the early church about a particular canonical text.

3. To broaden the base of biblical studies, Christian teaching and preaching to include classical Christian exegesis.

4. To stimulate Christian historical, biblical, theological and pastoral scholarship toward deeper inquiry into early classic practitioners of scriptural interpretation.

For Whom Is This Series Designed?

We have selected and translated these texts primarily for general and nonprofessional use by an audience that studies the Bible regularly.

In varied cultural settings around the world, contemporary readers are asking how they might grasp the meaning of sacred texts under the instruction of the great minds of the ancient church. They often study books of the Bible, verse by verse, book by book, in groups and workshops, sometimes with a modern commentary in hand. But many who study the Bible intensively hunger to have available to them as well the thoughts of some reliable classic Christian commentator on this same text. This series will give the modern commentators a classical text for comparison and amplification. Readers will judge for themselves as to how valuable or complementary are their insights and guidance.

The classic texts we are translating were originally written for anyone (lay or clergy, believers and seekers) who would wish to reflect and meditate with the great minds of the early church. They sought to illuminate the plain sense, theological wisdom, and moral and spiritual meaning of an individual book of Scripture. They were not written for an academic audience, but for a community of faith shaped by the sacred text.

Yet in serving this general audience, the editors remain determined not to neglect the rigorous requirements and needs of academic readers who until recently have had few full translations available to them in the history of exegesis. So this series is designed also to serve public libraries, universities, academic classes, homiletic preparation and historical interests worldwide in Christian scholarship and interpretation.

Hence our expected audience is not limited to the highly technical and specialized scholarly field of patristic studies, with its strong bent toward detailed word studies and explorations of cultural contexts. Though all of our editors and translators are patristic and linguistic scholars, they also are scholars who search for the meanings and implications of the texts. The audience is not primarily the university scholar concentrating on the study of the history of the transmission of the text or those with highly focused interests in textual morphology or historical-critical issues. If we succeed in serving our wider readers practically and well, we hope to serve as well college and seminary courses in Bible, church history, historical theology, hermeneutics and homiletics. These texts have not until now been available to these classes.

Readiness for Classic Spiritual Formation

Today global Christians are being steadily drawn toward these biblical and patristic sources for daily meditation and spiritual formation. They are on the outlook for primary classic sources of spiritual formation and biblical interpretation, presented in accessible form and grounded in reliable scholarship.

These crucial texts have had an extended epoch of sustained influence on Scripture interpretation, but virtually no influence in the modern period. They also deserve a hearing among modern readers and scholars. There is a growing awareness of the speculative excesses and spiritual and homiletic limitations of much post-Enlightenment criticism. Meanwhile the motifs, methods and approaches of ancient exegetes have remained unfamiliar not only to historians but to otherwise highly literate biblical scholars, trained exhaustively in the methods of historical and scientific criticism.

It is ironic that our times, which claim to be so fully furnished with historical insight and research methods, have neglected these texts more than scholars in previous centuries who could read them in their original languages.

This series provides indisputable evidence of the modern neglect of classic Christian exegesis: it remains a fact that extensive and once authoritative classic commentaries on Scripture still remain untranslated into any modern language. Even in China such a high level of neglect has not befallen classic Buddhist, Taoist and Confucian commentaries.

Ecumenical Scholarship

This series, like its two companion series, the ACCS and Ancient Christian Doctrine (ACD), are expressions of unceasing ecumenical efforts that have enjoyed the wide cooperation of distinguished scholars of many differing academic communities. Under this classic textual umbrella, it has brought together in common spirit Christians who have long distanced themselves from each other by competing church memories. But all of these traditions have an equal right to appeal to the early history of Christian exegesis. All of these traditions can, without a sacrifice of principle or intellect, come together to study texts common to them all. This is its ecumenical significance.

This series of translations is respectful of a distinctively theological reading of Scripture that cannot be reduced to historical, philosophical, scientific or sociological insights or methods alone. It takes seriously the venerable tradition of ecumenical reflection concerning the premises of revelation, providence, apostolicity, canon and consensuality. A high respect is here granted, despite modern assumptions, to uniquely Christian theological forms of reasoning, such as classical consensual christological and triune reasoning, as distinguishing premises of classic Christian textual interpretation. These cannot be acquired by empirical methods alone. This approach does not pit theology against critical theory; instead, it incorporates critical historical methods and brings them into coordinate accountability within its larger purpose of listening to Scripture.

The internationally diverse character of our editors and translators corresponds with the global range of our audience, which bridges many major communions of Christianity. We have sought to bring together a distinguished international network of Protestant, Catholic and Orthodox scholars, editors, and translators of the highest quality and reputation to accomplish this design.

But why just now at this historical moment is this need for patristic wisdom felt particularly by so many readers of Scripture? Part of the reason is that these readers have been longer deprived of significant contact with many of these vital sources of classic Christian exegesis.

The Ancient Commentary Tradition

This series focuses on texts that comment on Scripture and teach its meaning. We define a commentary in its plain sense definition as a series of illustrative or explanatory notes on any work of enduring significance. The word *commentary* is an Anglicized form of the Latin *commentarius* (or "annotation" or "memoranda" on a subject or text or series of events). In its theological meaning it is a work that explains, analyzes or expounds a biblical book or portion of Scripture. Tertullian, Origen, John Chrysostom, Jerome, Augustine and Clement of Alexandria all revealed their familiarity with both the secular and religious commentators available to them as they unpacked the meanings of the sacred text at hand.

The commentary in ancient times typically began with a general introduction covering such questions as authorship, date, purpose and audience. It commented as needed on grammatical or lexical problems in the text and provided explanations of difficulties in the text. It typically moved verse by verse through a Scripture text, seeking to make its meaning clear and its import understood.

The general western literary genre of commentary has been definitively shaped by the history of early Christian commentaries on Scripture. It is from Origen, Hilary, the *Opus imperfectum in Matthaeum*, John Chrysostom and Cyril of Alexandria that we learn what a commentary is—far more so than in the case of classic medical or philosophical or poetic commentaries. It leaves too much unsaid simply to assume that the Christian biblical commentary took a previously extant literary genre and reshaped it for Christian texts. Rather it is more accurate to say that *the Western literary genre of the commentary (and especially the biblical commentary) has patristic commentaries as its decisive pattern and prototype.*

It is only in the last two centuries, since the development of modern historicist methods of criticism, that modern writers have sought more strictly to delimit the definition of a commentary so as to include only certain limited interests focusing largely on historical-critical method, philological and grammatical observations, literary analysis, and socio-political or economic circumstances imping ing on the text. While respecting all these approaches, the ACT editors do not hesitate to use the classic word *commentary* to define more broadly the genre of this series. These are commentaries in their classic sense.

The ACT editors freely take the assumption that the Christian canon is to be respected as the church's sacred text. The reading and preaching of Scripture are vital to religious life. The central hope of this endeavor is that it might contribute in some small way to the revitalization of religious faith and community through a renewed discovery of the earliest readings of the church's Scriptures.

An Appeal to Allow the Text to Speak for Itself

This prompts two appeals:

1. For those who begin by assuming as normative for a commentary only the norms considered typical for modern expressions of what a commentary is, we ask: Please allow the ancient commentators to define *commentarius* according to their own lights. Those who assume the preemptive authority and truthfulness of modern critical methods alone will always tend to view the classic Christian exegetes as dated, quaint, premodern, hence inadequate, and in some instances comic or even mean-spirited, prejudiced, unjust and oppressive. So in the interest of hermeneutical fairness, it is recommended that the modern reader not impose upon ancient Christian exegetes modern assumptions about valid readings of Scripture. The ancient Christian writers constantly challenge these unspoken, hidden and often indeed camouflaged assumptions that have become commonplace in our time.

We leave it to others to discuss the merits of ancient versus modern methods of exegesis. But even this cannot be done honestly without a serious examination of the texts of ancient exegesis. Ancient commentaries may disqualify as commentaries by modern standards. But they remain commentaries by the standards of those who anteceded and formed the basis of the modern commentary.

The attempt to read a Scripture text while ruling out all theological and moral assumptions—as well as ecclesial, sacramental and dogmatic assumptions that have prevailed generally in the community of faith out of which it emerged—is a very thin enterprise indeed. Those who tendentiously may read a single page of patristic exegesis, gasp and toss it away because it does not conform adequately to the canons of modern exegesis and historicist commentary are surely not exhibiting a valid model for critical inquiry today.

2. In ancient Christian exegesis, chains of biblical references were often very important in thinking about the text in relation to the whole testimony of sacred Scripture, by the analogy of faith, comparing text with text, on the premise that *scripturam ex scriptura explicandam esse*. When ancient exegesis weaves many Scriptures together, it does not limit its focus to a single text as much modern exegesis prefers, but constantly relates it to other texts, by analogy, intensively using typological reasoning, as did the rabbinic tradition.

Since the principle prevails in ancient Christian exegesis that each text is illumined by other texts and by the whole narrative of the history of revelation, we find in patristic comments on a given text many other subtexts interwoven in order to illumine that text. In these ways the models of exegesis often do not correspond with modern commentary assumptions, which tend to resist or rule out chains of scriptural reference. We implore the reader not to force the assumptions of twentieth-century hermeneutics upon the ancient Christian writers, who themselves knew nothing of what we now call hermeneutics.

The Complementarity of Research Methods in this Series

The ACT series will employ several interrelated methods of research, which the editors and translators seek to bring together in a working integration. Principal among these methods are the following:

1. The editors, translators and annotators will bring to bear the best resources *of textual criticism* in preparation for their volumes. This series is not intended to produce a new critical edition of the original language text. The best urtext in the original language will be used. Significant variants in the earliest manuscript sources of the text may be commented on as needed in the annotations. But it will be assumed that the editors and translators will be familiar with the textual ambiguities of a particular text and be able to state their conclusions about significant differences among scholars. Since we are working with ancient texts that have, in some cases, problematic or ambiguous passages, we are obliged to employ all methods of historical, philological and textual inquiry appropriate to the study of ancient texts. To that end, we will appeal to the most reliable text-critical scholarship of both biblical and patristic studies. We will assume that our editors and translators have reviewed the international literature of textual critics regarding their text so as to provide the reader with a translation of the most authoritative and reliable form of the ancient text. We will leave it to the volume editors and translators, under the supervision of the general editors, to make these assessments. This will include the challenge of considering which variants within the biblical text itself might impinge on the patristic text itself, and which forms or stemma of the biblical text the patristic writer was employing. The annotator will supply explanatory footnotes where these textual challenges may raise potential confusion for the reader.

2. Our editors and translators will seek to understand the *historical context* (including socioeconomic, political and psychological aspects as needed) of the text. These understandings are often vital to right discernment of the writer's intention. Yet we do not see our primary mission as that of discussing in detail these contexts. They are to be factored into the translation and commented on as needed in the annotations but are not to become the primary focus of this series. Our central interest is less in the social location of the text or the philological history of particular words than in authorial intent and

accurate translation. Assuming a proper social-historical contextualization of the text, the main focus of this series will be on a dispassionate and fair translation and analysis of the text itself.

3. The main task is to set forth the meaning of the biblical text itself as understood by the patristic writer. The intention of our volume editors and translators is to help the reader see clearly into the meanings which patristic commentators have discovered in the biblical text. *Exegesis* in its classic sense implies an effort to explain, interpret and comment on a text, its meaning, its sources and its connections with other texts. It implies a close reading of the text, utilizing whatever linguistic, historical, literary or theological resources are available to explain it. It is contrasted with *eisegesis*, which implies that interpreters have imposed their own personal opinions or assumptions upon the text. The patristic writers actively practiced intratextual exegesis, which seeks to define and identify the exact wording of the text, its grammatical structure and the interconnectedness of its parts. They also practiced extratextual exegesis, seeking to discern the geographical, historical or cultural context in which the text was written. Our editors and annotators will also be attentive as needed to the ways in which the ancient Christian writer described his own interpreting process or hermeneutic assumptions.

4. The underlying philosophy of translation that we employ in this series is, like the ACCS, termed *dynamic equivalency*. We wish to avoid the pitfalls of either too loose a paraphrase or too rigid a literal translation. We seek language that is literary but not purely literal. Whenever possible we have opted for the metaphors and terms that are normally in use in everyday English-speaking culture. Our purpose is to allow the ancient Christian writers to speak for themselves to ordinary readers in the present generation. We want to make it easier for the Bible reader to gain ready access to the deepest reflection of the ancient Christian community of faith on a particular book of Scripture. We seek a thought-for-thought translation rather than a formal equivalence or word-for-word style. This requires the words to be first translated accurately and then rendered in understandable idiom. We seek to present the same thoughts, feelings, connotations and effects of the original text in everyday English language. We have used vocabulary and language structures commonly used by the average person. We do not leave the quality of translation only to the primary translator, but pass it through several levels of editorial review before confirming it.

The Function of the ACT Introductions, Annotations and Translations

In writing the introduction for a particular volume of the ACT series, the translator or volume editor will discuss, where possible, the opinion of the writer regarding authorship of the text, the importance of the biblical book for other patristic interpreters, the availability or paucity of patristic comment, any salient points of debate between the Fathers, and any special challenges involved in translating and editing the particular volume. The introduction affords the opportunity to frame the entire commentary in a manner that will help the general reader understand the nature and significance of patristic comment on the biblical texts under consideration and to help readers find their critical bearings so as to read and use the commentary in an informed way.

The footnotes will assist the reader with obscurities and potential confusions. In the annotations the volume editors have identified Scripture allusions and historical references embedded within the texts. Their purpose is to help the reader move easily from passage to passage without losing a sense of the whole.

The ACT general editors seek to be circumspect and meticulous in commissioning volume editors and translators. We strive for a high level of consistency and literary quality throughout the course of this series. We have sought out as volume editors and translators those patristic and biblical scholars who are thoroughly familiar with their original language sources, who are informed historically, and who are sympathetic to the needs of ordinary nonprofessional readers who may not have professional language skills.

Thomas C. Oden and Gerald L. Bray, Series Editors

TRANSLATOR'S INTRODUCTION

The identity of Ambrosiaster and the history of the transmission of his great commentary on the Pauline Epistles are two of the great questions of patristic scholarship, neither of which is likely to be resolved in the foreseeable future. In her very thorough examination of the evidence, Sophie Lunn-Rockliffe has concluded that a search for his true identity is futile and that all we can say about the three different recensions of his commentary is that they are likely to have come from the author himself.[1] His motives for producing different versions remain obscure, however, as does the order in which they were produced. The texts are with us in over seventy different manuscripts, but beyond that inescapable fact, all is speculation and uncertainty.

The Identity of the Author

The name Ambrosiaster seems to have been given to the author of the Pauline commentary by its Benedictine editors (1686-1690). Before that time it had been attributed to Ambrose of Milan (d. 397) for more than a thousand years, despite the fact that it differs remarkably in style and approach from the genuine writings of the great Milanese bishop. Augustine of Hippo, who knew the commentary, attributed it to a certain "Hilary," perhaps because he thought it came from the pen of Hilary of Poitiers, though this is most unlikely. A more plausible candidate is Decimus Hilarianus Hilarius, a prominent Roman layman of the late fourth century, but this too is no more than speculation. Other suggestions, which range from Isaac the Jew to Evagrius of Pontus, are equally uncertain and open to serious objections, as Lunn-Rockliffe has shown. The tone of the commentary suggests that the author was a clergyman, and if his comments on

---

[1]Sophie Lunn-Rockliffe, *Ambrosiaster's Political Theology* (Oxford: Oxford University Press, 2007), 11-32.

Philemon are anything to go by, it seems that he regarded lay involvement in church affairs as anomalous. Most likely he was a presbyter of the Roman church who wanted to instruct younger clergy on how to preach and teach the Pauline Epistles. He does not appear to have had any special expertise for this task, though it is clear that he was a follower of Nicene orthodoxy and that he had an eye for pastoral questions. Many of his comments end with moral maxims which summarize principles that look very much like the message of a sermon, and it is probable that he exercised a regular preaching and teaching ministry at Rome. It may be that he deliberately chose to remain anonymous, perhaps in order to avoid the unwelcome controversy that his writings were likely to generate.

Ambrosiaster had a strong interest in Jewish laws and customs, though the suggestion that he was a Jew himself probably goes too far, since at many points in his commentary he identifies himself with the Gentile world. He was not a biblical scholar in any deep sense, although he was aware of the existence of different manuscript traditions, and occasionally attempted to reconstruct what the original Pauline text would have been (see, for example, his remarks on Romans 5:14). His knowledge of Greek was rudimentary, and perhaps it is just as well that he made virtually no attempt to correct false or inadequate renderings in the Latin version he was using by reference to the original language.

We know from internal evidence that Ambrosiaster was writing during the pontificate of Damasus I (366–384), who commissioned Jerome to produce a definitive Latin translation of the Bible. He did not use the Latin Vulgate, which was the result of Jerome's labors, nor did he comment on it where his own version differed from that of Jerome, so we may assume that his work was complete before the Vulgate translation became known. There is also no mention of the decree making Christianity the official state religion (February 27, 380) or of the first council of Constantinople, held in 381. The impression we get is that Nicene orthodoxy was still fighting its various enemies—pagan, Jewish and heretical—and that the final outcome was sufficiently in doubt that congregations were in constant need of warning about the dangers posed by each of these. It probably took several years for the commentary to be written, so that we can make a good guess that the task was underway during the 370s. The surviving recensions shed no further light on this question, which suggests that they were produced fairly soon after the initial composition. If they were the work of literary executors, it is possible that Ambrosiaster died sometime before 380, but this is pure conjecture and the evidence of his other work, the *Quaestiones* which deal with disputed points in the Bible, suggests that he was still alive in 384. What is certain is that by the end of the fourth century Ambrosiaster's commentary had become a standard work of Latin biblical study and that it retained its influence even after the publication of Jerome's new Vulgate translation.

The Text and Its Translation

Ambrosiaster's commentary can be broken down into two, or possibly three, principal, recensions. Untangling these can be a delicate task, because in later centuries there was a good deal of cross-pollination, as monastic copyists incorporated elements from different recensions into their own text. It is possible that Ambrosiaster left his work in a semipolished state, which was then touched up for publication by literary executors who smoothed out some of its rough edges and filled in material that was either missing from the manuscript(s) they had or that was felt to be needed in order to make sense of what Ambrosiaster wrote. But it is also possible that Ambrosiaster produced the different versions himself, perhaps with a variety of audiences in mind. The style of the shortest recension is lapidary to the point of obscurity, and in some ways is more like a series of lecture notes than a finished commentary. It is often difficult or impossible to know what Ambrosiaster meant, and the second and third recensions were probably trying to explain the obscurities of the shortest text. Sometimes they are genuinely helpful and illuminate the commentary, but there are places when later hands digressed from Ambrosiaster's thought pattern and added material that is either irrelevant or contradictory. There is no reason to believe that anyone wanted to falsify Ambrosiaster's thought, though it is possible that the third recension contains comments that were felt to be more appropriate or helpful than the text of the primary and secondary ones. If they come from the pen of Ambrosiaster himself, then it would seem that he revised his work in the light of feedback received from readers of the earlier editions.

Given this situation, the task of a translator becomes extremely difficult. Reproducing the "original" Ambrosiaster is not a realistic goal, since even if this were possible, the result would be unreadable. Incorporating at least some of the later material is essential if we are to make sense of what Ambrosiaster was saying, and here we can only be guided by the weight of probability. Sometimes it appears as if whole phrases have gone missing or been transposed to other parts of the manuscript, but we cannot be certain of this. For this translation, editorial additions which round out the text and are uncontested by rival alternatives are included without further comment. Where a second possibility exists, it is put in a footnote. As a general rule the shorter version has been preferred for the main text and the longer one has been consigned to a footnote, on the assumption that the shorter text is more likely to be the older one. Interpolations which bear no relation to the rest of the text or which clearly contradict it have been omitted, though it should be said that there are very few of these. Possible transpositions have been ignored, though apparent lacunae have been filled in with conjectures that have been put in square brackets. The words and phrases thus supplied have been chosen in line with the general sense of the text, which makes them plausible, even if their accuracy cannot be guaranteed. In translating the commentary on the Corinthian correspondence, I was fortunate to be able to make use of an unpublished draft prepared by Janet Fairweather, and some of the Romans commentary has already appeared in my commentary on that book, which has appeared as *Romans* (New Testament 6, Ancient Christian Commentary on Scripture

[Downers Grove, Ill.: InterVarsity Press, 1998.])

Ambrosiaster knew nothing of chapter or verse divisions in the Bible, and so the passages that he isolated for comment do not always coincide with what we are familiar with today. Modern readers cannot be expected to find their place in the text without chapter and verse, so these have been added to the translation of the commentary. His quotations from other parts of Scripture are more problematic. Those taken from the Old Testament follow Latin versions of the Greek Septuagint rather than the Hebrew text, which is sometimes quite different, and not every quotation is full or exact. Often he omits parts of a verse or paraphrases it slightly, which makes it hard to know whether he was using a different translation or merely adapting the text in front of him to his own literary style. In the Psalms, he used the Greek numbering, which usually differs by one from the Hebrew but is relatively unfamiliar to English-speaking readers. The Greek numbering has been preserved in the text, with a note signaling the numbering in the Hebrew (and English) system; footnotes regularly supply references to modern verse numbering. For this translation, the text of the Revised Standard Version (RSV) has been followed, mainly because it was the one chosen for the Ancient Christian Commentary on Scripture, but quotations have been given in the form Ambrosiaster used, regardless of what the RSV says. When the commentary is based on a reading that is not in the RSV or is contradictory to it, this is pointed out in a footnote. Once again, the frequency of this should not be exaggerated, and at least ninety percent of the text is identical (or nearly so) in both Ambrosiaster and the RSV. Nevertheless, it is only fair to point out discrepancies where these occur and leave judgment on the underlying textual questions to the experts. Most of the time, it will be found that Ambrosiaster was using a text closer to that of the so-called Textus Receptus (which is essentially the one underlying the Authorized or King James Version of 1611), rather than the text(s) behind the RSV or other modern English translations, but this is not an invariable rule and each verse must be considered on its own merits.

What Latin version Ambrosiaster was using is unknown. It was probably the one known to Lucifer of Cagliari, who was writing about the same time. It contained some egregious errors which a knowledge of Greek would have corrected, but beyond that it is impossible to go. Whatever text he was using, it was no doubt the translation that was most familiar to him. This may have been the *Itala*, referred to by Augustine as the best of the Latin versions circulating in his time, but if so, we can only say that it provides clear evidence of the need for a fresh translation, which Jerome was even then being commissioned to provide. He seldom quotes from the deuterocanonical books of the Old Testament, although when he does he treats them as Scripture, but he did not regard the epistle to the Hebrews as Pauline. We have to admit that Ambrosiaster's interpretive skills are conditioned and sometimes constricted by a faulty text, leading him to conclusions that cannot be justified, but the extent of this problem should not be exaggerated. On the whole, he made sensible judgments and was careful to present alternative possibilities when the meaning of Paul's words was unclear to him. Only very occasionally does he go wrong for reasons that must be attributed to his own ignorance or speculation. An example of this can be found in his comment on 1 Corinthians 9:21, where he understands "those who are under the law" as a reference to the Samaritans, which is clearly not the case.

Such lapses are rare, however, and generally speaking, Ambrosiaster must be regarded as one of the greatest of the ancient biblical commentators, whose work can often stand alongside that of modern scholars. He was firmly wedded to the literal sense of interpretation and avoided allegory, though he was not averse to mentioning the spiritual dimension of the text when he thought that its grammatical or stylistic peculiarities required an explanation beyond the purely literal one. He was particularly sensitive to the rhetorical devices that the apostle Paul used, and sometimes we find interesting explanations of words taken from political, military or legal contexts that would have been well known to him but that might easily escape a modern reader less familiar with the Roman imperial context. One instance of this is his discussion of Paul's Roman citizenship, which he believed derived from a general enrollment of the people of Tarsus as Romans and not from a particular grant made to one of Paul's ancestors. Ambrosiaster clearly thought that grants of Roman citizenship were made collectively and not individually, but even if he was wrong in this case, his general sense of the way ancient societies functioned may give us a more faithful picture of the apostle Paul and his world than we usually get from modern commentaries.

The Social and Theological Context

The importance of Ambrosiaster's feel for the cultural context of the Pauline Epistles is most noticeable when we consider the way that he brings out the close connection between the church of his day and that of the first century. For example, the fourth-century church was full of newly converted pagans whose behavior, particularly in matters related to idol worship, was fairly lax from the standpoint of more rigorously orthodox Christians. He felt he had to stress the importance of distancing himself from such pagan practices, even if they were theologically matters of indifference. Ambrosiaster understood that perception is often as important as the reality, and so he counseled his readers to avoid even the appearance of wrongdoing, whatever their consciences might tell them. Behind the dumb idols, he claimed, there lurked active and malevolent demons who would do all in their power to lead Christians astray, and it was they, not the wood and stone figures, who had to be feared. The apostle Paul did not make that connection, as far as we know, but Ambrosiaster reminds us that Paul also inhabited a world in which pagan religious practices were often regarded as essentially demonic and that he would not have been surprised by Ambrosiaster's conclusion, even if he would not necessarily have shared it.

Like Paul, Ambrosiaster was writing at a time when it seemed possible that Jews might convert to Christianity in large numbers. He did not try to minimize the importance of the hardness of heart that they had shown in the time of Christ, but neither did he regard them as being completely beyond the pale. In his treatment of Romans 9–11 he held the door open to them, and put their refusal to accept Christ down to ignorance rather than to wickedness or malice of some kind. The implication must be that the triumph of Christianity across the Roman world was proof of their mistake, and that once they realized this, they would stream into the church in large numbers. By Judaism, Ambrosiaster understood four main things, which he constantly repeated every time the subject came up for discussion. These were circumcision, new moons, the sabbath and the food laws, all of which were ritual observances which set Jews apart from the Gentile world and which Gentiles found particularly difficult to come to terms with. When criticizing the law of Moses, Ambrosiaster had to walk a fine line between acknowledging that as God's Word it had once been required of believers and recognizing that much of it was "unspiritual" from the Christian standpoint. His favorite examples of this were the cases in which the Pentateuch spoke of the ritual impurity caused by dead mice and weasels; for some reason, this seems to have struck him as particularly absurd, and he returned to the theme on more than one occasion. What strikes the modern reader is the constant repetition of the same themes whenever Judaism is mentioned, a sure sign that Ambrosiaster was not engaging in polemic with Jews, but warning Christians not to be attracted by a "fundamentalist" reading of the Old Testament which ignored the effect of the coming of Christ.

Ambrosiaster's greatest worry was the prevalence of false teachers in the church, and here he felt a particular kinship with the apostle Paul, who also frequently warned against the influence of false apostles, who tried to subvert the congregations he had founded. In the fourth century, the enemies were different, but the principle was the same, and Ambrosiaster did everything he could to prove that the great heresies of his own time were often merely rehashes of what the apostle warned against. In the course of his many discussions of this subject, we learn that the greatest danger came from the Manichaeans, whose dualism was foreshadowed by some of the proto-Gnostics attacked by Paul. Somewhat surprisingly, Ambrosiaster says very little about Arius, although he defends the Nicene faith in ways which were clearly anti-Arian in their substance. The reason for that may well have been political, since until the defeat of Valens at Adrianople in 378, the imperial family was Arian or semi-Arian, and Ambrosiaster may have been reluctant to express his views in a way that might have led to a charge of political disloyalty. On the other hand, his deep concern for sound doctrine was never in doubt, and by that he meant the Athanasian interpretation of the decisions taken at Nicaea in 325.

As befits his Roman background, Ambrosiaster had a keen eye for moral issues. He came down heavily against sexual immorality of all kinds, but he also highlighted Paul's condemnation of slanderous gossip, greed and selfishness. He particularly appreciated the link Paul had made between false teaching and greed, which he regarded as one of the most prevalent evils of the church both in his own day and in the first century. We have no way of knowing how widespread this problem was in Ambrosiaster's time, but the influx of wealthy people into the church must have raised the problem of financial corruption, and Ambrosiaster's reaction to this is understandable.

Despite his close identification with Paul and the Pauline legacy, Ambrosiaster had a clear understanding of the developments that had taken place in the church since the first century. For example, he knew that the apostles had performed signs and wonders that were no longer current in his own day. He was not a "cessationist" in the modern sense, but put this down to the fact (as he saw it) that signs and wonders were intended to impress unbelievers; Christians had no need of them. To reinforce this view, he made a particular point of saying that some of the apostle's companions, like Epaphroditus, had bouts of serious illness which the apostle had to pray about, because he could not automatically cure them.

His Legacy

Ambrosiaster clearly belongs to the Latin theological tradition and was only minimally influenced by Greek, Jewish or other sources. He knew writers like Tertullian and Cyprian well enough to be able to quote them in support of his own views, and he was also familiar with the Roman schismatic Novatian. He never mentioned anyone from the Eastern church, apart from an occasional reference to Arius. He could have known Origen's biblical commentaries but apparently did not, presumably because Rufinus had not yet translated them into Latin. He could also have met Athanasius during one of his periodic exiles in the West, but if he did so, he said nothing about it. It is hard to believe that he was an original thinker, and many of his ideas presumably came from elsewhere. But since his is the oldest Latin commentary on the Pauline Epistles to survive from ancient times, it is not clear what his sources were. He never mentioned any, but reticence in such matters was characteristic of most writers before the modern era and tells us nothing one way or the other.

We know that he was read by Augustine with profit and that certain theological themes generally associated with the great bishop of Hippo can be traced back to him. This is particularly true of his treatment of original sin in Romans 5:12 and of the emphasis he places on predestination. On the other hand, it is clear that Ambrosiaster had not encountered the theology of Pelagius, which forced Augustine to be much more precise in his formulation of these doctrines than Ambrosiaster had been. Even so, it is fair to say that Ambrosiaster was an "Augustinian" *avant la lettre*, and his commentary is important evidence that Augustine's ideas were more traditional and less innovative than is often thought.

The links with Augustine are particularly noticeable when we compare him with his great contemporaries, Ambrose and Jerome. One might think that Ambrosiaster had some connection with Ambrose that would have justified the inclusion of his work with that of the bishop of Milan, but there is nothing that points clearly in that direction. Perhaps Ambrosiaster's work was edited by people close to Ambrose, but that is speculation and is not supported by any textual similarity between them. Nor is it clear to what extent Ambrosiaster knew Jerome or was known by him, although both men were probably in Rome in the early years of Pope Damasus I. Jerome was an accomplished linguist and therefore a better biblical scholar than Ambrosiaster could ever hope to be, and it would not be at all surprising if he had disliked Ambrosiaster's work and dismissed it as inferior to his own. Perhaps he did, but if so there is nothing in Jerome's works to tell us one way or another.

By the time Ambrosiaster's commentary was circulating widely, it had been subsumed under the name of Ambrose, and for more than a thousand years no one was aware of his separate identity. As the work of Ambrose, it was widely admired and imitated throughout the Middle Ages, when it did much to preserve both Pauline studies and a sense of the importance of the literal interpretation of Scripture. It was just as Ambrosiaster's distinct identity was being recognized that these two tendencies coalesced in a new outburst of scholarly energy that we associate with the Renaissance and the Reformation. But although Ambrosiaster was appreciated by humanists and reformers alike, his work was quickly surpassed, both in breadth of scholarship and in depth of theological insight, so that it never established itself as a standard reference for later biblical studies. His anonymity also worked against him at a time when there was an increasing focus on the accomplishments of particular individuals in the early church period. By showing that he was not Ambrose, his Benedictine editors effectively decanonized him, a disadvantage which persists to the present day and helps to explain why there has never before been a complete translation of his work, despite its obvious interest and importance.

Until very recently, Ambrosiaster was essentially unknown and disregarded by theologians, including those with a particular interest in the patristic tradition. He was better known to biblical scholars, but mainly because he regularly appears in the critical apparatus of the Greek New Testament as a witness to particular variant readings of the text. His skill as a commentator in his own right went unacknowledged, and it is only now that patristic biblical interpretation is coming into its own once more that his qualities are beginning to be more widely appreciated. It must be hoped that the publication of his commentaries on the Pauline Epistles will make it possible for a wider audience to hear and appreciate his message, and give him (at long last) the honored place in the history of biblical, and especially Pauline, studies, that he so richly deserves.

For Further Reading
The text of Ambrosiaster's commentary used for this translation is the one published

in the series Corpus Scriptorum Ecclesiasticorum Latinorum (CSEL), *Ambrosiastri qui dicitur Commentarius in Epistulas Paulinas*, edited under the name of H. J. Vogels (3 vols., Vienna: Hoelder-Pichler-Tempsky, 1966–1969), though much of the actual work was done by others. A new translation under the direction of Professor David Hunter of the University of Kentucky is due to appear in 2010, which will include a full critical apparatus and introduction to the text.

The most important study of his identity remains the work of Alexander Souter, *A Study of Ambrosiaster* (Cambridge: The University Press, 1905), though this must be supplemented by further details found in the introduction to the Vogels edition. The only substantial examination of his theology available in English is the recent study by Sophie Lunn-Rockliffe, to which reference has already been made.

AMBROSIASTER
Commentary on Romans

Preface

Everything needs an introduction if it is to be properly understood, and the plan of a work can be more easily explained if its origin is known. We shall therefore point out the form and purpose of the letter before us, so that what we are saying may be seen to be true.

Paul discusses four main points in his letter to the Romans. He begins with the statement that one part of the human race exists by its physical nature and the other exists through the law. This second group stands head and shoulders above the rest, and the other nations all learn what they know in and through it.

The first point he discusses is how [the human race] manifests itself, what it is now, what it was originally, and to whom it belongs, and in this way he disposes of heresies. The second point he makes is that human beings did not submit to the one God by the logic of nature, but instead engaged in dishonest and wicked activities for which they were rejected by God, so that those who believe are rewarded. The third point is that they disobeyed the law which had been given to them, with the result that God preferred the Jews to the Greeks.[1] The fourth point is that Paul teaches that when they rejected Christ, the Jews departed from the law and promise of God and became like the Gentiles, so that now both of them stand in need of the mercy of God, hoping for salvation not by the law but by faith in Christ Jesus.

It is clear that in the times of the apostles there were Jews living in Rome because they lived in the Roman Empire. Those of them who believed in Christ passed this belief on to the Romans, so that they too might keep the law by confessing Christ. Having heard reports of the power and virtue of Christ, the Romans were quick to believe in him, although they were cautious too, and not unreasonably, for some of them had been badly instructed and needed immediate correction, after which they remained faithful to him. Here we are given to understand that those Jews who believed in Christ did not accept that he was God from God, because they thought that this was a denial of monotheism.

For this reason Paul says that they did not receive the spiritual grace of God and so they lacked assurance of faith. These Jews were the same people who had undermined the [faith of the] Galatians, causing them to turn away from the teaching of the apostles. The apostle was therefore angry with them, because although they had been well taught, they had been easily led astray. He had no need to be angry with the Romans though. Instead, he praised their faith, particularly as they had not seen any signs of [miraculous] powers, nor had they received their faith in Christ from any of the apostles (even if this faith was more a matter of words than of substance), nor had the mystery of the cross of Christ been explained to them. As a result, when some people (like Aquila and Priscilla) turned up with the right doctrine, questions arose about the rights and wrongs of eating meat [which had been sacrificed to idols] and about whether the hope

---

[1]That is, non-Jews.

which they placed in Christ would be enough to save them, or whether they had to keep the law as well.

This is why Paul went to so much trouble to wean them away from the law, because *the law and the prophets are until John.*[1] The gospel established them in the faith of Christ alone and justified them more or less in opposition to the law, not by destroying it but by showing that Christianity was superior. For he asserts that Christ had been promised in such a way that the law would cease when he came, though not entirely. Rather, an abbreviated form of the law would emerge which would provide salvation. Many things had been handed down by their ancestors and had become a burden because of the hardness of their hearts, but the mercy of God had put an end to this through Christ, who forgave all that was past. Therefore, whoever wanted to go on living under the law was ungrateful for the mercy of God. For Moses had said: *So you shall make the children of Israel afraid*[2] so that whatever way they might turn they would still have the law and not be without the comfort [of God]. So, in order to tell them to put their hope of life and salvation in Christ apart from the law, and to teach them that he is the Lord of all things, Paul began his letter as follows.

Romans 1

¹Paul, a servant of Jesus Christ, called to be an apostle, set apart for the gospel of God,

Among our ancestors, names were given for a reason. Isaac was called after laughter and Jacob was so named because of the heel.[3] Saul was so called because of his restlessness, but after he was converted, he changed his name to Paul, and the change was permanent. *Saul* means *restlessness*, or *trial*, so when he came to faith in Christ he called himself *Paul*, in other words, *rest*, because our faith is peace. Whereas previously he had inflicted trials on the servants of God because of his desire to fulfill the law, later he himself endured trials on account of the hope which he had once denied, because of his love of Judaism.

In calling himself a *servant of Jesus Christ,* Paul showed that he had been delivered from the law. He put both names, Jesus and Christ, in order to signify the person of God and man, for in both he is Lord, as Peter the apostle testified, saying: *He is the Lord of all.*[4] And because he is Lord, he is also God, as David says: *For the Lord himself is God.*[5] The heretics deny this. Marcion, it seems, denied Christ and his body out of hatred for the law, although he confessed Jesus. The Jews and Photinus denied that Jesus was God, out of their zeal for the law. Whenever Scripture says either Jesus or Christ, it sometimes means the person of God, and sometimes the person of the man, for example: *there is one Lord Jesus Christ, through whom are all things.*[6]

Called to be an apostle. Because Paul acknowledged the Lord and confessed him, he became the perfect servant, he also showed that he had been promoted, saying that he was called to be an apostle, in other words, a messenger sent by the Lord to do his work. By this he showed that he had merit with God because he served Christ and not the law.

Set apart for the gospel of God. The gospel of God is good news, by which sinners are called to forgiveness. For since as a Pharisee the apostle had held a teaching post among the Jews, he now says that he has been set apart from the preaching of Judaism for the gospel of God, so that by abandoning the law, he might preach Christ, who justifies those who believe in him, which the law could not do. This does not go against the law, but affirms it, since the

---

[1]Lk 16:16. [2]A misreading of Lev 15:31. [3]On Isaac, see Gen 21:1-7. On Jacob, see Gen 25:26. He came out of the womb clutching his twin-brother Esau's heel. [4]Acts 10:36. [5]Ps 100:3. [6]1 Cor 8:6.

law itself says that this would happen in the future. In the words of Isaiah the prophet: *There will come from Zion one who will break and remove the captivity of Jacob, and this will be a testimony of me, when I shall take away their sins.*[1]

2which he had promised beforehand through his prophets in the holy scriptures

Which he had promised. In order to prove that the hope of faith was fulfilled and completed in Christ, Paul says that Christ's gospel was already promised by God beforehand, so that on the basis of the promise Paul could teach that Christ was the perfect author of (eternal) life. Before going to them, he showed them the testimony given to him, to which the apostle Peter also bore witness: *There is no other name given under heaven by which people must be saved.*[2]

Through his prophets. In order to show even more clearly that the coming of Christ was a saving event, Paul also indicated the people through whom God gave his promise, so that it might be seen from them just how true and magnificent the promise is. For nobody makes use of great forerunners to announce some minor thing.

In the holy Scriptures. Paul added this on top of his argument, in order to give greater confidence to believers and show his approval of the law. The Scriptures are holy because they condemn sins, and because they contained the covenant of the One God and of the incarnation of the Son of God for the salvation of mankind, [which was brought about] by the evidence of numerous signs.

3the gospel concerning his Son, who was descended from David according to the flesh

Concerning his Son. Since God promised his own Son to the world, it was fitting that he should promise him through great men, so that from them it might be known how very powerful the one who was being preached was, and so that he might include his future coming in the holy Scriptures. What is preached by the holy Scriptures cannot be shown to be false.

Who was descended from the seed of David according to the flesh. He who was the Son of God according to the Holy Spirit, that is, according to God (because God is Spirit and without any doubt holy), is said to have been made the Son of God according to the flesh by Mary, as it is written: *The Word became flesh.*[3] Christ Jesus is both Son of God and Son of Man, so that just as he is truly God, so also he is truly man. He would not be true man if he were not of flesh and soul, [which he needed in order to] be perfect. For although he was the Son of God in eternity, he was not known by the creation until God wanted him to be revealed for the salvation of mankind. At that point, God made him visible and corporeal, because he wanted him to be known by his power to cleanse people from their sins by overcoming death in the flesh. For that reason, he was made of the seed of David, so that just as he was born a king from God before the beginning of time, he would also acquire birth from a king according to the flesh. He was made from a virgin by the work of the Holy Spirit, in other words, born, so that, by the reverence reserved for him because of this fact, he who by his birth was distinguished from the law of nature might be recognized as being more than a man, just as had been predicted by Isaiah the prophet: *Behold a virgin will conceive in her womb.*[4] Thus, when the newborn child appeared to be worthy of honor, the providence of God could be discerned with regard to a future visitation of the human race.

---

[1]Cf. Is 27:9. [2]Acts 4:12. [3]Jn 1:1. [4]Is 7:14.

⁴and designated Son of God in power according to the Spirit of holiness by his resurrection from the dead, Jesus Christ our Lord,

When Paul speaks about the Son of God he is pointing out that God is Father, and by adding the Spirit of holiness he indicates the mystery of the Trinity. He who was incarnate obscured what he really was, but he was predestined according to the Spirit of holiness to be manifested in power as the Son of God by rising from the dead, as it is written in Psalm 85: *Truth is risen from the earth.*[1] Every ambiguity and hesitation was made clear and sure by his resurrection, so that when the centurion saw the wonders, he confessed that the man on the cross was the Son of God.[2] When Christ died, even his disciples doubted this, as Cleopas and Emmaus said: *We thought that he was the one who would begin to set Israel free.*[3] But the Lord himself had said: *When you have lifted up the Son of man, then you will know that I am he,*[4] and also: *When I am lifted up from the earth, I shall draw all men to myself.*[5] Note that Paul did not say: *because of the resurrection of Jesus Christ* but *because of his resurrection from the dead,* because the resurrection of Christ led to the general resurrection. This power and victory in Christ appears to be all the greater, in that a dead man could do the same things as he did when he was alive. By this fact he appeared to dissolve death, in order to redeem us. Thus Paul calls him our Lord.

⁵through whom we have received grace and apostleship to bring about the obedience of faith for the sake of his name among all the nations,

After the resurrection, Christ was revealed as the Son of God in power. He gave grace to make sinners righteous and appointed apostles, of whom Paul says here that he is one. The apostleship was granted by the grace of God's gift, and not because the apostles were Jews. They received this authority from God the Father through Christ the Lord. As his representatives, they could make his teaching acceptable by signs of power, so that the unbelieving Jews, who had been jealous of this power when they saw it in the Savior, might be all the more tormented at seeing it admired by the masses in his servants. For power bears witness to the teaching [of Christ], so that although what is preached is incredible to the world, it is made credible by deeds. Paul says that the apostles have been sent to preach the faith to all nations, so that they might obey and be saved. In this way, it would appear that the gift of God has been granted not only to the Jews but to all the nations, and that it is the will of God, to have pity on all in Christ and through Christ, by the preaching of his ambassadors, that is, *for his name.* As he says elsewhere: *For which mission we are appointed.*[6]

⁶including yourselves who are called to belong to Jesus Christ;

That is, by the mission of us who are preaching about the name of Christ to all the nations, among whom you too have been called, because the gift of God has been sent to all. When the Romans hear that they have been called along with others, they will know that they must not act as if they are under the law, since the other nations accepted the faith of Christ without the law of Moses.

⁷To all God's beloved in Rome, who are called to be saints:
Grace to you and peace from God our Father and the Lord Jesus Christ.

---

[1]Ps 85:11. [2]Cf. Mt 27:54. [3]Lk 24:21. Ambrosiaster mistook Emmaus for Cleopas's companion, rather than the name of the place where they lived. [4]Jn 8:28. [5]Jn 12:32. [6]Cf. 2 Cor 5:20.

To all God's beloved in Rome, who are called to be saints. Although Paul seems to be writing to the Romans in general, he specifies that he is really only writing to those who are in the love of God. Who are these people, if not those who believe the right things about the Son of God? They are the ones who are holy, and who are said to have been called. For someone who understands incorrectly is not said to have been called, just as those who act according to the law have not rightly understood Christ and have done injury to God the Father by doubting whether there is full salvation in Christ. Therefore they are not holy, nor are they said to have been called.

Grace to you and peace from God our Father and the Lord Jesus Christ. Paul says that grace and peace are with those who believe rightly. It is grace by which sinners have been cleansed, and peace, by which former enemies have been reconciled to the Creator, as the Lord says: *Whatever house you enter and they receive you, say: Peace be to this house.*[1] In order to teach that without Christ there is no peace or hope, Paul added that grace and peace are not only from God the Father, but also from the Lord Jesus Christ. He says that God is our Father because of our origin, since all things are from him, and that Christ is our Lord, because we have been redeemed by his blood and made sons of God.

8*First, I thank my God through Jesus Christ for all of you, because your faith is proclaimed in all the world.*

After finishing his introduction, and before going any farther, Paul bears witness to his joy as the apostle to the Gentiles, that although the Romans ruled the world, they had submitted to the Christian faith, which seemed lowly and stupid to the wise of this world. As there were many things about the Romans which

he could rejoice in—for they were mindful of discipline, and eager to do good works, more interested in doing right than in talking about it, which is not far from God's religion—nevertheless, he says that above all he rejoices in this: that word of their faith was circulating everywhere. For it seemed to be a wonderful thing that the lords of the Gentiles should bow before a promise made to the Jews. Even if they did not believe correctly, Paul was still pleased that they had begun to worship one God in the name of Christ and knew that they could advance further. For this reason he reveals his love for them, when he rejoices at their good start and encourages them to go on. He therefore says that he is giving thanks to God, even though they have not yet received everything, because God is the source of all things. The entire dispensation of our salvation is from God, indeed, but through Christ, not through the law or any prophet, which is why Paul says that he is giving thanks to God, but through Christ, because the report of their faith was an encouragement to many to attribute it to the providence of God through Christ. Either the others who believed rejoiced, having been strengthened by seeing their rulers and brothers established in the faith, or at least those who did not believe could easily have done so by following their example. For the lesser quickly copies what he sees being done by the greater.

9*For God is my witness, whom I serve with my spirit in the gospel of his Son, that without ceasing I mention you always in my prayers,*

In order to encourage brotherly love, Paul calls on God, whom he serves, as a witness, to whom he prays on their behalf, not by keeping the law but by the gospel of his Son, in other words, not by that which Moses the servant handed down, but by that which the most

---

[1]Lk 10:5.

beloved Son taught. For the servant is as far from his Lord as the gospel is from the law, not because the law is wrong, but because the gospel is better. Therefore Paul serves God in the gospel of his Son in order to show that it is God's will that men should believe in Christ.

Whom I serve. How? In my spirit, says Paul, not in the circumcision made with hands, nor in new moons, nor in the sabbath or the choice of foods, but in the spirit, that is, in the mind. Because God is a spirit, it is right that he should be served in spirit or in the mind for whoever serves him in his mind serves him in faith. This is what the Lord said to the Samaritan woman when she asked him whether God wanted to be worshiped on the mountain, saying: *The time is coming, and now is, when the true worshipers will worship the Father in spirit and in truth, for the Father is looking for such people to worship him. God is a spirit, and those who worship him must worship him in spirit and in truth,*[1] so that it is not the place but the devout mind which validates the prayer. This is what it means to worship God the spirit and Christ in spirit and in truth, the One from whom all things come and the one through whom are all things. The Father is looking for people like this to worship him.

Paul remembers them in his prayers, in order to sow brotherly love among them; indeed, he makes this his desire for them. For who would not love someone when he hears that that person remembers him? For if they had willingly listened to the teaching brought to them in the name of Christ by those who were not sent, how much more would they want to listen to Paul, whom they knew was an apostle, and whose words were accompanied by power!

[10]asking that somehow by God's will I may now at last succeed in coming to you.

Paul here indicates the point of his prayer for the Romans. He says that he asks God that he might come to Rome in order to strengthen them by the will of God, whose gift he preaches. That strengthening will only occur if what has to be done is done by the will of God. Therefore he prays that, whatever the excuse, an opportunity may be given to him to come to the city. He was already busy preaching to others and would consider his journey successful if he came by God's will, because the will of God would have prepared the way. A journey is successful if the labor of traveling has not been endured in vain. Paul asks that God will fill the Romans by calling them to [receive] his grace. He speaks with eagerness of mind, for he desires their response, knowing that it will be to their mutual advantage, as he says elsewhere: *For what is our joy and crown? Is it not you at our Lord's coming?*[2] The apostle will bear more fruit if he wins many over. If there is greater joy if the powerful people of this world are converted to Christ, because they are so much more serious enemies, how much more are they indispensable as converts, and the apostle will bear more fruit if he can win many of them over. By God's will, the opportunity [for Paul to go to Rome] was eventually given. He was arrested and appealed to Caesar, so that in the end, he was sent to the city of Rome for a different reason, but it was by God's will and in fulfillment of his own desires. When Paul was shipwrecked, God appeared to him and said: *Do not be afraid, Paul. For as you have borne witness to me at Jerusalem, so also will you do at Rome.*[3]

[11]For I long to see you, that I may impart to you some spiritual gift to strengthen you,

This confirmation requires three persons: God as helper, the apostle as minister, and the people as receiver. Paul here shows the will of his desire, and what his wish for the Romans is.

---

[1]Jn 4:23-24. [2]1 Thess 2:19. [3]Cf. Acts 27:24.

When he says: *that I might impart some spiritual gift to you*, he means that they have followed carnal ideas. Although they were acting in the name of Christ, they were not following what Christ taught, but those things which had been handed down to them by the Jews. Paul wants to come to them as quickly as possible in order to take them away from that tradition and give them a spiritual gift in order to win them for God and make them partakers of spiritual grace so that they might be perfect in faith and behavior. From this we learn that in the preceding verses it was not the content of their faith that he had praised, but their readiness and devotion to Christ. Though calling themselves Christians, they acted just as if they were under the law, as that had been handed down to them. For the mercy of God had been given for this reason: that they should give up the works of the law, as I have often said, because God, taking pity on our weakness, decreed that the human race was saved by faith alone, along with the natural law.

When he admonishes them in writing and draws them away from carnal thoughts, when he says that his presence is necessary in order to impart a spiritual grace to them, when what he writes is spiritual, what does this mean? He does not want his teaching to be applied in a way he does not intend, for that is what happens with heretics. So he desires to be present with them and pass on to them the gospel teaching in the precise sense in which he writes it, lest by the authority of his letter their error should be confirmed rather than removed. [Paul says that] if he were with them he would be able to convince them by power, if words failed to persuade them.

12that is, that we may be mutually encouraged by each other's faith, both yours and mine.

Paul says that he will be comforted by them if they understand spiritual things, because although he may rejoice at their faith, he nevertheless grieves that they have not received the faith rightly. The apostle was the type to grieve for the faults of others as if they were his own. *And we are comforted by this*, he says, *by one and the same faith*, because then the act of comforting is seamless. It is by the unity of faith that the Romans would be brought to maturity in Christ, and by this means the ministry of the spiritual grace, given by the apostle's preaching of the gospel, produces its own fruit.

13I want you to know, brethren, that I have often intended to come to you (but thus far have been prevented), in order that I may reap some harvest among you as well as among the rest of the Gentiles.

Paul here indicates his plan and intention. He does not doubt that they already know it from those brothers who had come to Rome from Jerusalem or the neighboring cities for some reason, perhaps because of their religion, as we read of Aquila and Priscilla, who would have told the Romans of Paul's intention. As he had often wanted to come but had been prevented, it came about that he wrote them a letter in case they should continue in their unwholesome habits for too long to be easily corrected. He calls them brothers not only because they had been born again, but also because there were some among them who believed rightly, however few they may have been. Incidentally, this is why he says that they are *called to be saints*.[1] What does it mean to be called to be saints? If they are already saints, how can they be called to be sanctified? But this is part of the foreknowledge of God, because God knows those who will be saints. Those who are already with him are saints and remain called forever. Yet Paul says that he has been prevented up to the time the epistle was

[1]Rom 1:7.

written, and prevented by God, who knew that the Romans were still unprepared and sent the apostle to other cities that were already able to receive the truth. Although they acted in the name of the Savior, they were as yet prevented by their negligence from being worthy to learn spiritual things. Paul and Silas had wanted to go to Bithynia, but they were prevented from doing so by the Holy Spirit.[1] Why was this, unless he knew that such a visit would have no result? Among the Corinthians too, Paul was reminded by God, who told him, *Speak and do not be silent, for I have many people in this city.*[2]

Paul did not say that he was prevented for no reason, but he wanted them to know why he was delayed, and he urged them to get ready, so that when they heard that a spiritual grace was to be given to them they would make themselves worthy to receive it.

Paul declared that he wanted to come to them for their common good so that they might receive the salvation of spiritual grace, having a reasoned profession of their faith, and that he might have some fruit of his ministry from God, having provoked them to the right faith by the example of the other Gentiles. For a person will be more eager for what is given to him if he sees many others responding to it.

[14]I am under obligation both to Greeks and to barbarians, both to the wise and to the foolish:

Paul says that he is under obligation to those whom he names because he was sent for the purpose of preaching to everyone. For this reason he states that they are all under obligation to believe in God the Creator, from whom and through whom are all things, for obligation and honor form part of the salvation of the believer. He wrote *Greeks* instead of *Gentiles*, but this includes those who are called Romans, whether by birth or by adoption, and barbarians, who are those who are not Romans,

who belong to a hostile race, and who are not Gentiles. He speaks of those who are wise, because they are learned in worldly sciences and are called wise in the world, whether they are stargazers, geometers, mathematicians, grammarians, orators or musicians. Paul shows that none of these things is of any advantage, nor are these people truly wise, unless they believe in Christ. He calls them fools because in their simplicity they lacked knowledge of spiritual things. He testifies that he has been sent to preach to them all, but he says nothing about the Jews because he is the teacher of the Gentiles. This is why he says that he is under obligation, because he has accepted this teaching in order to pass it on, and in passing it on, to acquire it himself.

[15]so I am eager to preach the gospel to you also who are in Rome.

Although Paul says that he has been sent to preach to all the nations, yet he asserts that he is eager to impart the gospel of the grace of God to the Romans, among whom the capital and seat of the Roman Empire lies. For it would be to the benefit and peace of the members if the head were not uncertain. Therefore he opts for the peace of the Romans, that Satan might not get too involved with them, and that he might have even richer fruits of his labor.

[16]For I am not ashamed of the gospel: it is the power of God for salvation to every one who has faith, to the Jew first and also to the Greek.

In saying this, Paul was referring to those from whom the Romans had received an incorrect faith. The teaching of the apostles was backed up by power, so that if what they preached seemed incredible, signs and won-

---

[1]Acts 16:7. [2]Acts 18:9-10.

ders performed by them were a testimony that the people should not be ashamed of what was said to them, because there was so much power in it. For there is no doubt that words must give way before power. It was precisely because the preaching of the false apostles was not backed up by signs that it was without the power of God. Therefore Paul does not say that he is ashamed of the gospel of God, but that they are ashamed of it, because what had been handed on to them had come into disrepute, had never been confirmed by any testimony and diverged from apostolic teaching. It is the power of God which calls men to faith and which gives salvation to all who believe, because it remits sins and justifies, so that a person who has been marked with the mystery of the cross cannot be bound by the second death. The preaching of the cross of Christ is a sign that death has been expelled, as the apostle John says: *The reason the Son of God appeared was to destroy the works of the devil.*[1] Thus no believer is bound by death, since he has a sign that death has been conquered.

To the Jew first and also to the Greek. This means to him who is of the race of Abraham, and to him who is from the Gentiles. By *Greek* Paul means Gentile, and by *Jew* he means a descendant of Abraham. These only began to be called Jews in the days of Judas Maccabaeus, who in a time of destruction resisted the sacrileges of the Gentiles and by trusting in God rallied the nation and defended his people. He was one of the descendants of Aaron. Although Paul puts the Jews first because of their ancestors, nevertheless he says that they must also accept the gift of the gospel in the same way as the Gentiles. Therefore, if the Jew can only be justified by faith in Christ, what need is there to be under the law?

[17]For in it the righteousness of God is revealed through faith for faith; as it is written, "He who through faith is righteous shall live."

Paul says this because the righteousness of God is revealed in the person who believes, whether Jew or Greek. He calls it the righteousness of God because God freely justifies the ungodly by faith, without the works of the law, just as he says elsewhere: *That I may be found in him, not having a righteousness of my own, based on law, but that which is through faith in Christ, the righteousness from God that depends on faith.*[2] He says that this same righteousness is revealed in the gospel, when God grants faith to man, through which he may be justified.

The truth and righteousness of God is revealed when a person believes and confesses. The righteousness is of God, because what he promised, he gave. Whoever believes that he has received what God had promised through his prophets proves that God is just and is a witness of his righteousness.

Through faith for faith. What does this mean, except that the faith of God is in him because he promised, and the faith of man is in him because he believes the one who promises, so that through the faith of the God who promises the righteousness of God might be revealed in the faith of the man who believes? To the believer God appears to be just, but to the unbeliever he appears to be unjust. Anyone who does not believe that God has given what he promised denies that God is truthful. This is said against the Jews, who deny that Christ is the one whom God promised.

As it is written: "He who through faith is righteous shall live."[3] Paul now moves over to the example of the prophet Habakkuk in order to declare that in the past it was revealed that a just man lives by faith and not by the law, in other words, that a man is not justified before God by the law but by faith.

---

[1] Jn 3:8. [2] Phil 3:9. [3] Hab 2:4.

[18] For the wrath of God is revealed from heaven against all ungodliness and wickedness of men who by their wickedness suppress the truth.

Just as the righteousness of God is revealed in the one who believes, as I mentioned earlier, so ungodliness and unrighteousness are revealed in the one who does not believe. From the very structure of heaven it appears that God is angry with unbelievers. For this reason he made the stars so beautiful, so that from them he might be known as their great and wonderful Creator and alone be adored. It is written in the eighteenth Psalm: *The heavens declare the glory of God, and the firmament shows his handiwork,*[1] and so the human race is made guilty by the natural law. For men could learn this by the law of nature, with the structure of the world bearing witness that God, its author, is the only one who ought to be loved, something which Moses later put down in writing. But the people became ungodly, not worshiping the Creator, and so unrighteousness appeared in them, because although they saw the truth, they suppressed it and did not confess the one God.

[19] For what can be known about God is plain to them, because God has shown it to them.

The knowledge of God is plain from the structure of the world. God, who by nature is invisible, may be known even from things which are visible. His work is made in such a way that it reveals its Maker by its very visibility, so that what is uncertain may be known by what is certain, and everyone may believe that he is God, because he made this work, which is impossible for anyone else to do.

[20] Ever since the creation of the world his invisible nature, namely, his eternal power and deity, has been clearly perceived in the things that have been made. So they are without excuse;

Paul here repeats the same thing in order to teach even more absolutely that although the power and majesty of God cannot by themselves be seen by the eyes of the creature, they may be known by the work of the structure of the world. In this way he indicts those who lived without law, whether natural or Mosaic. For by the habit of sinning they broke the law of nature, wiping out any memory of God. But they did not want to accept the law, which had been given for their reformation, and thus were doubly condemned.

God's power and deity are eternal, so that they are without excuse. In order that ungodliness might in no way be excused, Paul added that the power of God and his eternal divinity were known by men, who were prevented by some foolishness from honoring him, whom they knew existed and provided for their welfare. For no one doubts that he has ordained the things which ripen annually for human use. His eternal power is Christ, by whom he creates things that did not exist and in whom they abide, so that even if his person is not known, his works are nevertheless clear. This is his divinity, by which the elements subsist in the work which he has decreed, so that they are without excuse. For someone who is convicted in so many ways cannot be excused.

[21] for although they knew God they did not honor him as God or give thanks to him, but they became futile in their thinking and their senseless minds were darkened.

They were so far from being ignorant that they confessed that there was a single principle, from which all things, heavenly, earthly and infernal, derived their origin, and that there

---

[1] Ps 19:1 in English versions.

was only one being who decreed what properties and duties would belong to every thing by nature. Yet knowing this, they did not give thanks. Paul is speaking of the ancients, in order to correct his contemporaries and future generations.

Truly this is futility, that knowing the truth they decided to worship something else, which they knew was not true, so that hiding from God they might worship idols. A cloud of error covered their heart, because although they should have honored the Creator all the more from the beautiful things which he made, they clung to what they had, saying that the things which they could see were sufficient for their salvation.

22Claiming to be wise, they became fools,

They imagined that they were wise because they thought they had explored the natural sciences, investigating the courses of the stars and the quantities of the elements, while rejecting the God who made them. In fact they are fools, for if these things are worthy of praise, how much more is their Creator!

Yet people who ignore God often suffer shame and make the miserable excuse that they can get to him by such things, just as it is possible to speak to the king through his courtiers. Come now! Can anyone be so foolish or so unconcerned about his salvation as to try to transfer the king's honor to a courtier, when if other people could be found to pass judgment on the case, these would undoubtedly be condemned by the law of majesty? Yet they transfer the honor of God's name to creation and, abandoning the Lord, worship their fellow servants, as if this were more important than serving God, and do not think that they are guilty of anything. For it is possible to go to the king through tribunes and courtiers, because the king is only a man

and has no idea who to trust. In God's case though, nothing escapes him, and he knows what everyone is worth. Earning his favor is the task of a devout mind, not of a flunkey. God will answer such a person whenever he speaks to him.

23and exchanged the glory of the immortal God for images resembling mortal man or birds or animals or reptiles.

So blinded were their hearts that they altered the majesty of the invisible God, which they knew from the things which he had made, not into men, but what is worse and is an inexcusable offense, into the image of men, so that the form of a corruptible man was called a god by them, in other words, a depiction of a man. Moreover, they did not dare to honor living people with this name, but elevated the images of dead men to the glory of God! What great idiocy, what great stupidity, in that they knew they were leading them to their damnation, among whom an image was more powerful than the truth, and the dead were mightier than the living! Turning away from the living God they preferred dead men, among whose number they found themselves, as it is said in the Wisdom of Solomon: *A mortal man makes a dead thing with wicked hands.*[1]

Birds or animals or reptiles. Paul regarded people subject to such things as guilty of total idiocy, since they were beyond mere dullness and vanity. They so diminished the majesty and glory of God that they gave the title of *god* to the images of things which were small and tiny. For the Babylonians were the first to deify a notion of Bel, who was portrayed as a dead man and had supposedly once been one of their kings. They also worshiped the dragon serpent, which Daniel the man of God killed, and of which they had an image. The Egyptians worshiped a quadruped which they called

---

[1]Wis 15:17.

Apis, and which was in the form of a bull. Jeroboam copied this evil by setting up calves in Samaria, to which the Jews were expected to offer sacrifices, and vultures, because the pagans have their *Coracina sacra*.[1] The Egyptians worshiped idols of all the things which I have mentioned as well as others, which I have no need to talk about right now. These things were done by people who thought they were wise in the world, but because by doing this, those who knew the invisible God did not honor him, they were unable to be wise in the things which are visible. For someone who has problems with the big things will not be wise in the little things either.

[24]Therefore God gave them up in the lusts of their hearts to impurity, to the dishonoring of their bodies among themselves,

Paul says that because the Gentiles had deified relics and images of things, to the detriment of the Creator God, they were given over to illusions, and given over, not so that they could do what they did not want to do, but so that they could carry out what they desired. And this is the goodness of God. For had it been right for them to be subjected, so that they would do what they did not want to do, they would have been crucified—for even the good, if it is done unwillingly, is bitter and evil—but they themselves voluntarily turned away from God and were handed over to the devil.

To *hand over* means to permit, not to encourage or to force, so that they were helped by the devil to put into practice the things which they conceived in their lusts. They never thought of doing anything good, and so they were handed over to uncleanness and damaged each other's bodies with abuse. Even now there are still men of this type, who are said to dishonor each other's bodies. When the thought of the mind is wrong, the bodies are said to be dishonored. Is not a stain on the body a sign of sin in the soul? When the body is contaminated, nobody doubts that there is sin in the soul.

[25]because they exchanged the truth about God for a lie and worshiped and served the creature rather than the Creator, who is blessed for ever! Amen.

They changed the truth about God into a lie to the point that they gave the name of the true God to these things, which are false gods. Ignoring what rocks and wood and other metals really are, they gave them an honor which does not belong to them, because the truth of God is turned into a lie when a rock is called God. This behavior drove out the God who is true, and when true and false shared a common name, it was easy for the true God to be regarded as false. This is what it means to change what is true into falsehood, for those things were not called rock or wood, but God. This is to worship the creature rather than the Creator, which is what they did. They did not deny God, but worshiped a creature as God. In order to justify this, they gave these things the honor due to God, so that their worship did injury to him. For that reason he hastened to punish them, because although they knew God, they did not honor him *who is blessed for ever. Amen.* This is true!

Blessing to God, he says, for ever, because God is eternal. Unbelief attributes honor to the gods of the Gentiles for a time only. For that reason it is not genuine, but truth resides in God. Elsewhere, Paul attributes this same blessing to the Son of God, saying among other things: *Christ is of them according to the flesh, who is God blessed above all for ever. Amen.*[2] Either both of these apply to Christ or else he said the same things about the Son as he said about the Father.

---

[1]This was a sacred rite of initiation in Mithraism, which involved the cult of ravens. [2]Rom 9:5.

26For this reason God gave them up to dishonorable passions. Their women exchanged natural relations for unnatural,

Paul tells us that these things came about, that a woman should lust after another woman, because God was angry at the human race on account of its idolatry. Those who interpret this verse differently do not understand the force of the argument. For what is it to change the use of nature into a use which is contrary to nature, if not to take away the former and adopt the latter, so that the same part of the body should be used by each of the sexes in a way for which it was not intended? Therefore, if this is the part of the body which they think it is, how could they have changed the natural use of it if this use had not been given to them by nature? He had said earlier that they had been handed over to uncleanness, but he did not explain in detail what he meant by that, which is why he goes on to state what follows next.

27and the men likewise gave up natural relations with women and were consumed with passion for one another, men committing shameless acts with men and receiving in their own persons the due penalty for their error.

It is clear that because they changed the truth of God into a lie, they changed the natural use into that use by which they were dishonored, and were condemned to the second death. For since Satan cannot make another law, having no power to do so, it must be said that they changed to another order, and by doing things which were not allowed, fell into sin.

Paul says that the due penalty comes from contempt of God, and that it is wickedness and obscenity. This is the prime cause of sin. What is worse, what is more harmful than that sin which deceives even the devil, and binds man to death? For just as idolatry is a most ungodly

and serious sin, its reward is the most horrible and disgusting suffering.

28And since they did not see fit to acknowledge God, God gave them up to a base mind and to improper conduct.

Because of the error of idols the Gentiles were handed over to doing evil things with each other, as has already been said. Because they thought they could get away with it, and that God would look the other way, and were therefore prone to neglect what they were doing, Paul adds here that they were more and more reduced to idiocy, and became ever readier to tolerate all kinds of evils, to the point that they imagined that God would never avenge things which no one doubted were offensive to humanity as well. He now lists all the evils which were added to these, so that if they should be converted to normal reason, they might recognize that these evils came upon them because of God's wrath.

29They were filled with all manner of wickedness, evil, covetousness, malice. Full of envy, murder, strife, deceit, malignity, they are gossips,

Paul put wickedness at the head of the list, because he thought that evil and covetousness depended on it. He then added malice, from which flows envy, murder, strife and deceit. After this he put malignity, which generates gossip and slander.

30slanderers, haters of God, insolent, haughty, boastful, inventors of evil, disobedient to parents,

Because these things were displeasing to God, Paul says that they were hateful to him, and because they are also displeasing to other people, he adds that they are insolent, haughty, boastful and inventors of evil, not just followers of it. For becoming true imitators of their father the devil, they invented the evil of idolatry, through which all the vices in the world originated, as well as the greatest perdition. For although the devil, whom Scripture says was a sinner from the beginning,[1] gloried in his tyrannical presumption, he never dared go so far as to call himself God. For among other things, he says to God: *All these things have been given to me,*[2] not: *All these things are from me.* In the book of Job the devil asks for power to be given to him,[3] and in the prophet Zechariah he thinks that he can contradict the priest, but does not claim power for himself.[4]

For this reason the idolaters are even worse, because they proclaim the divinity not only of the elements, but also of imaginary things. They were seized with such insolence that they did not even acknowledge their parents, who had given them birth! They rejoiced in their children, but despised those by whom they had come into being.

[31]foolish, faithless, heartless, ruthless.

They were foolish and faithless, and had no feelings either for God or for men. That is why they were heartless and ruthless. For someone who is cruel to his own family will be even more cruel to others!

[32]Though they know God's decree that those who do such things deserve to die, they not only do them but approve those who practice them.

Those who knew by the law of nature what God's righteousness was realized that these things were displeasing to God, but they did not want to think about it, because those who do such things are worthy of death, and not only those who do them, but those who allow them to be done, for consent is participation.

All these evil things constitute a body of sinners. They have become tied to sin by its power, so that they do things which are deserving of punishment. The cause of these evils began with the Sodomites who offended God, as was said above, and it has extended its branches into almost every part of the world, the cause of idolatry which heralds the wrath of God and is the first part of error and ungodliness. Paul condemns this first of all, because once it has been put right, their moral vices will also be corrected. Once the seed of evil is taken away, the fruits of wickedness dry up, for if the tree does not bring forth fruit its roots are cut out.

Therefore Moses recorded the [evil] deeds of Sodom and Gomorrah and did not pass over their result in silence, so as to scare people into avoiding them. This vice and corruption of a dishonored life is not tolerated by someone who meditates on God in his mind.

There are those who think that they are not guilty if they do not do what is wrong, but they are tolerant of those who do. But to tolerate such things when they should be condemned is to give silent assent to them or even to delight in hearing about them. Someone who is impure and wicked is fully aware of what he is doing and does nothing to avoid it, but rather glories in being that kind of person as if it were a point of honor. He is not ashamed of these things, especially when he sees that he can get away with them and that he is being supported by those who are not like himself. So it is with those who encourage their crimes, and therefore it is right that they should be considered equally guilty of them. Again, there are people who not only do evil things but also tolerate others who do, so that they not only do them themselves but also consent to seeing them done.

Their wickedness is double, for those who do such things but prevent others are not so

---

[1] Jn 3:8. [2] Lk 4:6. [3] Job 2:6. [4] Zech 3:1.

bad, because they realize that these things are evil and do not justify them. The worst people are those who do these things and approve of others doing them as well, not fearing God but desiring the increase of evil. They do not try to justify them either, but in their case it is because they want to persuade people that there is nothing wrong in doing them.

Romans 2

¹Therefore you have no excuse, O man, whoever you are, when you judge another; for in passing judgment upon him you condemn yourself, because you, the judge, are doing the very same things.

Paul shows that both the man who does evil and the one who approves of others who do it are deserving of death, in case someone who does evil himself but does not approve of others who do it (and says openly that he does not approve of them) thinks that he can excuse himself thereby. Paul teaches that such a person is inexcusable. It is not right to tolerate someone who pretends to be better than others when in fact he is worse. Something is wrong when a person who ought to be punished appears to be worthy of honor instead.

²We know that the judgment of God rightly falls upon those who do such things.

This means that we are not unaware that God will judge these people in truth, for we judge them ourselves. If what they do is displeasing to us, how much more will it be so to God, who is truly just and efficient in carrying out his work. When Paul says that God will judge these things, he is really instilling fear [in his readers]. Although the ungodly say that God does not care, in fact he will judge the wicked and most strictly render to each one according

to his deserts, not sparing anybody.

³Do you suppose, O man, that when you judge those who do such things and yet do them yourself, you will escape the judgment of God?

Paul does not want the Romans to entertain the hope that they can be pardoned, since that would be unjust, when they have been given the ability to judge evil and wrongdoing, and to avoid it. So if they cannot manage to avoid it in this life, they will not be able to escape the judgment of God in the future either. For God, with whom there is neither flattery nor respect of persons, will judge them on his own authority.

If someone thinks he ought to be immune from such punishment, let him say so. But if it is not right that he should escape, let him believe that God will judge, and judge rightly, and that it is true that God, the Creator of the world, will reward the merits of his creation with due attention and care.

If God had made the world and then neglected it, he would be called a bad Creator, because he would be demonstrating by his neglect that what he had made was not good. But since it cannot be denied that God made good things—for it is unworthy and impossible for one who is good to make bad things—it is necessary to say that he is also concerned about them. This is because it would be a crime and a reproach to him if he were to neglect the good things which he had made, and because in fact life itself is governed by his servants the elements, who act according to his pleasure and plan, as the Lord himself says: *He makes his sun rise on the evil and on the good, and sends rain on the just and on the unjust.*[1] Therefore, if he does all that, will he not take care to look after what he has made by rewarding those who love him and condemning those who reject him?

---

[1]Mt 5:45.

4Or do you presume upon the riches of his kindness and forbearance and patience? Do you not know that God's kindness is meant to lead you to repentance?

Paul says this so that no one should think that he has escaped, just because God's goodness has allowed him to go on sinning, nor should he think that God's patience is to be despised, as if he did not care about human affairs. Rather, he ought to understand that God conceals himself, because his judgment is not promised in this life. It is for the future, so that in the next life the man who did not believe that God is a judge will repent. It was in order to reveal the terror of future judgment and [warn us] that his patience should not be despised, that God said: *I have been silent. But shall I be silent for ever?*[1] Thus the man who has been punished and has not repented will repent when he sees the future judgment of God, which he has spurned. At that time, anyone who thought that the long-suffering of God's goodness was something to laugh at will not hesitate to beg for mercy.

5But by your hard and impenitent heart you are storing up wrath for yourself on the day of wrath when God's righteous judgment will be revealed.

The one who hopes he can get away with his sins not only remains unconvertible and intractable, but in addition sins more seriously still, convinced that there will be no future revenge. He has an impenitent heart, and is not aware that he is storing up wrath for himself on the day of wrath.

6For he will render to every man according to his works:

Such a person must be punished more severely, even to the point of being tortured in eternal fire, because despite a long stay of execution, not only did he not want to change, but he increased his sinning, adding to his contempt for God. The day of wrath is for sinners, because it is the day on which they will be punished. Therefore the wrath is on those who receive punishment on the day when the just judgment of God is revealed. For it will be revealed and made known, even though it continues to be denied as long as it is in the future. Thus when what is believed not to exist is pointed out, it is revealed. It is pointed out to those who deny it—because it is clear to believers—so that they will confess, even against their will, that the judgment of God is just when he renders to each one according to his works. Will they not admit that it is just when they see their evil deeds avenged?

7to those who by patience in well-doing seek for glory and honor and immortality, he will give eternal life;

Paul preaches that the judgment of God is just, as he has declared the future will be good. He says that those who recognize that the patience of God is designed partly for concealment and partly for greater revenge on those who do not correct themselves, repent of their previous works and live rightly, armed with confidence in their faith in God, will not have to wait long before receiving their promised reward of eternal life. For God will give them glory and honor. And to avoid invidious comparisons with this life, where men are also glorious and honored, Paul added *immortality*, so that people would realize that the glory and honor which they will obtain will be of a different order altogether, when it is accompanied by immortality. In this life honor and glory are frequently lost, for the one who gives them, the things he gives and the one who receives them

---

[1]Cf. Is 42:14.

are all mortal, but on the day of God's judgment, honor and glory will be given to the immortal and will be eternal, for this substance of ours will be glorified by a certain change of properties. Therefore, those who seek eternal life are not merely those who believe correctly, but those who live correctly as well.

8but for those who are factious and do not obey the truth, but obey wickedness, there will be wrath and fury.

Those who doubt that there will be a future judgment of God through Christ, and who for that reason despise his patience, do all they can to discredit it as being true and certain, because they believe in wickedness. For wickedness is to deny what God has foretold. Paul mentions three things which are fitting punishments for unbelief—wrath, fury and tribulation. Wrath is not in the one who judges, but in the one who is judged, because he is made guilty. God is said to get angry because he is believed to take vengeance, but in reality the nature of God is immune from such passions. And so that we should believe that God not only gets angry, but that he will take revenge, Paul added: *and fury.* This means that God will seek vengeance, adding to his anger the injury which has been done to him.

9There will be tribulation and distress for every human being who does evil, the Jew first and also the Greek,

Tribulation refers to the punishment which the condemned sinner will suffer. Evil is not just a matter of deeds but of unbelief as well. Here Paul is speaking about the unbeliever, which is why he has said *for every soul*[1] so that you will understand that the punishment is spiritual and not physical, for the soul is subject to invisible punishments. Paul always puts

the Jew first, whether he is to be praised or blamed, because of his privileged ancestry. If a Jew believes, he will be all the more honored, because of Abraham, but if he doubts, he will be treated that much worse, because he has rejected the gift promised to his forefathers.

10but glory and honor and peace for every one who does good, the Jew first and also the Greek.

Just as Paul mentioned three woes for unbelievers, so now he mentions three benefits for believers: genuine honor as sons of God, unchanging glory, and peace, so that those who live rightly may live in peace in the future, undisturbed by any commotion. For everyone who keeps himself from wrongdoing has a judge who will be favorable to him.

11For God shows no partiality.

Paul shows that neither Jews nor Greeks will be rejected by God if they believe in Christ, but that both are justified by faith. He also says that those who do not believe are equally guilty, since circumcision without faith is worthless but uncircumcision with faith is acceptable. For God does not recognize any privilege of race, which would make him accept unbelievers on account of their ancestors and reject believers because of the unworthiness of their parents. On the contrary, he rewards or condemns each one on his own merits.

12All who have sinned without the law will also perish without the law, and all who have sinned under the law will be judged by the law.

How can someone sin without the law, when Paul says that everyone is subject to the law of nature? Here he is speaking about the law of Moses, to which the Jews are subject, al-

---

[1]The word "soul" is rendered "human being" in the English translation.

though they do not believe, and the Gentiles also, but only because they have chosen not to attach themselves to it. Gentile unbelievers are doubly guilty, because they have neither assented to the law given through Moses, nor have they received the grace of Christ. Therefore it is quite right that they should perish. But just as the person who sins without the law will perish, so also the one who has kept the law without knowing it will be justified. For the keeper of the law maintains his righteousness by nature. If the law is given, not for the righteous but for the unrighteous, whoever does not sin is a friend of the law. For him, faith alone is the way by which he is made perfect, for avoiding evil will not gain him any advantage with God unless he also believes in God, so that he may be righteous on both counts. The one righteousness is temporal, but the other is eternal.

Just as the Gentiles, even if they keep the natural law, will perish if they do not accept the faith of Christ—for it is a greater thing to confess belief in one Lord, since God is one, than it is to avoid sinning (for the first of these has to do with God, the second with us)—so also the Jews who live under the law will be accused and judged by the law, since they have not accepted the Christ who was promised to them in the law. And if you wonder about this, the fate of the Jews will be worse than that of the Gentiles, for it is worse to lose what was promised than not to receive what was not hoped for in the first place. In other words, whereas the unbelieving Gentile has not entered the kingdom of God, the unbelieving Jew has been thrown out of it.

13For it is not the hearers of the law who are righteous before God, but the doers of the law who will be justified.

Paul says this because those who hear the law

are not justified unless they believe in Christ, whom the law itself has promised. This is what it means to keep the law. For how does someone who does not believe the law keep it, when he does not receive the one to whom the law bears witness? But the one who appears not to be under the law, because he is uncircumcised in his flesh, may be said to have kept the law if he believes in Christ. And he who says he is in the law, in other words, the Jew, is not a doer of the law but a hearer only, because what is said in the law does not penetrate to his mind, for he does not believe in the Christ who is written about in the law, as Philip said to Nathanael: *We have found Jesus, of whom Moses in the law and also the prophets wrote.*[1]

14When Gentiles who have not the law do by nature what the law requires they are a law to themselves, even though they do not have the law.

Paul calls the Gentiles Christians because he is the teacher of the Gentiles, as he says elsewhere: *For I speak to you Gentiles.*[2] These people are uncircumcised and do not keep new moons or the sabbath or the law of foods, yet under the guidance of nature they believe in God and in Christ, in other words, in the Father and the Son. This is what it means to keep the law—to acknowledge the God of the law. For this is the first part of wisdom—to fear God the Father, from whom all things come, and the Lord Jesus, his Son, through whom all things come. Therefore, nature itself acknowledges its Creator by its own judgment, not by the law but by reason, for the creature recognizes its Maker in itself.

15They show that what the law requires is written on their hearts, while their conscience also bears witness and their conflicting thoughts accuse or perhaps excuse them

---

[1]Jn 1:45. [2]Rom 11:13.

The meaning here is that those who believe under the guidance of nature do the work of the law, not through the letter but through their conscience. For the work of the law is faith, which although it is revealed in the Word of God, also shows itself to be a law for the natural judgment, since it goes beyond what the law commands and believes in Christ. These people believe because of the inner witness of their conscience, because they know in their conscience that what they believe is right—for it is not inappropriate for the creature to believe and worship his Creator, nor is it absurd for the servant to recognize his Lord.

Paul said that unbelieving Jews will be judged by the law—for the law will accuse them, because it promised them Christ and when he came they did not want to accept him. But those Gentiles who have chosen not to believe will be judged first of all by other believing Gentiles, just as the Lord said that his disciples would judge the unbelieving Jews: *They themselves will be your judges.*[1] The unbelief of the Jews will be judged by the faith of the apostles who, although Jews themselves, believed in Christ while the rest of their people rejected him. Similarly the Gentiles will be accused by their own thoughts if, touched by the faith and power of the Creator, they refuse to believe. But if because of some ignorance a man does not consciously believe the words or deeds of the Lord, his conscience will defend him on the day of judgment, because he did not think that he was obliged to believe. He will be judged not as an intentional malefactor but as one who was merely ignorant, although he will not escape future punishment, since that cannot be overlooked.

Paul divides the Gentiles into two types, those who believe and those who do not. Earlier he was speaking about Gentile believers, but later he added these reflections about those Gentiles who do not believe, to the effect that just as those who believe are praised by their consciences, so those who do not believe are accused by theirs. For although someone who does not believe may not appear guilty of anything at all in his own eyes, because he has not taken this idea on board, he is nevertheless convicted because he has not persuaded himself that these things are true, even though he has seen them confirmed by powerful testimonies which many have accepted.

If this whole issue is believed to refer to believing Gentiles, I think that it can be understood as follows, for he says: *For what have I to do with judging outsiders?*[2] And: *He who does not believe is condemned already.*[3] And: *The ungodly will not rise in the judgment.*[4] Those whom Paul says will be accused or defended on the day of judgment are Christians. Those who differ from the mainline church, either because they think differently about Christ or because they disagree about the meaning of the Bible in the tradition of the church (e.g., Montanists, Novatianists, Donatists and other heretics) will be accused by their own thoughts on the day of judgment. Likewise the man who recognizes that the mainline faith is true but refuses to follow it because he does not want it to appear that he has been corrected and is ashamed to give up what he has so long held will be accused by his own thoughts on the day of judgment.

[16]on that day when, according to my gospel, God judges the secrets of men by Christ Jesus.

There are two thoughts inside a man which will accuse each other—the good and the evil. The good accuses the evil because it has denied the truth, and the evil accuses the good because it has not done what it knows to be right. In this way a man who knows that the mainline church is good and true but persists in his heresy or schism will be judged guilty.

---

[1]Mt 12:27. [2]1 Cor 5:12. [3]Jn 3:18. [4]Ps 1:5.

His thoughts will excuse each other because he has always thought that it was expedient to do what he did. He will say: "In my mind I have always thought it expedient to do what I have done. This was my faith." He will have a better case, even though he will still have to be corrected, because his conscience will not accuse him on the day of judgment. This is how the secret things of men will be judged by Jesus Christ our Lord on the day of judgment.

[17]But if you call yourself a Jew and rely upon the law and boast of your relation to God

They are called Jews because it was their ancestral right to be called Israelites. Nevertheless, if we wish to understand everything which is relevant to the case, we must note that the name *Jew* had three different meanings. First, it meant the children of Abraham, who because of his faith was made the father of many nations. Next it refers to Jacob, who because of his increasing faith was called Israel, for the dignity which began with the father was honored in the sons. Third, they are called Jews not so much because of Judah as because of Christ, who was born of Judah according to the flesh, since in Judah was made known what later would be revealed in Christ. For it is said: *Judah will be your master*,[1] and: *Judah, your brothers praise you.*[2] This praise was not given to Judah as such, but to Christ, whom nowadays all those whom he deigns to call his brethren praise. For he said to the women: *Go and say to my brothers that I shall go before you into Galilee.*[3] The Jews themselves do not understand the meaning of their name, and claim that it refers to the human Judah.

[18]and know his will and approve what is excellent, because you are instructed in the law,

It is no great deal if a Jew should believe, since because he has been taught by the law, it is dangerous for him not to believe—he has the law as his guide. But in order for the believer to be exalted, Paul extols the merit of the forefathers, since even though someone might come to maturity by himself, he is nevertheless strengthened by their example.

[19]and if you are sure that you are a guide to the blind, a light to those who are in darkness, [20]a corrector of the foolish, a teacher of children, having in the law the embodiment of knowledge and truth—

These things are true, because it is the task of the law to teach the ignorant, to subject the wicked to God and to provoke those who by the worship of idols are ungodly to trust in a better hope by the promise which is given through the law. The teacher of the law is right to glory in these things, because he is teaching the form of truth. But if the teacher does not accept him whom the law has promised, he glories in vain in the law, to which he is doing harm as long as he rejects the Christ who is promised in the law. In that case he is no more learned than the fools, nor is he a teacher of children, nor is he a light to those who are in the darkness, but rather he is leading all of these into perdition.

[21]you then who teach others, will you not teach yourself? While you preach against stealing, do you steal?

This means: *You who complain about the Gentiles, because they are without the law and God, are accusing yourself, because you do not believe in the Christ promised by the law but find this belief in those you are complaining about.* The Jew does what he preaches should not be done. For by denying the Christ promised to

---

[1]Judg 20:18. [2]Gen 49:8. [3]Mt 28:7.

us in the law, he removes faith by false interpretation, and thus does what he preaches against.

22You who say that one must not commit adultery, do you commit adultery? You who abhor idols, do you rob temples?

The Jew adulterates the law by removing the truth of Christ from it and putting lies in his place. In another of his epistles, Paul writes: *They are adulterers of God's Word.*[1] A man is sacrilegious when he denies Christ, whom the law and the prophets call God. Isaiah says: *God is in you, and apart from you there is no God, for you are God and we did not know, the God of Israel, the Savior whom Jesus made plain.*[2] Did the Jews ever say: *You are God and we did not know it* of God the Father, when the entire law proclaims the authority of God the Father, by whom all things are made? But when the Son of God appeared, what was hidden was revealed after the resurrection. It was then that it was said of him: *You are God and we did not know it.* The one who, in the time of the law, was thought to be only an angel and the leader of the Lord's army, was revealed as the Son of God, and then it was said with thanksgiving: *You are God and we did not know it.* This therefore means that it was he who appeared to the patriarchs as God, and was afterward incarnated, although he was not recognized by everyone.

23You who boast in the law, do you dishonor God by breaking the law?

The breaker of the law is the one who ignores the meaning of the law, which speaks of the incarnation and divinity of Christ, and dishonors God by not accepting the testimony which he gave concerning his Son. For the Father said: *This is my beloved Son.*[3]

24For as it is written, "The name of God is blasphemed among the Gentiles because of you."[4]

Isaiah the prophet said this because God's name was being blasphemed among the Gentiles when the Jews, by their misdeeds, did not observe the things which were handed down to them, but instead gave glory to idols, giving the impression that they had defeated the God of the Jews by conquering them. So also at the time of the apostles, God's name was being blasphemed in Christ, because the Jews, by denying that Christ was God, were blaspheming the Father also, as the Lord said: *Whoever receives me does not receive me, but him who sent me.*[5] Therefore God was blasphemed among the Gentiles, because when they believed in Christ, the Jews tried to persuade them not to call Christ God, so that the blasphemy of the Gentiles originated among the Jews.

25Circumcision indeed is of value if you obey the law; but if you break the law, your circumcision becomes uncircumcision.

An opponent might say: *If circumcision is of value, why was it stopped?* But it is only of value if you keep the law. Circumcision may be retained, therefore, but if it is to be of any value, the law must be observed. So why did Paul prohibit what he shows to be of value if the law is observed?

Paul answers by saying that if the law is not kept, the Jew effectively becomes a Gentile. But he claimed that circumcision had been given for [defining] the race of Abraham, because circumcision was from Abraham. He could not build the things which he had torn down. For he says this in order to teach that it was of benefit to be of the race of Abraham if the law were kept. To keep the law is to believe

---

[1]2 Cor 2:17. [2]Is 45:14-15. [3]Mt 3:17. [4]Is 52:5. [5]Lk 9:48.

in Christ, who was promised to Abraham. Those who are justified by faith have their own merit, and are included in the honor shown to the patriarchs. For every mention of salvation in the law refers to Christ. Therefore the man who believes in Christ is the man who keeps the law. But if he does not believe then he is a transgressor of the law, because he has not accepted Christ, of whom the law prophesied with regard to the righteousness which was to come but which it could not itself give. It is no advantage for him to be called a son of Abraham, because the only person who deserves to be called a son of Abraham is one who follows Abraham's faith, by which he is made worthy before God. This is why Paul said: *Your circumcision has become uncircumcision*, that is to say: *You have become like a Gentile, because you do not believe in the one who is the son of circumcision promised to Abraham.*

26So, if a man who is uncircumcised keeps the precepts of the law, will not his uncircumcision be regarded as circumcision?

Faith in Christ is the righteousness of the law, as Paul says elsewhere: *Christ is the end of the law for the justification of all who believe.*[1] whence it is clear that if a Gentile believes in Christ he becomes a son of Abraham, who is the father of faith.

27Then those who are physically uncircumcised but keep the law will condemn you who have the written code and circumcision but break the law.

The Gentile who believes under the guidance of nature condemns the Jew, to whom Christ was promised through the law and who refused to believe in him when he came. For as much as the Gentile is worthy of glory for having

known the author of nature by nature alone, as the apostle Peter says: *You killed the author of life,*[2] so the Jew deserves to be punished all the more, because he did not know Christ the Creator, either by nature or by the law.

28For he is not a real Jew who is one outwardly, nor is true circumcision something external and physical. 29He is a Jew who is one inwardly, and real circumcision is a matter of the heart, spiritual and not literal. His praise is not from men but from God.

It is clear why Paul denies that the circumcision of the flesh has any merit with God. For Abraham was not justified because he was circumcised; rather he was justified because he believed, and afterward he was circumcised. It is the circumcision of the heart which is praiseworthy before God; to circumcise the heart means to cut out error and recognize the Creator. And because the circumcision of the heart was to come in the future, Moses said: *Circumcise the hardness of your heart,*[3] and Jeremiah also: *Circumcise the foreskin of your heart.*[4] He said this to Jews who were following idols. For there is a veil over the heart, which the one who is converted to God circumcises, because faith removes the cloud of error and grants those who are perfect knowledge of God in the mystery of the Trinity, which was unknown in earlier times. The praise of this circumcision is from God but is hidden to men, for it is the merit of the heart which God looks for, not that of the flesh. But the praise of the Jews is from men, for they glory in the circumcision of the flesh, which comes from their ancestors. This is why in another letter Paul says the following, among other things: *They glory in their shame, who mind earthly things,*[5] that is, who think that the circumcision of the flesh is their glory. For whoever glories in the

---

[1]Rom 10:4. [2]Acts 3:15. [3]Deut 10:16. [4]Jer 4:4. [5]Phil 3:19. Ambrosiaster reads "shame" as *pudenda* in Latin, referring primarily to the sexual organs.

flesh minds earthly things, whereas whoever glories in the Spirit—his praise is from God, because his belief proceeds from the Spirit and not from the flesh.

Romans 3

¹Then what advantage has the Jew? Or what is the value of circumcision? ² Much in every way. To begin with, the Jews are entrusted with the oracles of God.

Although Paul says that there are many things which pertain to the honor and merit of the seed of Abraham, he records only one of them openly, because their greatest boast was that they were judged worthy to receive the law, by which they learned to distinguish right from wrong. Only after that was it possible for the value of other things to be understood. But as far as the Jews according to the flesh are concerned (that is, the unbelievers among them), Paul shows that the witness of their race is of no advantage to them. But so as not to appear to be treating them all, including the believers among them, badly, he teaches that the law is very useful to Jewish believers, because they are children of Abraham. For it was to them that the oracles of God were entrusted, until by the merits of their ancestors they received the law, which had been reformed (for it had almost gone out of use by the sins of men, who did more or less what they liked in front of God), and were called God's people. Egypt was hit by different plagues because of the wrongs which it did to them; they dined on heavenly manna; they were a terror to all nations, as Rahab the harlot bore witness. Moreover, it was to them that Christ the Savior was promised, for their sanctification. Therefore Paul says that in many ways it was useful to the Jews, because they were the children of Abraham,

and came ahead of the Gentiles, but only if they believed.

³What if some were unfaithful? Does their faithlessness nullify the faithfulness of God?

Paul says this because it was not foreordained that believing Jews would be thought unworthy to receive what God had promised just because the others were unbelieving, for the promise was such that the gift of grace would be given to those who believed.

Therefore, God is not put out because of the unbelief of the Jews, and will grant eternal life to other believers, which he promised would be given to those who believed in Christ. Those who did not believe excluded themselves from consideration, without doing the rest any injury. Having said this, Paul commends Jewish believers, because it was not their fault that many of their kinsmen refused to believe.

⁴By no means! Let God be true though every man be false, as it is written, "That thou mayest be justified in thy words, and prevail when thou art judged."[1]

Because God is true, he gives what he has promised. To fail is human, for the times and the foolishness of nature make man unstable, in that he does not have foreknowledge. But God, for whom there is no future, remains unchanging, as he says: *I the Lord do not change.*[2] Therefore Paul says that all men are liars, and this is true. For nature is fallible, and is not unreasonably called a liar. It may be a liar intentionally or accidentally, but we must not expect God to be like that, for he is perfect and full of good will, and will accomplish what he has promised. He even confirms this by the prophetic oracle: *Thou art justified in thy sentence and blameless in thy judgment.*[3]

The prophetic word bears witness that God

---

[1]Ps 51:4. [2]Mal 3:6. [3]Ps 51:4.

is just in his promises and in his words, nor is his faith lessened by the unfaithfulness of some people, which it overcomes by giving. Unfaithful people say that God will never give anything, which is why he will give what he is assumed not to give, and by doing so will disprove the claim that he will not do it. Thus the ungodliness which does not believe and denies that the things God has promised are true will be proved wrong. It will see the resurrection, which it denies actually taking place, and will thereby know that unbelief will be overcome by the promise and truth of God. This is because God is truthful, whereas every human being who denies what will come to pass is a liar.

In order to back up what he has said above, which is that God is faithful to his promise and every human being [who doubts this] is a liar, Paul quotes a prophetic example from Psalm 51 in order to show that God is justified in what he says and that man is a liar because of his unbelief. In the book of Psalms we find it said both that God is just and truthful, and that all men are liars. It says that a man is a liar when he does not believe what God has promised, for by denying that God will give what he has promised he becomes a liar.

Although man is a liar for many reasons, he calls God a liar when he does not believe in his promises. Therefore God says that every man is a liar if he does not believe in the promises of God. This refers primarily to the Jews, whose case Paul examines in this passage. They saw Christ but denied that he was the one whom God had promised, and for this reason they are condemned as liars. For God is truthful and has sent Christ as he promised to do, and he overcomes when he is judged, because he will give what it was said he would not give.

Therefore, whoever does not believe in God is judged a liar. When he gives what it is thought he will not give, he overcomes [the opposition] by showing that he is truthful and that the man who does not believe in his words is a liar. For he will see the Son of God, whom he denies, [coming] in majesty, and he will see the resurrection of the flesh and thus know that unbelief will be defeated by the promise and truth of God. Christ too overcame when he was judged. For he was unjustly put to death and made the devil guilty. He had already defeated him by not sinning, so that when he was later "defeated" he could liberate those whom the devil was keeping in hell. This is what it means to say that all men are liars and that God alone is truthful.

⁵But if our wickedness serves to show the justice of God, what shall we say? That God is unjust to inflict wrath on us? (I speak in a human way.)

The apostle added this according to the words of the prophet David. Because David had sinned on account of Uriah the Hittite,[1] and knew that the promise would not be given to sinners, he pleads that the righteousness of the words of God might overrule the judgment which said that the promise should not be given to sinners, and that it might sanctify the penitent in order to give him what God had promised he would give to the righteous. This is why Paul adds: *If our wickedness serves to show the justice of God,* et cetera. If God is justified merely because we are sinners, it would be wrong of him to pardon us on that account. This is true, if it can really be said that our wickedness is of some advantage to God. But it is dangerous to speak like that. God is not unjust if he judges, because our unrighteousness is of no benefit to him, as if he would somehow be justified by our sins, in other words, as if he would somehow rejoice at our sins, which make him alone appear to be righteous.

---

[1] 2 Sam 11:4–12:25.

This way of thinking suits men, but not God, because it does not happen that God should ever be unjust, only man. Nor does our unrighteousness make God righteous, if he gives to us sinners what he promised to the saints, for although we are sinners, we are reformed by repentance, so that it is not as sinners but as those who have been cleansed that we deserve to receive the promise.

This is not the meaning of the prophet David when he says: *Against you only have I sinned and done this evil in your sight, so that you might be justified in your words and win out when you pass judgment*,[1] although the false interpretation of wicked people claims that the sins and bad deeds of men contribute to the righteousness of God, because he looks good when we do wrong and our wickedness highlights his righteousness. Therefore, since God is not unjust when he imposes his anger, neither is he justified by our sins, for if he were justified by our sins, he would be unjust if he were to punish us for this. This is absurd! God does not want us to sin, and for that reason he is just if he brings his anger to bear.[2]

[6] By no means! For then how could God judge the world?

It is true that it would not have been just if God had judged the world if its sins were of some benefit to him, so that whenever sinners received forgiveness at his nod, God would appear to be good, and that if they had not sinned, he would not appear to be righteous. For if they had not sinned there would be nothing to forgive, and God would not be good. But this kind of thinking is absurd!

[7] But if through my falsehood God's truthfulness abounds to his glory, why am I still being condemned as a sinner?

It is clear that if human sin benefits the glory of God by making it appear that he is the only one who is true, sinners would not be so called because they sin, for it would not be by their own will but by God's impulse that they sinned, which is absurd.

[8] And why not do evil that good may come?—as some people slanderously charge us with saying. Their condemnation is just.

Here is why the apostle asked himself this question. The matter was raised by opponents, as if those who preached the forgiveness of sins meant that they should do evil and good would come of it. In other words, they should sin, so that by forgiving their sins God would appear to be good, according to what has just been said above. Paul calls this blasphemy and rejects it as a misinterpretation of God's teaching. Faith is not meant to encourage people to sin, particularly since it preaches that God will judge. Rather it gives sinners a remedy, so that having recovered their health, they may live under the law of God and not sin again.

Their condemnation is just. That is to say, the condemnation of those men who, out of jealousy toward us, attribute what was said above to us, is just. The Jews launched these charges in order to discredit the apostles' teaching, saying that when the latter preached the forgiveness of sins, what they were really doing was encouraging further sinning. Their claim was that people who had assurance of forgiveness would be quick to sin, when in fact it is dangerous to sin after accepting the faith, and equally dangerous for this idea to be preached to believers.

[9] What then? Are we Jews any better off? No, not at all; for I have already charged that all men, both Jews and Greeks, are under the power of sin,

---

[1]Ps 51:4. [2]Another version replaces this sentence with: "Let no one say that God is unjust. This idea suits the man whom God says goes wrong, is deceived and deceives [others], for God remains immutable and cannot stop loving what he has made."

Paul is saying: *Why go on talking like this? For we have shown by the examples given that all, Jews and Gentiles alike, are guilty, and that the law is being kept in vain.* First he showed that the Gentiles are guilty according to the law of nature, and also because they did not accept the law of Moses, for which reason their case is very bad indeed. Then he showed that the Jews were also guilty, because although they appeared to be living under God's law and defended their privilege by the merit of their ancestors, in fact they brought the grace of God into disrepute because they rejected the promise made to their ancestors. To back up this assertion he quotes Psalm 14 as follows:

[10]as it is written:
   "None is righteous, no not one";[1]

From unrighteousness Paul goes on to list their evil deeds, and even adds some worse ones in order to show that there was no hope for them unless they cried out for the mercy of Christ, who forgives sins.

   [11]"no one understands, no one seeks for God."

It is true that if someone were to make the effort to understand, he would not be unrighteous. Nor is it a secret that if he understood what the benefit to him would be, he would seek God, and not be like Asa the king of Judah, who after receiving many blessings from God fell so far that when he suffered lameness in his feet he would not seek God, even though there was a prophet present.[2]

   [12]"All have turned aside, together they have gone wrong;
      no one does good, not even one."

No one doubts that those who do not look to God for help are inclined to seek help from

vanity, and vanity is an idol. Those who disregard God become useless. Once that happens, they cannot do good either, for those who have already fallen just go from bad to worse.

   [13]"Their throat is an open grave,
   they use their tongues to deceive.
   The venom of asps is under their lips."[3]

Already chained to evil, they wanted, if possible, to devour the good, so that just as a sepulcher is open to receive corpses, so their throat is open to devour the good. Those who had fallen for such evil deeds and talked about them were deceived. The words of men are like tiny mice. They speak in order to deceive, and just as poison flows from the lips of a serpent, so trickery and deceit flow from their lips.

   [14]"Their mouth is full of curses and
      bitterness."[4]

It is clear and obvious that evil people are always throwing curses and bitterness at the good, in an attempt to harm and distract them.

   [15]"Their feet are swift to shed blood,"[5]

Scripture says this about the murder of the prophets, whom they killed without hesitation—slow to do good, but swift to murder.

   [16]"in their paths are ruin and misery,"

Since they hastened to do evil, Paul calls their path a ruinous and unhappy way.

   [17]"and the way of peace they do not know."

Having chosen the way of hostility, along which they were heading toward the second

---

[1]Ps 14:1-3; 53:1-3. [2]Cf. 2 Chron 16:12. [3]Ps 5:9; 140:3. [4]Ps 10:7. [5]Is 59:7-8.

---

death, they did not want to know about the way which leads to eternal life, which is called the way of peace, because with God as its guardian, it will have no disturbance. Men of good will will have this rest with God.

[18]*"There is no fear of God before their eyes."*[1]

Since people of this kind have no sense, they have no fear of God. For *the fear of God is the beginning of wisdom,*[2] says Solomon. But Scripture did not say that they did not have the fear of God; it said: *There is no fear of God before their eyes.* For seeing how evil their works were, and not being horrified by them, they are said not to have the fear of God before their eyes.

The prophet Jeremiah also referred to all these people when he said: *Then they all rose up against the prophet of the Lord and wanted to kill him,*[3] and then a little later: *Not all the people went along with this.*[4]

Paul therefore uses the word *all* to mean first the wicked and then the good. When he says that *all have turned away,* he does not mean every last person, but only that part of the people which contained all the wicked ones (as the above-mentioned prophet also says). There have always been two nations in the one people. Here Paul is speaking of the nation which the Lord rebukes under the name of Jerusalem, when he says: *Jerusalem, Jerusalem, who kill the prophets,* et cetera.[5] Elsewhere he speaks of *a wicked and adulterous generation*[6] and of *a nation of vipers.*[7]

Isaiah the prophet also complains about them when he says: *Woe to the sinful nation, a most wicked seed.*[8] They are *a most wicked seed* because of the ill will by which they bring forth bad fruit. But the apostle shows that if they want to, they can be converted, as he says in another letter: *We too were once children of wrath by nature,* et cetera.[9]

[19]*Now we know that whatever the law says it speaks to those who are under the law, so that every mouth may be stopped, and the whole world may be held accountable to God.*

It is clear that the law censures those who first of all did not believe their leader, Moses, nor their ancestors the prophets, whom they killed, nor the apostles who were their kinsmen according to the flesh, whose blood they spilled. They were always ungodly and rebellious against God, so as to be condemned by the law, whose authority they thought should be despised. For just as in evil, one thing is the cause of all the rest, so it is also with the good. Therefore the wickedness of everyone like them is proved by their behavior. These things refer to the disobedience of the Jews, who bore witness to themselves and to their ancestors on the basis of the law.

Paul says this because, with the Jews bound in sin, the whole world has become subject to God. For there is no doubt that the pagans were immersed in sins and wickedness, and that for that reason the whole world bowed before God, in order to obtain forgiveness. The whole world includes both Jews and Gentiles, from whom believers are set apart. Therefore, when Paul affirms that the Jews, who had received God's law and to whom the promise had been given, were bound in sin, there is no doubt that all the Gentiles were also guilty of death. For this reason, he says that *every mouth is stopped and the whole world is made accountable to God.* For all have been found guilty and need the mercy of God, whether they be Jews or Gentiles.

[20]*For no human being will be justified in his sight by works of the law, since through the law comes knowledge of sin.*

Paul never says that men will not be justified

---

[1]Ps 36:1. [2]Prov 1:7. [3]Jer 26:8. [4]Cf. Jer 26:16. [5]Mt 23:37. [6]Mt 12:39. [7]Mt 3:7. [8]Is 1:4. [9]Eph 2:3.

before God because they have not kept the law of righteousness in the commandments, but because they have refused to believe the sacrament of the mystery of God, which is in Christ. For it is by that that God has declared that men should be justified, and not by the law, which justifies for a time, but not [eternally] before God. Therefore those who keep the law in time are justified, but not before God, because faith, by which men are justified before God, is not in them. For faith is greater than the law, since the law pertains to us but faith pertains to God. The law has a temporary righteousness, but faith has an eternal one. When Paul says *all flesh*[1] he means every human being, just as the prophet Isaiah says that *all flesh shall see the salvation of God*,[2] which means that every human being will see the Christ of God, in whom the salvation of everyone is found. But when he says *in the flesh*, he means those who are bound by sin. For just as righteousness makes men spiritual, so also sins make men carnal, and men take the name from the deed.

By faith the law is abolished, and faith then follows. What then is this law, through which he says that sin is made known? Made known how? For we see that the patriarchs were not ignorant of sin, because Joseph was thrown into prison, albeit by the wickedness of others, and both the butler and the baker of Pharaoh were in prison because of their sins. In what way then, did sin lie dormant? In fact, the law has three parts to it. The first part concerns the mystery of God's divinity; the second is what is fitting according to natural law, which forbids sin, and the third is the deeds of the law, in other words, sabbaths, new moons, circumcision, et cetera. This here is the natural law, which was partly reformed and partly confirmed by Moses, which made sin known to those who were bound in wickedness, not that

it was hidden, as I said before, but Paul shows that these sins will not go unpunished in the sight of God. The law shows the coming judgment of God and that no sinner will escape punishment, in case someone who has escaped for a time thinks that the law is an illusion. The law shows that sin will be dealt with by God.

21 But now the righteousness of God has been manifested apart from law, although the law and prophets bear witness to it,

It is clear that the righteousness of God has now appeared apart from the law, but this means apart from the law of the sabbath, the circumcision, the new moon and revenge, not apart from the sacrament of God's divinity, because the righteousness of God is all about God's divinity. For when the law held them guilty, the righteousness of God forgave them, and did so apart from the law, so that until the law was brought to bear, God forgave them their sin. And lest someone think that this was done against the law, Paul added that the righteousness of God had a witness in the law and the prophets, which means that the law itself had said that in the future someone would come who would save mankind. But the law had no authority to forgive sin.

Therefore, what is called the righteousness of God appears to be mercy, because it has its origin in the promise, and when God's promise is fulfilled, it is called the righteousness of God. For it is righteousness when what is promised has been delivered. And when God accepts those who flee to him for refuge, this is called righteousness, because wickedness would not accept such people.

22 the righteousness of God through faith in Jesus Christ for all who believe. For there is

---

[1] Ambrosiaster's text read: "All flesh shall not be justified." The phrase "all flesh" is a Hebraism which has been smoothed out in the English version to give the more idiomatic rendering, "no human being." [2] Is 40:5.

no distinction, ²³*since all have sinned and fall short of the glory of God,*

What else comes through faith in Jesus Christ except the righteousness of God, which is the revelation of Christ? For it is by faith in the revelation of Jesus Christ that the gift long ago promised by God is acknowledged and received.

Because Paul had said that the righteousness of God was over everyone, both Jews and Greeks, he added this verse in order to prove his point. For he says: *All have sinned.* This must be understood in universal terms, which is why he added: *There is no distinction.* For *all* here includes even the saints, in order to show that nobody can keep the law without faith. For the law was given in such a way that faith was also contained in it, and this faith looked for a future salvation. Thus the death of Christ benefits everyone, because both here in this world, it has taught what is to be believed and observed, and it has delivered everyone from hell.

²⁴*they are justified by his grace as a gift, through the redemption which is in Christ Jesus,*

They are justified freely, because they have not done anything nor given anything in return, but by faith alone they have been made holy by the gift of God. Paul testifies that the grace of God is in Christ, because we have been redeemed by Christ according to the will of God, so that once set free we may be justified, as he says to the Galatians: *Christ redeemed us by offering himself for us.*[1] For he achieved this despite the fierce attacks of the devil, who was outwitted. For the devil received Christ (in hell), thinking that he could hold him there, but because he could not withstand his power, he lost not only Christ but all those whom he held, at the same time.

²⁵*whom God put forward as an expiation by his blood, to be received by faith. This was to show God's righteousness, because in his divine forbearance he had passed over former sins;*

Paul says this, because in Christ God put forward, in other words, appointed, himself as a future expiation for the human race, if they believed. This expiation was by his blood, because we have been set free by his death, so that God might reveal him and condemn death by his passion. This was in order to make his promise clear, by which he set us free from sin, as he had promised before. And when he fulfilled this promise, he showed himself to be righteous.

God knew the purpose of his loving-kindness, by which he determined to come to the rescue of sinners, both those living on earth and those who were held bound in hell. He waited a very long time for both, nullifying the sentence by which it seemed just that everyone should be condemned, in order to show us that long ago he had decided to liberate the human race, as he promised through Jeremiah the prophet, saying: *I will forgive their iniquity and I will remember their sin no more.*[2] And in case it might be thought that this promise was for the Jews only, he said through Isaiah: *My house will be called a house of prayer for all peoples.*[3]

For although the promise was made to the Jews, God knew in advance that the ungodly Jews would reject his gift and therefore he promised that he would allow the Gentiles to share in his grace, at the sight of which the ungodly Jews would be angered.

²⁶*it was to prove at the present time that he himself is righteous and that he justifies him who has faith in Jesus.*

The present time means our time, in which God has given what long before he had prom-

---

[1]Gal 3:13. [2]Jer 31:34. [3]Is 56:7.

ised to give at the time at which he gave it. Paul has rightly said that God gave what he promised in order to appear righteous. For he had promised that he would justify those who believe in Christ, as he says in Habakkuk: *The righteous will live by faith in me,*[1] and whoever has faith in God and Christ is righteous.

27Then what becomes of our boasting? It is excluded. On what principle? On the principle of works? No, but on the principle of faith.

Paul tells those who live under the law that they have no reason to boast, basing themselves on the law and claiming either to be of the race of Abraham or to have accepted the precepts of God from Moses, seeing that no one is justified before God except by faith.

28For we hold that a man is justified by faith apart from works of law.

Paul says that a Gentile can be sure that he is justified by faith without doing the works of the law, in other words, without circumcision or new moons or the veneration of the sabbath.

29Or is God the God of Jews only? Is he not the God of Gentiles also? Yes, of Gentiles also,

Undoubtedly there is only one God for everybody. For even the Jews cannot claim that their God is not the God of the Gentiles also, because they believe that the origin of all people is from the one Adam, and that no one who comes willingly to the law may be prevented from accepting it. Some Gentiles actually went with the Israelites into the desert of Egypt, and the Israelites were ordered to accept them as long as they agreed to be circumcised and eat unleavened bread, or the Passover, together with the rest of them.[2] Then again, Cornelius, a Gentile who was not judaized, received the

gift of God, and it is clear from Holy Scripture that he was justified.[3]

30since God is one; and he will justify the circumcised on the ground of their faith and the uncircumcised through their faith.

By *the circumcised*, Paul means the Jews who have been justified by their faith in the promise and who believe that Jesus is the Christ whom God had promised in the law. By *the uncircumcised*, he means the Gentiles who have been justified with God by their faith in Christ. Thus God has justified both Jews and Gentiles. For because God is one, everyone has been justified in the same way. What benefit then is there in circumcision? Or what disadvantage is there in uncircumcision, when only faith produces worthiness and merit?

31Do we then overthrow the law by this faith? By no means! On the contrary, we uphold the law.

Paul says that the law is not nullified by faith, but fulfilled. Its status is confirmed when faith bears witness that what it said would come has actually happened. Paul says this because of the Jews who thought that faith in Christ was inimical to the law, because they did not understand the true meaning of the law. For Paul does not nullify the law when he says that it must come to an end, because he asserts that at the time it was given it was rightly given, but now it does not have to be kept any longer. In the law itself it is said that a time would come when the promise would be fulfilled and the law would no longer have to be kept.

For among other things, the angel Gabriel showed the prophet Daniel, when he wanted to know this, that at the coming of Christ, the anointing, that is to say the royal unction, would cease. This refers to power, because

---

[1]Hab 2:4. [2]Cf. Ex 12:48-51. [3]Cf. Acts 10:31.

then kings will have ceased to exist, and *there will be no more judgment*, which means no more law, and *my sacrifice will cease.*[1] He says *my* so that it will be understood that the sacrifices of the old law will come to an end. The Savior clarifies this sense when he says: *The law and the prophets were until John.*[2] And because once the law of Moses comes to an end, God will give better precepts, Jeremiah the prophet prophesied, saying: *Behold the days are coming, says the Lord, when I will make a new covenant with the House of Israel and the House of Judah, not like the covenant which I made with their fathers,*[3] meaning with those who believed the promise and received Christ at his coming. Therefore the Savior said: *I have not come to abolish the law and the prophets, but to fulfill them.*[4] And because in the future the house of God will no longer be exclusively in Jerusalem, but in other places too, Zechariah the prophet said: *I shall place Jerusalem among all the nations,*[5] meaning by this the church.

Romans 4

[1]*What then shall we say about Abraham, our forefather according to the flesh?*

After showing that no one can be justified before God by the works of the law, Paul goes on to say that Abraham could not merit anything according to the flesh either. In saying *the flesh*, Paul meant circumcision, because Abraham sought nothing on the basis of his circumcision, since he was already justified before he was circumcised.

[2]*For if Abraham was justified by works, he has something to boast about, but not before God.*

This is a rhetorical argument. Abraham does indeed have glory before God, but this is only because of the faith by which he was justified, since nobody is justified by the works of the law in a way which would give him glory before God. And because those who keep the law are still being justified, Paul adds: *If Abraham was justified by works, he has something to boast about, but not before God.* Rather, before the world, lest he appear to be bound by the current law. But before God it is those who have faith who are justified.

[3]*For what does the scripture say? "Abraham believed God, and it was reckoned to him as righteousness."*[6]

Paul revealed that Abraham had glory before God not because he was circumcised, nor because he abstained from evil, but because he believed in God. For that reason he was justified, not by the present, but by the future heavenly righteousness, and he would receive the reward of praise in time to come.

[4]*Now to one who works, his wages are not reckoned as a gift but as his due.*

It is certain that no merit is imputed for reward to the man who is subject either to the law of works, in other words, of Moses, or to the law of nature, so that he might have glory before God. The person who is obliged to keep the law is a debtor, because a necessity is imposed upon him by the law to keep it, whether he wants to or not, so as not to be made guilty, as Paul says in another passage: *Those who resist will incur judgment.*[7] On the other hand, to believe or not to believe is a matter of choice. No one can be obliged to believe something which is not obvious, but he is invited—he is not forced, but persuaded. Therefore he obtains merit, for like Abraham he believes what he does not see, but hopes for.

[5]*And to one who does not work but trusts him*

---

[1]Dan 9:26. [2]Lk 16:16. [3]Jer 31:31-32. [4]Mt 5:17. [5]Cf. Zech 12:2. [6]Gen 15:6. [7]Rom 13:2.

who justifies the ungodly, his faith is reckoned as righteousness.

This refers to somebody who is bound by sin and who therefore does not do what the law commands. Paul says this because to an ungodly person, that is, to a Gentile, who believes in Christ without doing the works of the law, his faith is reckoned for righteousness just as Abraham's was. How then can the Jews think that they have been justified by the works of the law in the same way as Abraham, when they see that Abraham was not justified by the works of the law, but by faith alone? Therefore, there is no need of the law, when the ungodly person is justified before God by faith alone.

Thus Paul says that it has been decreed by God that when the law comes to an end, the grace of God will demand faith alone for salvation.

6So also David pronounces a blessing upon the man to whom God reckons righteousness apart from works:

Paul backs this up by the example of the prophet David, who says that those are blessed of whom God has decreed that, without work or any keeping of the law, they are justified before God by faith alone. Therefore he foretells the blessedness of the time when Christ was born, just as the Lord himself said: *Many prophets and righteous men longed to see what you see and to hear what you hear, and did not hear it.*[1]

7"Blessed are those whose iniquities are forgiven, and whose sins are covered; 8blessed is the man against whom the Lord will not reckon his sin."[2]

Obviously they are blessed, whose iniquities are forgiven without labor or work of any kind, and whose sins are covered without any work

of penitence being required of them, as long as they believe.

Forgive, cover, not reckon—it all amounts to one and the same thing, for all three are given and received in the same way. Some people think that there is a three-part logic in these terms, because the apostle makes use of different words and moves from the plural to the singular. He has expanded his vocabulary because the words of God come in an abundance of grace, corresponding to the different kinds of sin, which all have different names. Nevertheless, the words all point to the same thing, because what he has covered he forgives, and what he has forgiven he does not reckon [to the sinner]. He expands on what he wants to say in order to magnify and praise the grace of God.

Paul has made three categories to cover the different types of sin. The first category is that of wickedness or ungodliness, in that the Creator is not acknowledged. The second category is that of the more serious sins, and the third is that of the less serious ones. All of these are wiped out in baptism, and these three categories cover the entire range of sin.

How can these words apply to a penitent, when we know that penitents obtain the forgiveness of sin with much struggle and groaning? How can they be applied to a martyr, when we know that the glory of martyrdom is obtained by sufferings and pressures? But the prophet, foreseeing a happy time when the Savior comes, calls them blessed, because their sins are forgiven, covered and not reckoned to them, and this without labor or work of any kind.

Yet because of the fullness of the times and because there is more grace in the apostles than there was in the prophets, the apostle brings out the greater things, which we receive by the gift of baptism. He states that not only do we receive the forgiveness of sins, but we

---

[1]Mt 13:17. [2]Ps 32:1-2.

are also justified and made children of God, so that this blessedness may have perfect assurance and glory.

⁹Is this blessing pronounced only upon the circumcised, or also upon the uncircumcised? We say that faith was reckoned to Abraham as righteousness.

Is this blessedness given to the children of Abraham only, or to the Gentiles also? If in those days the Gentiles were not forbidden to come under the law and the promise made to Abraham, how could it be that in the time of Christ they should be prevented from coming to grace, when God has clearly invited them? In the context of the law, *faith was reckoned to Abraham as righteousness.* Paul starts with the source so as to exclude all willful backsliding, because what is not allowed to the head has no chance of ever being considered [in anyone else].

¹⁰How then was it reckoned to him? Was it before or after he had been circumcised? It was not after, but before he was circumcised.

Abraham believed in God before he was circumcised. What did Abraham believe? He believed that he would have a descendant, that is, a son, in whom all the nations would be justified by faith while they were still uncircumcised, as Abraham then was.

¹¹He received circumcision as a sign or seal of the righteousness which he had by faith while he was still uncircumcised. The purpose was to make him the father of all who believe without being circumcised and who thus have righteousness reckoned to them,

Abraham received circumcision as a sign of the righteousness of faith. For believing that

he would have a son, he received the sign of the thing which he believed, that it might be known that he was justified because of what he believed. Circumcision has no special value; it is just a sign. The children of Abraham received this sign, both so that it would be known that they were the children of him who had received it because he believed in God, and so that they would imitate their father's faith and believe in Jesus, who was promised to Abraham. Isaac was born as a type of Christ, for the nations are not blessed in Isaac, but in Christ, *for there is no other name under heaven given among men by which we must be saved,* says the apostle Peter.[1]

¹²and likewise the father of the circumcised who are not merely circumcised but also follow the example of the faith which our father Abraham had before he was circumcised.

Paul says this because by believing, Abraham became the forefather of the circumcision. But this was the circumcision of the heart, not only of those who descended from him but also of those Gentiles who believed in the way he did. He is the father of the Jews according to the flesh, but according to faith he is the father of all believers.

¹³The promise to Abraham and his descendants, that they should inherit the world, did not come through the law but through the righteousness of faith.

It is clear that the law had not yet been given, neither was there as yet circumcision, when the promise was made to Abraham the believer and to his seed, which is Christ, who would cleanse the sins of all men. Therefore Abraham was made heir to the world not by the merit earned from keeping the law, but by faith. The heir of the world is the heir of

---

[1] Acts 4:12.

the earth, which he obtained in his children. For Christ is the heir of the nations, as David sings: *I will make the nations your heritage, and the ends of the earth your possession.*[1] For we shall die and live again with him.

[14]If it is the adherents of the law who are to be the heirs, faith is null and the promise is void.

Those who live under the law inherit under the law. It is clear that if one's inheritance is from the law, the promise which was made to Abraham by faith is nullified, since the promise was not made through the law, but the inheritance comes through the righteousness of faith. The apostle shows that there is something wicked in hoping for an inheritance under the law.

[15]For the law brings wrath, but where there is no law there is no transgression.

In order to show that no man can be justified before God by the law, nor can the promise be given through the law, Paul says that *the law brings wrath.* It was given in order to make transgressors guilty. But faith is the gift of God's mercy, so that those who have been made guilty by the law may obtain forgiveness. Therefore faith brings joy. Paul does not speak against the law, but gives priority to faith, because it is not possible to be saved by the law, but we are saved by God's grace through faith. Therefore the law is not itself wrath, but it brings wrath, in other words, punishment, to the sinner, for wrath is born from sin. For this reason Paul wants the law to be abandoned so that the sinner will take refuge in faith, which forgives sins, that he may be saved.

Paul says that *where there is no law there is no transgression,* because once the guilty have been removed from the power of the law and given forgiveness, there is no transgression. For those who were sinners because they had

transgressed the law are now justified. For the law of works has ceased, that is, the observance of sabbaths, new moons, circumcision, distinction of foods, and the expiation by a dead animal or the blood of a weasel.

[16]That is why it depends on faith, in order that the promise may rest on grace and be guaranteed to all his descendants—not only to the adherents of the law but also to those who share the faith of Abraham, for he is the father of us all,

The promise could not be certain to every offspring, that is, to every man from every nation, unless it were by faith. The source of the promise is faith and not the law, because those who are under the law are guilty, and the promise cannot be given to those who are guilty. For this reason they must first be purified by faith, so that they may become worthy to be called the children of God, so that the promise may be certain. For if they say they are children of God when they are still guilty, that is to say, under the law, it is not certain, because the children of God have been set free from sin. So those who are under the law must be rescued from the law in order to deserve to receive the promise, which is all the greater because it is apart from the law. It is not worthwhile therefore to put yourself under the law if you are looking for a shortcut to the heart of the problem.

This applies equally to the Jews who are under the law and to the Gentiles who share Abraham's faith, because the Gentile has believed that he is justified without the law, just as Abraham did. Therefore, Abraham is actually closer to the Gentiles, so that the promise is assured to those who believe in the God in whom Abraham believed.

[17]as it is written, "I have made you the father

---

[1]Ps 2:8.

of many nations"[1]—in the presence of the God in whom he believed, who gives life to the dead and calls into existence the things that do not exist.

Paul confirms by quoting the law that Abraham is the father of all who believe, and so the promise is firm if they abandon the law on account of their faith, because the promise of the kingdom of heaven is given to the righteous, not to sinners. Those who are under the law are under sin, because all have sinned, and it is not possible for anyone who is under to law to receive grace, as he says to the Galatians: *You are severed from Christ, you who would be justified by the law; you have fallen away from grace.*[2]

In order to teach that there is one God for all, Paul tells the Gentiles that Abraham believed in God himself and was justified in his sight. The Gentiles also believe in him, that they may be justified, and so there is no difference between Jew and Greek in faith, for when the circumcision and the uncircumcision are taken away they are made one in Christ, because Abraham also believed when he was still uncircumcised and was justified.

Having said this, Paul invites the Gentiles to share the faith of Abraham, who believed God while he was still uncircumcised. Now that that faith is preached in Christ, he has been raised from the dead, along with his wife. For when they were already very old they sprang back to life, so that Abraham did not doubt that he would have a son by Sarah, whom he knew to be sterile, and who had long since ceased to have her menstrual period. Paul said this so that they would not worry about circumcision or uncircumcision, but that they would respond eagerly because of their faith, secure in the knowledge that the one in whom they believe is no other than the one who gives life to the dead, and that when he wants to bring things which do not exist into being, they appear immediately by his mere willing [them to be].

Therefore Abraham was called a father [of many nations] even before he became one and he believed, secure in the power of God. The identity of the God in whom Abraham believed with the Father of Jesus Christ is assured by the sign given to Zachariah and Elizabeth, when the promise comes back into the world at the coming of Christ. It was the same sign as was given to Abraham and Sarah, when the promise was first announced, that in the same way, bodies worn out by old age would bear the holy John just as Isaac was born.

[18]*In hope he believed against hope, that he should become the father of many nations; as he had been told, "So shall your descendants be."*[3]

It is clear that since Abraham had no hope of having a son, he believed God and had faith against hope that he would have a son, knowing that with God all things are possible.

The quotation is from Genesis, where God shows Abraham the stars of the sky and says: *So shall your descendants be*, because believing, he was justified. For Abraham believed what seems impossible to the world, because it does not occur in the order of nature that old people should have children and know that their seed will increase to such an extent that it will be impossible to count them. Therefore faith is precious, because it believes in the future, even against what it now sees or knows. For it consoles itself in this hope, that it is God who promises. For this reason it is fair to say that there is more to be known than human weakness can grasp.

[19]*He did not weaken in faith when he consid-*

---

[1]Gen 17:5. [2]Gal 5:4. [3]Gen 15:5.

ered his own body, which was as good as dead because he was about a hundred years old, or when he considered the barrenness of Sarah's womb. [20]No distrust made him waver concerning the promise of God, but he grew strong in his faith as he gave glory to God, [21]fully convinced that God was able to do what he had promised. [22]That is why his faith was "reckoned to him as righteousness."[1]

Paul claims that Abraham is worthy of this praise because, although he knew that he could not do it himself, he strengthened his weakness by faith, so that he believed that with God's help he could do what he knew was impossible by the laws of the universe. He was of great merit before God because he believed God over against his own knowledge, not doubting that because he was God he could do things which he knew were impossible according to the world's wisdom. It is quite certain that God exists outside the rationality of this world, for there is no one within the created order who can be said to have made it, and so the person who attributes more to God his maker than he himself knows is to be congratulated for doing that. It would not make any difference if everyone thought exactly the same thing, but the faith of those who believe stands out in the presence of God when contrasted with the unbelief of so many others.

Paul therefore urges the Gentiles to believe as firmly as Abraham did, so that they might receive the promise of God and his grace without any hesitation, secure in the example of Abraham, that the praise given to a believer increases if he believes what is incredible and seems to be foolish to the world. For the more foolish what he believes is thought to be, the more honor he will have, and indeed it would be foolish to believe it, if it were said to occur without God.

Therefore Abraham's faith is much more

praiseworthy than that of anyone else because it was not brought about by any miraculous signs. For since the world is governed by a particular law and power and is ruled in a way determined by God but human beings have despised God its Creator out of a love of the flesh which is based on scientific reasoning, God has willed that it should be preached that what is impossible for the world he can and has done, so as to remove this error. Thus those who believe this will be saved one by one, being bound to the rule of God, while those who have despised God, because they are puffed up with the wisdom of the world, will be damned.

[23]But the words, "it was reckoned to him," were written not for his sake alone,

Paul says that in Abraham a model was given to both Jews and Gentiles, so that by his example we might believe in God and Christ and the Holy Spirit, and that it might be reckoned to us as righteousness.

[24]but for ours also. It will be reckoned to us who believe in him that raised from the dead Jesus our Lord,

Although what is now believed is different, faith has one and the same gift. Therefore, we receive this gift because we believe. And believing that Christ is the Son of God, we are adopted as sons, for God could give no greater gift to believers than to call them sons of God once they had renounced their sins. For we are called sons of God, but they are not worthy even to be called servants.

Out of his infinite greatness, God has given to those who love him what is worthy of his majesty and not what human beings deserve. In the gift it is the excellence of the giver more than that of the receiver which is considered, and for that reason he receives greater praise

---

[1]Gen 15:6.

when he distributes large gifts to small people through Christ, who for our sake allowed himself to be killed, in order to rescue us from a second death, that is, from the pain of hell, so that out of the joy of the triumph over vanquished death he might make us, by the grace of justification, worthy to be called sons of God.

25who was put to death for our trespasses and raised for our justification.

Those who were baptized before Christ's passion received only the remission of their sins, for the love of which Satan killed the Savior. But after the resurrection, those who were baptized before and those who were baptized after were all justified by the set form of faith in the Trinity, and they received the Holy Spirit, who is the sign of believers that they are children of God. And so that he might top off our justification, after his resurrection he gave authority by his commandments, that by imitating them we might increase our merits. Having obtained grace through these merits, we may appear shining in the kingdom of God, in that faith by which, once we are justified, we cannot be held by death. For by the Savior's passion death is vanquished. Once it was dominant because of sin, but it does not dare to hang on to those who have been justified by God.

Romans 5

1Therefore, since we are justified by faith, we have peace with God through our Lord Jesus Christ.

Faith gives us peace with God, not the law, for it reconciles us to God by taking away those sins which had made us God's enemies. And because the Lord Jesus is the minister of this grace, it is through him that we have

peace with God. Faith is greater than the law, because the law is our thing, whereas faith belongs to God. Furthermore, the law is concerned with our present life, whereas faith is concerned with eternal life. But whoever does not think this way about Christ, as he ought to, will not be able to obtain the rewards of faith, because he does not hold the truth of faith.

2Through him we have obtained access to this grace in which we stand, and we rejoice in our hope of sharing the glory of God.

It is clear that in Christ we have access to the grace of God. For he is the mediator between God and men, who builds us up by his teaching and gives us the hope of receiving the gift of his grace if we stand in his faith. Therefore if we stand (because we used to be flat on the floor), we stand as believers, glorying in the hope of the glory which he has promised to us.

3More than that, we rejoice in our sufferings, knowing that suffering produces endurance,

Since it is through tribulations that we must enter the kingdom of God, Paul teaches that we should rejoice in them. For suffering added to hope increases our reward. Suffering is the measure of how much hope we have, and it testifies to the fact that we deserve the crown we shall inherit. This is why the Lord said: *Blessed are you when they persecute you and say all kinds of evil things against you on account of God's righteousness. Rejoice and be glad, for your reward in heaven is great.*[1] For to despise present sufferings and hindrances and not to give in to pressure, because of hope for the future, has great merit with God. Therefore a person should rejoice in suffering, believing that he will be all the more acceptable to God, as he sees himself

---

[1]Mt 5:11-12.

made stronger in the face of tribulation.

Suffering produces endurance as long as it is not the result of weakness or doubt.

[4]and endurance produces character, and character produces hope,

It is clear that if endurance is of the quality we have said, our character will be quite strong. That there should be hope in someone who has been tried and tested is perfectly reasonable, for one who is worthy is sure to receive a reward in the kingdom of God.

[5]and hope does not disappoint us, because God's love has been poured into our hearts through the Holy Spirit which has been given to us.

Hope does not let us down, even though we are considered by evil people to be stupid and naive, because we believe in things which are impossible in this world. For we have in us the pledge of God's love through the Holy Spirit, who has been given to us. The Holy Spirit of God demonstrates that he has been promised to believers because people speak in unknown languages in order to confirm their hope. He also strengthens God's love in us because he calls us *beloved*. It is possible for us to be sure of the promise, because it is God who has promised and it is to those whom he wants to be his beloved that he has promised. For because human words are inadequate to express the reason of our faith, by the witness of power which "shouts while being silent,"[1] it is shown to be reasonable, to the consternation of the wise men of this world, who in the audacity of their verbiage struggle with earthly weapons against heavenly things and with carnal ones against spiritual realities, and are not ashamed to call themselves wise. Just as a vagabond comes from some foreign country, even though

we cannot prove it, so the truth of our faith wanders as a stranger on the earth. Because its nature cannot be explained in words, it is judged by the witness of its power, which is a much greater thing.

[6]While we were yet helpless, at the right time Christ died for the ungodly.

If Christ gave himself up to death at the right time for those who were unbelievers and enemies of God—for he died at a particular time and rose again on the third day—how much more will he protect us with his help if we believe in him! He died for us in order to obtain life and glory for us. If he died for his enemies, just think what he will do for his friends! In human terms, that is to say, in time, he appeared to die, when in fact he was alive in hell and breaking down its gates by the strength of his power.

Times exist in the world, where the sun rises and sets, the moon waxes and wanes, and day and night rotate with one another. A thing which is subject to time and age is always changing. Therefore when Christ left his body he died to time. Now he is alive where time and age do not exist, and not only alive, but victorious over them as well.

[7]Why, one will hardly die for a righteous man—though perhaps for a good man one will dare even to die.

Paul wanted to commend the Savior's love to us when he said this. Christ died for the ungodly. Now if someone will hardly die for a righteous man, how can it be that he would die for ungodly people? And if someone might volunteer to die for one good man (or not volunteer, since the phrase is ambiguous), how can it be that someone would dare to die for a multitude of the ungodly? For if someone dares to

---

[1]The reference is to Cicero *Catiline Orations* 1.21.

die for a righteous or good man, it is probably because he has been touched with some sort of pity or been impressed by his good works. But in the case of the ungodly, not only is there no reason to die for them, but there is plenty to make us want to cry when we look at them!

Christ, however, died for the ungodliness of a people which was not yet his, and made everything which the world disbelieves believable. He made two kinds of people— the righteous and the good. Even though a righteous man ought to be called good as well, he nevertheless created these distinct types of people, the difference being that the righteous person has achieved that status by self-discipline whereas the good person was born that way and is innocent in the simplicity of his nature. Thus, although there is greater merit in being a righteous person than in being merely a good one, it is still true, says Paul, that someone might volunteer to die for a good person, meaning by this that since the cause of his innocence is less noble, someone might possibly be pressured into this. Finally, parents choose to die for their good children, and perhaps even wives might die for good husbands.

For if we have to make a choice between the righteous person and the good one, we sometimes prefer the righteous and other times the good. For if a person is righteous according to the law of God, he is better than a good one, but only because the latter has not yet gotten to work on himself in order to develop his good points. For a righteous person will improve the goodness of his nature by self-discipline. But if the righteous person is righteous according to the [standards of the] world, the good person is to be preferred to him because of his innocence, because that kind of righteousness is ungodly. Therefore everything natural is good. The righteousness which comes from the law of God is a development which is compatible with nature. Therefore righteousness is goodness, which is why the righteous can always be

called good as well, but the good are not always righteous, because they are not called good on account of their works, but because of their innocence. For righteousness is perfect goodness, bringing the goodness of its nature to perfection by its labors.

⁸*But God shows his love for us in that while we were yet sinners Christ died for us. ⁹ Since therefore, we are now justified by his blood, much more shall we be saved by him from the wrath of God.*

God shows his love by being so merciful to his enemies that he saved them when they had done nothing to deserve it. Paul says this, because if God allowed his Son to be killed for sinners' sake, what will he do for those who have been justified, except save them from wrath, that is, preserve them unharmed from the deception of Satan, so that they will be safe on the day of judgment, when revenge will begin to destroy the wicked. For since the goodness of God does not want anyone to perish, he has shown mercy on those who deserved death in order to increase the honor and glory of those who understand the grace of God and make the ungrateful more worthy of punishment. The ungrateful are those who reject the call of God and refuse his grace in order to continue in the path of error and wickedness.

¹⁰*For if while we were enemies we were reconciled to God by the death of his Son, much more, now that we are reconciled, shall we be saved by his life.*

The God who acts on behalf of his enemies will not be able to love his friends any less than that. Therefore, if the death of the Savior benefited us while we were still ungodly, how much more will his life do for us who are justified when he raises us from the dead? For just as his death freed us from the devil, so his life will deliver us from the day of judgment.

[11]Not only so, but we also rejoice in God through our Lord Jesus Christ, through whom we have now received our reconciliation.

Paul teaches us that we should thank God, not only for the salvation and assurance which we have received, but that we should also rejoice in God through our Lord Jesus Christ, because through his Son the Mediator, God has been pleased to call us his friends. Therefore we can rejoice that we have received every blessing through Christ, that through him we have come to know God. As we rejoice in him, let us therefore honor the Son equally with the Father, as he himself bears witness, saying: *That they may honor the Son as they honor the Father.*[1] Therefore, after talking about the providence of God the Father and the gift which he gave through Christ, Paul added what follows in order to make us appreciate his person, because we have been redeemed by one God and Father through one Christ.

[12]Therefore as sin came into the world through one man and death through sin, and so death spread to all men because all men sinned—

Having already shown how the grace of God has been given to us through Christ according to the pattern of truth, Paul now expounds what that pattern of the one God and Father [working] through his one Son Christ actually is. Because the one Adam (that is, Eve, for she too is Adam) sinned and affected everyone, so the one Christ, the Son of God, has conquered sin in everyone. Because he declares the offer of God's grace toward the human race in order to reveal these origins of sin, he starts with Adam, who was the first man to sin, in order to teach us how the providence of the one God has turned everything around by one [other]

man, since it was by one man that the human race had fallen and been drawn into death. Therefore it is also one man through whom we have been saved. We owe him the same reverence that we give to God the Father, which the Father himself desires, as he says elsewhere: *He who thus serves Christ is acceptable to God.*[2] For it is written: *You shall worship the Lord your God, and him only shall you serve.*[3] So if Scripture says that we are to serve God alone and also commands us to serve Christ, [it is clear that] Christ belongs to the unity of God and is not an inferior or different deity, for although the law admonishes us to serve God alone, it also says that serving Christ is pleasing to God. Therefore, just as sin entered into the world through one man and death through sin, so the condemnation of sin and eternal life has come into the world through the one Christ, as he goes on to explain.

Paul says that all have sinned in Adam, even though he really meant the woman, because he was not referring to the particular person but to the universal human race. For it is clear that all have sinned in Adam as though in a lump. For being corrupted by sin himself, all those whom he fathered were born under sin. For that reason we are all sinners, because we all descend from him. He lost God's blessing because he transgressed, and was made unworthy to eat of the tree of life. For that reason he had to die. Death is the separation of body and soul. There is another death as well, called the second death, which takes place in hell. We do not suffer this death as a result of Adam's sin, but his fall makes it possible for us to get it by our own sins. Good men were protected from this, as they were only in hell, but they were still not free, because they could not ascend to heaven. They were still bound by the sentence meted out in Adam, the seal of which was broken by the death of Christ. The sentence passed on Adam was that the human

---

[1]Jn 5:23. [2]Rom 14:18. [3]Deut 6:13; Mt 4:10.

body would decompose on earth, but the soul would be bound by the chains of hell until it was released.

¹³sin indeed was in the world before the law was given, but sin is not counted where there is no law.

Paul says that everyone has sinned in Adam, as I mentioned above, but that until the law was given this sin was not imputed to anyone. Before the law was given, men thought that they could sin with impunity before God, but not before other men. For the natural law, of which they were well aware, had not completely lost its force, so that they knew better than to do to others what they did not want to suffer themselves. Sin was certainly not unknown among men at that time. For example, when Laban, Jacob's father-in-law, asked him whether he had taken his idols and found out that Jacob had stolen them, he judged him deserving of death.[1] Joseph too was bound in prison as a guilty man, even if the charge against him was false. Likewise, Pharaoh's baker and his cook suffered because of some crime, and Moses, frightened by the law after having killed an Egyptian, fled away.

How is it then that sin was not imputed when there was no law? Was it all right to sin if the law was absent? There had always been a natural law, and it was not unknown, but at that time it was thought to be the only law, and it did not make men guilty before God. It was not then known that God would judge the human race, and for that reason sin was not imputed, almost as if it did not exist in God's sight and God did not care about it. But when the law was given through Moses, it became clear that God did care about human affairs, and that in the future wrongdoers would not escape without punishment, as they had done up to then.

For if they figured out under the tutelage of nature that sins should not go unavenged among themselves, how much more should they recognize that God, whom they knew to be the Creator of the world, would demand recompense, as when Sodom and Gomorrah were sentenced to perish by fire. God kept relatively quiet about this, but Moses revealed it in writing in order to confirm that God would henceforth be a judge. But when mentally depraved people turned away from God and began to worship idols, they spurned the first part of the natural law.

For the natural law has three parts, of which the first is this, that the one recognized as Creator should be honored and that neither his glory nor his majesty should be attributed to any of his creatures. The second part is moral, that is, that we should live properly under the control of modesty, for it is right that someone who has some understanding of his Creator should control his life by law, so that this understanding might mean something. But the third part of the law must be learned, which is that knowledge of the Creator must be passed on to others as an example of moral behavior, so that they may learn to what extent merit is located in the Creator. This is true and Christian wisdom.

¹⁴Yet death reigned from Adam to Moses, even over those whose sins were not like the transgression of Adam, who was a type of the one who was to come.

Although sin was not imputed before the law of Moses was given, death nevertheless reigned in the supremacy of its own seizure of power, knowing those who were bound to it. Therefore death reigned in the security of its dominion both over those who for a time escaped punishment and over those who suffered punishment for their evil deeds.

[1]Gen 31:30-31.

Death claimed everyone as its own, because whoever sins is the servant of sin.[1] Imagining they would get away with it, people sinned all the more, and were more prone to wrongdoing because the world abetted it as if it were legal. Because of all this, Satan rejoiced, knowing that he was secure in his possession of man, who because of Adam's sin had been abandoned by God. Thus it was that death reigned.

It is clear that not everyone has sinned in the manner of Adam's transgression, that is to say, not everyone has sinned by despising God. Who are those who have sinned by despising God, if not those who have ignored the Creator and served gods which they have made for themselves out of the creation, whom they worship to God's detriment? For even Terah, the father of Abraham, Nahor and Laban had their own gods, and the sin of Adam is not far from idolatry, because he transgressed by thinking that even though he was only a man he would become a god himself. He thought that it was more advantageous to do what the devil persuaded him to do than to do what God had commanded and thus set up the devil in the place of God, by which act he became subject to the devil.

Likewise those who disobey God by serving a creature sin in a similar way even if it is not exactly the same, because *likeness* applies to something which is basically different, and it cannot be said that these people had received a commandment from God not to eat of the tree, as Adam had. There were also those who sinned without any previous knowledge of God, but rather according to the natural law. For if someone who has understood and worshiped God and has not given the honor of his name and majesty to anyone else sins (and it is impossible not to sin), he does so under the law which he has broken. Therefore death does not reign in them, but it does reign in those who

have served the devil in the shape of idols and thus despised their Lord.

Because the law had not yet been promulgated in all its authority, these people had no inkling that God was a judge. Most of the world had no idea that God would ever judge them. There were very few in whom death did not reign. Those in whom death did reign, after this death which is called the first death, were exempted from the second one and held for future punishment and destruction. As for those in whom death did not reign because they had not sinned in the likeness of the transgression of Adam, they were set aside in the hope that a savior would come to free them, as is said of Abraham. Although he was in hell, he was kept apart from the rest for a long time, because there was a great gulf fixed between the righteous and sinners who were all the more unrighteous. The righteous were kept refrigerated but the sinners were left in the heat. There was fire for the ungodly, so that even before the judgment it was quite clear what each person deserved, and for that reason death reigned in them, because it saw that the works of its cleverness had reached them as a punishment inflicted on enemies. Nor was it unknown that God had placed human beings in the world so that they might proclaim the sovereignty of the one God, which Satan had transgressed.

Some Greek manuscripts say that death reigned even in those who had not sinned in the way that Adam had. If this is true, it is because Satan's jealousy was such that death, that is, dissolution, held sway even over those who did not sin, and they die because they are given over to Satan. If this were true, it would not be right to say that *death reigned from Adam to Moses,* when in fact it reigns from beginning to end in everyone. Could it be that Paul has created different stages here, so that death reigned first from Adam to Moses, then

---

[1]Cf. Jn 8:34.

from Moses to Christ and finally from Christ to the end [of the world]? What purpose would such an expression serve, when it is not even clear that he said this at all? For he said: *Sin reigned from Adam until Moses*, because the law had not yet been revealed, the point being that once the law had been given, people would live under its authority and know to beware lest death should reign in them.

Therefore, how can it be said that death reigned in someone who, guided by nature, kept what the law later commanded before the law itself came? Look what Paul says about such a person: *Sin was not imputed when there was no law*. And he added: *death reigned from Adam to Moses*, that is to say, during the time when there was no law. It is therefore appropriate to say that because death reigned before the law was given, it should be said to have reigned in those who had sinned after the likeness of Adam's transgression, as we have recorded above.

For just as after the giving of the law death reigned in those who served fornication or idols and ignored the lawgiver, so before the coming of the law, death did not reign in those who sensed what it was all about and honored its author regardless. Death is said to have reigned when the knowledge of the one God had disappeared from the earth. Finally, this is how the law which was actually given begins: *I am the Lord your God, who brought you up out of the land of Egypt, out of the house of bondage. You shall have no other gods before me, and you shall not make for yourselves any idol or likeness.*[1]

The law was given, therefore, so that death might no longer reign, and the human race might follow the one God once its earlier sins had been wiped out. As the same apostle says in another place: *Let not sin reign in your mortal body, to make you obey it.*[2] Having said this, he shows that death is still reigning whenever the law is ignored. For what is the reign of death, other than the doing of its will, when it commands things which are to the destruction of whoever obeys it? Desire for death's rule starts with idolatry.

At least this is what is prescribed to us on the basis of the Greek manuscripts, as if there was no discrepancy among them. Disagreement is the result. Somebody who could not win his argument altered the words of the text, in order to make them say what he wanted them to say, so that not rational argument, but the authority of the text, would determine the issue. However, it is known that there were Latin-speakers who translated ancient Greek manuscripts, which preserved an uncorrupted version from earlier times. But once these problems were raised by heretics and schismatics who were upsetting the harmony of the church, many things were altered so that the biblical text might conform to what people wanted. Thus even the Greeks have different readings in their manuscripts. I consider the correct reading to be the one which reason, history and authority all retain. For the reading of the modern Latin manuscripts is also found in Tertullian, Victorinus and Cyprian. Thus it was in Judea that the destruction of the kingdom of death began, since God was made known in Judea.[3] But now it is being destroyed daily in every nation, since many who were once sons of the devil have become sons of God. Therefore, death did not reign in everyone, but only in those who sinned in the same way as Adam had sinned, as I said above.

I think that this is irrelevant, because the apostle says that death has reigned for the reason that sin was not imputed when the law had not yet been given. For almost everyone served idols. In an idol there is the worship of the devil, and for that reason death reigned. For if death reigned even in those who did not sin in the likeness of Adam's transgression,

---

[1]Ex 20:2-4. [2]Rom 6:12. The Latin does not make it clear whether the obedience is to the body or to sin. [3]Ps 76:1.

because they died, and still reigns, because even the saints die, even if it reigned solely because of idolatry, it would still reign. But it does not reign, because death did not reign solely because of idolatry, but also because of the wickedness of people's lives, and every day children of God become children of the devil instead. Death does not reign because the law has been given, so that those who have been captured under the law will be charged on the day of judgment as subjects of God, not of the devil. For this reason, once the law is given, death's rule starts to end, for everyone begins to realize that the Creator God will judge the human race and so little by little it retreats from death's dominion.

Adam was the type of the one who was to come, because even then, God had secretly decided to redeem Adam's sin through the one Christ, as it says in the Revelation of John: *The Lamb of God which was slain before the foundation of the world.*[1] Paul then continues as follows:

15But the free gift is not like the trespass. For if many died through one man's trespass, much more have the grace of God and the free gift in the grace of that one man Jesus Christ abounded for many.

Paul said that Adam was a type of Christ, but in order to assure us that they were not alike in substance, he says that the gift is not like the trespass. The only similarity between them is that just as there was one man who sinned, so there was also one man who put things right.

If by the trespass of one man many have died by imitating his transgression, how much more has the grace of God and his gift abounded in those who flee to him for refuge! For there are more who have received grace than who have died because of Adam's trespass. From this it is clear that Paul was not

talking about ordinary death, which is common to us all, since everybody dies but not everybody receives grace. But death does not reign in everyone. It only reigns in those who have died because of the sin of Adam, who have sinned by a transgression like his. Paul is talking only about these when he says that although many have died because of Adam's sin, many more have received grace. For both to those who sinned in a way similar to Adam, and to those who did not sin in that way, but who were nevertheless confined to hell because of God's judgment on Adam's sin, the grace of God has abounded by the descent of the Savior to hell, granting pardon to all and leading them up to heaven in triumph.

16And the free gift is not like the effect of that one man's sin. For the judgment following one trespass brought condemnation, but the free gift following many trespasses brings justification.

There is an obvious difference between the fact that those who have sinned in imitation of Adam's transgression have been condemned and the fact that the grace of God in Christ has justified men, not from one trespass but from many sins, giving them forgiveness of sins. Paul says this in order to glorify the faithfulness of God and Christ, since on account of Adam's sin many are held by the second death in the depths of hell, yet the gift of God's grace not only forgives those who ought by right to be punished, but also justifies them.

17If, because of one man's trespass, death reigned through that one man, much more will those who receive the abundance of grace and the free gift of righteousness reign in life through the one man Jesus Christ.

It must be observed that there is one mean-

---

[1]Rev 13:8.

ing here, and one only. Paul says that death reigned, not that it is now reigning, because those who understood through the law what the future judgment of God would be have been delivered from its control. It reigned, because without the revelation of the law there was no fear of God on earth. But the higher meaning is that since death reigned from Adam to Moses over those who sinned according to the transgression of Adam, how much more will grace reign by the abundance of God's gift of life through the one Jesus Christ? For if death reigned, why should grace not reign even more, since it has justified far more people than the number over whom death reigned? How much more believable it is that grace reigns, because it confers life through Christ!

[18]Then as one man's trespass led to condemnation for all men, so one man's act of righteousness leads to acquittal and life for all men.

This means that just as everyone has deserved condemnation because of the sin of one man since they are also sinners, so everyone who believes will be justified by the righteousness of one man. Some people think that because the condemnation was universal, the acquittal will also be universal. But this is not so, because not everyone believes.

[19]For as by one man's disobedience many were made sinners, so by one man's obedience many will be made righteous.

When Paul said *all men* in the preceding verses, what he meant was *most* or *many*. For many sinned by following Adam, but not all. Likewise, many are justified by faith in Christ, but not all. (Therefore death did not reign in those who did not sin in the likeness of Adam's transgression.)[1]

[20]Law came in, to increase the trespass; but where sin increased, grace abounded all the more,

This means that the law was given in writing in order to make it clear. For it was already present in nature and was freely accepted by those Jews who said to Moses: *Whatever the Lord God says, we shall do.*[2] The law came in, though, because once it was freely accepted it demonstrated that those who had sinned earlier on were guilty. They then remembered that God would require the fruit of the seed of righteousness, which he had planted in nature. Therefore, [in this context] *to come in* means to enter in humility and end up in control. It was for this reason that after the law came in, sin abounded, because it showed that our ancestors were sinners both before and after the coming of the law, and more after the law, because the enemy fanned the flames of jealousy even more when he realized that God was taking care of the human race. The devil wanted to make us feel guilty because of the law, so that we would not pay any attention to God.

An objector might say: *If the law merely served to increase sin, it should never have been given. If there was less sin before the law came, there was no need of the law.* Obviously the law was necessary, both to show that sins, which many thought they could get away with, actually counted before God, and so that people might know what they ought to avoid.

This is why the prophet Isaiah said: *The law was given to help.*[3] The seeds of righteousness have somehow been planted in nature itself, to which the law has been added, by the authority and prestige of which the natural mind might progress to the point of producing the fruits of righteousness. For just as a baby dies if it has no nourishment on which to grow, so the natural inclination toward righteousness will not easily

---

[1]This sentence may have been inserted here by mistake. [2]Ex 24:7. [3]Cf. Is 8:20.

progress if it has nothing to respect and look up to. Instead it will grow sick and give way to supervening sins. It is crushed by the habit of sinning and cannot bear fruit, so it dies as a result. Therefore the law was given providentially, as the prophet testifies, but the people merely increased their sins because they continued in their old habits. In this way they ended up sinning more than they had done before. Thus it happened that the result was that instead of declining, sin became more prevalent after the giving of the law. The apostle is showing here what happens when the law is given, not what the law itself does. How could sin have increased by the fault of the law, when the law warns people not to sin? Yet it is said to have come in so that sin might increase!

The truth is that although it originally came in with great hopes for the future and in humility, later on it started to take control of the people because it had ordered them not to sin and they went on doing so. The law began to show how prevalent sins were, and the more it forbade them the more people committed them. That is why it is said that the law was given so that sin might increase. So when commending the faith by which sins are wiped out, the apostle said that the law had created a situation in which sin would abound, as I said above. It was not given so that sin would be taken away, but so that it might become more prevalent, because it showed that sinners had existed before the law came and afterward it held that they were all guilty.

It is obvious that when sin abounded, grace abounded even more, for the gift of God came as promised and covered over the sins of everyone, so that the devil's jealousy might grieve at having achieved nothing; the providence of God toward the human race would stay as it was and would not be alienated by his cleverness. For it was because the law was given to be of benefit to the human race that the devil tried to overturn it by persuading us to do unlawful things, and because it was given

as a promise that he took the opposite tack by despising its commands, so that the beneficial effects of the law would not be felt to the praise of God's grace, but only its judgment as punishment. Then, in order to nullify the pride of Satan, who rejoiced in his victory over man, the just and merciful God decreed that his Son would come to forgive every sin, so that there would be more happiness from the gift of grace than there had been sorrow from the coming of sin. For the joy of God's gift was a great blessing to those over whom Satan could not triumph. Therefore grace abounded more than the sin which Satan was encouraging people to commit.

21so that, as sin reigned in death, grace also might reign through righteousness to eternal life through Jesus Christ our Lord.

Sin reigned when it saw that it was driving sinners into death, in which it rejoiced, in much the same way as grace will reign through righteousness for eternal life through Jesus Christ our Lord, so that just as sin began to reign through Adam, so grace began to reign through Christ.

Grace reigns through righteousness if we follow righteousness after receiving the forgiveness of sins. Then grace, seeing that it bears fruit in those whom it has redeemed, will reign for eternal life, knowing that we shall live forever. Therefore grace abounds even more, because while sin reigns for a time, grace reigns for eternity. The kingdom of God is the reign of grace, just as the kingdom of the devil is the reign of sin. It all goes back to Christ, so that the entire grace of God may be taught in Christ. Therefore, in answer to the above interpretation, Paul says what follows.

Romans 6

1What shall we say then? Are we to continue in sin that grace may abound?

The question here is whether we should go on sinning so that the gift of God might abound, covering our sins, so that we might always exalt the grace of Christ, trusting in the forgiveness of those sins because God is faithful. Not at all! For God took pity on us through Christ, so that we should no longer sin but instead should gain merit for ourselves and ensure that the grace of God will reign in us.

The believer who returns to his former way of life rejects the kingdom of God's grace and returns to sin, in other words, to the pattern of his previous life. For we have received mercy for two reasons: first, that the kingdom of the devil might be removed, and second, that the rule of God might be proclaimed to the ignorant, for it was by this means that we came to desire this dignity.

²By no means! How can we who died to sin still live in it?

Paul says this because when we lived for sin we were dead in God's eyes. To sin is to live for sin, and not to sin is to live for God. Therefore when the grace of God through Christ and through faith came upon us, we began to live for God by the spiritual rebirth of baptism, and we died to sin, which is the devil. This is what dying to sin means—to be set free from sin and to become a servant of God. Therefore, having died to sin, let us not go back to our earlier evils, lest by living once again to sin and dying to God, we should incur the penalty from which we have escaped.

³Do you not know that all of us who have been baptized into Christ Jesus were baptized into his death?

Paul says this so that we might know that once we have been baptized we should no longer sin, since when we are baptized we die with Christ. This is what it means to be baptized into his death. For there all our sins die, so that, renewed by the death we have cast off, we might be seen to rise as those who have been born again to new life, so that just as Christ died to sin and rose again, so through baptism we might also have the hope of resurrection. Therefore baptism is the death of sin, so that a new birth might follow, which, although the body remains, nevertheless renews us in our mind and buries all our old evil deeds.

⁴We were buried therefore with him by baptism into death, so that as Christ was raised from the dead by the glory of the Father, we too might walk in newness of life.

In saying this, Paul means, first of all, that Christ raised his own body from the dead. For he is the power of God the Father, as he said: *Destroy this temple and I will raise it again in three days.*[1] He was saying this about the temple of his own body; because Christ has risen to a new life, he is now a stranger to death. It also means that we now have a new way of life, which has been given to us by Christ. For by baptism we have been buried together with Christ, in order that from now on we may live according to the life into which Christ rose from the dead. Baptism is the sign and symbol of the resurrection, which means that we ought to abide in the commandments of Christ and not go back to what we were before, for the person who dies does not sin; death is the end of sin. This is symbolized by water, because just as water cleanses the dirt of the body, so we believe that we have been spiritually cleansed by baptism from every sin and renewed, for what is incorporeal is cleansed invisibly.

⁵For if we have been united with him in a death like his, we shall certainly be united with him in a resurrection like his.

---

[1]Jn 2:19.

Happily Paul says that we can rise again if we have been united with Christ in the likeness of his death, in other words, if we have laid aside all our wickedness in baptism and, having been transferred into a new life, no longer sin. In this way we shall be like him in his resurrection, because the likeness of his death presupposes a similar resurrection. The apostle John states this in his epistle when he says: *For when he appears, we shall be like him.*[1] This is what it means to rise again immortal and glorious. The likeness does not mean that there will be no difference at all between us, of course. We will be like him in the glory of his body, not in the nature of his divinity.

[6]We know that our old self was crucified with him so that the sinful body might be destroyed, and we might no longer be enslaved to sin. [7]For he who has died is freed from sin.

Paul underlines and repeats a good deal, in order to teach the baptized that they must not sin, and above all that they must not return to idolatry, which is a very serious crime and the root of all errors, lest they lose the grace which they have received through Christ. He calls our former behavior *our old self*, because just as the man who has a pure life through Christ and faith in him is said to be new, so the same man is said to be old through unbelief and evil deeds. Paul says that these deeds have been crucified, which means that they are dead, that the body of sin (i.e., all our misdeeds) may be destroyed. Paul calls all our sins a body, which he says has been destroyed by the cross of Christ, for on the cross the devil, who is the author of sin, has been destroyed.[2]

[8]But if we have died with Christ, we believe that we shall also live with him.

It is clear that those who have crucified the body, in other words, the world, with its vices and lusts, die to the world and die together with Christ, and that they are also conformed to his eternal and saving life, so that they might deserve to be made like Christ in his glory. But the flesh, in other words, the body, is crucified in such a way that the lusts which arise in it as a result of the sin in it, which comes from the transgression of the first man, are trampled underfoot. For the devil is crucified in our flesh; it is he who deceives us through the flesh. But note how the word *flesh* is sometimes to be understood as the world, in other words, the elements, sometimes as the human body and sometimes as the soul which is affected by corporeal vices.

[9]For we know that Christ being raised from the dead will never die again; death no longer has dominion over him. [10]The death he died, he died to sin once for all, but the life he lives he lives to God.

Paul shows that in the Savior's resurrection we have the assurance of eternity, to which we shall attain if we live a better life. For whoever lives to God by doing good is truly alive here and now, and has eternal life.

[11]So you also must consider yourselves dead to sin and alive to God in Christ Jesus.

Paul says this in order to show that there is no other way of dying to sin and living to God, because all our hope is in Christ, whom he calls our Lord. Nothing in the law will be of any help toward our salvation in the next life, when no one will live to God in any way other than through Christ.

[12]Let not sin therefore reign in your mortal bodies, to make you obey their passions.

---

[1] Jn 3:2. [2] An alternative, but probably less authentic reading of the last clause is "(destroyed by) a good life and by orthodox belief."

The body is mortal because of the sin of Adam, but by faith in Christ we believe that it will be immortal. In order for it to inherit the promise, Paul says that it must not listen to the voice of sin, so that sin may not reign in our mortal body. Sin reigns as long as it is in control. But if it does not reign, the body will no longer appear to be mortal, because it dwells in the hope of eternal life. Paul did not say that the body is mortal because it will disintegrate, but because of the pain of hell, so that the man who is sent to hell is said to be mortal because whoever hearkens to sin will not escape the second death, from which the Savior has delivered those who believe in him. Therefore the mortal body refers to the entire human being, because those who hearken to sin are said to be mortal. For Scripture says: *The soul which sins shall surely die,*[1] which means the whole human being. For nobody will be judged apart from his body.

[13]*Do not yield your members to sin as instruments of wickedness, but yield yourselves to God as men who have been brought from death to life, and your members to God as instruments of righteousness.*

Paul shows that the devil fights against us by using our members. For the opportunity is given to him by our sins, so that when God abandons us he acquires the power to deceive and destroy us. Therefore we must protect our members from every work of iniquity so that our enemy may be left defenseless and subdued. Paul did not say: *Present your bodies,* but: *Present your members,* for a person goes wrong when his members, and not his whole body, lead him wherever sin dictates.

Death in this context means ignorance and unbelief, combined with an evil life, because *life* is to know God through Christ. Just as nobody acquires life without a parent, everything has obtained life through Christ. Therefore whoever does not recognize that God is the Father of all through Christ, is said not to have life, in other words, what he has here on earth does not count as life. For such a person denies himself, as long as he thinks he can live without God as his Father. Therefore ignorance and a wicked life are death. For wickedness obtains death, not the death which is common to us all, but the death of hell, as I mentioned above. Likewise, knowledge of God the Father and holy behavior are life, not that life which is subject to death, but the life of the world to come which is called eternal. For this reason Paul says that you should present yourselves to God, for by knowing him you will go on to salvation. Having turned away from an evil life you will be like people who have risen from the dead.

Such great modesty ought to govern our conduct that our behavior will lead to the righteousness of God, not to earthly righteousness. For the righteousness of this world is without faith in Christ, and without that it is death, not life. Let us then yield our members to him so that he can defend us. For when we yield our members to him through good works, we make ourselves worthy to be aided by God's righteousness, because that righteousness is not given to those who are unworthy to receive it. Where God's righteousness is, there the Holy Spirit dwells and helps our infirmity. Just as we yield our members to sin when we act wrongly, so we yield them to righteousness when we behave rightly, protecting them from all wickedness.

[14]*For sin will have no dominion over you, since you are not under law but under grace.*

If we walk according to the commandments which he gives, Paul says that sin will not rule over us, for it rules over those who sin. For if we do not walk as he commands we are under

---

[1]Ezek 18:4.

the law. But if we do not sin we are not under the law, but under grace. If, however, we sin, we fall back under the law, and sin starts to rule over us once more, for every sinner is a slave to sin. It is necessary for a person to be under the law as long as he does not receive forgiveness, for by the law's authority sin makes the sinner guilty. Thus the person to whom forgiveness is given and who keeps it by not sinning anymore will neither be ruled by sin nor be under the law. For the authority of the law no longer applies to him; he has been delivered from sin. Those whom the law holds guilty have been turned over to it by sin. Therefore the person who has departed from sin cannot be under the law.

15 What then? Are we to sin because we are not under law but under grace? By no means!

Paul starts by saying that the law is from God so as to avoid possible opposition from someone who would make this objection. But if this is the case, why do we not have to be under it? Paul deals with this problem and teaches that by the will of God, who is the author of the law, we have been set free from it by Christ. Although it was right for the law to be given—for it was given in order to show that those who sinned against it were guilty before God, and in order to dissuade people from continuing to sin—yet because of the weakness of its infirmity the human race was unable to restrain itself from sin and had become subject to the death of hell. God was moved by the righteousness of his mercy, by which he always comes to the aid of the human race, and through Christ he provided a way by which he could reward those who were without hope. By forgiving their sins he released them from the law which had held them subject. Restored and made whole again by the help of God, they could reject the sins by which they had previ-

ously been held down. Therefore we did not sin in rejecting the law but rather we followed the providence of God himself through Christ.

16 Do you not know that if you yield yourselves to anyone as obedient slaves, you are slaves of the one whom you obey, either of sin, which leads to death, or of obedience, which leads to righteousness?

Paul warns us not to say one thing and do another, so that when we are said to be servants of God we should be found by our actions to be servants of the devil. He proclaims that we are servants of the one whose will we do, and that it is not fair to confess God as Lord but do the works of the devil. For God himself notices this and attacks it: *This people honors me with their lips, but their hearts are far from me,*[1] and the Lord says in the Gospel: *No man can serve two masters,*[2] and in the Law it is written: *God is not mocked.*[3]

17 But thanks be to God, that you who were once slaves of sin have become obedient from the heart to the standard of teaching to which you were committed, 18 and, having been set free from sin, have become slaves of righteousness.

We are said to be slaves to whomever we give obedience. As it is right to obey Christ, for he is himself righteousness and what he commands is righteous, Paul therefore says that we have become servants of righteousness *from the heart*, not from the law; voluntarily, and not out of fear, so that our confession of faith might be manifested by the judgment of our mind. We have been led to faith by nature, not by the law, and have been made in this form of teaching for the rule of God, who created nature. For by nature we know by whom and through whom and in whom we were created.

---

[1] Is 29:13. [2] Mt 6:24. [3] Gal 6:7.

Therefore the form of teaching is that into which our Creator has led us naturally. This is what he said above: *They are a law unto themselves,*[1] when their own natures see what they believe, and that what the law and the prophets predicted to the Jews concerning Christ is what the Gentiles have confessed from the heart. For this reason Paul gives thanks to the Lord, because when we were still slaves to sin we obeyed from the heart, believing in Christ, so that we might serve God, not according to the law of Moses, but according to the law of nature.

[19]I am speaking in human terms, because of your natural limitations. For just as you once yielded your members to impurity and to greater and greater iniquity, so now yield your members to righteousness for sanctification.

In recalling the weakness of the flesh, Paul wants to say that he is demanding less from us than the worship of God would normally require. In order to remove from us any reason to be afraid of coming to faith, because that might seem to us to be unbearable and tough, Paul commands us to serve God with the same degree of zeal that we previously served the devil with. We ought to be more willing to serve God than the devil, given that God brings salvation and the devil damnation, yet our spiritual physician does not demand any more from us, lest in avoiding the more difficult precepts on account of our weakness we should remain in death. Whence the Lord says: *Take my yoke upon you, for my yoke is easy and my burden is light.*[2]

[20]When you were slaves of sin, you were free in regard to righteousness.

It is clear that whoever is free from God is a slave of sin. For as long as he sins he goes away from God and comes under sin.

[21]But then what return did you get from the things of which you are now ashamed? The end of those things is death.

What are the fruits of sin? Learning from them what a good life is we are ashamed by the way we lived so wickedly before. It is not only the opinion of the pagans that is wicked, but also the heresy which is found most of all in Phrygia, to which only a morally corrupt person would belong, in which there is no sacrament and Christian piety has died out.[3] It is a freedom full of sin and bound by wickedness, whose deeds have only shame as their reward and whose end is death! Our departure is the end of this life and its deeds, and either death or life will succeed it. But here the word *death* has a double meaning, for it shifts from one kind of death to another.

[22]But now that you have been set free from sin and have become slaves of God, the return you get is sanctification and its end, eternal life.

If we receive the forgiveness of sins and become imitators of good deeds, we shall acquire holiness and obtain eternal life at the end, for we shall pass from death, which Paul said was the end, to life, which is without end.

[23]For the wages of sin is death, but the free gift of God is eternal life in Christ Jesus our Lord.

Paul says that the wages of sin is death because death comes through sin, and thus whoever refrains from sin will receive eternal life as his reward. Those who do not sin will not undergo the second death.

Just as those who follow sin obtain death,

---

[1]Rom 2:14. [2]Mt 11:29-30. [3]This is Montanism, a heresy which originated in the second century but was still alive two hundred years later.

so those who follow the grace of God, that is, the faith of Christ, which pardons sins, will have eternal life. They will therefore rejoice at being dissolved for a time, knowing that they will eventually obtain a life which is free of all care and has no end. It was when he saw this from afar that St. Simeon asked to be released from this world, that he might go into peace,[1] that is, into a life which allows no disturbance. And he bears witness that this gift is given to us by God through Christ our Lord, so that we should offer thanks to God through no one other than his Son.

Romans 7

[1]*Do you not know, brethren—for I am speaking to those who know the law—that the law is binding on a person only during his life?*

To strengthen their minds in the divine teaching, Paul uses an example drawn from human law, so that once again he argues for heavenly things on the basis of earthly ones, just as God also is known by the creation of the world.

Because all things come from one source, they often have similarities to one another in certain respects, even though they are apparently quite different. Thus the Romans know what law is, because they are not uncivilized, and they understand natural justice, partly on the basis of their own traditions and partly from those of the Greeks, just as the Greeks have picked some things up from the Hebrews. Before Moses the law was not nonexistent; it merely lacked order and authority. For laws were brought to the Romans from Athens. Therefore it was to people who knew what law was that Paul says: *The law is binding on a person only during his life.* It is no secret that every human life comes under natural law, which is given to the world. This law is universal. Now, however, he has proposed another, particular

law (although it too is universal, only becoming "particular" because it is not accepted by everybody), by which he intends to prove his assertion. His intention is to teach the truth one step at a time, and therefore he says what follows.

[2]*Thus a married woman is bound by law to her husband as long as he lives; but if her husband dies she is discharged from the law concerning the husband.*

This law comes from the gospel, not from Moses or from human justice. Those who learned something from the guidance of nature and those who learned something from the law of Moses have both been made perfect by the gospel of Christ. Thus in the following example ·he argues more openly that Christianity has been set free from the law of works, but not from all law, so that now there is no advantage in staying under the law. Someone who returns to life under the law will nullify the grace of God, because the grace of God has set people free from the law, so that we may serve him in spirit, that is to say, in mind.

[3]*Accordingly, she will be called an adulteress if she lives with another man while her husband is alive. But if her husband dies she is free from that law, and if she marries another man she is not an adulteress.*

Just as a woman is freed by the death of her husband from the law of her husband, but not from the law of nature, so also they will be set free by the grace of God from the law by which they were held captive. It will be dead for them and they will not be adulterers by being joined to Christianity. For if the law lives in them they are adulterers and have no right to be called Christians, since they will be subject to punishment. Nor will he who is joined to

---

[1]Lk 2:29.

the gospel after the death of the law, and later returns to the law, be an adulterer to the law, but to the gospel. For when the law's authority ceases, it is said to be dead.

Those who have been delivered from the law and united with Christ by receiving the forgiveness of sins have not committed adultery against the law, because the law is dead as far as they are concerned. However, if those who keep the law think that they can have access to the gospel, they will be guilty of adultery because they will have joined themselves to the faith while the law is still alive [in their eyes] and thus they will be double adulterers.

⁴Likewise, my brethren, you have died to the law through the body of Christ, so that you may belong to another, to him who has been raised from the dead in order that we may bear fruit for God.

Since the Savior allowed the devil to crucify his body, knowing that this was for us and against him, Paul says that we have been saved by the body of Christ. For to die to the law is to live to God, since the law rules over sinners. Therefore the one whose sins are forgiven dies to the law; this is what it means to be set free from the law. We receive this blessing through the body of Christ, for by giving up his body the Savior conquered death and condemned sin. The devil sinned against him when it killed him, even though he was innocent, and entirely without sin. When the devil claims a man for himself because of sin, he is found to be guilty of the thing he accuses him of. Thus it happens that all who believe in Christ are delivered from the law because sin has been condemned. For sin, which is the devil, has been conquered by the body of Christ. Now he has no authority over those who belong to Christ, by whom he has been conquered. Because Christ was sinless yet was killed as if he were guilty, he conquered sin by sin; that is to say, he defeated the devil by causing him to

sin. And what he allowed to get into the devil he condemned, thereby destroying the penalty which had been decreed because of the sin of Adam. When he rose again from the dead an image of new life was given to those who believe in him, so that they cannot be bound by the second death. For this reason we have died to the law by the body of Christ. Thus whoever has not died to the law is still guilty, and whoever is guilty cannot escape the second death.

Paul says that we *belong to another* because we have died to the law so that in the future we may be slaves of Christ alone, and this will bear fruit for God. Whoever perseveres in the grace of Christ belongs to God and is worthy of the promised resurrection.

⁵While we were living in the flesh, our sinful passions, aroused by the law, were at work in our members to bear fruit for death.

Although he is in the flesh, Paul denies that he is in the flesh, even though he is in the body. In this passage *living in the flesh* means following something which is forbidden by the law. Therefore *living in the flesh* can be understood in many different ways. For every unbeliever is in the flesh, in other words, is carnal. A Christian living under the law is in the flesh. Anyone who puts his trust in men is in the flesh. Anyone who does not properly understand Christ is in the flesh, and if a Christian leads an extravagant life, he is in the flesh. Nevertheless, in this passage we should understand being *in the flesh* as meaning that we were in the flesh before we believed. For then we lived under the flesh, in other words, following our carnal desires we were subject to wickedness and sin. For the mind of the flesh is not to understand spiritual things, for example, that a virgin might conceive without intercourse with a man, that a man may be born again of water and the Spirit, and that a soul delivered from the bondage of the flesh may rise again in it. Anyone who doubts these things is in the flesh.

It is clear that whoever does not believe acts under sin and is led by his captivity to indulge in wickedness and to bear fruit worthy of the second death. When such a person sins, death makes a profit. Paul says that evil works in the members, not in the body itself, so that there will be no excuse for mistreating the body. The tongue is made bitter by speaking evil, the hand is corrupted by theft, the ears are pricked by [the sound of] hypocrisy and so on. All these things proceed from the heart, but they become visible in the functions of the members.

This discussion concerns the Jews and all those who say they are Christians yet want to live under the law. Its purpose is to teach them that they are carnal, so that they will abandon the law. Nevertheless Paul says that the sins which rule over those who commit them in the flesh are revealed by the law; they are not caused by the law. For the law is the measure of sin, not its cause, and it makes sinners guilty.

6But now we are discharged from the law, dead to that which held us captive, so that we serve not under the old written code but in the new life of the Spirit.

We are set free from the law when we receive the forgiveness of sins. It has no power over us, but controls only unbelievers and sinners. The law is called the law of death because it punishes the guilty and puts sinners to death. It is not therefore evil, but righteous. For although evil is inflicted on its victims by the law, the law itself is not evil, because it executes wrath justly. Therefore it is not evil to sinners, but just. But to good people it is spiritual. For who would doubt that it is spiritual to forbid sin? But because the law could not save men by for-

giving sin, the law of faith was given in order to deliver believers from the power of sin and bring those whom the law had held in death back to life. For to them it is a law of death, and it works wrath in them because of sin.

Although Paul regards the law as inferior to the law of faith, he does not condemn it. Rather he says that we have been delivered from the law of death so that we might obey the law of faith, which gives us a saving protection which the old law could not give, lest we appear to cancel out the benefit of grace by continuing to serve the old law. The law of Moses is not called old because it is evil, but because it is out of date and has ceased to function. But the law of the Spirit is the law of faith, because faith is in the mind and is believed in the heart, not calculated by works. The mind itself understands that what it believes shares its own nature, that it cannot be perceived by the eyes or touched by the hands, and that the gifts for which it hopes are not earthly but spiritual. The old law was written on tablets of stone, but the law of the Spirit is written spiritually on the tables of the heart, that it might be eternal, whereas the letter of the old law is consumed with age. There is another way of understanding the law of the Spirit, which is that where the former law restrained evil deeds, this law, which says that we ought not to sin even in our hearts, is called the law of the Spirit, because it makes the whole man spiritual.

7What then shall we say? That the law is sin? By no means! Yet, if it had not been for the law, I should not have known sin. I should not have known what it is to covet if the law had not said, "You shall not covet."[1]

Paul has just said that the law is a law of death; he rejoices in that we have been delivered from it, and he says that it is not possible

---

[1]Ex 20:17; Deut 5:21.

to serve God by it. But to avoid giving the impression that he is saying that it is unjust, he adds this statement. Here Paul shows that the law is not sin but the yardstick of sin. For Paul demonstrated that sins lie dormant in us and that they will not go unpunished by God. When a man finds this out he becomes guilty, and does not thank the law for it. For who would be grateful to someone who tells him that he is running the risk of punishment? But he gives thanks to the law of faith, because the man who was made guilty by the law of Moses has been reconciled to God by the law of faith. Even though the law of Moses is just and good in itself (because it is good to show that danger is near), he gives greater thanks for the law of faith, because by it he has been rescued from danger and lives.

Paul does not distinguish covetousness from sin, but merely observes that as long as he was unaware that it was not allowed by God, he did not know that it was a sin. Paul takes on a particular role in order to expound a general principle. The law forbids covetousness, but because it is a matter of desire, it was not previously thought to be sin. Nothing could be easier than to covet something which belongs to a neighbor; it is the law which called it sin, for to men of the world nothing seems more harmless and innocent than desire.

⁸But sin, finding opportunity in the commandment, wrought in me all kinds of covetousness. Apart from the law sin lies dead.

By *all kinds of covetousness* Paul means every sin. In the last verse he mentioned covetousness according to the law, and now by adding other sins he shows that all covetousness works in man by the impulse of the devil, whom he calls *sin*, so that the law was given to man to promote the opposite. When the devil saw the help provided by the law for man, whom he was delighted to have snared as much by his own sin as by the sin of Adam,

he realized that this was done against him. When he saw man placed under the law he knew that he would escape from his control, for now man knew how to escape the punishment of hell. For this reason his wrath was kindled against man, in order to turn him away from the law, and by getting him to do what was forbidden, man would again offend God and fall back into the devil's power. The devil begins not by commanding but by deceiving, since when the law was given the devil lost his power, knowing that in the future the human race would come under the judgment of God.

Apart from the law sin lies dead. This is to be understood in two ways. First, you should realize that the devil is meant when the word *sin* is used and, second, that it also refers here to sin itself. The devil is said to have died, because before the law came he did not conspire to deceive man, and was quiet, as if unable to possess him. But sin was also dead, because it was thought that it would not be reckoned by God. For that reason it was dead as far as man was concerned, as if he could sin without being punished. In fact sin was not absent, as I have already indicated, but this was not realized, because God would decide what became clear by the giving of the law, in other words, that sin would revive. But how could it revive unless it had previously been alive and after the fall of man was thought to be dead, when in fact it was still living? People thought that sin was not being reckoned to them, when in fact it was. Thus something which was alive was assumed to be dead.

⁹I was once alive apart from the law, but when the commandment came, sin revived and I died;

What does it mean to live without the law, if the law was always there, unless, as I have often shown, man lived without the fear of God, secure that God would not judge human deeds? Therefore Paul said that sin had sprung back to life in order to indicate that it had once been alive but that later it had been considered dead because of human laziness, even though it was still alive, just as false rumors have a way of spreading about strangers. This therefore means that in the beginning, sin was indeed reckoned as guilt before God, which means that it was alive, but that when the habit of sinning had obscured this, it was considered dead, so that the crime might be thought to have faded away with the person.

To say that sin revived because it was dead means that it came back to life because it began to be recognized as something for which guilt was imputed.

[10]the very commandment which promised life proved to be death to me.

Man died when he realized that he was guilty before God, when he had previously thought that he would not be held accountable for the sins which he committed. It is true that the law was given for life, but because it made man guilty, not only for the sins which he committed before the coming of the law but also for those which he committed afterward, the law which was given for life turned out to bring death instead. But as I have said, this was for the sinner, because for those who obeyed, it led to eternal life.

[11]For sin, finding opportunity in the commandment, deceived me and by it killed me.

Sin in this verse is to be understood as the devil, who is the author of sin. He found an opportunity through the law to satisfy his cruelty by the murder of man, so that as the law threatened sinners, man by instinct always did what was forbidden. By offending God, he incurred the penalty of the law, so that he was condemned by that which had been given to him for his own good. For as the law was given to man without his asking for it, it inflamed desires to man's disadvantage, in order to stain him even more with sinful lusts, and he could not escape its hands.

[12]So the law is holy, and the commandment is holy and just and good.

Paul commends the law in this way, so that no doubts about it might remain, and therefore states that it is not only righteous, but also holy and good. It is the language of the Gospel which tells us that the word *commandment* means the law, for it says: *If you want to come to life, keep the commandments.*[1]

[13]Did that which is good, then, bring death to me? By no means! It was sin, working death in me through what is good, in order that sin might be shown to be sin, and through the commandment might become sinful beyond measure.

By no means, indeed! How can it possibly be that something which is good should be regarded as death? Paul says that the devil seized the opportunity offered by something good in order to do harm to the human race by tricking him into death. For the law revealed in writing was given in order to show that those things which had been done out of an excess of desire before it came were in fact sins and ought to be avoided in the future.

Satan was so incensed by the goodness which he saw being offered to the human race that he enticed it into illegal activities, so that instead of obtaining life through the law we would get death instead. It is therefore the fault of human wickedness, which has so weakened the power of its nature by sinning that [the law] can no longer suppress the sug-

---

[1]Mt 19:17.

gestions of the adversary.

Yet the enemy, whom he refers to when he talks about sin, in order to appear as the enemy he is, took the opportunity offered by the good (law) to bring death to the human race. Although even before the law came, the devil obtained death for man because of the first sin of Adam, nevertheless after the law came, he found still greater punishments for him in hell, where death followed him. For to have sinned before the coming of the law was a lesser crime than to have sinned after it.

Beyond measure suggests that there is a limit imposed on sinners beyond which it is not permitted to go. But these are the words of God: *The sins of the Amorites are not yet complete.*[1] By this God shows that there is some limit to sin, and when sinners reach it, they will be judged completely unworthy of life. Pharaoh was an example of this, because when he reached his limit, the signs and powers of God were revealed against him, by which the terrified people [of Egypt] did all they could to obtain the benefits of life, and so life was made known in death.

But it is also *beyond measure* when the devil cajoles people to sin more after the giving of the law than they had sinned before, so that they would do whatever was contrary to the providence of God when they should have sinned less out of fear of the law. Therefore, in order to defeat the jealousy of the devil and confirm his providence toward the human race, God turned everything around by sending Christ the Savior, who both defeated the devil and confirmed the statutes of God made for the benefit of human beings.

[14]We know that the law is spiritual; but I am carnal, sold under sin.

Paul is speaking here to those who knew the law. He calls man carnal, because he sins or used to sin. He calls the law of Moses, which was given on the tablets, spiritual. It is spiritual because it prohibits sinning, and especially because it forbids the worship of visible and carnal things. This is all part of his commendation of the law. He does not want guilt to be thought valuable because it has had such bad effects on sinners. He calls people carnal because they sin.

To be sold under sin means to trace one's origin to Adam, who was the first to sin, and to subject oneself to sin by one's own transgression, as Isaiah the prophet says: *You are sold to your sins.*[2] For Adam sold himself first, and because of this all his descendants are subjected to sin. Thus people are weak and unable to keep the precepts of the law unless they are strengthened by God's help. This is why Paul says: *The law is spiritual but I am carnal, sold under sin.* This means that the law is firm and just and without fault, but man is weak and bound either by his own or by his inherited fault, so that he cannot obey it in his own strength. That is why he has to take refuge in God's mercy, so that he may escape the severity of the law and, pardoned for his sins, may in the future resist the enemy with God's help. For what does it mean to be subjected to sin other than having a body corrupted by the wickedness of the soul which is dominated by sin?

Thus the Lord said, among other things: *The devil came and took away what was sown in their heart, so that they should not be saved.*[3] Thus too the same apostle said in another letter: *Our struggle is not against flesh and blood, but against princes and powers, against the spiritual forces of wickedness in the heavenly places,*[4] which he declares are puppets of Satan. Before the transgression of man and before he bound himself to death, these things did not have the power to gain access to the inner parts of a man and plant contrary thoughts in him. It was by his cleverness that the devil got around

---

[1]Gen 15:16. [2]Is 50:1. [3]Lk 8:12. [4]Eph 6:12.

this by talking to man through a serpent. But after he had wormed his way in and subjugated man, he obtained power over him to attack his inner being by joining himself to his mind, so that it would no longer be possible for him to distinguish what was his idea and what was the devil's, unless he turned to the law.

¹⁵I do not understand my own actions. For I do not do what I want, but I do the very thing I hate.

Paul does not understand what he does, because he sees that he knows one thing by the law and does another.

¹⁶Now if I do what I do not want, I agree that the law is good.

Paul proves that the law was right to forbid things when he confesses that he did what the law forbids even against his will. He also says that what the law commands accords with his nature, because he says that he hates himself when he transgresses it.

¹⁷So then it is no longer I that do it, but sin which dwells within me.

Since Paul sees that what he does is contrary to the law and agrees that this should not happen and that he is acting under some alien impulse, he declares that this is sin. He always calls it sin when he knows that it is the devil and his angels at work, because if the first man had not sinned these things would never have happened. It is sin because he does them all.

¹⁸For I know that nothing good dwells within me, that is, in my flesh. I can will what is right, but I cannot do it.

Paul does not say that the flesh is evil, as some think, but that what dwells in the flesh is not good, in other words, sin. How does sin dwell

in the flesh when it is not a substance, but the perversion of what is good? Since the body of the first man was corrupted by sin and became dissolvable, this same corruption of sin remains in the body because of the state of transgression, retaining the strength of the divine judgment given in Adam, which is the sign of the devil, at whose prompting Adam sinned. Because of this, sin is said to dwell in the flesh, to which the devil comes as if to his own kingdom. The flesh is sinful and sin remains in it in order to deceive man by evil temptations, so that man will not do what the law commands.

Man can agree that what the law commands is good; he can say that it naturally pleases him and that he wants to do it. But in spite of all that, the power and the strength to carry out his wishes is lacking, because he is so oppressed by the power of sin that he cannot go where he wants nor can he make contrary decisions, because another power is in control of him. Man is burdened by his habit of sinning and succumbs to sin more readily than to the law, which he knows teaches what is good. Even if he wants to do what is good, habit, backed by the enemy, prevents him.

¹⁹For I do not do the good I want, but the evil I do not want is what I do.

Paul repeats this often in order to make it clear. This is exactly what he said above, because he is forced to do it as if in bondage to the above-mentioned causes, because he does not want the sin which controls him.

²⁰Now if I do what I do not want, it is no longer I that do it, but sin which dwells within me.

This is the same as he has already mentioned above, because pressured by sin and in its power, he does its will and not his own. Is the sinner compelled to sin by a power outside himself? Should he be regarded as innocent because he has acted against his will? Not at all. It was by his own fault that these evil things began, for whoever binds himself to sin voluntarily is ruled by its law. Sin persuades him first, and when it has conquered him it takes control. In order to exalt the grace of God, the apostle records the number of evils from which it has liberated the human race in order to show that whatever liabilities he has inherited from Adam, he has received benefits from Christ, which even the law could not bring him.

²¹So I find it to be a law that when I want to do right, evil lies close at hand.

Paul says that the law of Moses agrees with his will against sin, which dwells in his flesh and forces him to do something other than what he and the law want to do.

²²For I delight in the law of God, in my inmost self,

Paul says that the mind delights in the things which are taught by the law. This is *our inmost self*, because sin does not dwell in the mind but in the flesh, which lies at the root of sin and by descent all flesh has become sinful. It may be true that the soul is also passed on by descent and that it dwells in the flesh, because the soul of Adam sinned more than his flesh did, but the sin of the soul has corrupted the body. Therefore sin dwells in the flesh, at the door of the soul as it were, so as to prevent the soul from doing what it wants to do. If it dwelt in the mind it would derange it, so that man would not know himself. As it is, he does know himself and takes delight in the law of God.

²³but I see in my members another law at war with the law of my mind and making me captive to the law of sin which dwells in my members.

Paul mentions two laws here. One of these he sees in his members, in other words, in the outer self, which is the flesh or the body. This law is hostile to us. It wars with his mind, leading him captive in a state of sin and preventing him from getting out of it and finding help. The other law is the law of the mind, which is either the law of Moses or the law of nature which is innate in the mind. This law is attacked by the violence of sin, and by its own negligence, for because it loves evil, it subjects itself to sin and is held captive by the habit of sinning. Man, after all, is a creature of habit.

For Paul, there are four kinds of law. The first is spiritual. This is the law of nature, which was reworked by Moses and made authoritative; it is God's law. Then there is the law of the mind, which agrees with God's law. Thirdly, there is the law of sin, which is said to dwell in man's members because of the transgression of the first man. The fourth appears in our members and tempts us to sin, before retreating. But these four laws can be reduced to two—the law of good and the law of evil. For the law of the mind is the same as the spiritual law or the law of Moses, which is called the law of God. But the law of sin is the same as the law which appears in our members, which contradicts the law of our mind.

²⁴Wretched man that I am! Who will deliver me from this body of death?

Paul says that a man born in sin is wretched. Indeed, how could man not be wretched when he has succeeded to this inheritance of sin, having this enemy sin with him, through which Satan has access to him? Adam invented steps by which the despoiler came up to his descendants, yet the most merciful God, moved by pity, gave us his grace through Christ so that it might be revealed that the human race, once it accepted the forgiveness of sins, might repent and put sin to death. A man who is pardoned for his sins and cleansed can resist the power of the enemy which is aimed against him, provided that God continues to help him.

Here Paul introduces a third, more powerful law, which is a law of faith that he also calls grace, which takes its origin from the spiritual law, since by it the human race is set free. Thus Moses gave the law and so did the Lord; they are said to be two different laws but are understood to be the same as far as their meaning and purpose is concerned. The former is the initiator of salvation and the latter is the accomplisher of it.

I have spoken here of the law which was given on the tablets, not of that part of it which deals with new moons, circumcision and food, but rather of what belongs to the covenant and [spiritual] discipline of God. For by the grace of God the human race has been liberated by Christ from this body of death. Paul speaks of this death, which, as he showed earlier, is found in the murder of man by sin in hell, which is called the second death. The body of death is the full complement of sins, for they all form part of the body of the second death, being each of them members attached to a single source. By the grace of God the human race has been rescued from these sins by baptism and has escaped the above-mentioned second death. For being in a carnal body right now, Paul does not say that he has been rescued from it; rather he was referring to that body which was destroyed by baptism and by keeping the law. For when he talks about the body of death he shows that there is another body which is not subject to death.

25Thanks be to God through Jesus Christ our Lord! So then, I of myself serve the law of God with my mind, but with my flesh I serve the law of sin.

The law of God means both the law of Moses and the law of Christ. *With my flesh I serve the law of sin.* I myself, that is, I who have been liberated from the body of death. He is in the body, for what does it mean to be liberated from the body of death, except to be delivered from all evil? The forgiveness of sins takes away all sin. Therefore, being delivered from the body of death by the grace of God through Christ, *I serve the law of God with my mind, but with my flesh I serve the law of sin*, that is, of the devil, who puts wicked thoughts into my soul through the flesh which is subjected to him. Man is two-sided, consisting of both flesh and soul. Paul said that he served the law of God with his mind, because his soul was devoted to God and having recovered its strength was able to do battle with the sin which works through the flesh. For because the flesh is corrupt and subject to death, yet was so made that by its fellowship and union with the soul it should not die, it has received desires, the burden of which it transfers to the mind, so that it will degenerate as well. But whoever rejects the flesh will escape death by the grace of God.[1]
A free mind which has been called back to good habits by the help of the Holy Spirit can repulse evil temptations. For it has recovered its power to resist the Enemy. If it is no longer subject [to sin], then Satan cannot appear uninvited. Flesh by itself has no judgment nor is it able to discern anything, because it is brute nature. It cannot close the door to the enemy, nor can it come in and persuade the mind to do the opposite of what the mind intends.

Because man consists of both soul and flesh, the part which knows this serves God and the part which is mute serves the law of sin. But if man perseveres in the form in which he was created, the enemy would have no power to reach the flesh and persuade it to act against the will of the soul. But because the whole man was not restored to his pristine state by the grace of Christ, the sentence pronounced on Adam remains in force, for it would be unjust to abolish a sentence which was rightly pronounced. So although the sentence re-

---

[1]The Latin here is obscure and ungrammatical.

mains in force, a cure has been found by the providence of God, so that the salvation which man had lost by his own fault might be given back to him. Now that he is born again he can believe, because his adversary, defeated by the power of Christ, would not dare to rely on the sentence of the first death, which has now been superseded in the reconciled race of Adam, nor would Adam, now that he is fully and permanently immortal, be called to account for his first [terrestrial] origin.

Romans 8

1There is therefore now no condemnation for those who are in Christ Jesus.

It is true that there will be no damnation for those who are Christians, serving the law of God with a devout mind.

2For the law of the Spirit of life in Christ Jesus has set me free from the law of sin and death.

Paul promises us assurance by the grace of God, so that we shall not be tempted by the suggestions of the devil, as long as we reject them. There will be nothing to hurt us at the second death, because the law of faith, which is of the Spirit, has delivered us from the second death by condemning sin. Nothing will harm us because of the sin in our flesh, as long as we reject it with God's help. We shall instead be rewarded if we repel the counsels of that sin which remains in us, for it demands great skill to avoid the tricks of the enemy within. *The law of the Spirit of life* is the law of faith. Even the law of Moses is spiritual, in that it forbids us to sin, but it is not the law of life. It has no power to pardon those who are guilty of sins which deserve death, and thereby to bring them back to life. This is why the law of the Spirit of life is called what it is, because it

does not allow us to sin and it calls us back to life. It does not consist of the letter but of the Spirit, because it is believed in the heart, and it is the Spirit who is believed. Therefore it is the law in Christ Jesus, that is to say, through faith in Christ, which frees the believer from the law of sin and death. The law of sin, which Paul says dwells in our members, tries to persuade us to sin, and the law of Moses is a law of death, because it puts sinners to death.

In another letter Paul says this, among other things, about the authority of the law: *If the dispensation of death carved in stone was in glory.*[1] It is not to be wondered at that the spiritual law is also called a law of death, because that is also true of the gospel. In another place Paul says: *To one a fragrance from death to death, to another a fragrance from life to life,*[2] because the gospel brings life to believers but death to unbelievers. The report of wonders or great deeds which have been seen or heard drew some to faith, and for those people it was the fragrance of life. But in other cases the power at work merely angered some people into denying it, and for them the preaching of the faith was the fragrance of death. So although there is only one faith, it affects people in different ways, just as the sun, which is one and the same in itself, melts wax but hardens mud. In the same way, how a person reacts to the fragrance of the faith will determine the effect it has on him.

Now someone might ask: *If faith has the same effect as the law, why is it not also called a law of death, seeing as it brings death to nonbelievers?* But this does not follow. Faith is given to and justifies those who turn to it. It forgives those whom the law held to be guilty so that, acting in faith, they might be free from sin, because acting under the law they had been in bondage. Those who do not obey the faith are not killed by faith but by the law, because by not coming to the faith they are held guilty

---

[1]2 Cor 3:7.　[2]2 Cor 2:16.

by the law. Therefore everyone who hears[1] the words of faith with the wrong attitude remains in death. Now let us consider what it means to say that the law is spiritual, or of the Spirit. The point is that it is called a spiritual law because it gives precepts by which it is possible not to sin, and whoever does not sin is called spiritual, the imitator of the heavenly beings above us. It is called the law of the Spirit because God, whose faith it is, is a spirit. The words thus correspond to the reality. They come from God, and God himself is in them.

[3]For God has done what the law, weakened by the flesh, could not do: sending his own Son in the likeness of sinful flesh and for sin, he condemned sin in the flesh,

Paul says this in order to reassure those who have been baptized and set free from sin. For whom was the law unable to act? For us, of course, because we could not fulfill the commandment of the law, since we were subject to sin. For this reason God sent his Son in the likeness of sinful flesh. It is called the "likeness" of our flesh, because although it is the same as ours is, it was sanctified in the womb and born without sin, nor did the Son sin in it. The womb of a virgin was chosen for the divine birth, so that the divine flesh might differ from ours in its holiness. It is like ours in origin, but not in sinfulness. For this reason Paul says that it is similar to our flesh, since it is of the same substance, but it did not have the same birth, because the body of the Lord was not subject to sin. The Lord's flesh was sanctified by the Holy Spirit, in order that he might be born in the same kind of body as Adam had before he sinned. By sending Christ, God used sin to condemn sin. He says this because sin was condemned by sin itself. How? Christ was crucified by sin, which is Satan; sin operated in the flesh of the Savior's body. In this way,

God condemned sin in the flesh, in the very place where it sinned, as he says elsewhere: *Triumphing over them in himself.*[2]

It is customary to explain the reason why a condemned person has been condemned—for homicide, let us say. In this way sin is condemned in the flesh, that is to say, in the sin which it has allowed into the flesh. Therefore Satan, who has been condemned for this sin, has lost his power to keep souls in detention, and does not dare to hold in the second death those who have been signed with the sign of the cross, by which he has been conquered. The apostle explains this in order to reassure us.

[4]in order that the just requirement of the law might be fulfilled in us, who walk not according to the flesh but according to the Spirit.

Paul says that sin has been condemned in order that the righteousness of the law given by Moses might be fulfilled in us. Once we are removed from the power of the law we become the law's friends. Those who have been justified are friends of the law. For how is this righteousness fulfilled in us unless the forgiveness of sins is given to us, so that once we have been justified by the removal of our sins we might serve the law of God with our minds? This is what it means to walk according to the Spirit and not according to the flesh. The devotion of the mind, which is the spirit, will not succumb to the desire of sin, which sows lusts in the soul by means of the flesh, because sin dwells in it. But if sin has been condemned, how can it be indwelling?

Sin has been condemned by the Savior in three different ways. In the first place, he condemned sin by saying that a person should turn away from it and not sin. Next, sin is said to have been condemned on the cross, because it actually committed sin itself. The power by

---

[1]The original text has "smells," to agree with the notion of fragrance mentioned earlier. [2]Col 2:15.

which it held people in hell because of Adam's sin was then taken away, because it was itself a sinner. After that it would no longer dare to hang on to anyone who had been signed with the sign of the cross. In the third place, God condemned sin by canceling it out in the case of those who had received forgiveness for their sins. For although a sinner ought to be condemned for his sin, God forgave him and condemned the sin in him instead. So if we follow our Savior's example and do not sin, we are condemning sin.

5For those who live according to the flesh set their minds on the things of the flesh, but those who live according to the Spirit set their minds on the things of the Spirit.

Paul says this because whoever obeys the temptation which comes through the flesh knows what the things of the flesh are, for what it leads to seems agreeable to him. Going against what it right, he seeks out the behavior and attitude inherent in the error of the flesh, for the sin of this world is marked on the flesh wherever you look. Those who live according to the Spirit are those who have stomped on the lusts of the flesh by attacking sin. They have put the world behind them, and although they still walk in the flesh they do not struggle according to the flesh. Their glory is not from men but from God. Dwelling in these spiritual works, they know what the things of the Spirit of God are and walk in his commandments.

6To set the mind on the flesh is death, but to set the mind on the Spirit is life and peace.

The wisdom of the flesh is death because sin is serious, and it is through sin that this death comes. It is called wisdom, even though it is a foolish thing, because to worldly people, sins against the law of God which are conceived on the basis of what is visible, whether in thought or in deed, appear as wisdom, especially because those who sin are full of energy and cleverness. The fact that they take so much trouble over it makes them appear wise, even though there is nothing more foolish than sinning. Moreover, there is yet another wisdom of the flesh, which is puffed up by earthly reasoning and denies the possibility of miracles, which is why it laughs at the virgin birth and the resurrection of the flesh. The wisdom of the Spirit, on the other hand, is true wisdom, which leads to life and peace. Whoever follows spiritual things and despises the enticements of this present life will have this, eternal life with peace, that is without disturbance, because where there is disruption there is also punishment.

7For the mind that is set on the flesh is hostile to God; it does not submit to God's law, indeed it cannot;

Paul did not say that the flesh itself is hostile, but rather that *the wisdom of the flesh* is. *The wisdom of the flesh* means, in the first place, any argument about the unknown which men have come up with, and in the second place, a preference for what can be seen. Both these things are hostile to God, because they reduce the Lord of the elements and the Creator of the world to the level of what he has made, and assert that nothing can happen unless there is a rational cause for it. For this reason they deny that God made a virgin give birth or that he raises the bodies of the dead. They say that it is absurd that God should do anything beyond what man can understand, and therefore he did not do it. O, wise men of this world, who think that God must never do anything beyond the power of his creatures, as if he was one of them! These people are so blinded that they do not see how greatly they are insulting God, for the work which he was pleased to do in order that his praise should be proclaimed, they condemn and claim is unbelievable and absurd. For this reason such a mind cannot be subject to the law of God, because it spends all its energy trying to reject God's works.

8and those who are in the flesh cannot please God.

The wise of this world are in the flesh because they cling to their wisdom, by which they reject God's law. Whatever goes against the law of God is of the flesh, because it is of the world. The whole world is flesh and every visible thing is consigned to the flesh; indeed everything in the world is related to it. So whoever follows earthly things is carnal [by definition].

9But you are not in the flesh, you are in the Spirit, if the Spirit of God really dwells in you. Anyone who does not have the Spirit of Christ does not belong to him.

Those who are physically in the flesh are said not to be in the flesh if they agree with the apostle John and do not love the things of the world.[1] It is as if a man's thinking fashions his nature, so that it is defined by what he thinks.

Paul speaks somewhat ambiguously, because those who had been inducted into the law did not yet have a perfect faith, although Paul saw some hope for perfection in them. For this reason he sometimes speaks to them as if they are perfect and sometimes as if they are yet to become perfect. This is why sometimes he praises them and sometimes he warns them, so that if they maintain the law of nature according to what has been said above, they will be said to be in the Spirit, because the Spirit of God cannot dwell in anyone who follows carnal things.

Here Paul says that the Spirit of God is the Spirit of Christ, for everything which belongs to the Father belongs to the Son as well. Therefore he says that whoever is subject to

the above-mentioned sins does not belong to Christ. Such a person does not have the Spirit of God, even if he has accepted that Christ is God's Son. The Holy Spirit abandons people for one of two reasons, either because they think carnally or because they act carnally. Therefore Paul exhorts them to good behavior, because although human beings have been made by the goodness of God it is hard for them to be called children of God unless they live in a way which is not too unworthy of the name given to them.

10But if Christ is in you, although your bodies are dead because of sin, your spirits are alive because of righteousness.

Paul asserts that the bodies of those whom the Holy Spirit has abandoned because of sin are dead, nor does the Spirit of God feel like a murderer, since he cannot sin. He is given for righteousness, in order to make people righteous by his assistance, and therefore, because he cannot sin, he is life and cannot die. Death comes through sin. It is for this reason that a sinner dies to himself, and not to the Spirit, whom he receives. It is not the Spirit who will be called to account, because it was his desire to justify [the sinner], and his presence in a man is the sign of his justification, so that by the fact that he dwells in him the justified [sinner] appears as a child of God. The Holy Spirit cannot dwell in a fake man, nor in a body which is subject to sin, as Solomon says.[2]

If a believer returns to the life of the flesh, the Holy Spirit will leave him and he will die in his unrighteousness. In saying the body, Paul means that the whole person will die because of sin, just as by using the word *soul* the prophet meant the whole man, as if a part can stand for the whole. As he says: *The soul that sins, it shall die.*[3] Will this happen without

---

[1]Cf. 1 Jn 2:15-16. [2]Wis 1:4. [3]Ezek 18:4.

the body? Hardly! Paul uses *body* for the whole person; Ezekiel uses *soul*; and another prophet uses *flesh* to say exactly the same thing: *All flesh shall see the salvation of our God.*[1]

Because the Holy Spirit is given to everyone who is baptized, that person's spirit is also called *holy*. Therefore Paul has here called the rest of man the *body* for the purpose of comparison, because the soul, when it sins, is called *flesh*. It is called by what it follows, as I have said many times already. In a similar way, the Lord during his passion did not want it to be thought that his divinity was struggling [against evil], but rather that he had taken the place of man [on the cross], and so he said: *The Spirit is willing but the flesh is weak,*[2] meaning by this that the Spirit is God and the flesh is man.

[11]If the Spirit of him who raised Jesus from the dead dwells in you, he who raised Christ Jesus from the dead will give life to your mortal bodies also through his Spirit which dwells in you.

Paul continues with the same logic as above. When he says *bodies* he means the whole person. And because he has already said that the body dies a second death because of sin, he here promised that their mortal bodies, that is to say, their whole being, would be reanimated in order to live a good life.

[12]So then, brethren, we are debtors, not to the flesh, to live according to the flesh—

It is right and clear that we are not obliged to follow Adam, who lived according to the flesh, and who by being the first to sin, left us an inheritance of sin. On the contrary, we ought rather to obey the law of Christ who, as was demonstrated above, has redeemed us spiritually from death. We are debtors to him who in baptism has washed our spirits, which

had been sullied by carnal sins, who has justified us and who has made us children of God. As dwellers in the flesh we used to live in subjection to sin, following the example of Adam, but now that we have been delivered we ought to pay homage to the Redeemer. This homage does nothing for him of course, because he lacks nothing, but it obtains eternal life for us. He loves us so much that he imputes to himself what he has promised to us.

[13]for if you live according to the flesh you will die, but if by the Spirit you put to death the deeds of the body you will live.

Nothing is truer than this, that if we live according to Adam we shall die. By sinning, Adam was consigned to the flesh and sold himself to sin, for all sin is flesh. It is because vices and sins start outside us, when we look at them, and not from within the mind, that they are attached to the flesh, for every thought of sin which looks outside ourselves brings on transgression. Even in the case of the first man, sin began outside himself. Therefore to live according to the flesh is death, for the life of the flesh is completely outside the bounds of the law.

The body wants to be governed by the law of the spirit, which is why Paul shows that if we are led by the Holy Spirit, the acts and desires of the flesh, which are made up by the instigation of the powers of this world, are repressed, so as to be unable to act. Then we shall enjoy eternal life. When they cease they are said to die, because there is no sin if nothing happens.

[14]For all who are led by the Spirit of God are sons of God.

Paul says that those in whose works the de-

---

[1]Is 40:5; 52:10; Lk 3:6. [2]Mt 26:41.

signs of the princes and powers of this world are not to be seen are those who are moved by the Spirit of God. Those in whom such things are to be seen are children, not of God but of the devil, because *whoever is born of God does not sin*, says the apostle John.[1] It is this that proves who are the children of God and who are the children of the devil. As the Lord said to the Jews who behaved badly and even contemplated parricide: *You are of your father the devil.*[2]

[15]For you did not receive the spirit of slavery to fall back into fear, but you have received the Spirit of sonship. When we cry, "Abba! Father!"

Paul says this because once we have received the Holy Spirit we are delivered from all fear of evil deeds, so that we might no longer act in a way which would make us afraid once more. We used to be under fear, because after the law was given, everyone was considered guilty. Paul called the law the spirit of fear, because it made people afraid on account of their sins. But the law of faith, which is what is meant by *the Spirit of sonship*, is a law of assurance, because it has delivered us from fear by pardoning our sins and thus giving us assurance, so it is not called a spirit of fear according to this world.

Set free from fear by the grace of God, we have received the Spirit of sonship, so that considering what we were and what we have become by the gift of God, we must govern our life with great care, lest the name of God the Father be disgraced by us and we incur all the punishments we have escaped from. We have received such grace that we can dare to say to God: *Abba! Father!* For this reason, Paul warns us not to let our trust degenerate into pride. If our behavior does not correspond to our voice, when we cry *Abba! Father!* we insult

God by calling him Father. Indeed, God in his goodness has indulged us with what is beyond our capacity, for what we were unworthy of by nature we have earned by our deeds.

[16]it is the Spirit himself bearing witness with our spirit that we are children of God,

When we do what is right the Spirit of God dwells in us, and for this reason he becomes our voice and our mind, by which we cry in prayer: *Abba*, that is, *Father*. The Spirit of God bears witness, when he dwells in us, so we are bold to say *Abba, Father*, for then we live a life worthy of this cry. The witness of children is that by the Spirit they should be seen to bear the sign of the Father.

[17]and if children, then heirs, heirs of God and fellow heirs with Christ, provided we suffer with him in order that we may also be glorified with him.

This is an enormous challenge, because as Paul predicts that we shall receive even greater blessings from God, he warns us that we must make ourselves all the more worthy to receive them, so that we may live better and better lives, as the future coheirs of Christ.

Since there is no way that God the Father can be said to have died, Christ the Son is said to have died because of his incarnation. How is it that he who died is always said to be the heir of the Living One, when heirs are normally heirs of the dead? The answer, of course, is that Christ died in his humanity, not in his divinity. For with God, which is where our inheritance lies, the Father's gift is poured into his obedient children, so that one who is alive may be the heir of the Living One by his merit, and not by reason of death.

Thus the Lord indicated in the gospel, by both human and divine reasoning, that as a liv-

---

[1]1 Jn 3:9-10. [2]Jn 8:44.

ing being he imparted his nature to the living, and there is no absurdity in this statement. In order to make us ready to obey God the Father, he exhorts us by this hope, saying that we are the future heirs of God and coheirs with Christ, so that because the hope of reward is so great, we shall be all the more inclined toward the things of God, laying aside the care of worldly things.

What it means to be a fellow heir with Christ we are taught by the apostle John, for among other things he says: *We know that when he appears we shall be like him.*[1]

Paul declared how we can become coheirs with Christ when he said: *If we suffer with him we shall also be glorified with him.* Let us consider what this means. To suffer together with Christ is to endure persecutions in the hope of future rewards and to crucify the flesh with its evils and lusts, in other words, to reject the pleasures and pomp of this world. For when all these things are dead in a man, then he has crucified this world, believing in the life of the world to come, in which he believes that he will be a fellow heir with Christ.

[18]*I consider that the sufferings of this present time are not worth comparing with the glory that is to be revealed to us.*

This exhortation relates to what we have just read, where Paul shows that the things which we might suffer at the hands of the wicked here below are small in comparison with the reward which awaits us in the next life. We ought to be prepared for every eventuality, because the rewards which are promised to us are so great, so that our mind may be consoled in tribulation and grow in hope. We know how long and hard we have to work for the money we have and for the little we shall get in the future, and sometimes there is no reward at all,

because this life is weak and uncertain.

Think of the enormous storms and tempests that sailors endure in order to make a living, when they know full well that in their profession death is more likely to stare them in the face than life! And soldiers are quick to take the sword in the hope of present reward, even when victory is highly uncertain. How much more therefore should we be ready to suffer for Christ, whose blessings are spread out before us, who offers us great things in exchange for little ones, heavenly things in exchange for earthly ones and eternal rewards in exchange for temporal ones? We are said to suffer for Christ, and yet it is we and not he who benefits from it! But because he looks for an opportunity to reward us, this is what he prescribes. Like a good and generous benefactor, he looks for ways of giving to those who are either unworthy or embarrassed. He even supplies the strength which they need to be able to endure receiving such benefits!

[19]*For the creation waits with eager longing for the revealing of the sons of God;*

Because Paul says that the sufferings of the present time are unworthy to be compared to our future glory, he adds that the creation is waiting until the number of the children of God destined for eternal life is complete, so that then it too can be discharged from the office of a servant and enjoy eternal rest.

[20]*for the creation was subjected to futility, not of its own will but by the will of him who subjected it in hope;*

The creation is placed in the power of the Lord and Creator, and has not chosen to be subject to futility. This subjection of the creation is not for its benefit but for ours. What does it mean to be subject to futility, but that

---

[1] Jn 3:2.

what it produces is worthless? The creation works in order to bring forth corruptible fruit, but corruption is itself futility. Everything which is born into the world is weak, worthless and corruptible, and is therefore futile, futile because it cannot retain its original condition. All things are constantly decaying and returning to the primordial confusion of their nature. Solomon also spoke of this when he said that *all is vanity*,[1] and is created—not eternal but futile. David agreed with this when he said: *Surely every living man is vanity*.[2] For is it not futile to eat, drink and care for the things of this world? Yet even this futility has its purpose, because it helps the people who are born in this world, when they feel the excitement of these things in their bodies, to study the mystery of their Creator. In comparison with eternal things they are futile, but in themselves they are good and even necessary. What hope is, he goes on to explain in the next verse.

21*because the creation itself will be set free from its bondage to decay and obtain the glorious liberty of the children of God.*

Because the creation cannot contradict its Creator, it is in bondage because of him, though it is not without hope. For in its travail it has this comfort, that it will have rest when all those who will believe, and for whose sake it was subjected in the first place, will have come to faith.

22*We know that the whole creation has been groaning in travail together until now;*

To groan in travail is to suffer. The meaning here is that the whole creation groans in its daily labor and suffers up to now. *Up to now* means for as long as it says. The elements themselves show forth their works with care,

for both the sun and the moon fill the spaces allotted to them but not without travail, and the spirits of the animals demonstrate their servitude by loud groanings. All of these are waiting for rest, and to be set free from their servile labor. Now if this service were of any benefit to God, the creation would be rejoicing, not suffering. But every day it watches its labor disappear. Every day its work appears and vanishes. Therefore it is right to say that it is suffering, because its work leads not to eternity, but to corruption.

As far as we can understand, all this is happening for the benefit of our salvation, for we know that the sooner we acknowledge our Creator the sooner we shall obtain our deliverance. Knowing this, we ought to make ourselves worthy by every form of care and diligence, so that we may also set an example to others. We should not be motivated by our own sufferings only, but also by those of him who for our sake patiently groaned day and night. Indeed, we ought to be even more concerned for the sake of others.

23*and not only the creation, but we ourselves, who have the first fruits of the Spirit, groan inwardly as we wait for adoption as sons, the redemption of our bodies.*

Paul adds that like the earthly creation, we too should be waiting and longing for God, so that all of us who are predestined to life may be set free. For Christians, this world is like the ocean. Just as the sea is whipped up by adverse winds and produces storms for sailors, so also this world is moved by the scheming of wicked men and disturbs the minds of believers. The enemy does this in so many different ways that it is hard to know what to avoid first, for sources of tribulation are by no means wanting.

24*For in this hope we were saved. Now hope*

---

[1]Eccles 1:2. [2]Ps 39:5.

that is seen is not hope. For who hopes for what he sees?

Paul says this because we have made ourselves worthy of deliverance by hoping for what God has promised to us in Christ. Therefore we have been set free in the hope that what is coming in the future will be no different from what we believe. It is clear that hope is not what is seen but what is unseen, and by this those who hope are made ready for their rewards, because they hope for what they do not see.

25But if we hope for what we do not see, we wait for it with patience.

There is no doubt that what is hoped for is not yet seen; it is an expectation of the future. This expectation is patience, which is greatly approved of by God, for by daily waiting it desires the coming of the kingdom of God, and does not doubt just because it delays.

26Likewise the Spirit helps us in our weakness; for we do not know how to pray as we ought, but the Spirit himself intercedes for us with sighs too deep for words.

Since the text has just recalled that we groan in our prayers, and we either suffer or want things which are said to be still far off in the future either to happen or to be taken away much sooner so that we may obtain merit, our prayers seem to be weak because their effect is denied. They are weak because they ask for things contrary to reason, which is why Paul shows that this weakness in us is helped by the Holy Spirit who has been given to us. The Holy Spirit helps because he does not allow anything we ask for to happen before the proper time, or against God's wishes.

Paul says that the weakness of our prayers

means ignorance. We go wrong because we think that the things we are asking for will be beneficial for us, when they are not. Finally, the same apostle prayed three times for his trials to go away because they were happening so frequently, but the Lord said: *My grace is sufficient for you, for my strength is made perfect in weakness.*[1] The meaning of this is that a person will find merit when he is found patiently enduring suffering. Therefore he taught that what he was asking for was against his own interests. Then too, sometimes a petition can be arrogant and stupid, like the one of the apostles James and John, whose inappropriate and outrageous requests received the answer: *You do not know what you are asking.*[2]

Paul says that the Spirit intercedes for us not with human words but according to his own nature. For when what comes from God speaks to God, it is obvious that he will speak in the same way as the one from whom he comes speaks. The Spirit given to us overflows with our prayers, in order to make up for our inadequacy and lack of foresight by his actions, and to ask God for the things which will be of benefit to us.

27And he who searches the hearts of men knows what is the mind of the Spirit, because the Spirit intercedes for the saints according to the will of God.

It is clear that the prayer of every spirit is known to God, from whom nothing is secret or hidden. How much more then should he know what the Holy Spirit, who is of his own substance, is saying. The Spirit does not speak by beating the air, nor does he talk like the angels or like other creatures, but in a way which is compatible with his divinity. When he appears to us to be silent, he is speaking to God, just as he sees us when he is not seen [by us], and he

---

[1]Cor 12:9. [2]Mt 20:22.

asks for what he knows God will like and will be of benefit to us. Then the Spirit intervenes on our behalf, because he knows that we are asking for things in ignorance, not because we deliberately want the opposite.

28We know that in everything God works for good with those who love him, who are called according to his purpose.

Paul says this because the prayers of those who love God, even if they are inept, will not fail them. God knows the intention of their heart and their ignorance, and will not give them things they ask for if they are harmful. Rather he teaches them what ought to be given to people who love God. This is what the Lord said in the Gospel: *For your Father knows what you need, even before you ask him.*[1] Those who are called according to the promise are those whom God knew would be true believers in the future, so that even before they believed they were known.

29For those whom he foreknew he also predestined to be conformed to the image of his Son, in order that he might be the first-born among many brethren.

Those whom God foreknew would believe in him he also chose to receive the promises. Those who appear to believe but do not persevere in the faith are not chosen by God, because whomever God chooses will persevere. Some people are chosen only for a time, like Saul and Judas, not on the basis of foreknowledge but on that of temporary righteousness.

Conformed to the image of his Son. This is because they are predestined to this in the future age, when they will be like the Son of God, as I have already mentioned above.

Christ is rightly called the *firstborn* because he was not made before the rest of Creation,

but begotten, and God has chosen to adopt men as his children following Christ's example. He is the firstborn in the regeneration of the Spirit, in the resurrection from the dead and in the ascension into heaven. Therefore the firstborn in all things is said to be our brother, because he chose to be born as a man, but he is also Lord, because he is our God, as the prophet Jeremiah said: *This is our God.*[2]

30And those whom he predestined he also called; and those whom he called he also justified; and those whom he justified he also glorified.

To *call* is to help somebody who is already thinking about faith, or else to put pressure on him in the knowledge that he will listen.

Paul says this because those whom God has foreknown would be devoted to him persevere as believers, which would not be possible if God had not foreknown it. He has also justified them and glorified them so that they may become like the Son of God. As for those whom God has not foreknown, there is no concern for them in this grace, because he has not foreknown them. If they believe or are chosen for a time because they seem to be good and do not appear to have rejected righteousness, they do not persevere until they are glorified. Examples of this are Judas Iscariot or those seventy-two who were chosen but who stumbled and fell away from the Savior.[3]

31What then shall we say to this? If God is for us, who is against us?

This is clear because God has borne witness to us as to who he is. Who would dare attack us when the Judge himself has foreknown us and pronounced us to be suitable?

32He who did not spare his own Son but gave

---

[1]Mt 6:8. [2]Bar 3:35. [3]Cf. Jn 6:67, 71; Lk 10:1, 17.

him up for us all, will he not also give us all things with him?

Paul urges us to rest assured on account of our faith by showing us that God gave up his Son to death on our behalf, even before we had ceased being sinners, because he knew in advance that we would believe. He says that God long ago decided that all those who believed in Christ would be rewarded. So if God is prepared to give us the greatest things, even to the point of sacrificing his own Son on our behalf, how can we not believe that he will give us the lesser things as well? The believer's rewards are already waiting, and giving them to us is not nearly as difficult as handing Christ over to death for our sake.

[33] *Who shall bring any charge against God's elect? It is God who justifies;*

It is clear that nobody would dare or be able to override the judgment and foreknowledge of God. Who could reject what God has approved, given that nobody is equal to God?

It is God who justifies.[1] This comes from Isaiah the prophet, though Paul quotes it almost as if it were his own idea, for there is no one else who could object to what God approves of. Could God himself become our accuser? Hardly, since he cannot accuse those whom he justifies.

[34] *who is to condemn? Is it Christ Jesus, who died, yes, who was raised from the dead, who is at the right hand of God, who indeed intercedes for us?*

Paul says that we cannot accuse God, because he justifies us, nor can we condemn Christ, because he loved us to the point of dying for us and rising again to intercede for us with the Father. Christ's prayers on our behalf are not to be despised, because he sits at God's right hand, that is to say, in the place of honor, since he is himself God. So let us rejoice in our faith, secure in the knowledge of God the Father and of his Son Jesus Christ who will come to judge us.

From this comes what the Lord said to the apostle Peter: *Behold, Satan demanded to sift you like wheat, but I have asked for you, that your faith may not fail.*[2] This is how the Son intercedes for us. He knows the impudence and arrogance of our enemy, and when he moves against us, if we do not give in to him, the Savior intercedes for us, so that he will not try anything violent against us and we may be protected from his insolence. The Son is said to intercede, because although he controls everything and is equal to God the Father, we are not to think that the Father and the Son are one and the same person. The Scriptures speak of the distinction of the persons in such a way as to convey the message that the Son is not inferior, and that the Father is so called both because he is the Father of the Son, and because everything comes from him.

[35] *Who shall separate us from the love of Christ? Shall tribulation, or distress, or persecution, or famine, or nakedness, or peril, or sword?*

This means: *Who will turn us away from the love of Christ, who has given us such great and innumerable gifts?* Nobody, because no torments will overcome the love of a mature Christian. Love is stirred up all the more in those who love him if an attempt is made to prevent them from loving the one whose blessings they experience. For anyone who thinks he can reject God's merits merely draws attention to his blessings.

It is clear that all the events which he lists, tribulations, sufferings and death, cannot

---

[1]Cf. Is 50:8. [2]Lk 22:31-32.

be likened or compared to the love of Christ which he has planted in us. For the blessings which we have are far greater than everything which appears to be against us.

[36]*As it is written,*

   "For thy sake we are being killed all the
      day long;
   we are regarded as sheep to be
      slaughtered."[1]

[37]*No, in all these things we are more than conquerors through him who loved us.*

The quotation is from Psalm 43.[2] If we die for him, something which appears to be the most serious thing mentioned in this passage, he also died for us. But since he is a blessing to us, our death does not benefit him but us. We sacrifice our earthly life in order to get eternal life in return. Why be surprised if slaves die for a good master, when the Lord has died for slaves and wicked people? In this way they win blessings and encourage the mind to persevere on account of the one who loved us.

[38]*For I am sure that neither death, nor life, nor angels, nor principalities, nor things present, nor things to come, nor powers,* [39]*nor height, nor depth, nor anything else in all creation, will be able to separate us from the love of God in Christ Jesus our Lord.*

These are all the things which have come upon us since we were kidnapped by the devil. Paul lists them in order to steel us against them if they should appear, so that, confident of the hope and help of Christ and armed with faith, we might be able to fight against them. What then? If death has been brought in, does not its greatest value lie in the fact that it gives us the opportunity to get to the promised kingdom faster? Even if the present life promised to us

were clothed with dignity, it must not turn us away from the hope and benefits of Christ, whom we know, because he is a blessing to us not only in the future but also in the present life. Even if an angel appears to us in order to draw us away because he is bound to the lies of his father the devil, he must not prevail against us, because we know that nothing can come before Christ, who is the angel of great counsel. Even if a miracle is performed by someone, as we are told was the case with Simon Magus, who is said to have flown up into the air in order to scandalize Christ's people,[3] this should in no way lessen our faith, since we know that the Savior ascended above all the heavens with a cloud to accompany him. Even if Satan should reveal himself to us in the height of his power, concerning which the same apostle says: *Are you unaware of the heights of Satan?*[4] it ought not to deflect us from our devotion to the Lord Jesus, whom we know came down from heaven in order to unite earthly things with spiritual ones.

Even if he should try to seduce us in a dream by opening up horrible depths and thereby frightening us to give in to him, it would be unworthy of us to break faith with Christ, whom we know descended into the depths of the earth for our sake, where he subdued death and set the human race free. Not even if he should pledge to us the future blessings which he promised to Eve should we assent to him independently of Christ, whom we believe and know to be God in power and by nature. Even if by trickery and the excellence of his cleverness he should bring forth another creature for a moment in time, in the way that Jannes and Jambres did before Pharaoh,[5] it would not be right for us to turn away from God our Creator merely for that reason, when we know that through Christ his Son he founded the creation which exists for eternity.

---

[1]Ps 44:22. [2]Ps 44 in English versions. [3]The legend is told in the *Acts of Peter and Paul* 4. [4]Cf. 2 Cor 2:11; Rev 2:24. [5]Ex 7:11-12; 2 Tim 3:8.

Some people think that when Paul refers to *another creature* he is talking about idols. But this is not true, for this was meant to stand for what Satan might appear to create under the attraction of his deceiving power. Who among the those who believe would be attracted to those things which he gave up once their error had been revealed? But Satan thinks about and makes these things, by which he can deceive even the elect. There is nothing which can separate us from the love of Christ which is in Christ Jesus, for God showed us his love in Christ, when he gave him up for us.

Romans 9

¹I am speaking the truth in Christ, I am not lying; my conscience bears me witness in the Holy Spirit, ²that I have great sorrow and unceasing anguish in my heart. ³For I could wish that I myself were accursed and cut off from Christ for the sake of my brethren, my kinsmen by race.

Since it appears that earlier he was speaking against the Jews, who thought that they were justified by the law, Paul now shows his desire and love for them, and says that his conscience bears witness in Christ Jesus and in the Holy Spirit that their faith cannot be considered as something hostile to God. Therefore he calls on Christ Jesus and the Holy Spirit, whom nothing escapes, as his witnesses. Their testimony cannot be rejected, and they bear witness to the apostle when they commend him by the power of the signs which they did through him.

It is because he shows how great the protection of Christ is and how ready his love is toward the human race, as well as the glorious dignity and immortal rewards promised by him, that Paul grieves for his own people, as they were according to the flesh, who have deprived themselves of this eternal and saving blessing by their unbelief. He says: *I could*

wish, not *I wish*, because he knows that it is impossible for such an honorable member as he was to be cut off from the body of Christ without having done anything wrong. But by saying this, he shows his own feeling of love toward his own people.

⁴They are Israelites, and to them belong the sonship, the glory, the covenants, the giving of the law, the worship, and the promises; ⁵to them belong the patriarchs, and of their race, according to the flesh, is the Christ. God who is over all be blessed for ever. Amen.

Paul proves that he is right to grieve when he sings the praises of his people, because although they were once adopted children, they have nullified the love and grace of God the Father. He added this here in order to make others grieve for them as well.

Paul lists so many instances of the nobility and dignity of the Jewish people and of the promises they received in order to deepen their grief for these things, because by not accepting the Savior they lose the privilege of their fathers and the merit of the promises, and they became worse than the Gentiles, whom they had previously detested when they were without God. It is a worse evil to lose a dignity than never to have had it.

As there is no mention of the Father's name in this verse, and Paul is talking about Christ, it cannot be disputed that Christ is called God here. When Scripture is speaking about God the Father and adds the Son, it often calls the Father God and the Son Lord. If someone does not think that it is said here about Christ that he is God, then let him name the person about whom he thinks it is said, for there is no mention of God the Father in this verse.

It is hardly surprising that here Paul should speak openly of Christ as God over all, when elsewhere, in another letter, he confirmed this idea by saying: *That at the name of Jesus every knee shall bow in heaven and on earth and under the earth.*[1] These are all the things over which Christ is God. There are no exceptions made, as if there were some things over which Christ is not God, nor can the knees of every creature bow to anything except to God. Finally, when the apostle John in ignorance wanted to worship an angel as if he were God, he was told by the angel: *Do not do this, for I am a fellow servant with you. Worship God.*[2]

Christ the Lord would not allow himself to be worshiped if he were not God. Otherwise it would have to be said that he had usurped the place of God and sinned, which is absurd, considering that he himself reproached the devil [with the reminder] that the Lord God alone was to be worshiped and served. Therefore there is no prejudice to God the Father when Christ is worshiped as God, because when it is said that only God is to be served, this includes Christ. As Paul says elsewhere: *Whoever serves Christ in these things pleases God.*[3] What more is there to be said, except that if the Father is God and the Son is God, yet there is only one God, then both of them are God? If someone worships either the Father or the Son, he is said to be worshiping the one God, and to serve the Father or the Son is to demonstrate service to the one God. There is no discrepancy here, because whoever serves the Son serves the Father, and whoever serves the Father serves the Son. And to show that this confession of Christ's deity is not a form of flattery, Paul put *Amen*, that is, *It is true* at the end, in order to demonstrate that Christ is God over all things in truth, blessed be he forever!

[6]But it is not as though the Word of God had failed. For not all who are descended from Israel belong to Israel, [7]and not all are children of Abraham because they are his descendants; but "Through Isaac shall your descendants be named."[4]

The Word of God has not failed. He said: *In Isaac shall your seed be called.* This happened in the sense that what God said was meant to be future, so that it was not those who were descended from Abraham according to the flesh who would be called his seed, but those who accepted the faith by which Isaac was born and which was reproduced in the time of Christ. It was no longer restricted to one nation but made universal, so that what Abraham believed about Isaac, Christians would believe about God and Christ, for the Son of God was born in order to restore salvation to the human race.

What Paul wants us to understand is that not all the children of Abraham are worthy for that reason alone, but only those who are children of the promise, that is, whom God foreknew would receive his promise, whether they are Jews or Gentiles. For these are the ones who deserve to be called Israelites, that is to say, those who have seen God and believe. Indeed, they are all children of Abraham through Isaac, because all the offspring of the Jewish race came from Abraham through Isaac. But as I said, these are the true children of Abraham, because they follow the promise which was made in Isaac.

Because of this, the other children are not really Abraham's. Abraham believed and received Isaac on account of his faith, because he believed in God. By this the mystery of the future faith was indicated, that they would be brothers of Isaac who had the same faith by which Isaac was born, because Isaac was born as a type of the Savior by the promise. Thus whoever believes that Christ Jesus was promised to Abraham is a child of Abraham and a brother of Isaac. Abraham was told that all the nations would be blessed in his offspring. This did not happen in Isaac, but in him who was promised to Abraham in Isaac, that is, Christ, in whom all the nations are blessed when they

---

[1]Phil 2:10. [2]Rev 19:10. [3]Rom 14:18. [4]Gen 21:12.

believe. Therefore the other Jews are children of the flesh, because they are deprived of the promise and cannot claim Abraham's merit, since they do not follow the faith by which Abraham is counted worthy.

⁸This means that it is not the children of the flesh who are the children of God, but the children of the promise are reckoned as descendants.

It is clear that the children of God cannot be called children of the flesh, for they are born by the lust of the flesh, whereas the children of God are born spiritually by faith, according to what was promised to Abraham, that those who believed would be regarded as his children.

⁹For this is what the promise said, "About this time I will return and Sarah shall have a son."[1]

This prefigures Christ, because Christ was promised to Abraham as a future son, in whom the word of the promise would be fulfilled, that all the nations of the earth would be blessed in him. For when the promise was made to Abraham and he heard that *in your seed shall all the nations be blessed,*[2] Christ was also promised to him in the descent of Isaac, in whom we see this promise fulfilled.

¹⁰And not only so, but also when Rebecca had conceived children by one man, our forefather Isaac,

Paul says that Sarah was not the only one to give birth in a typological manner. Rebecca, the wife of Isaac, did the same, though in a different way. Isaac was born as a type of the Savior, but Jacob and Esau were born as types of two peoples, believers and unbelievers, who come from the same source but are nevertheless very different. Each of these individuals stands for a whole nation, because believers and unbelievers are both united in a single people. One person represents the entire race, not because he is their physical ancestor but because he shares their relationship to God. There are children of Esau who are children of Jacob, and vice versa. It is not because Jacob is praised that all those descended from him are worthy to be called his children. Nor is it because Esau was rejected that all those descended from him are condemned, for we see that Jacob the deceiver had unbelieving children, and Esau had children who were faithful and dear to God. There is no doubt that there are many unbelieving children of Jacob, for all the Jews, whether they are believers or unbelievers, have their origin in him. And that there are good and faithful children of Esau is proved by the example of Job, who was a descendent of Esau, five generations away from Abraham, and therefore Esau's grandson.[3]

¹¹though they were not yet born and had done nothing either good or bad, in order that God's purpose of election might continue, not because of works but because of his call, ¹²she was told, "The elder will serve the younger."[4] ¹³As it is written, "Jacob I loved, but Esau I hated."[5]

Paul proclaims God's foreknowledge by citing these events, because nothing can happen in the future other than what God already knows. Therefore, knowing what each of them would become, God said: *The younger will be worthy and the elder unworthy.* His foreknowledge chose the one and rejected the other. And in the one whom God chose, his purpose remained, because nothing other than what God knew and purposed in him, to make him worthy of salvation, could happen. Likewise the purpose of God remained in the one whom he rejected. However, although God knew

---

[1]Gen 18:10. [2]Gen 22:18. [3]There is no indication of this in the Bible itself. [4]Gen 25:23. [5]Mal 1:2-3.

what would happen, he is not a respecter of persons, and condemns nobody before he sins, nor does he reward anyone until he conquers.

These things are said of the Jews, who defend their privilege of being the children of Abraham. The apostle consoles himself, for he had said that he was constantly grief-stricken in his heart because of the unbelief of those who possessed the adoption of children and the constitution of the law, and from whom Christ the Savior had come, just as he himself had said: *Salvation is of the Jews.*[1] However, on reading the law, he discovered that not all who are called children of Abraham deserve to be so called, as I have already pointed out.

Therefore Paul restricts his grief to the fact that he discovered that it was long ago predicted that not all would believe, and he only grieves for them because they refused to believe out of jealousy. They had had the opportunity, however, as Paul demonstrates. At the same time, there was no point in grieving over those who were not predestined to eternal life, for God's foreknowledge had long ago decreed that they would not be saved. Who would cry over someone who is long dead? When the Gentiles appeared and accepted the salvation which the Jews had lost, Paul's grief was stirred, but this was mainly because they were the cause of their own damnation.

God knew those who would turn out to be people of ill will, and he did not number them among the good, although the Savior said to the seventy-two disciples whom he chose as a second class, and who later abandoned him: *Your names are written in heaven.*[2] This was for the sake of justice, since it is just that each person should receive his reward. Because they were good they were chosen for this service and so their names were written in heaven for the sake of justice, as I have said,

but according to foreknowledge they were among the number of the wicked. For God judges according to his justice, not according to his foreknowledge. Thus he said to Moses: *If someone sins against me, I shall delete him from my book.*[3] The person who sins is deleted according to the justice of the Judge, but according to his foreknowledge his name was never in the Book of Life. The apostle John described these people as follows: *They went out from us but they were never of us, for if they had been of us they would have remained with us.*[4] There is no respect of persons in God's foreknowledge. For God's foreknowledge is that by which it is defined what the future will of each person will be, in which he will remain, by which he will either be condemned or rewarded. Some of those who will remain among the good were once evil, and some of those who will remain among the evil were once good.

The problem is solved, because God is no respecter of persons. Even Saul and Judas Iscariot had been good at one time. Scripture says of Saul: *He was a good man and there was none better in Israel.*[5] And of Judas Iscariot the apostle Peter says: *he was numbered among us and allotted a share in this ministry of performing signs and wonders.*[6] How could someone who was not good have a share in the Savior's ministry? In the plan of God it was decided that he would be considered worthy for the time for which he was chosen, like the seventy-two I mentioned above. But after confessing his crime he was moved with remorse and committed suicide. [It is not to be wondered at that these men were considered good, because all nature is good and no substance is evil, but rather transgression, which arises from the will. It is the will which is betrayed by error.][7]

---

[1]Jn 4:22. [2]Lk 10:20. [3]Ex 32:33. [4]1 Jn 2:19. [5]1 Sam 9:2. [6]Acts 1:17. [7]An alternative version of this sentence reads, "It is not possible for the good in anyone to be totally wiped out, for nature itself cannot be changed but only the will, yet even then not in everything, because there remains in human nature something which continues to bear witness to the Creator."

¹⁴*What shall we say then? Is there injustice on God's part? By no means!*

Is God not unjust because he loves the one and hates the other? Not at all—he is perfectly just. He knows what he is doing and his judgment cannot be taken back. This is what it says in the prophet Malachi: *Jacob have I loved but Esau have I hated.*[1] He says this about judgment, but earlier he speaks about foreknowledge, when he says: *The elder shall serve the younger.*[2] In the same way he condemned Pharaoh from foreknowledge, knowing that he would not reform, and chose the apostle Paul when he was still persecuting the church, knowing that he would turn out to be good later on. Therefore God anticipated Paul before time, because he was needed, and condemned Pharaoh in advance of the judgment, so that people would believe that it was coming.

¹⁵*For he says to Moses, "I will have mercy on whom I have mercy, and I will have compassion on whom I have compassion."*[3]

That is: *I will have mercy,* he says, *on the one whom I know in advance that I will show mercy to, because I know that he will be converted and remain with me. And I will show compassion to the person whom I know will come back to me, having put his heart right after his error.* In other words, God will give to the one who is meant to be given to and not give to the one who is not meant to be given to, so that he will call whomever he knows will obey, and he will not call whomever he knows will not obey. For to call someone is to compel him to accept the faith.

¹⁶*So it depends not upon man's will or exertion, but upon God's mercy.*

Rightly so, because it is not the will of the one who asks but the decision of the one who gives what there is to be given. What is asked for must be weighed by the judgment of the giver, who judges justly. When Saul asked forgiveness for his sin he did not receive it, but when David confessed his sin, he did receive it.[4] However, it cannot be said on this basis that God judged unjustly by granting forgiveness to the one and withholding it from the other. This is because the one who looks on the heart knows in what spirit the penitent is making his request, and whether it deserves to be heard. And although it is dangerous to try to figure out God's judgment, yet for the sake of unbelievers, who reap the reward of their own minds, let us examine the matter in deeds rather than in words, so that they will not think that the judgment of God is unjust and say: *He calls one and ignores the other,*[5] and decide on that basis that those who are to be condemned are not guilty. When we look at actual cases, nobody will dare to question this or offer any sort of excuse.

David and Saul were two different people. Look at their stories and ask yourself what happened to them after God's judgment. Did Saul do what was right after he was refused mercy? Did he prove that God's judgment was unjust? Did David, after receiving mercy, turn his back on God? Or did he remain in him from whom he received mercy? Each of them had to take on the burden of ruling the kingdom before the answers to these questions could be known.

How great was David's burden, when even his son wanted to take the kingdom from him! In those dire straits, David wept and journeyed barefoot. The king and chief of God's people fled in great humiliation, to the point where he did not even answer the servant who was cursing him, so that by his suffering he could make God, by whom he believed the kingdom was preserved for him, look favorably

---

[1]Mal 1:2-3. [2]Gen 25:23. [3]Ex 33:19. [4]1 Sam 15:24-31. [5]Lk 17:34.

on him. Saul on the other hand was never in such dire straits, because a civil war is worse than a foreign one, and on top of that Saul was furious because on two occasions when he was upset he was not heard. But rather than keep on praying and thereby gain merit for himself which would have made him worthy, he grew impatient and angry at God's judgment, and turned for help to idols which he had previously condemned as being worthless. See then how it is clear that the judgment of God's foreknowledge is just, even to those who do not want to accept it.

[17]For the scripture says to Pharaoh, "I have raised you up for the very purpose of showing my power in you, so that my name may be proclaimed in all the earth."[1]

Paul says this because this Pharaoh (this was a royal title among the Egyptians and not a personal name, just as the rulers of Rome are called Caesars) was guilty of a great many crimes and unfit to live. He would never repent or in any way earn the right to live with God. But if anyone thinks that God made a mistake, or that he was unable to take revenge on Pharaoh, let him listen to what God says. He had raised Pharaoh up so that in him the other nations would learn that there is no God other than the one who was the God of the Jews and became the God of the Christians, although they were also Christians back then, just as we are now Jews because of Judah, from whom came Christ according to the flesh. The ancient Jews were Christians because they hoped for the coming of Christ, their future redeemer.

Rahab the harlot told the Jewish scouts sent by Joshua, who had previously been called Hoshea: *The wonders and plagues which were done by your God in Egypt have been heard of here, and people are terrified; they are afraid of*

your face.[2] Pharaoh was used by God in order that many signs and plagues might be revealed through him. Even though he was really dead, he appeared to be alive for a short while, so that all those who were without God might be frightened by the punishment and the torments which they saw being inflicted on him and confess the one true God, by whom this revenge was being wreaked. In the same way, the ancient physicians used to open up the bodies of people who deserved to die while they were still alive in order to find out what the causes of their disease might be and thus by punishing the dying bring saving health to the living.

[18]So then he has mercy upon whomever he wills, and he hardens the heart of whomever he wills.

Here Paul assumes the role of an objector who thinks that God is gracious to somebody without regard for justice, so that faced with two people who are identical, he accepts one and rejects the other. This is what actually happens. He compels one to believe and hardens the other so that he will not believe. God answers the objector on the basis of his authority, but justice is maintained on the basis of the foreknowledge that I mentioned above.

[19]You will say to me then, "Why does he still find fault? For who can resist his will?"

Paul teaches us first that nobody can resist God's will, because he is more powerful than anyone else. Next he teaches us that God is the Father of all, and therefore does not want anyone to suffer evil. What God has made, he wants to remain unharmed. It does not follow that he is unjust, when his benevolence appears to be such that not only does he make

---

[1]Ex 9:16. [2]Cf. Josh 2:9.

things out of nothing but also adorns them with life itself and glory, so that his work may reflect something of his majesty. Therefore it must not be doubted that someone who is so thoughtful and good is also just.

²⁰*But who are you, a man, to answer back to God? Will what is molded say to its molder, "Why have you made me thus?"*[1]

It is a great indignity and presumption for a man to answer back to God—the unjust to the Just, the evil to the Good, the imperfect to the Perfect, the weak to the Strong, the corruptible to the Incorrupt, the mortal to the Immortal, the servant to the Lord, the creature to the Creator! Paul takes over the quotation from the prophet Isaiah and makes it his own. He uses it to show that a work cannot complain about its author, because it is in the power of the author, who wanted to make such a creature.

²¹*Has the potter no right over the clay, to make out of the same lump one vessel for beauty and another for menial use?*

It is clear that some vases are made for beauty, because they are required for decorative uses, while others are made for menial tasks in the kitchen. The substance of the clay is the same, but the will of the potter is different. Likewise God made us all of the same substance and we all became sinners, but he had mercy on one and rejected another, not without justice. The potter has only a will, but God has a will and justice to go with it. For he knows who ought to be shown mercy, as I have already said.

²²*What if God, desiring to show his wrath and to make known his power, has endured with much patience the vessels of wrath made for destruction,*

This means that unbelievers are made ready for punishment by the will and long-suffering of God, which is his patience. For although he has waited a long time for them, they have not repented. He waited a long time so that they should be without excuse, for God knew all along that they would not believe.

²³*in order to make known the riches of his glory for the vessels of mercy, which he has prepared beforehand for glory,*

It is God's patience and long-suffering that, just as he prepares the wicked for destruction, so also he prepares the good for their reward. For the good are those who have the hope of faith. God preserves everyone, knowing what the destiny of each will be. Therefore it is a sign of his patience that those who have been rescued from evil or who persevere in good works, he prepares for glory. The riches of glory are a many-sided dignity which is prepared for believers. But those who start out good and turn bad, or who persist in their evil ways, he prepares for burial.

This is what it means for God to manifest his power in much patience, for just as people think he will not take revenge because he has kept quiet about it for so long, when he starts to do so his power will appear. Although he can take revenge in an instant, he prolongs the process so that none of those who are damned can claim that he is deceitful. To *prepare* here means to let each one know what he will be in the future.

²⁴*even us whom he has called, not from the Jews only but also from the Gentiles?*

God has called those whom he has prepared for glory, whom he knew would persevere in faith, whether they are near at hand or far away.

---

[1]Is 45:9.

²⁵*As indeed he says in Hosea,*
  "Those who were not my people
  I will call 'my people,'
  and her who was not beloved
  *I will call 'my beloved.'"*¹

It is clear that this was said about the Gentiles, who once were not God's people, but afterward, to the chagrin of the Jews, received mercy and are called God's people. Once they were not loved, but when the Jews fell away they were adopted as children and are now loved, so that where once they were not called God's people, now they are called children of the living God.

²⁶*"And in the very place where it was said to*
  them, 'You are not my people,'
  they will be called 'sons of the living
  *God.'"*²

At one time nobody was called a child of God except in Judea, that is, in Jerusalem, where God's house was, as it says in Psalm 75: *In Judah is God known.*³ Later on, he says in Zechariah: *I will put Jerusalem in all the peoples,*⁴ in other words, wherever the children of God will be in the future, and the house of God, which is the church, will be in all places. Thus the Lord says to the Jews: *Therefore the kingdom of God will be taken away from you and given to a nation producing the fruits of it.*⁵

²⁷*And Isaiah cries out concerning Israel:*
"Though the number of the sons of Israel be as
the sand of the sea, only a remnant of them will
*be saved;"*⁶

Paul says this because Isaiah was crying out for those who believe in Christ. It is these who are the true Israel, as the Lord said to Nathanael: *Behold a true Israelite in whom there*

*is no guile.*⁷ Most of the Jews have gone away from the merit and promise of their ancestors, because they have not accepted it. These have remained, because by believing they have kept faith in the promise made to their fathers. The others have gone away from the law because they have not believed in him whom the law promised would alone be sufficient for salvation. So they became apostate, because by not accepting Christ, they became lawbreakers. Therefore of that great number, only those whom God foreknew would believe have been saved.

²⁸*"for the Lord will execute his sentence upon*
the earth with rigor and dispatch."

The Lord promises that those whom he calls the remnant will be saved by the just execution of the sentence on the earth (for it is right that the creation should receive salvation only in the name of its Lord and Creator), that is, by faith, because now that new moons, the sabbath, circumcision, the food laws and animal sacrifices have all been abolished, it is faith alone which is given for salvation. What is executed by the law and what by faith is contained in the law itself, as the Savior said: *Moses wrote about me.*⁸ Therefore when the law is executed, a remnant will be saved, but the rest cannot be, because they have rejected the conditions by which God decreed that the human race would be saved.

²⁹*And as Isaiah predicted,*
  "If the Lord of hosts had not left us
    children,
  we would have fared like Sodom and been
    *made like Gomorrah."*⁹

This seed, which alone remains and is reserved for the conversion of the human race is Christ

---

¹Hos 2:23. ²Hos 1:10. ³Ps 76:1 in English versions. ⁴A misreading of Zech 12:2. ⁵Mt 21:43. ⁶Is 10:22-23. ⁷Jn 1:47. ⁸Jn 5:46. ⁹Is 1:9.

and his teaching, as he himself said: *The seed is the Word of God.*[1] Therefore what was long ago promised to us who have been delivered from the burden of the law remains for our redemption, so that by receiving the forgiveness of sins we might not be punished by the law and perish as Sodom did.

Paul says that the Savior was left to us for the promotion of life, which the law could not provide. God decreed from the beginning that he should be born, and because he would be the only man without sin, he would wipe out the sins of everyone once the enemy of the human race was defeated.

This is what the Revelation of John says: *No one in heaven or on earth or under the earth was found who could open the book and its seals,*[2] except the Savior who overcame death. This is the seed which God promised long ago and kept in reserve so that it might bear fruit when the sins of all the Jews as well as all the Gentiles had reached their full number. His fruit is the forgiveness of sins. If Christ had not been kept in reserve—this is why he is called the seed, because it was through him that the human race was restored—Abraham's offspring would have perished because they were riddled with sin, and the law could do nothing to help them. Therefore Paul teaches that Christ came afterward and brought the assurance of life.

[30] What shall we say, then? That Gentiles who did not pursue righteousness have attained it, that is, righteousness through faith;

Since there is righteousness in the law, which is believed by the world and which forbids sinning, Paul is not saying here that the Gentiles do not understand this righteousness, which is known from mother nature, but that righteousness which is by faith in Christ. As far as God is concerned, that is the true and lasting righteousness, if it is acknowledged. For what is more righteous that to know God the Father, from whom all things come, and Christ his Son, through whom all things come? The first part of righteousness is to acknowledge the Creator, and the next part is to keep what he commands. Therefore the Gentiles, who in the past did not pursue righteousness, that is to say, the law which bears witness to the Creator, at the coming of Christ found a righteousness greater than that of the scribes and Pharisees. So those who never followed the lesser righteousness afterward discovered one which was greater, whereas the Jews, who were born under the law and who ought to have benefited more, fell away instead.

[31] but that Israel who pursued the righteousness which is based on law did not succeed in fulfilling that law.

Faith is the fulfilling of the law. It is because the Gentiles have faith that they appear to fulfill the whole law. But since the Jews, out of envy, did not believe in the Savior, claiming instead the righteousness which is commanded in the law, in other words, the sabbath, circumcision et cetera. they never arrived at the law. In other words, they did not fulfill the law, and those who do not fulfill the law are guilty of it. The person who fulfills the law is the one who comes from the law of Moses to the faith of Christ.

[32] Why? Because they did not pursue it through faith, but as if it were based on works. They have stumbled over the stumbling stone,

The Jews rejected faith, which as I have said, is the fulfillment of the law, and instead claimed that they were justified by works, that is, by the sabbath, the new moons, circumcision and so on. They forgot that Scripture says that *the just shall live by faith.*[3] By the righteousness of the law is meant, therefore, that which by the

---

[1] Lk 8:11. [2] Rev 5:3. [3] Hab 2:4.

just judgment of God was given to the Jews because of the hardness of their hearts. So if someone stepped on a dead weasel or touched dead animals, or if a mouse ran into a pot, he would be declared unclean. Because of this, people took great care to make sure that they did nothing which might make them unclean. If the weasel's blood were in the house, the stain would not be treated lightly.

They also had to abstain from richer foods. Both the sabbath and circumcision had their own righteousness for a time, because they were given as types [of what was to come]. The Lord demonstrated this, among other things, in the words of the prophet Ezekiel, when he said: *Moreover I gave them statutes that were not good,*[1] because they were irreverent and ungodly.

But at the coming of Christ, who would give the gift of salvation, God reveals the future through the prophet Jeremiah, saying: *I will give them a new covenant, not like the covenant which I gave to their fathers.*[2] He calls this covenant the law which, as I mentioned above, they did not inherit.

When Jewish believers wanted to impose this burden of observances on Gentiles who had believed, the apostle Peter said: *Why are you putting a yoke on the neck of our brothers, which neither our fathers nor we were able to bear?*[3] For since the coming of Christ, the indulgence promised in the law has been given as the prophet Isaiah said: *There will come from Zion one who will take away and remove ungodliness from Jacob. And this will be a covenant with them from me, when I take away their sins.*[4] This is the new covenant promised by God in Christ.

[33]*as it is written,*

> "*Behold, I am laying in Zion a stone that*
> *will make men stumble,*
> *a rock that will make them fall;*

and he who believes in him will not be put to shame."[5]

This quotation is from Isaiah. There are many passages of Scripture where Christ is portrayed as a rock or a stone. The prophet Daniel calls him a stone which detached itself without hands from the mountain, hitting and threatening all the kingdoms and filling the whole earth.[6] This clearly refers to Christ. And in the law, the rock from which the waters flowed is called Christ: *They drank from the spiritual rock which followed them, This rock was Christ,*[7] says Paul. And the apostle Peter says to the Jews: *This is the stone which the builders rejected.*[8] The stone of stumbling placed in Zion is Christ, Zion being generally regarded as Jerusalem or the temple. When nonbelievers looked on his body, they were offended. They were scandalized by his body and said: *Are not his mother and his brothers among us? How can he say then, that he came down from heaven?*[9]

The Jews did not want to compare Christ's words with his deeds, lest perhaps they might recognize that it was not absurd for him to say that he had come down from heaven, as if the body were operating on its own and God were not concealed in it, revealing himself by his works in the body. This was the rock of offense as far as the Jews were concerned. The rock was undoubtedly the human flesh of the Savior. It detached itself without hands, because it was made of a virgin by the Holy Spirit, without the participation of a male.

Romans 10

[1]*Brethren, my heart's desire and prayer to God for them is that they may be saved.* [2]*I bear them witness that they have a zeal for God, but it is not enlightened.*

Since Paul wants to liberate the Jews from the

---

[1]Ezek 20:25. [2]Jer 31:31-32. [3]Acts 15:10. [4]Is 59:20; 27:9. [5]Is 28:16. [6]Dan 2:34-35. [7]Cf. 1 Cor 10:4. [8]Acts 4:11. [9]Jn 6:42.

law, which is a veil over their faces, but does not want to appear to desire this out of any hatred for Judaism, he shows his love for them and says many good things about the law. But he teaches that the time for obeying the law has come to an end, and by doing this bears witness that he is concerned for them, if only they will listen to him and not assume that he is their enemy, seeing that he bears witness to them of nobility and ancestral tradition.

³For, being ignorant of the righteousness that comes from God, and seeking to establish their own, they did not submit to God's righteousness.

Paul says that the Jews did not believe in Christ because they were ignorant. They wanted to show their zeal for God, but not knowing his will or plan, they acted against him even though they claimed to be defending him. Paul says of them that it was not out of malice or envy but out of ignorance that they did not accept Christ. The apostle Peter says to them: *I know, brothers, that you did this evil in ignorance, as did your rulers.*[1] Not realizing that this was the Christ whom God had promised, they said they were waiting for someone else, preferring the righteousness which they had from the law over him who is the righteousness of God in faith. He is righteousness, because in him God fulfilled what he had promised.

⁴For Christ is the end of the law, that every one who has faith may be justified.

Paul says that this is because whoever believes in Christ has the perfection of the law. Nobody was justified by the law because nobody fulfilled it, apart from the man who hoped in the promised Christ. Therefore faith was given, which believes in the perfection of the law, so that everything else can be left aside

and faith can stand in for the whole of the law.

⁵Moses writes that the man who practices the righteousness which is based on the law shall live by it.

Paul says this because the righteousness of the law of Moses did not make people guilty as long as they kept it, that is to say, they lived by keeping the law, because they were debtors. This is what it says in Numbers and in Leviticus.

⁶But the righteousness based on faith says, Do not say in your heart, "Who will ascend into heaven?" (that is, to bring Christ down) ⁷or "Who will descend into the abyss?" (that is, to bring Christ up from the dead).[2]

The quotation is from Deuteronomy, and is interpreted here with reference to Christ. The last phrase is the apostle's own addition. He says that someone who does not doubt about the hope of God which is in Christ has the righteousness of faith. (The question marks here are not due to unbelief on the speaker's part.) Christ therefore suffered so that once hell was looted and death defeated, he might rise again with the souls he had rescued and ascend into heaven. Everyone who languished in hell and who hoped for salvation through him was delivered from it on seeing the Savior. The apostle Peter testified to this when he said: *He was also preached to the dead.*[3] So whoever does not doubt these things in his heart is justified by faith, whereas justification by the law comes through fear. A man fears the law when he sees its punishment inflicted on sinners. Thus the righteousness of the law is not great, nor does it earn merit with God, but only for the present age. Faith, however, though it is foolishness to unbelievers, has its reward with God and hopes for what it cannot see.

---

[1]Acts 3:17. [2]Deut 30:12-13. [3]1 Pet 4:6.

---

[8]*But what does it say? The word is near you, on your lips and in your heart (that is, the word of faith which we preach);*[1]

This is said in Deuteronomy in order to show that belief [in Christ] is not all that foreign to our mind or to our nature. Even though we cannot see him with our eyes, what we believe is not out of harmony with the nature of our minds and our way of speaking. There are seeds, as it were, planted in our nature which, if they are tended by hearing and the will, will bear the fruit of witness to the Creator. Paul says that he does not preach any work of the law, but only the faith which is to be given in the cause of Christ.

[9]*because, if you confess with your lips that Jesus is Lord and believe in your heart that God raised him from the dead, you will be saved.* [10]*For man believes with his heart and so is justified, and he confesses with his lips and so is saved.*

What Paul spoke about above he now makes clear, that the rule of faith is to believe that Jesus is Lord and not to be ashamed to confess that God raised him from the dead and has taken him up to heaven with his body, whence he will come to be incarnate. The person who believes this will not incur the judgment of the Gospel, which says: *Many, even of the authorities, believed in him but for fear of the Jews they did not confess it openly, for they preferred the glory of men to the glory of God.*[2]

[11]*The scripture says, "No one who believes in him will be put to shame."*[3]

On the day of judgment, when everything will be examined and all false opinions and teachings will be overthrown, then those who believe in Christ will rejoice, seeing it revealed to all that what they believed is true, and what was thought to be foolish was wise. For they will look at others and see that they alone are glorified and wise, when they had been considered contemptible and crazy. This will be the real test, when rewards and condemnation are decreed.

[12]*For there is no distinction between Jew and Greek; the same Lord is Lord of all and bestows his riches upon all who call upon him.*

Paul says that in general everyone is lumped together because of unbelief or else exalted together because of their belief, because apart from Christ there is no salvation in God's presence, only punishment or death. For neither the privileges of their ancestors nor the law can do the Jews any good if they do not accept the merit and promise made to them. Neither do the Gentiles have anything to boast about in the flesh if they do not believe in Christ.

It is clear that this applies to everyone, whether Jews or Greeks, because nobody can live with God if he does not call upon the name of Christ. He is the Lord of all, an opinion shared by the apostle Peter, who said: *He is Lord of all.*[4] However, he is generous only to those who call upon him, because they are the ones who will receive a reward. He is not generous to the ungodly, because they do not share in his goodness, nor will they receive anything since they have not believed in him who will give it. Yet Paul did not say that God is generous to those who believe in him, but to those who call upon him. Once a mind has put its faith in him, it will not cease to implore him, because it has been taught by the Lord to pray without ceasing. In the Gospel of Luke, for example, it says that we must always pray because of our enemy, who is subtle and cunning.[5] However, forgiveness of sins is given only to those who believe. It follows therefore

---

[1]Deut 30:14. [2]Jn 12:42-43. [3]Is 28:16. [4]Acts 10:36. [5]Lk 18:1.

that someone who has been consecrated by prayer will be set free from evil and be able to receive what God has promised to those who are watchful with all their heart.

¹³For, "every one who calls upon the name of the Lord will be saved."[1]

God himself, when he was seen by Moses, said to him: *My name is the Lord.*[2] This is the Son of God, who is said to be both an angel and God, so that he might not be confused with the One from whom all things come but might be acknowledged as the One through whom all things come and to whom all things belong. He is called God, because the Father and the Son are one, and he is also called an angel, because he was sent by the Father to announce the promised salvation. He says that he was sent so that people would not mistake him for the Father, but recognize that he was begotten from him. Therefore, *everyone who calls upon the name of the Lord will be saved.* Moses said the same thing: *Whoever does not listen to that prophet will be destroyed from among the people.*[3] If he is the Lord of all, then he is called on by his servants, and because this is the case, Paul adds what follows.

¹⁴But how are men to call upon him in whom they have not believed? And how are they to believe in him of whom they have never heard? And how are they to hear without a preacher?

Of course the Jews themselves do not believe in Christ, whom Paul called the Lord. As I said above, you have to believe first if you are going to have the faith to ask for anything. It is obvious that Christ cannot be believed in if he is not obeyed. It is likewise clear that whoever rejects a preacher does not accept the one who sent him either.

¹⁵And how can men preach unless they are sent? As it is written, "How beautiful are the feet of those who preach good news!"[4]

There is no question about this, because nobody can be a true apostle unless he is sent by Christ, nor will he be able to preach without a mandate to do so, for his testimony will not reflect these signs of power.

Paul quotes the prophet Nahum.[5] By talking about feet, he means the coming of the apostles who went around the world preaching the coming of the kingdom of God. For their appearance enlightened mankind by showing them the way toward peace with God, which John the Baptist had come to prepare. This is the peace to which those who believe in Christ are hastening. Then the holy Simeon, seeing the discord in the world, rejoiced at the coming of the Savior, saying: *Lord, now let your servant depart in peace,*[6] because the kingdom of God is peace, and all discord is taken away when everyone bows the knee to the one God. Finally, the Jerusalem which is above means the city of peace, which is our mother.[7]

¹⁶But they have not all heeded the gospel; for Isaiah says, "Lord, who has believed what he has heard from us?"[8]

It is true that even though the world is enlightened by the splendor of the Lord's teaching, there are still those who reject it and who call the light darkness. The understanding of their minds is so clouded by their error that they cannot receive the splendor of the true light. The Gospel accuses them when it says: *The light shines in the darkness, and the darkness has not comprehended it.*[9]

Isaiah says: *Lord, who has believed our report?*[10] This means: *Who believes what we have heard from you and talk about?* With this

---

[1]Joel 2:32. [2]Ex 6:3. [3]Deut 18:19. [4]Is 52:7; Nahum 1:15. [5]Nahum 1:15; cf. also Is 52:7. [6]Lk 2:29. [7]Gal 4:26. [8]Is 53:1. [9]Jn 1:5. [10]Is 53:1.

quote from the prophets, Paul supported [his statement that] the Jews are opponents of gospel truth—for the law rebukes the Jews— and what was true in ancient times still holds good today. Paul is here referring to the [large] number who do not accept the faith.

[17]*So faith comes from what is heard, and what is heard comes by the preaching of Christ.*

It is obvious that unless something is said, it can neither be heard nor believed.

[18]*But I ask, have they not heard? Indeed they have; for*
"Their voice has gone out to all the earth, and their words to the ends of the world."[1]

This means that they heard but did not want to believe. For there are some who, in spite of the fact that they hear, do not believe. They hear but do not understand, because their heart is blinded by wickedness. Paul testifies that up to his time the Jews had heard the preaching of God, to the point where the entire world was full of the divine message, because even if the body was not present, its sound and reputation were everywhere, just as the report of the wonders done in Egypt had reached all nations, as Rahab the harlot testified.[2] If the sound of the gospel has gone out to the entire world, it is not possible that the Jews have not heard it, and so none of them can be pardoned from the sin of his unbelief.

[19]*Again I ask, did Israel not understand?*
First Moses says,
"I will make you jealous of those who are not a nation;
with a foolish nation I will make you angry."[3]

Paul means here that of course Israel knew. In

order not to appear to be complaining about every single Israelite when quoting the foregoing examples in order to denounce the people of Israel for their unbelief, Paul does not deny that Israel knew, nor that it received what was promised to it in the law, but he meant that Israel of the spirit, which is greater than the Israel of the flesh and which God had foreknown would believe. They all heard, but they did not all believe, which explains why Moses said what he did.

The words are those of someone who is angry because the Jews are still unbelievers, and Moses assigns one origin and cause to all their troubles. Although he attacks his contemporaries, he is really more interested in future generations, to whom this is particularly relevant. For there is one condemnation common to all of them if they remain in their unbelief. Their jealousy arose from their envy at seeing a people which earlier had been without God and barbarous claim the Jewish God as their own and receive the promise which had originally been made to the Jews. Because of the jealousy which they suffered on their account, the Jews were bloated with anger and so paid the price of their wickedness and unbelief. Nothing destroys a man so much as jealousy, which is why God made it the avenger of unbelief, because that is a great sin. Those who are given over to anger are always tortured when they hear that the law and the prophets belong to us who believe in Christ.

[20]*Then Isaiah is so bold as to say,*
"I have been found by those who did not seek me;
I have shown myself to those who did not ask for me."[4]

Having made use of the words of Moses to talk about the rejection of the Jews, Paul here added the testimony of the prophet Isaiah in

---

[1]Ps 19:4. [2]Cf. Josh 2:9-10. [3]Deut 32:21. [4]Is 65:1.

order to make it even clearer that after expelling the Jews, God proclaimed his grace to the Gentiles, to the shame and destruction of the Jews. (Isaiah here is speaking in the person of Christ.)

21But of Israel he says, "All day long I have held out my hands to a disobedient and contrary people."[1]

Here *Israel* refers to the Israel of the flesh, those who are children of Abraham, but not according to faith. For the true Israel is spiritual, and sees God by believing in him. *All day long* means *always*, because they are always being reproved. This is because those who are not going to believe feel rebuked, because they know that they are the cause of their own damnation. This passage may also refer to the Savior, who held out his hands on the cross to plead forgiveness for those who were killing him. That event also proclaims the criminal behavior of the Jews. Earlier on, Isaiah had dared to say that those who had once been enemies of God would become his friends, and that those who were called Israelites would be rejected as enemies because of their disobedience.

Romans 11

1I ask, then, has God rejected his people? By no means! I myself am an Israelite, a descendant of Abraham, a member of the tribe of Benjamin.

Paul has already shown that the people of Israel did not believe, but in order that it should not be thought that he has said that Jews were all unbelievers, he points out that God has not rejected the inheritance which he promised to the descendants of Abraham. He would not have promised them a kingdom if he knew that

none of them would believe, since according to the law, the "inheritance of the Lord" means the children of Abraham, but only those who believe. By using himself as an example, Paul shows that the part of Israel which God foreknew would be saved had already been saved, and that the part which had been consigned to perdition because of its constant unbelief might yet be saved.

2God has not rejected his people whom he foreknew. Do you not know what the scripture says of Elijah, how he pleads with God against Israel?

This is what the Savior says: *Father, I have kept those whom you gave to me, and none of them is lost but the son of perdition.*[2]

3"Lord, they have killed thy prophets, they have demolished thy altars, and I alone am left, and they seek my life."[3] *4But what is God's reply to him? "I have kept for myself seven thousand men who have not bowed the knee to Baal."*[4]

This is clear. Paul shows that it was not only Elijah who remained devoted to God, and did not worship idols, but that there were many who remained faithful to him, just as there were not a few Jews who believed in Christ. History bears this out, because there were many who hid in caves on account of Ahab, the king of Israel, and his wife Jezebel, who listened to the false prophets and persecuted the prophets of God, forcing the people to worship idols.

5So too at the present time there is a remnant, chosen by grace.

Even though many have fallen away, those whom God foreknew have remained in the

---

[1] Is 65:2. [2] Jn 17:12. [3] 1 Kings 19:10. [4] 1 Kings 19:18.

promise of the law. Those who have accepted Christ as he was promised in the law have remained in the law, but those who rejected Christ have fallen away from it.

⁶But if it is by grace, it is no longer on the basis of works; otherwise grace would no longer be grace.

It is clear that because grace is the gift of God, it is not a reward due for works, but granted freely because of the free mercy which intervenes. It is true that if it is a reward it is not grace, but because it is not a reward, it is undoubtedly grace, since to grant pardon to sinners is nothing other than grace, granted to those who are not asking for it but offered so that they may believe. Grace has two aspects to it. It is a characteristic of God, who abounds in mercy, and it seeks out those whom he cures free of charge.

⁷What then? Israel failed to obtain what it sought. The elect obtained it, but the rest were hardened,

These are the carnal Israelites, who thought they were justified by the law and did not realize that they were justified by faith before God, because through the law they were all guilty, for: *Cursed is everyone who does not keep all the things which are written in the book of the law, to do them.*[1] Those who believed that they were justified by faith received the election, so that as justified children of God they might recall the text of Scripture which says: *The just shall live by faith,*[2] that is, not by the law.

**⁸as it is written,
"God gave them a spirit of stupor,
eyes that should not see and ears that
should not hear,
down to this very day."**[3]

**⁹And David says,
"Let their feast become a snare and
a trap,
a pitfall and a retribution for them;**[4]
**¹⁰let their eyes be darkened so that
they cannot see,
and bend their backs for ever."**

He curses the feasts of the wicked because the innocent are often deceived there. They are tricked into coming to dinner so that they may be ruined. This is how Amnon, the son of David, was deceived, and the wicked Holofernes thought he could do the same to the holy Judith during a feast. It was also at the table of the criminal Herod that wicked people clamored for the head of John the prophet.[5] The two prophets agree about this kind of people, who started off as faithless and objectionable enemies of the good, although some of them later mended their ways and reformed, albeit rather late in the day. The others who persisted in their rebellion were bent forever and did not escape the severity of their punishment. They were the ones who were blinded and unable to see the way of truth, which in their wickedness they had rejected and gone away from, so that they could no longer come to the grace of salvation.

The above-mentioned examples taken from the prophets reveal that there are two kinds of blind people. The first kind consists of those who are blinded forever, who will never be saved. These people are of such evil disposition that they openly say that they do not understand what they hear. They are the ones who said of the Savior: *What is he saying? We do not know what he is talking about. What did you hear from him? He has a demon and is insane.*[6] But others who belonged to the true Israel contradicted them and said: *These are not the words of someone who has a demon. For what demon can open the eyes of the blind?*[7]

---

[1]Deut 27:26. [2]Hab 2:4. [3]Is 29:10; Deut 29:4. [4]Ps 69:22-23. [5]2 Sam 13:27; Jdt 12:1; Mk 6:28. [6]Jn 10:20. [7]Jn 10:21.

Because they were jealous of the Savior, they did not want to understand what they were hearing, and because it seemed that he was not understood by the jurists and Pharisees, people generally thought that he was saying absurd things which were unlawful and might turn others away from the faith. For this reason they heard the Savior tell them: *You have the key of knowledge, but you will not enter in yourself, nor do you allow others to enter in.*[1] Who would not follow the counsel and advice of jurists and Pharisees, considering that they were not superficial but quite serious people who seemed to be defenders of the law? After all, they told those who were members of the true Israel: *Have any of the authorities believed in him?*[2] By these means they tried to make it appear as though those who did not believe were justified, if they could make many others join their conspiracy [against Jesus], because whatever is defended by only a few people is unlikely to prove to be true.

Thus they were blinded and prevented from seeing and being saved. They were strengthened in their resolve, by declaring false what they knew to be true, and so considered what was true to be false, as they wished.

The second type consists of those who, although they try to live according to the law, do not accept the righteousness of Christ. These people are not doing this out of the envy of an evil will, but by an erroneous imitation of the tradition of their ancestors. They are blinded for a time, for although they ought to recognize the great works of Christ which cannot be mistaken, because his outstanding power appears in his deeds, they have instead neglected to compare his preaching with the new covenant promised by the prophets, which would have led them to confess that he was the one they had promised, and are now against God and attracted to human beings. For this reason they are blinded, so that when the Gen-

tiles have all been accepted into the promise on account of their jealousy (for they envy the Gentiles), they may return to the faith of God.

11So I ask, have they stumbled so as to fall? By no means! But through their trespass salvation has come to the Gentiles, so as to make Israel jealous.

Paul says here what I have mentioned above, that these people have not fallen into unbelief in such a way as to make their ultimate conversion impossible. In other words, they are not so blinded by their dishonesty that they cannot be cured, as we read of the devil's fall, in the words of the prophet Isaiah: *How did Lucifer fall from heaven?*[3] Paul labeled his fall apostasy but says that the Jews have not offended in this way and fallen as a result, but are merely deafened for a time because of their offense.

Paul means here that salvation was given to the Gentiles because of the sin of the Jews who have rejected the gift of God. But by that very suffering they will be converted, because they are zealous for the promise made to their fathers.

12Now if their trespass means riches for the world, and if their failure means riches for the Gentiles, how much more will their full inclusion mean!

It is clear that the world will benefit if, by the trespass of the Jews, it ends up having even more good people—for the Gentiles are far more numerous than the Jews—and their decline, which is the reward of the promise, turns out to mean riches for the Gentiles because they have gained eternal life and are so much more in number! It is clear that the world will be richer in good men if those who are now blinded are also converted. A large part of the world has already been saved. The *world* here

---

[1]Lk 11:52. [2]Jn 7:48. [3]Is 14:12.

means the human race, as it is said of the Savior: *Behold, the whole world has gone after him.*[1]

[13]Now I am speaking to you Gentiles. Inasmuch then as I am an apostle to the Gentiles, I magnify my ministry [14]in order to make my fellow Jews jealous, and thus save some of them.

Paul is showing the Gentiles here how much he loves the Jews, for he magnifies his ministry, by which he is the apostle to the Gentiles, if by loving his own people he wins them to the faith as well. Indeed, he is more honored still if he wins to eternal life those to whom he has not been sent, for he who finds his lost brothers will have the greatest honor with his parents.

[15]For if their rejection means the reconciliation of the world, what will their acceptance mean but life from the dead?

Paul says this because if the Gentiles have been reconciled to God while the Jews remain unbelievers, to the benefit of the world with respect to the faith of Christ, what will it mean, and how great will the fullness of salvation be, if the Jews too are incorporated into the faith of Christ? Will it not be as if the world has been brought back to life by people who have risen from the dead? This is why Paul worked so hard for the conversion of the Jews, since the handicap of their blindness will be removed at the time when their sin is paid for, so that they may get the free exercise of their will back again.

[16]If the dough offered as first fruits is holy, so is the whole lump; and if the root is holy, so are the branches.

It is clear that they are one and the same

substance, so it is impossible for the offering to be holy and the lump unclean, given that the offering comes from the lump. Thus Paul shows that those whose ancestors believed cannot be regarded as unworthy to receive the faith, for if some of the Jews have believed, why can it not be said that the others may also believe? The second part of the verse merely repeats the first, giving a different example.

[17]But if some of the branches were broken off, and you, a wild olive shoot, were grafted in their place to share the richness of the olive tree,

If some Jews have not believed, then they have been cut out and the Gentiles have been grafted in faith in the hope of the promise, thus becoming a source of grief to the Jews. The Gentiles, who were from a bad root, were grafted into a good tree, which is the opposite of what happens in agriculture, where it is the good branch which is grafted onto a bad root. This is why he says that the graft has been into an olive tree, because the graft bears the fruit of the root and shares in its effects.

[18]do not boast over the branches. If you do boast, remember it is not you that support the root, but the root that supports you.

This means that we should not rejoice in the unbelief of the Jews. It displeases God if someone rejoices at the misfortune of others, as Solomon says.[2] In any case, the Jews were not rejected for the sake of the Gentiles. Rather, it was because they were rejected that they gave an opportunity for the gospel to be preached to the Gentiles. If you boast against those onto whose root you have been grafted, you insult the people which has accepted you, so that you might be converted from bad to good. You will

---

[1]Jn 12:19.　[2]Cf. Prov 24:17.

not continue like that if you destroy the thing on which you stand.

[19]*You will say, "Branches were broken off so that I might be grafted in."*

A believing Gentile says that he can rejoice that the Jews did not believe, saying that their condemnation made room for the Gentiles. But the Jews were not condemned by God in order to let the Gentiles in. They condemned themselves by rejecting God's gift, and by doing that they gave the Gentiles an opportunity to be saved. Paul wants to stop this boasting, so that we might rejoice in our salvation rather than insult the weak. For the man who [rejoices in the wrongdoings of others][1] is easily deceived.

[20]*That is true. They were broken off because of their unbelief, but you stand fast only through faith. So do not become proud, but stand in awe.*

This means that it is not because of you but because of their fault (for they do not believe) that you have been called to salvation, so as to make them jealous. You ought to thank God for his gift in Christ and not insult them, but rather pray that if their wickedness has led to your salvation, that they too might return to their roots. Then you will please God who has shown you mercy, for he called you so that by making them jealous of you he might bring them to grace as well.

Because the Jews fell away due to their unbelief, Paul says that the Gentiles stand by faith. Before, they were lying down flat because of their treachery, but now that they believe they have begun to stand up straight.

[21]*For if God did not spare the natural branches, neither will he spare you.*

This is true, because if God has blinded those who enjoyed the prerogatives of their ancestors, to whom the promise that they would be adopted as children of God had been given, because of their unbelief, what will he do to those who come with no such background and who have been honored when they had no dignity they could claim, if they should doubt or start boasting about themselves?

[22]*Note then the kindness and severity of God: severity toward those who have fallen, but God's kindness to you, provided you continue in his kindness; otherwise you too will be cut off.*

Paul testifies that God is good to the Gentiles, because although they followed idols and deserved to die, he waited for them in his patience, and even though they did not seek him, he called them and forgave their sins. But God is severe toward the Jews and has even blinded them because they rejected God's gift. Here Paul is referring to those Jews who, because of their wickedness, have been permanently blinded. For this reason he says that they have fallen, whereas the others, whom I mentioned above, have not fallen, even though they have sinned, because Paul shows that they have been blinded only for a time. But God has been severe to these, because they have become eternally blind and apostate.

[23]*And even the others, if they do not persist in their unbelief, will be grafted in, for God has the power to graft them in again.*

Paul shows that God's justice will not continue in its severity toward those whom he has blinded for a time, because he has not cut them off in such a way that he cannot graft them in again if they are converted. He said through the prophet: *Those who come back to me I shall*

---

[1]An alternative reading here is "insults a sinner."

replant,[1] so that, knowing this, Christians should not insult Jews, because they know that the mercy of God has been set aside for them, even though they have fallen away.

[24]For if you have been cut from what is by nature a wild olive tree, and grafted, contrary to nature, into a cultivated olive tree, how much more will these natural branches be grafted back into their own olive tree.

Let us agree that the olive tree represents faith, through which Abraham has been justified, whereas the wild olive refers to wickedness, because it is rustic and unfruitful by nature. So, if those who have always been enemies of God are converted to the faith of Abraham and grafted into an alien tree, how much more will the Jews be grafted back into God's promise if after a period of unbelief they should accept the faith and thus return to their ancestral nature?

[25]Lest you be wise in your own conceits, I want you to understand this mystery, brethren: a hardening has come upon part of Israel, until the full number of the Gentiles come in, [26]and so all Israel will be saved; as it is written,
"The Deliverer will come from Zion,
he will banish ungodliness from Jacob";[2]

It is clear that at the time of their blinding, a hardness was given to the Jews, so that although they are jealous for the law, they cannot see the gift which has come as promised by God, and which was preached by Christ. They were blinded by zeal, thinking that the law of works would never come to an end, which is why they were so jealous of the sabbath. Because of this offense, they were partially hardened, so that during the time of their unbelief, the Gentiles might be admitted into the faith. The Jews were hardened for a time, so that they would not see the way which leads to salvation, but when the full number of the Gentiles has been admitted, the darkness will be taken away from their eyes so that they may believe. [This will happen because their unbelief is the result of error rather than malice.][3]

Paul quotes Isaiah in order to prove that God has reserved a gift for them, in order to teach that they can be set free by the same grace by which the believing Jews have already been set free, because he is not empty, but always full of grace.

[27]"and this will be my covenant with them when I take away their sins."

The covenant will always be there, however long it takes for the Jews to believe. For this is the Lord Jesus, who has promised to come from heaven in order to set the human race free. Every day he forgives the sins of those who turn to God, nor does he condemn unbelievers straightaway, but waits for them, knowing that they may come to a knowledge of God.

[28]As regards the gospel they are enemies of God, for your sake; but as regards election they are beloved for the sake of their forefathers.

Because of their unbelief the Jews are enemies of the gospel, so that their error and sin may open the way to enter into the faith before time, as I have already said above. For at first the preaching was intended for all the Jews, and only then was it right for God's Word to be believed by the Gentiles too. But because they did not believe, the kingdom was taken away from them and given to the Gentiles.

---

[1]Jer 24:6. [2]Is 59:20-21. [3]An alternative reading says, "They will mend their ways and afterward be saved. God will give them back the free exercise of their will so that, because their unbelief did not spring from malice but from error, they may be put right and afterward be saved."

He says this so as not to insult those whose sin has been of benefit to the Gentiles, because the one who ought to be insulted is the one whose sin has stood in the way of others [coming to faith]. Their unbelief is not a matter for rejoicing but for sorrowing. If they are slow to be converted, the Gentiles ought to be glad that they have been saved by their sin, and so rejoice in the Jews' conversion. For by their fall, the Gentiles have received God's grace faster [than they would otherwise have done].

However seriously the Jews may have sinned by rejecting the gift of God, and however worthy they may be of death, nevertheless, because they are the children of good people, whose privileges and many benefits from God they have received, they will be received with joy when they return to the faith, because God's love for them is stirred up by the memory of their ancestors.

29For the gifts and the call of God are irrevocable.[1]

This is true, because the grace of God in baptism does not demand groaning or crying or anything else, but only a profession of faith from the heart. This is because crying and groaning belong to those who have done great wrong by not receiving the promise of God and because they commit serious sins, that they need such things for forgiveness. But in order that these people should not think that it is impossible for them to receive mercy because they have not been seen to grieve sufficiently for their sins, Paul shows that these things are promised in stages which lead to faith and are not required at the start, because God's gift freely pardons sins in baptism.

30Just as you were once disobedient to God but now have received mercy because of their dis-

obedience, 31so they have now been disobedient in order that by the mercy shown to you they also may receive mercy.

Paul recalls the unbelief of the Gentiles so that, being ashamed of it, they may not insult the Jews who have not believed, but rejoice when they accept the promise of God. He says in effect: You Gentiles rejected the words of God when the Jews believed them, but now you have received mercy, not because of any merit of yours, but in order to bring shame on them, for why should they not receive even greater mercy if they are converted, seeing that they were familiar with the law of God long before you and that the promise had been made to them?

32For God has consigned all men to disobedience, that he may have mercy upon all.

From earliest times [all] nations lived in ungodliness and ignorance, because they were without God. For this reason the law was revealed, by which the worst ones could be restrained. By the activity of the adversary, sins began to multiply, so that through the commandment man was considered more guilty still. Then God, who in the mercy of his goodness always took care of man, seeing that even without the law sin still existed and that by the law it could be wiped out, decreed that he would demand only faith, by which the sins of all men might be abolished. Thus although man had no ground for hope through the law, he was nevertheless saved by the mercy of God. To consign everything to disobedience means that this decree comes as a gift from God at a time when everyone was laboring in unbelief, so that grace might appear to be the freest of all rewards. Therefore nobody should boast, for the one who is proud of his ignorance is to be pitied.

---

[1]Ambrosiaster interpreted the meaning here to be: "The gifts and calling of God are without repentance." In other words, there is no need to shed copious tears in order to receive it.

[33]*O the depth of the riches and wisdom and knowledge of God! How unsearchable are his judgments and how inscrutable his ways!*

Paul testifies with all praise and thanksgiving that God is high and immense in the riches of his wisdom and knowledge, for his counsel and judgment are beyond understanding. God knew from the beginning what man's behavior and works would be like, and that the human race could not be saved except by the severity of his justice, nor could it reach perfection except by his mercy. So at a particular time he decreed what should be preached, whereas before that time he allowed each person to decide for himself, because righteousness was recognized under the guidance of nature. And because the authority of natural righteousness was weakened by the habit of sin, the law was given so that the human race would be held back by the fear engendered by the revealed law. But because they did not restrain themselves and were counted guilty under the law, mercy was proclaimed, which would save those who took refuge in it but would blind those who rejected it for a time. During that time this mercy would invite the Gentiles, who earlier on had not wanted to follow the law given to Moses, to share in the promise, so that the Jews might become jealous of their salvation and because of that jealousy turn again to the source of the root, which is the Savior. This is *the depth of the riches and wisdom and knowledge of God*, who by his many-sided providence has won both Jews and Gentiles to eternal life.

[34]*"For who has known the mind of the Lord, or who has been his counselor?"*[1]
[35]*"Or who has given a gift to him that he might be repaid?"*[2]

It is clear that it is only God who knows everything and who lacks nothing, because everything comes from him. No one can understand or measure this knowledge, because the inferior cannot comprehend what is superior to it. Jewish believers could not understand how the salvation of the Gentiles could be God's plan and will. Likewise, it seemed unlikely and incredible to the Gentiles that the Jews, who had not believed, could be converted or be accepted as believers. This is part of the counsel of God which was hidden and could not be understood.

[36]*For from him and through him and to him are all things. To him be glory for ever. Amen.*

By saying this Paul revealed a meaning which had been hidden from the world. Because God is the Creator of all things, everything comes from him, and because everything comes from him, it comes through his Son, who is of the same substance and whose work is the Father's work too.

Therefore, because the Father works through the Son, everything comes into being through the Son. And because what is from God and through God is then born again in the Holy Spirit, everything is in him as well, because the Holy Spirit is from God the Father, which is why he knows what is in God. Therefore the Father is also in the Holy Spirit, because what is from the Father is from God. It cannot be otherwise because the Father is God.

All things that are from him and through him and in him can only exist by finding their origin in him. They cannot know his mind and his counsel, but he knows everything, because all things are in him. Here Paul laid bare the mystery of God, which he said above should not be unknown to them.

Romans 12

[1]*I appeal to you therefore, brethren, by the*

---

[1]Is 40:13-14. [2]Job 35:7; 41:11.

mercies of God, to present your bodies as a living sacrifice, holy and acceptable to God, which is your spiritual worship. [2]Do not be conformed to this world but be transformed by the renewal of your mind, that you may prove what is the will of God, what is good and acceptable and perfect.

Paul does not plead with them on the basis of their salvation, nor through Christ, although the mercy of God is found in Christ, but through the mercy of God, by which they began to return to life from the dead, so that they should be mindful of this and behave carefully in order to keep their salvation. This is a warning that they should remember, that they have received God's mercy and that they should take care to worship the one who gave it to them, by whom they were freely justified while they were still ungodly. They know that this is the living sacrifice which is holy and acceptable to God, that we should keep our bodies untainted and be different from the people of this world who go after earthly desires.

God's will is our sanctification,[1] for bodies subject to sin are not considered to be alive, but dead, since they have no hope of obtaining the promise of eternal life. It is for this purpose that we are cleansed from our sins by God's gift, so that from now on we should lead a pure life and stir up the love of God in us, not making his work of grace of no effect. The ancients killed sacrifices which were offered in order to signify that men were subjected to death because of sin. But now, since by the gift of God men have been purified and set free from the second death, they must offer a living sacrifice as a sign of eternal life. It is no longer the case that bodies are sacrificed for bodies, because instead of bodies, it is the sins of the body which must be put to death.

If our worship is to have any benefit for us, we must guard our righteousness and stay chaste. To serve God with the mind means to be conformed to spiritual things by the operation of righteousness, working out by the patience of the Spirit we have received what is pleasing to God and then doing those things, because that is the perfect goodness which God likes.

[3]For by the grace given to me I bid every one among you not to think of himself more highly than he ought to think, but to think with sober judgment, each according to the measure of faith which God has assigned him.

Here Paul shows openly that we ought to know that the bounds of righteousness must not be transgressed, so that not only will it be of service to us, but it will not harm anyone else either. This is wisdom, that one should help people rather than harm them, be content with the lot which God has given to the merit and faith of each one, and not to claim what has not been granted. This is the meaning of *not to think . . . more highly*, because not everything can be given to a single individual. If someone lives a moral life, he must not on that basis lay claim to doctrinal wisdom also, or if someone is skilled in the law, he ought not to demand the office of priesthood as well. Paul therefore urges and teaches that wisdom is given by grace. This grace is understood as mastery of the Lord's teaching, by which we are committed to the study of humility and righteousness.

[4] For as in one body we have many members, and all the members do not have the same function,

By using the example of the body, Paul teaches that it is impossible for any one of us to do everything on our own, for we are members of each other and need one another. For this

---

[1] 1 Thess 4:3.

95

reason we ought to behave toward one another with consideration, because we need each other's gifts.

5 so we, though many, are one body in Christ, and individually members one of another.

This is what it means to love Christ, that we should encourage one another to live in a way which corresponds to the way in which the body is made perfect in Christ.

6 Having gifts that differ according to the grace given to us, let us use them: if prophecy, in proportion to our faith;

Paul now lists the offices which have been assigned to the members on the basis of faith, so that when a member sees what office has been assigned to him, he will not seek another which he sees being assigned to someone else, but rejoice because the Lord's body has been perfected.

Paul begins with prophecy, which is the first proof that our faith is rational, for believers prophesied when they received the Spirit. This is given in proportion to the recipient, that is, as much as is necessary for the purpose for which it is given.

7 if service, in our serving; he who teaches, in his teaching;

The minister is strengthened for the service of the church to the extent that he believes he ought to serve, lest he labor beyond his faith and exhaust himself in serving to his ruin, because this happens to everyone who tries to do his best. Likewise Paul says that the teacher is aided in his teaching, so that he will be inspired to transmit the heavenly doctrine to the extent that he has the faith to teach.

8 he who exhorts, in his exhortation; he who contributes, in liberality; he who gives aid, with zeal; he who does acts of mercy, with cheerfulness.

The exhorter is helped in the same way as the above, and is prepared by the Spirit to have the grace to provoke, for he stirs up the brethren to do good and unbelievers to accept the faith. The contributor is likewise given a spirit of generosity, so that he will not stop giving [without seeking anything in return][1] as Solomon says: *Whoever gives to the poor will not be wanting.*[2]

He who takes care of his brethren will receive vigilance and authority in proportion to his faith, so that he can continue doing this for those under his authority without any sense of shame. Likewise he who does acts of mercy according to his intention will do them with a cheerful heart, and not as if somebody was twisting his arm, being established and strengthened by God, so that he will have the resources he needs to be merciful and a reward will be set aside for him in the future. To be generous in simplicity is almost the same thing as being merciful with joy, though mercy is more fundamental, for there are many actions which are contained under that name.

It is an act of mercy to forgive sinners, and mercy to bring help to someone who finds himself placed in or weighed down by some kind of necessity. It is an act of mercy to intercede with someone on behalf of another, and to give to someone who has nothing. Therefore if someone has done these things readily and without regretting it, he will get help in this life and a reward in the next.

Every act of mercy should be done without

---

[1] This seems to be the meaning of the Latin word *simpliciter*, which some manuscripts explain in a note which reads, "The meaning of giving *simply* is that the person who gives does not merely pretend, so that praise will be given to him by other people, but so that he may receive merit from God for what he has done." [2] Prov 28:27.

ulterior motives and with joy, because straight-forwardness rules out hypocrisy and joy bears witness to our reliance on future hope.

⁹Let love be genuine; hate what is evil, hold fast to what is good;

The Spirit will come to the aid of the mind which meditates on this, that it should love its brother, not in order to get praise in this life, but because this is pleasing to God the Creator. Anyone can accomplish his duties if he puts his mind to it. He has heard what the Lord said: *A new commandment I give to you, that you should love one another.*[1]

¹⁰love one another with brotherly affection; outdo one another in showing honor.

Paul says that it is not much to avoid evil, if there is no clinging to the good in consequence, nor is there any benefit in brotherly love unless it is mutual.

¹¹Never flag in zeal, be aglow with the Spirit, serve the Lord.

This is what the prophet Jeremiah says: *Cursed by God is the person who does the Lord's work negligently.*[2] To be lazy in the things of God is to be without hope. Therefore Paul adds what follows.

Be aglow with the Spirit means that we should not be lukewarm in doing God's work or the law, as God says in the Revelation of John: *Because you are lukewarm, I shall spit you out of my mouth.*[3] Daily meditation removes laziness and makes people vigilant.

Serving time.[4] The Greek here apparently reads *serving the Lord* but this does not fit the context. What would be the point of making this the sum of all devotion when Paul is listing the individual members which belong to

the worship and service of God? Full service to God is manifested in all the things that he lists here.

What it means to *serve time* Paul explains elsewhere, when he says: *redeeming the time, for the days are evil, so that you may know how to answer each one.*[5] Since he has just said: *Be aglow with the Spirit*, he immediately added: *Serving the time* so that they would not understand this to mean that they should go around shoving religion down everyone's throats even when the time was not right, and so cause enormous scandal. Paul wanted them to talk about their faith moderately and honestly, in the right places, to the right people and at the right time. There are some people, even in this day and age, which is one of peace for the church, who get so worked up when they hear the words of God that they blaspheme the way of Christ in great anger. Even Paul himself "served the time" when he did what he did not want to do, for he unwillingly circumcised Timothy and purified himself by shaving his head according to the law when he went up to the temple, in order to silence the madness of the Jews.[6]

¹²Rejoice in your hope, be patient in tribulation, be constant in prayer.

Even if the times do not allow us to speak publicly about our faith, nevertheless we must rejoice in tribulation, for this sadness brings joy. With the joy of hope we can endure tribulation, knowing that the things which are promised to those who suffer are much greater. Prayer is essential, for if we are to survive tribulation we need to pray.

¹³Contribute to the needs of the saints, practice hospitality.

It is clear that whoever wants his prayers to be heard must imitate the life of the saints,

---

[1]Jn 13:34. [2]Jer 48:10. [3]Rev 3:16. [4]This was the reading of Ambrosiaster's Latin text. [5]Eph 5:16; Col 4:6. [6]Acts 16:3; 21:24.

which he will acquire and share with others by copying their actions. We ought to share with those who are lacking in resources, as Paul says elsewhere: *Concerning the collections which are being made among the saints,*[1] and to the Galatians: *That we should be mindful of the poor.*[2] The imitator and lover of the saints will practice hospitality following the example of Abraham and Lot, a righteous man.

[14]Bless those who persecute you; bless and do not curse them.

God makes Christians new people in every respect, so that here too he wants to take away from us the habit which is common to everyone. Instead of cursing others in anger, which we once did so easily, we ought rather to overcome our anger and bless them, so that the Lord's teaching might be praised.

[15]Rejoice with those who rejoice, weep with those who weep.

When somebody is a consolation to a brother in need, he raises his spirits and obtains merit with God, because he loves a member of the body of Christ, and if he weeps with an unbeliever, he may provoke him to accept the Lord's teaching.

[16]Live in harmony with one another; do not be haughty, but associate with the lowly; never be conceited.

To live in harmony with one another is to share in the tribulations of a brother, as Paul said elsewhere: *Consider yourself, so that you will not be tempted also. Bear one another's burdens.*[3]

To be haughty is pride, which is how the devil fell. There should be none of that haughtiness of mind which assumes that its own actions are above reproach and does not sympathize with a brother, but rather rebukes him as if he were a sinner or merely careless. This is pride, which can be very harmful. When someone puts himself forward, he causes offense. The Lord also remarks on this, saying: *Take the beam out of your own eye and then you will see clearly and be able to take the mote out of your brother's eye.*[4] Haughtiness of this kind is a sin, as if the person concerned were not a sinner, which is impossible, because he becomes a sinner by being proud. Finally, Solomon says that *God resists the proud.*[5]

Put pride aside and make other people's cares your own and your own foreign to you, so that you may have grace with God, because *whoever exalts himself will be humbled.*[6]

Never be conceited. This is written in the prophet Isaiah, though Paul quotes it here as if it were his own.[7] Righteousness must be the same for everyone, and nobody can be righteous in his own eyes but unrighteous in the eyes of others.

[17]Repay no one evil for evil, but take thought for what is noble in the sight of all.

This is what the Lord says: *Unless your righteousness exceeds the righteousness of the scribes and the Pharisees, you will not enter the kingdom of God.*[8] The commandment in the law was: *Love your neighbor and hate your enemy.*[9] This is righteousness as far as it goes, but in order for the righteousness of Christians to go beyond it, they are taught not to render evil for evil, so that they may be blameless and that a reward may be given to them for this in the judgment of God. This righteousness is surpassed when what is permitted is not done, so that it can be better. For the righteousness of the world, given to it by God, makes a person innocent, but the heavenly righteousness makes him perfect, so that he has merit with God.

---

[1]1 Cor 16:1. [2]Gal 2:10. [3]Gal 6:1-2. [4]Mt 7:5. [5]Prov 3:34. [6]Lk 14:11. [7]Is 5:21. [8]Mt 5:20. [9]Lev 19:18.

To *take thought* is to keep the future good in mind, so as to bring it about as far as possible, so that afterward it will not be criticized but all the more greatly praised, both by God and by other people. Lest anyone imagine that lawful things are not displeasing to God, and so there is no need to worry about whether they might cause scandal to a brother, Paul here reminds us that what must be done is what is both pleasing to God and not a scandal to a brother. But if he does something which scandalizes a brother, he does not please God, because God wants us to be more concerned about salvation [than about anything else].

Thus good things are brought about before both God and man, if things which are allowable are done in a way which does not cause scandal.

¹⁸*If possible, so far as it depends upon you, live peaceably with all.*

Paul wants everyone who keeps God's righteousness to be peaceful. It is clear that if someone disturbs this peace, he will be at odds with any righteous person, either because he does not want to be rebuked by him or because he is jealous of his possessions, although what belongs to him does not conflict with those who do good. The person who is not peaceful is the one who has rejected the law of God and who follows his own law instead, as David said: *I was peaceful with those who hate peace.*[1]

This is necessary because of the power of egotism. Yet even the man whom pride exalts to the point where he despises the commandments can be defeated by humble behavior. Therefore Paul says: *if possible, so far as it depends on you*, so that those who behave well may have peace. Even if the other person is not a lover of peace, you should want to be peaceful insofar as you can be. However, if someone is irreverent and blasphemous and you cannot have peace with him, you will not be held accountable for this, because the apostle John would not even allow people to greet those who deny that Christ came in the flesh.[2] We must therefore be ready to have peace with everyone as far as we can. If others refuse it will become impossible, but not because of us, since the problem does not depend on us. (Whoever harms no one appears to be peaceful.)

¹⁹*Beloved, never avenge yourselves, but leave it to the wrath of God; for it is written, "Vengeance is mine, I will repay, says the Lord."*[3]

Paul warns us to avoid anger, especially because so often anger is the chief cause of sin. Someone who is motivated by wrath will demand more than the cause of the sin merits, or will put himself out to do more harm while seeking revenge if he tries to avenge the more serious sins when he is incompetent to do so. In the end he will destroy someone when he could have corrected and restored him instead. Thus Solomon says: *Be not righteous overmuch, for there are some who die in their righteousness.*[4] Wanting to respond to individual sins, a person might find death on account of his revenge, both for himself and for the person he is punishing, for it is common for punishment to be overdone.

Paul not only forbids us to seek revenge from those under us, but also from those who are our equals or superiors. We must not seek to avenge ourselves against brethren who may have sinned against us, but rather to commit everything to God's judgment, so that an enemy will find no way of promoting or advancing what is against our interest while we are too angry to notice what is happening.

Paul quotes what is written in Proverbs to back up his point: *Vengeance is mine and I will repay, says the Lord.* If we do not do what God

---

[1]Ps 120:6. [2]2 Jn 7. [3]Lev 19:18; Deut 32:35. [4]Eccles 7:16.

teaches, he will show us contempt. But if we give revenge over to God it benefits us in two ways. It overcomes our anger and makes us perfect and justified in God's sight.

[20]No, *"if your enemy is hungry, feed him; if he is thirsty, give him drink; for by so doing you will heap burning coals upon his head."*[1]

Paul teaches us not just to let God take revenge, but also to give good things to our enemies, so that we may demonstrate that we do not have these enemies because of anything we have done. Rather, we are trying to get them to desist from evil by doing them service. If by their ungodliness they continue in their evil ways, our service to them will lead to punishment for them, or else, by the persistence of our service, they will be pricked and spring back to life like dying coals. Thus the Lord not only forbids us to repay our enemies in kind but also exhorts us to seek friendship by acts of kindness, both because that serves to make us perfect and because it is a means of winning others to eternal life.

[21]*Do not be overcome by evil, but overcome evil with good.*

The interpretation of the apostle is that he is urging us not to take revenge on our enemies, as is said. It will do us much good if we refrain from evil. The person who appears to be overcome by evil for a time in fact is overcoming evil, just as the Savior overcame evil by not resisting it. Evil works against itself, and when it is overcome it thinks that it has won! Our enemy acts in such a way as to divert us from our purpose, looking for an opportunity to make us sin. Therefore if we are provoked by him and do not reply in kind, we overcome him with good. Therefore we do not resist, in order to serve the good by ignoring the demands of

justice for retribution, for justice urges us to seek retribution.

Romans 13

[1]*Let every person be subject to the governing authorities. For there is no authority except from God, and those that exist have been instituted by God.*

As Paul has already ordered that the law of heavenly righteousness be followed, he now commends earthly law as well, so as not to appear to be slighting it. For if the earthly law is not kept, the heavenly law will not be kept either. The earthly law is a kind of tutor, who helps little children along so that they can tackle a higher level of righteousness. For mercy cannot be imputed to anyone who is not righteous.

Therefore, in order to back up the authority and fear of the natural law, Paul bears witness to the fact that God is the author of both and that the ministers of the earthly law have his permission to act. That is why he added: *Those that exist have been instituted by God.* So that no one should despise it as a merely human construction, they see the divine law as being delegated to human authorities. A man who does not do what is forbidden out of the fear of God is subject to the governing power.

[2]*Therefore he who resists the authorities resists what God has appointed, and those who resist will incur judgment.*

Paul writes this against those who believe that because of their own power they cannot be apprehended, and so they can play fast and loose with the law. He shows them that this is the law of God, and that those who by some subterfuge avoid it for a time will not escape God's judgment. It is clear that everyone will either

---

[1]Prov 25:21-22.

be justified or condemned by his own works, so those who hear the law and sin against it are without excuse.

³*For rulers are not a terror to good conduct, but to bad. Would you have no fear of him who is in authority? Then do what is good, and you will receive his approval,*

Rulers here are kings who are created in order to correct behavior and prevent bad things from happening. They have the image of God, because everyone else is under his head. *Approval* comes from the authorities when someone is found to be innocent.

⁴*for he is God's servant for your good. But if you do wrong, be afraid, for he does not bear the sword in vain; he is the servant of God to execute his wrath on the wrongdoer.*

It is clear that rulers have been appointed so that evil will not occur. Therefore we must be warned that if someone stands in contempt of the law, the ruler will punish him. Since God has ordained that there will be a future judgment, and he does not want anyone to perish, he has ordained rulers in this world who, by causing people to be afraid of them, act as tutors to mankind, teaching them what to do in order to avoid future punishment.

⁵*Therefore one must be subject, not only to avoid God's wrath but also for the sake of conscience.*

Paul rightly says that we must be subject [to the authorities], not only because of wrath, that is, immediate revenge—for wrath produces revenge—but also because of the coming judgment, for whoever escapes now will be punished then, his own conscience accusing him.

⁶*For the same reason you also pay taxes, for the authorities are ministers of God, attending to this very thing.*

Paul says that to pay tribute, or what are called taxes, is to show subjection. By doing this, people know that they are not free, but act under authority, which is from God. They are subject to their ruler, who acts as God's deputy, just as they are subject to God. This is what Daniel says: *The kingdom is God's and he will give it to whom he wills.*[1] And so the Lord says: *Render to Caesar what is Caesar's.*[2] The people must therefore be subject to their ruler as they are to God, and the proof of their subjection is that they pay him tribute.

⁷*Pay all of them their dues, taxes to whom taxes are due, revenue to whom revenue is due, respect to whom respect is due, honor to whom honor is due.*

Paul wants everyone to give what he owes, for even the authorities are debtors to their inferiors and have to respect their merits. First of all he orders what is owed to the royal power to be paid, because that is the most important thing or need. The authorities are to be feared because fear stops sin. It must also be shown to parents or earthy lords, so that they will give thanks for their child or for their Christian servant. Giving honor to the powers that be in this world may have the effect that, if they see the humility of Christ's servants, they may praise rather than curse the gospel's teaching.

⁸*Owe no one anything, except to love one another; for he who loves his neighbor has fulfilled the law.*

Paul wants us to have peace with everyone but to love the brethren. When we do this, honor is maintained. Paul says that we are debtors,

---

[1] Dan 5:21. [2] Mt 22:21.

because it is right and proper for us to defer to any man who is worthy of honor, whether present or future. Everyone defers to the man from whom he receives honor, and therefore he is said to be a debtor. If you do not do this to your ruler, you are proud, for he is to be honored whether because of his merit or because of his age.

He who loves his neighbor has fulfilled the law of Moses, for the commandment of the new law is that we should love our enemies also.

⁹The commandments, "You shall not commit adultery, You shall not kill, You shall not steal, You shall not covet," and any other commandment, are summed up in this sentence, "You shall love your neighbor as yourself."

Moses received this writing from God in order to reform the natural law. *You shall love your neighbor as yourself* is found in Leviticus.[1] Paul means that above all the other laws there lies one which must be fulfilled in love. Although there may be other laws which Paul has not mentioned, love is the fulfillment of them all. If the human race had loved from the beginning, there would never have been any wickedness on earth, for the result of unrighteousness is discord.

¹⁰Love does no wrong to a neighbor; therefore love is the fulfilling of the law.

Paul says that love does what is good, and therefore it is the fulfillment of the law, because not doing what is evil fulfills the law by love. For whoever loves his enemies fulfills the law to the point where it is not only fulfilled but fulfilled to overflowing. For to fulfill something is more than merely to fill it. The overflow of the law is contained in the precepts of the gospel, which he says are heavenly,

because they make human beings resemble God the Father. Paul is using the words of the law to arrive at the meaning of the gospel. Therefore, when he mentions the fulfilling of the law, he ties it to the gospel, demonstrating that both have a single author. Yet in the time of Christ it was necessary to add something, namely, that we should love our enemies as well as our neighbors, whence *Love is the fulfilling of the law,* so that righteousness is to love one's neighbor, but overflowing and perfect righteousness is to love one's enemies. What does it mean to love an enemy, except to choose not to hate him any longer and to seek to do him no harm? This is what it means to love him—to choose out for him those things by which God's righteousness is satisfied. This is the heavenly righteousness which makes us like God the Father, who bestows annual gifts on those who do not worship him. For the Lord himself prayed for his enemies when he was on the cross, in order to demonstrate what the fullness of righteousness, which he had taught, actually was.

¹¹Besides this you know what hour it is, how it is full time now for you to wake from sleep. For salvation is nearer to us now than when we first believed;

Paul says that the time has come when we must hasten to perfect our merit. This is what it means to wake up from sleep—to do good as if it were day, in other words, openly. Unlawful things happen at night, that is, in secret. Now that we have been made aware of what is in God's mind, we ought to recognize what we must do and get to work on it, so that by pure living we may come to the promised reward, having stamped out sleep, that is to say, ignorance or negligence.

It is clear that if we live well after baptism and strive for love, we are not far from the

---

[1]Lev 19:18.

reward of the promised resurrection. The good life of a Christian is the sign of future salvation. When a person is baptized he is forgiven, but not rewarded, but later on, as he walks in newness of life, he comes closer to eternal life.

[12]the night is far gone, the day is at hand. Let us then cast off the works of darkness and put on the armor of light;

Night means the old man, who is renewed through baptism. Paul says that he has passed away like the night, and that the day is near, in other words, the sun of righteousness, by whose light the truth appears to us so that we may know what to do. Before, we were in the dark because we were ignorant of Christ, but when we learned of him the light dawned on us and we passed from the false to the true.

The darkness refers to carnal sins, which are done by worldly enticements. They are worthy of the darkness, as the Lord says: *Take him and tie his hands and feet and throw him into the outer darkness.*[1] But to *put on the armor of light* is to do good deeds. Just as evil deeds are consigned to the darkness because they are done in secret so those who do good do it in the open, because they are not afraid but rejoice. Good deeds are the arms of light, doing battle with the darkness, which means the vices of the flesh.

[13]let us conduct ourselves becomingly as in the day, not in reveling and drunkenness, not in debauchery and licentiousness, not in quarreling and jealousy.

It is true that people do not sin in public, so let us behave as if we were constantly in the public eye, for there is nothing more public than the truth.

Revels are extravagant parties which are celebrated when everyone gets together. They sometimes take place after weddings, when nobody is supposed to be ashamed if he says or does something inappropriate, because each guest is meant to feel right at home, and it is only in someone else's house that one is expected to behave oneself. The result is that crimes are hatched in large supplies of wine, and many kinds of lust are stirred up. Parties of this kind are therefore to be avoided. After mentioning extravagant revels and drunkenness, Paul adds what follows, that is debauchery, which is the result of this sort of lasciviousness. Paul was right to warn them against quarreling and jealousy, because both of these things lead to enmity. Paul calls all these things *darkness*, because they cannot come into the presence of the light.

[14]But put on the Lord Jesus Christ, and make no provision for the flesh, to gratify its desires.

Paul wants everything the law forbids not to be desired, or if it is desired, to be overcome. These are the works of the flesh, and those who have put on Christ, that is to say, who have been renewed by Christ, must stay away from such evils. To put on Christ means to cut oneself off from every sin and wickedness, so that at the wedding banquet one will not be found without a new garment, and be shamefully thrown out into the darkness. If they do anything less, they have not put on Christ Jesus the Lord but have covered their new robes with their old rags. They still have to put off the old man in newness of life.

Romans 14

[1]As for the man who is weak in faith, welcome him, but not for disputes over opinions.

As I mentioned in my prologue to the epistle, those who led the Romans to faith had mixed it

---

[1]Mt 22:13.

up with the law because they were Jews, which is why some of them thought that they should not eat meat. But others, who followed Christ apart from the law, thought otherwise, that it was permissible to eat meat, and for this reason there were disputes among them. The apostle tried to solve these disputes by arguing that the person who abstained from eating gained no advantage in the sight of God, nor did the one who ate lose anything. He says that the person who is afraid to eat because the Jews had forbidden it is weak. He wants this person to be left to his own judgment, so as not to be hurt and depart from that love which is a mother of souls. Leave him alone with his troubled mind, for Christians should be peaceful and quiet.

2One believes that he may eat anything, while the weak man eats only vegetables.

The faithful reader of Scripture will not doubt that everything which is given for human use is fit to be eaten, for it says in Genesis that everything God created is good.[1] Therefore nothing is to be rejected, for neither Enoch, who was the first to please God, nor Noah, who was the only one found to be righteous at the time of the flood, nor Abraham, who was the friend of God, nor Isaac nor Jacob, both righteous men and friends of God, nor even Lot, nor any other righteous men are said to have abstained from these things.

    If someone thinks it right to be a vegetarian he is not to be persuaded to eat meat, because if he ignores his own principles and eats with reluctance he will appear to be sinning.

3Let not him who eats despise him who abstains, and let not him who abstains pass judgment on him who eats; for God has welcomed him.

What we eat or do not eat is a matter of personal choice and therefore it should not become a subject for argument. Everything was made for the purpose of being subordinated to the will, because the whole creation is subject to human dominion. God has welcomed the abstainer since he has been called to grace.

4Who are you to pass judgment on the servant of another? It is before his own master that he stands or falls. And he will be upheld, for the Master is able to make him stand.

It is clear that a servant must not be arrested by someone who wants to pass judgment on him, for the law was not given for that purpose. God is the judge of whether he eats or does not eat in conscience, because he is God's servant. The servant will be able to stand before his master because he is not guilty whether he eats or not, as long as he does what he does in a spirit of devotion and does not avoid it for the opposite reason.

5One man esteems one day as better than another, while another man esteems all days alike. Let every one be fully convinced in his own mind.

This means that some people eat certain things on certain days only. There are people who have decreed that it is wrong to eat meat on Tuesdays, others who eat it [only] on Saturdays and still others who eat it from Easter to Pentecost. The person who regards all days alike never eats meat. Everyone must make his own decision about this.

6He who observes the day, observes it in honor of the Lord. He also who eats, eats in honor of the Lord, since he gives thanks to God; while he who abstains, abstains in honor of the Lord and gives thanks to God.

---

[1] Cf. Gen 1:31.

It is true that someone who always abstains thinks that he is pleasing God. He eats for the Lord because he gives thanks to the Creator. He gives thanks to God when he says that the creation was made by God and that all created things are good. He cuts himself off from it [to some extent], but does not condemn it [as evil].

⁷*None of us lives to himself, and none of us dies to himself.*

A man would be living for himself if he did not act according to the law. Whoever is controlled by the brake of the law is not living for himself, but for God, who gave the law so that it might be possible to live according to his will. Likewise, whoever dies dies to God, for he is the Judge who will either crown him or condemn him.

⁸*If we live, we live to the Lord, and if we die, we die to the Lord; so then, whether we live or whether we die, we are the Lord's.*

The meaning here is the same. It is true that we are all servants in the control and power of the Redeemer, and each of us will be judged according to his merits.

⁹*For to this end Christ died and lived again, that he might be Lord both of the dead and of the living.*

The creation was made by Christ the Lord, but because of sin it has become separated from its Maker and taken captive. But God the Father sent his Son from heaven to earth to teach his creation what to do in order to escape the hands of its captors, so that his work should not perish. For this reason he allowed himself to be killed by his enemies, so that by going down to hell he could condemn sin, because he was killed as an innocent man, and liberate those whom the devil held there. Therefore, since he showed the way of salvation to the living and offered himself for them, and also delivered the dead from hell, he is Lord of both the living and the dead, for he has turned those who were lost into his servants.

¹⁰*Why do you pass judgment on your brother? Or you, why do you despise your brother? For we shall all stand before the judgment seat of God;*

Paul teaches that we must not pass judgment in this matter because it is not contained in the law, especially since we are waiting for God the Judge to come.

¹¹*for it is written,*
"As I live, says the Lord, every knee shall bow to me,
and every tongue shall give praise to God."[1]

This is written in Isaiah, because every tongue will confess to God in the faith of Christ. For having been killed, the future Judge rose from the dead, and therefore he rightly said: *As I live, says the Lord.* For not only do I live, but I will come to judge, and my enemies will confess my name and kneel before me, acknowledging that I am God from God.

¹²*So each of us shall give account of himself to God.*

Since we are not going to give account of each other, says Paul, let us not condemn one another over the issues mentioned above.

¹³*Then let us no more pass judgment on one another, but rather decide never to put a stumbling block or hindrance in the way of a brother.*

---

[1]Is 45:23.

In other words, since we know this, let us stop quarreling. In this matter Paul advises that we should decide what is profitable and can be defended on the authority of the law, which is that no stumbling block should be put in the way of one of the brothers because of what he eats or does not eat.

14I know and am persuaded in the Lord Jesus that nothing is unclean in itself; but it is unclean for any one who thinks it unclean.

It is clear that by the Savior's blessing everything is clean, because he rescued human beings out from under the yoke of the law and by justifying them gave them back the condition of their original freedom, so that they might make use of the whole creation, just as the saints of old did. Those who are still under the law cannot use or eat what the law prohibits, since they have rejected the dispensation offered. Unclean things are what they are, not because of their own nature but because they are eaten against the law. For in the law it says: *They will be unclean for you.*[1] If either a Jewish Christian or a Gentile believer thinks that something of this kind should be avoided, it is he whom Paul describes above as *weak*, because he is weakened by his doubts. As far as he is concerned, what he thinks ought not to be eaten is unclean, and because he does this, not out of superstition but out of fear, he is left to make up his own mind.

15If your brother is being injured by what you eat, you are no longer walking in love. Do not let what you eat cause the ruin of one for whom Christ died.

In another epistle Paul says: *Food is meant for the stomach and the stomach for food, and God will destroy both one and the other.*[2] Since God does not care one way or the other about food, Paul tells us to maintain a spirit of charity,

by which God has seen fit to deliver us from sin. As he says: *God, out of his great love, had mercy on us.*[3] Therefore whoever is mindful of this blessing honors this love and lets nothing come before it but puts aside even the greatest things, which he knows cannot compare with the promise [we have] with God.

We know how much the salvation of a brother is worth from the death of Christ. Whoever knows how much he is worth ought to back him up and not offend him by causing him anxiety over some trivial thing, making him hesitate as to whether he should eat meat or not, when previously he had been quite simply eating with a good conscience. When controversies arise, such a person will get upset and start to sin against God's creation. This will in turn insult the Creator, which will only hasten the damnation of the doubter.

16So do not let what is good to you be spoken of as evil.

Since God's teaching is good and salutary, it should not be blasphemed because of something trivial. Yet it is blasphemed when doubts are cast on the goodness of God's creation. Another way of interpreting this verse is to read it as saying that our good is blasphemed, because if someone who has good works is caught doing something wrong, his good is obscured and starts to be blasphemed because of his wrongdoing, as it is written in Ezekiel: *The righteousness of the righteous man is of no use if he has sinned.*[4] It is as if some handsome person has a scar on his forehead or nose. Is that not a disfigurement? Therefore Paul urges us to choose things which will not destroy people's approval of the good which remains in us.

17For the kingdom of God does not mean food and drink but righteousness and peace and joy in the Holy Spirit;

---

[1]Lev 11:4. [2]1 Cor 6:13. [3]Eph 2:4. [4]Ezek 33:12.

It is clear that nobody can please or displease God simply by the food he eats. Paul says that the people who enter the kingdom of God are those who follow righteousness and have that Christian peace which the Lord gave, when he said: *My peace I give you, my peace I leave with you,*[1] out of which comes joy in the Holy Spirit. Disagreement, however, does not bring joy, but anger. Therefore the Holy Spirit does not honor it, because he rejoices only in those who are peaceful. We make him sad [by our behavior], but he rejoices in us.

¹⁸*he who thus serves Christ is acceptable to God and approved by men.*

Since it is Christ who redeems us, Paul says: *He who thus serves Christ is acceptable to God.* There is no doubt that whoever serves the one whom God sent serves God, as the Lord himself said: *Whoever does not honor the Son does not honor the Father.*[2] The man who is acceptable to God is approved by men. Why? Because he has accepted the gift through which he appears worthy in the sight of God.

¹⁹*Let us then pursue what makes for peace and for mutual upbuilding.*

Since disagreement leads to discord, Paul teaches us to be peaceful and to avoid arguments over eating or not eating. Instead, he encourages us to follow the way of upbuilding, so that we may put together with peace the things by which we build ourselves up, separate them out from those things which are unfruitful and reject things which are completely the opposite. Such an assemblage can help us, and even excite the mind, but only if we forget about trying to win the argument. That is the kind of thing which starts quarrels.

²⁰*Do not, for the sake of food, destroy the work*

of God. Everything is indeed clean, but it is wrong for any one to make others fall by what he eats;

Man is the work of God by creation, and again by his renewal in regeneration, and food is God's work as well. But man was not made for food; food was made for man, which is very different! Therefore, says Paul: *I do not want this work of God, which is superb, to be ruined by something so unimportant.* That is to say, you should be more concerned for your brother's salvation than for what you are going to eat, if that will upset him. Whoever drives his brother back to sinning after he has been delivered from it nullifies God's blessing by destroying the works which Christ has done in him in order to set him free from sin.

It is true and obvious that all things are clean, especially since we read in Genesis that everything which God has made is very good.[3] Therefore, although everything is good and clean by nature, it becomes unclean to those who doubt and will be a cause of stumbling to someone who eats when he doubts. When that happens, the conscience is not clean, because it is doing something which it thinks is unhelpful to it. There is therefore no contradiction in what Paul says here.

²¹*it is right not to eat meat or drink wine or do anything that makes your brother stumble.*

Although the issue involves only meat, Paul adds drink here as well, in order to nurture those who abstain from both of these things, so that they will not be hurt by those who eat and drink, on the ground that it is lawful to do so. Paul gives them peace of mind by telling them to make their own decision and putting an end to the disagreement through which the dispute had arisen. No one will dispute that either option is legitimate in itself. For the

---

[1] Jn 14:27. [2] Jn 5:23. [3] Gen 1:31.

creation was given for voluntary use; there is no necessity imposed on anybody, one way or the other. Paul then says the same thing again, that it is wrong to make a brother who has formed a weak mind in himself question what to eat, lest he should get upset and sin, not knowing what to think.

22*The faith that you have, keep between yourself and God; happy is he who has no reason to judge himself for what he approves.*

In other words, who are you, who eat in the confidence that God's creation is good? There is no need to judge anyone else. Rather you should be at peace with your brother, for this is what God wants. Food is useful for the flesh, but peace helps both the flesh and the soul, which is why this kind of disagreement ought to stop and each person should feel right in his heart about what he is doing. Paul says that in his judgment anyone who does something which he says he ought not to do should be condemned, and the one who only does what he is certain will be helpful to him is blessed.

23*But he who has doubts is condemned, if he eats, because he does not act from faith; for whatever does not proceed from faith is sin.*

It is true that if someone thinks it wrong to eat but does so anyway, he is condemned. For he makes himself guilty when he does what he says is unhelpful to him. A person who objects to eating something but who then eats it anyway is not eating in faith. Paul quite rightly says it is a sin to do something other than what is approved of. When the Romans had been instructed in the law, as I mentioned in the preface to this letter, there were people who came along thinking that they had a more correct faith. Questions arose about eating or not

eating meat, and those who thought it right to eat seemed to be better, because everything is very good in itself. Paul called those who refused to eat *weak*, whether they were Jews or Gentiles, and told them to make up their own minds, since it was neither harmful to eat nor helpful as far as God is concerned. He did not want them to get tied up in knots and end up sinning because they were eating against their better judgment.

Romans 15

1*We who are strong ought to bear with the failings of the weak, and not to please ourselves;*

Paul says the right thing here. We ought to do this because it is necessary for teachers to strengthen the weak and instruct the ignorant with tenderness, so that they will not be provoked into argument or feel humiliated and then do ever worse things. We should not just defend what is to our advantage and what we like, but consider our brother's welfare, which is our concern as well.

2*let each of us please his neighbor for his good, to edify him.*

Here Paul is talking about himself. He advises them, as people trying to love, to please their neighbors for their benefit. Elsewhere he had said the same thing: *I please everyone in everything.*[1]

3*For Christ did not please himself; but, as it is written, "The reproaches of those who reproached thee fell on me."*[2]

In Psalm 68[3] it says that the Savior did not come to please himself but God the Father. It was because he said: *I did not come down from heaven to do my will, but the will of him*

---

[1] 1 Cor 10:33. [2] Ps 69:9. [3] Ps 69 in English versions.

who sent me,[1] that the Jews objected and put him to death as a sinner. Therefore the Psalmist puts himself in Christ's place and says: *The reproaches of those who reproached thee fell on me.*[2] This means, *Although I do your will, they say that I am sinning against you. By not accepting me, whom you have sent, they are insulting you.* Not only were the Jews sinning against God by not accepting the Christ whom he sent, but they went further and killed him, thereby deliberately sinning against God, and so the sins of those sinning against God fell on Christ. They said that he ought to die because he was sinning against God. He was innocent of all sin but was put to death for blasphemy, as is written in the Gospel.

[4]For whatever was written in former days was written for our instruction, that by steadfastness and by the encouragement of the scriptures we might have hope.

It is clear what whatever is written has been written for our instruction, so that by that encouragement we may advance in hope, not losing faith in the promises, even though they have still not been realized.

[5]May the God of steadfastness and encouragement grant you to live in such harmony with one another, in accord with Christ Jesus,

As if he had been sent for their salvation, the apostle charges the people with a good wish, praying that God may grant them a common understanding of his wisdom according to Christ Jesus, so that they may be wise in the teaching of Christ. For then they will be able to please God by following the example of the Lord, who said: *Greater love has no man than this, that a man should lay down his life for his friends and his brethren.*[3]

[6]that together you may with one voice glorify the God and Father of our Lord Jesus Christ.

Those who are wise in Christ praise God with a single voice.

[7]Welcome one another, therefore, as Christ has welcomed you, for the glory of God.

Just as we have been welcomed by Christ, who accepts our weaknesses and has borne our sicknesses, we must follow his example and shore up each other's infirmities by patience, so that God's name of honor assumed by us will not lose its meaning; for by the grace of Christ we are called children of God.

[8]For I tell you that Christ became a servant to the circumcised to show God's truthfulness, in order to confirm the promises given to the patriarchs,

Paul recalls the origin of the Jews. By the term *sons of circumcision*[4] he means the children of Abraham, to whom Christ was sent and ministered the grace promised to their ancestors. Thus the Savior said: *I am in your midst not to be served but to serve,*[5] as the truth in the promise made to the fathers is proved. For the circumcision of the flesh was given to Abraham as a figure of the circumcision of the heart, which later on the prophet said referred to the future: *Circumcise the hardness of your heart.*[6] Christ is the minister, that is to say, the preacher of this promised circumcision, and so are the apostles after him. They have come to minister the circumcision of the heart to those who are already circumcised in the flesh. As he says: *Just as you have sent me into this world, so I also have sent them into this world.*[7] The circumcision of the heart means removing the cloud of error and acknowledging God the Father as Creator and Christ his Son, by whom

---

[1]Jn 6:38. [2]Ps 69:9. [3]Jn 15:13. [4]A Hebraism translated here as "circumcised." [5]Lk 22:27. [6]Jer 4:4. [7]Jn 17:18.

he has created all things, so that the truth of God might be fulfilled. God had promised that he would give mercy, and had promised this to the ancestors of the Jews. As he had said to Abraham: *In your seed all the nations shall be blessed,*[1] and to David he said: *Of the fruit of your womb I shall place upon your seat,*[2] and *A star will arise from Jacob.*[3]

[9]*and in order that the Gentiles might glorify God for his mercy. As it is written,*
> *"Therefore will I praise thee among the Gentiles,*
> *and sing to thy name";*[4]

Since there was no promise made to the Gentiles, almost as if they were unworthy of one, it was only by mercy that they were accepted for salvation, so that they might honor God by their confession, because unbelievers do not honor God. He proves this by a quotation from the prophets. It is written in Psalm 17 that the Gentiles will be admitted to the grace of God in order to receive salvation.[5] This is the voice of Christ, which predicted what would happen in the future, that his name would be preached among the Gentiles, who would confess God and give him the glory for the gift they had received. This is why Christ says in the Gospel: *I confess to you, Father, Lord of heaven and earth, that you have hidden these things from the wise and prudent and revealed them to little ones, for so, Father, it seemed good to you.*[6] This is a confession of the One God in Trinity, from which springs joy, because after confessing the truth, the happy person will sing of the mercy and gift of God.

[10]*and again it is said,*
> *"Rejoice, O Gentiles, with his people";*[7]

This is from a song in Deuteronomy.

[11]*and again,*
> *"Praise the Lord, all Gentiles,*
> *and let all the peoples praise him";*[8]

God long ago decreed in Psalm 116[9] that by the intervention of his mercy Jews and Gentiles would be united. The Gentiles would be granted grace to become fellow heirs with the Jews, who by the grace of God were long ago named as his people. While the Jews were noble, the Gentiles were ignoble, but now by God's mercy the Gentiles have been made noble as well, so that all may rejoice together by acknowledging the truth. In the praise of the Gentiles all the peoples magnify God. In that of the twelve tribes, the Jews magnify the One God, because he has increased the number of his people by the addition of the Gentiles. Finally, when the Jews disagreed with the apostle Peter over Cornelius, they changed their tune when he explained the reason, and magnified God, saying: *Perhaps God has allotted repentance to the Gentiles also, so that they may receive life.*[10]

[12]*and further Isaiah says,*
> *"The root of Jesse shall come,*
> *he who rises to rule the Gentiles;*
> *in him shall the Gentiles hope."*[11]

In order to give the Gentiles greater assurance and a surer hope, Paul confirms by many examples that God's decree had been that all the nations would be blessed in Christ. There would be no sympathy for the insolence of the unbelieving Jews, nor would the minds of the Gentiles be unsettled by the thought that they were promising themselves hope to no purpose. Once they accepted the God of Abraham, the faith of his children was given to them, so that they might grow in the same joy and assurance.

Why is Christ said to be from the root of

---

[1]Gen 22:18. [2]Ps 132:11. [3]Num 24:17. [4]Ps 18:49; 2 Sam 22:50. [5]Ps 18:49 in English versions. [6]Mt 11:25-26. [7]Deut 32:43. [8]Ps 117:1 [9]Ps 116 in English versions. [10]Acts 11:18. [11]Is 11:10.

Jesse, and not from the root of Boaz, a righteous man, or of Obed? It is because he is said to be the Son of David on account of the kingdom, and just as he was born of God to be king, so also he was born of David according to the flesh. Therefore, the root of Jesse is the tree of David, which bore fruit on the branch which is the Virgin Mary, who gave birth to Christ.

13May the God of hope fill you with all joy and peace in believing, so that by the power of the Holy Spirit you may abound in hope.
14I myself am satisfied about you, my brethren, that you yourselves are full of goodness, filled with all knowledge, and able to instruct one another.

These are words of encouragement. By praising the Romans, Paul is exhorting them to better understanding and behavior. One who sees himself praised develops the work he has been given, so that the things which are said of him might be true. Therefore he did not say that they should teach one another but that they should encourage one another. Encouragement normally takes place when it becomes clear that something is undermining the mind, or that it has grown slack. The rest is clear and needs no explanation.

15But on some points I have written to you very boldly by way of reminder, because of the grace given me by God 16to be a minister of Christ Jesus to the Gentiles in the priestly service of the gospel of God, so that the offering of the Gentiles may be acceptable, sanctified by the Holy Spirit.

Paul says he has been given authority by the grace of God to embolden him to write to all the Gentiles, exhorting and confirming their calling in Christ, so that he might show his concern in the service of the gospel as a teacher of the Gentiles and so that their sacrifice

might be reckoned acceptable because of their sanctification in the Holy Spirit. Whatever is offered with a pure faith and a sober mind is purified by the Holy Spirit.

17In Christ Jesus, then, I have reason to be proud of my work for God. 18For I will not venture to speak of anything except what Christ has wrought through me to win obedience from the Gentiles, by word and deed,

Paul says that he has glory with God through Christ Jesus. By believing and serving Christ Jesus with a pure conscience, Paul has made himself worthy in the sight of God the Father, to the point that he can say that there is nothing which Christ has not done through him for the encouragement of the Gentiles. Christ has even used him to perform signs and wonders, so that their power might support the preaching of the gospel.

This is why he says that he has glory in Christ before God, for by serving Christ he has glory before God. He has not had any divine power which has not been given to him by God, but confesses that he has received everything which might help in the conversion of the Gentiles by the power of signs from him, who is the perfect dispenser. As a result, Paul can show that he is in no way inferior to the other apostles, who were with the Lord, nor did God do fewer or lesser miracles among the Gentiles, so that by Paul's witness they might grow when they saw that they had received the same grace that the Jews, who claimed the special privileges of their ancestors, had obtained.

19by the power of signs and wonders, by the power of the Holy Spirit, so that from Jerusalem and as far round as Illyricum I have fully preached the gospel of Christ, 20thus making it my ambition to preach the gospel, not where Christ has already been named, lest I build on another man's foundation,

It was not without reason that Paul says that he tried to preach in places where Christ had not been named. For he knew that false apostles went about sharing Christ in ways which were wrong, in order to ensnare the people by some other teaching under the name of Christ, which was then very difficult to put right afterward. Therefore he wanted to get there first, in order to lay the foundation of Christ's name in the right way. Later on they were persuaded of something else, which they absorbed differently. Because he was given as a master to the Gentiles, Paul had to take this mission seriously and teach in places where Christ had not yet been proclaimed, in order to confirm his authority and receive the full fruit of his labors from those whom he had planted. This is why he established a church in every place. Later on heresies would arise to corrupt the meaning of the law and faith by the subtlety of their wickedness, using the name of Christ as their pretext. He backs this up by quoting the law as follows.

[21]*but as it is written,*
> *"They shall see who have never been told of him,*
> *and they shall understand who have never heard of him."*[1]

Paul says that he was always quick to fill the Gentiles with the truth of the gospel, so that their understanding of the true Son of God might be correct and unshakable.

[22]*This is the reason why I have so often been hindered from coming to you.* [23]*But now, since I no longer have any room for work in these regions, and since I have longed for many years to come to you,* [24]*I hope to see you in passing as I go to Spain, and to be sped on my journey there by you, once I have enjoyed your company for a little.*

Here Paul explains what he has already mentioned at the beginning of the epistle,[2] and excuses himself by saying that although he wanted to come to them, he was obliged to shut out the wicked teachings of the false apostles. After finishing his preaching tour, Paul says that he will depart for the city of Rome, as he had long ago wanted to do. In the meantime he is encouraging the Romans, who had been instructed in the law, by letter. As for those who had not yet accepted the preaching of the gospel, he thought it would be better for them to be taught by him personally, so that once grounded in the right faith they would be much less likely to accept anything else. In order to prepare their minds, he also says that he would come to them when he was on his way to Spain, because Christ had not yet been named there.

Since the false apostles would have found the journey to Rome difficult, Paul thought that it would do no harm if he postponed his visit for a while.

[25]*At present, however, I am going to Jerusalem with aid for the saints.* [26]*For Macedonia and Achaia have been pleased to make some contribution for the poor among the saints at Jerusalem;*

Paul says that first he must go minister to the saints at Jerusalem. He wants the Romans to understand that they ought to be concerned with good works, for those who live because of mercy and who are justified before God ought to show their devotion to their brethren.

[27]*they were pleased to do it, and indeed they are in debt to them, for if the Gentiles have come to share in their spiritual blessings, they ought also to be of service to them in material blessings.*

Paul says that the Gentiles are debtors to Jew-

---

[1]Is 52:15. [2]Rom 1:13.

ish believers because they have been allowed to share in their spiritual gifts, and so now they must contribute to their bodily necessities. In this way the believers among the Jews would rejoice at God's providential saving of the Gentiles through their ministry. For these Gentiles, by giving themselves completely to the service of God and not caring at all about the things of this world, offered an example of good behavior to believers.

The apostle also wants us to be sympathetic and merciful, so that we may feel obliged to give alms and to do good works with a willing heart, because whoever hopes for mercy from God must be merciful, in order to prove that he has some reason for his hope. For if a man is merciful, how much more is God! For this is the payment or reward, that those who receive mercy should be merciful. As the Lord said: *Blessed are the merciful, for God will be merciful to them.*[1]

28*When therefore I have completed this, and have delivered to them what has been raised, I shall go on by way of you to Spain; *29*and I know that when I come to you I shall come in the fullness of the blessing of Christ.

Assured of the dispensation and grace of God, Paul promises that he will come to them with an abundance of the blessing of Christ, whom he preaches. The blessing refers to the miracles by which they have been strengthened.

30*I appeal to you, brethren, by our Lord Jesus Christ and by the love of the Spirit, to strive together with me in your prayers to God on my behalf, *31*that I may be delivered from the unbelievers in Judea, and that my service for Jerusalem may be acceptable to the saints,

Paul asks for their prayers so that he may escape the hands of unbelieving Jews, not because he deserves them, but because he is following the principle that the church ought to pray for its pastor. When many humble people come together and agree they become great, and the prayers of many people cannot be ignored, so if the Romans want to see the apostle, let them pray earnestly that he may be set free and that they may receive him in the joy of brotherly love.

32*so that by God's will I may come to you with joy and be refreshed in your company.

Paul also asks them to pray that his administration of the gifts might be accepted by the saints at Jerusalem, because he shows that he does everything with God's will behind him. Paul's mind is dedicated to delivering the gifts, and so he wants their mind to respond to him by the judgment of God, so that having understood his love for them, they might with one accord give thanks to God on his behalf. He was a great blessing to them because many were made happy by his ministry and are now praising God.

He would have great success if the majority of the brothers were united [behind him in prayer], particularly as the Lord says: *If two of you agree, whatever they ask my Father for will be done for them.*[2]

33*The God of peace be with you all. Amen.

The God of peace is Christ, who said: *My peace I give to you, my peace I leave with you.*[3] This is what he prays for them, knowing that the Lord said: *Behold I am with you always, even to the end of the world.*[4] Paul therefore wants them to be the kind of people in whom the Lord Jesus Christ dwells, who has shown them that all the discord caused by human sin has been taken away and who has given them what is true, that they may live peacefully in that truth.

---

[1]Mt 5:7. [2]Mt 18:19. [3]Jn 14:27. [4]Mt 28:20.

Romans 16

¹I commend to you our sister Phoebe, a deaconess of the church at Cenchreae, ²that you may receive her in the Lord as befits the saints, and help her in whatever she may require from you, for she has been a helper of many and of myself as well.

Paul commends Phoebe as *our sister*, that is, in the sense meant by the law. He commends her highly and says that she is a deaconess of the church at Cenchreae. She has been a great help to many, and Paul says that she should also be helped on her journey. In order to ensure that she would be consistently well treated and helped in all her needs if she came and approached them, Paul testifies that she had been with him also, so that the greater his person was in the sight of others, the more they would do their duty in love by doing what he asked of them.

³Greet Prisca and Aquila, my fellow workers in Christ Jesus, ⁴who risked their necks for my life, to whom not only I but also all the churches of the Gentiles give thanks; ⁵greet also the church in their house. Greet my beloved Epaenetus, who was the first convert in Asia for Christ.

These were Jews who, after their conversion, became coworkers with the apostle because they had believed correctly and were thus able to persuade others to accept the right faith. Apollos, for example, although he was learned in the Scriptures, was nevertheless taught the way of the Lord more correctly by them. This is why Paul calls them his fellow workers *in Christ Jesus*, for they worked with him in the gospel of God.

Aquila was the husband of Priscilla, and it is clear that they had gone to Rome on a mission, for they were very keen in their devotion to God. All the people whom Paul greets are understood to have been in Rome for the strengthening of the Romans. For that reason, Paul says that not only he but all the churches give thanks for them. He includes the Romans in this, so that they will be obedient to these people whom they hear are laboring for the benefit of the Gentiles by encouraging them to put their faith in the truth of Christ.

Paul also praises them because they have not run away from danger for his sake. They have not refused to suffer the enmity both of Jews and of false brethren in order to assist the apostle in service and love. The false brethren were those who believed in Christ but said that it was still necessary to keep the law, because they did not think that Christ was sufficient for the full effect of salvation. The apostle demolished this idea, which is why he suffered persecutions from them. He also greets their servants and employees, whom he calls the church, because they were disciples of holy men in the faith.

Paul mentions Epaenetus's claim to fame, in order to show that important people believe and turn to the faith, and in order to invite the leaders of the Romans to accept Christ, and if they have already done so, to become humble.

⁶Greet Mary, who has worked hard among you.

Paul reminds them of the name of Mary, whom we understand had labored unstintingly to encourage them, so that they would thank her for that.

⁷Greet Andronicus and Junias, my kinsmen and my fellow prisoners; they are men of note among the apostles, and they were in Christ before me.

They were Paul's kinsmen in flesh and in Spirit, as the angel said to Mary: *Behold, your kinswoman Elizabeth.*[1] He also declares by his own testimony that they followed the earlier apostles and shared his captivity for the sake of the faith. (The Jews had incited the Gentiles to persecute or imprison them.) For this reason they were to be all the more greatly honored.

8Greet Ampliatus, my beloved in the Lord.

Paul greets him as a friend, but as a friend in the Lord, because he had not shared Paul's work or his imprisonment.

9Greet Urbanus, our fellow worker in Christ, and my beloved Stachys.

Not only does Paul call Urbanus a fellow worker of his, but also an associate of others in spreading the faith. Paul calls Stachys his *beloved*, but even so he ranks him behind Urbanus as a colleague in the work of the gospel.

10Greet Apelles, who is approved in Christ. Greet those who belong to the family of Aristobulus.

Paul does not greet Apelles as a friend or fellow worker, but because he has been tried in temptations and found to be faithful to Christ. Aristobulus is to be understood as having assembled the brethren in Christ. Paul approves of this so much that he regards those whom he has gathered together to be worthy of greeting as well.

11Greet my kinsman Herodion. Greet those in the Lord who belong to the family of Narcissus.

When Paul calls Herodion his kinsman and nothing more, he shows that he was faithful in the love of the new birth, but he does not mention his perseverance. Narcissus is said to have been a presbyter of the time, and this is what we find in other manuscripts. He was not in Rome at the time, which is why you see Paul greeting those of his household in the Lord as saints. This presbyter Narcissus went about encouraging believers by his preaching. And since Paul did not know what the merits were of those who had been with him, he asks the Romans to greet those of his household who had put their trust in the Lord and who were therefore worthy of his greeting.

12Greet those workers in the Lord, Tryphaena and Tryphosa. Greet the beloved Persis, who has worked hard in the Lord.

Paul declares that Tryphaena and Tryphosa are worthy of equal honor in Christ. Persis appears to be more honored than the other two, because she has worked hard in the Lord. This work is one of encouragement and of service to the saints for Christ's sake, when they are under pressure and in need, because they had fled their homes and were being attacked by unbelievers.

13Greet Rufus, eminent in the Lord, also his mother and mine.

Paul mentions Rufus ahead of his mother because of the dispensation of God's grace, in which a woman has no place. For he was chosen, that is, promoted by the Lord to do his work. Nevertheless he had such a holy mother that the apostle calls her his mother also.

14Greet Asyncritus, Phlegon, Hermes, Patrobas, Hermas, and the brethren who are with them.

Paul greets these together because he knew that they agreed with one another in Christ and were loyal friends. He also greets the brethren who were with them, but omits their names.

---

[1]Lk 1:36.

15Greet Philologus, Julia, Nereus and his sister, and Olympas, and all the saints who are with them.

These are understood to have been of one mind because it was for that reason that Paul greeted them together. He knew of their worth from those who had been with them. He calls them saints because they seemed to him to be worthy of salvation.

16Greet one another with a holy kiss. All the churches of Christ greet you.

Paul asks that all those to whom he has written and whom he names be greeted with a holy kiss, that is, in the peace of Christ, not in the desire of the flesh, because these kisses are spiritual, not physical.

By saying *churches of Christ* Paul is saying that there is a church which is not Christ's. David called the company of evildoers a church of the wicked.[1] Therefore Paul says that the churches of all those places greeted them, so that they might grow in their faith. He refers this back to the earlier meaning in order to show that it is Christ in whom salvation is to be found, he to whom the faithful Christian people belong, and by his will that the whole creation lives, for he is the author of life, as the apostle Peter says,[2] and not the keeping of the law, as some of them thought.

17I appeal to you, brethren, to take note of those who create dissensions and difficulties, in opposition to the doctrine which you have been taught; avoid them. 18For such persons do not serve our Lord Christ, but their own appetites, and by fair and flattering words they deceive the hearts of the simple-minded. 19For while your obedience is known to all, so that I rejoice over you, I would have you wise as to what is good and guileless as to what is evil;

Now Paul goes on to mention the false apostles, whom he warns against throughout the epistle, just as he does here as well, but he attacks their teaching without saying what it was. They were forcing believers to become Jews, and thereby making the benefits of God worthless, as I said above. They compiled long genealogies and used them to support their teaching, by which they were deceiving the hearts of the simple. *Your obedience is known to all*, Paul says, which means what he said at the beginning of the letter: *Your faith is proclaimed in all the world.*[3] The doctrine which he says they have followed is not the same as what he has been expounding throughout the letter, but what they had learned at their conversion. Paul wants them to benefit from those whom he is greeting.

I rejoice over you. Here too the meaning refers back to the earlier part of the letter. Paul rejoices because the Romans, who appeared to have an empire, submitted themselves to the Christian faith.

Being *wise as to what is good* means doing good works, while being *guileless as to what is evil* means having no knowledge of bad works, that is to say, not knowing how to do evil.

20then the God of peace will soon crush Satan under your feet. The grace of our Lord Jesus Christ be with you.

Paul say this about his own coming to them, for then he will crush the devil so that they will be able to receive spiritual grace. Satan gets angry at that, because he wants people to remain in sin. The grace which he has promised he will give them when he comes, he now prays that they will have. For if they deserve to receive that grace, then he is already with them in spirit.

21Timothy, my fellow worker, greets you; so do

---

[1]Cf. Ps 26:5. [2]Cf. Acts 3:15. [3]Rom 1:8.

Lucius and Jason and Sosipater, my kinsmen.

Timothy was a fellow worker of Paul's as a cobishop, and he governed the church with great care. The Jews hated him to the point that he was circumcised because of it,[1] since his mother was Jewish and he could not be a teacher without being circumcised. Paul calls these people his kinsmen, partly by blood and partly by faith.

22I Tertius, the writer of this letter, greet you in the Lord.

Tertius was his name, not a number (third). He was the scribe who wrote the epistle, and Paul allowed him to send his own greetings to the Romans to whom he was writing, so that they might greet the others whom he names. At that time there were heads of churches in very few places.

23Gaius, who is host to me and to the whole church, greets you. Erastus, the city treasurer, and our brother Quartus, greet you.

I think that this is the same Gaius to whom John wrote, rejoicing in the love which he showed to the brethren and being always ready to meet their needs.[2] Earlier Paul had said: *All the churches of Christ greet you,*[3] which he now repeats—I think for a good reason. A man as great and flexible as Paul never wrote anything that was unnecessary. Because earlier he had said *all the churches of Christ greet you*—that is, all the saints, as he says elsewhere: *Those who belong to Christ have crucified the flesh*[4]— he now adds greetings to those who follow, thereby covering the entire membership of the church twice, because in every church there are two different types of people. It is possible that he was referring to the churches of two provinces, so that in the first instance he meant all the churches of one province and in the next all the churches of the other, but more probably he meant the churches of the Jews and of the Gentiles.

24The grace of our Lord Jesus Christ be with you all. Amen.[5]

Paul places Christ through whom we were made and again remade by his grace at the end of his epistle, so that he might stick in our minds, for if we are mindful of his benefits he will always look after us, as he said: *Behold, I am with you always, even to the end of the world.*[6]

25Now to him who is able to strengthen you according to my gospel and the preaching of Jesus Christ, according to the revelation of the mystery which was kept secret for long ages 26but is now disclosed and through the prophetic writings is made known to all nations, according to the command of the eternal God, to bring about the obedience of faith—27to the only wise God be glory for evermore through Jesus Christ! Amen.

Paul gives glory to God the Father, from whom are all things, that he might be pleased to fill the congregation of the Romans with his grace, as he can do, by confirming their minds in faith, for the advancing of the gospel and the revelation of the mystery hidden for long ages, which has now been made manifest in Christ.

The mystery which is eternally hidden in God was revealed in the time of Christ, for God is not alone, but from all eternity he has his Word and the Paraclete with him. God decreed that every creature was to be saved by coming to a knowledge of this truth. The truth of this mystery had been indicated by the prophets in symbols, and it was known

---

[1]Acts 16:3. [2]3 Jn 1-3. [3]Rom 16:16. [4]Gal 5:24. [5]In Ambrosiaster's text, this verse comes at the very end of the epistle. [6]Mt 28:20.

only to God. Paul wanted all the Gentiles to share in God's grace, which was unknown to the human race. God alone is wise, because all wisdom comes from him, as Solomon says: *All wisdom comes from the Lord God and has always been with him.*[1] This wisdom is Jesus Christ, who is from God and was with God forever, through whom be glory to him forever and ever. Amen.

Without Christ nothing is complete, because all things are through him. It is acknowledged that praise is given to God the Father through him, because it is understood that *through Christ* means *through his wisdom*, in whom he has saved believers. Therefore glory to the Father through the Son is glory to both in the Holy Spirit, because both are present in the one glory.

[1] Sir 1:1.

AMBROSIASTER
Commentary on 1 Corinthians

Preface

Prompted by the Lord's command, Paul stayed with the Corinthians for eighteen months and taught the Word of God among them. It is because of this that he treats them with great confidence and loving affection, sometimes warning and censuring them, and sometimes treating them fondly as if they were his own children. There are many reasons why he was writing to them. The first is that some godly people were disagreeing with one another like heretics, wanting to be called followers of Paul, of Peter or of Apollos, rather than of Christ, and Paul strongly disapproved of this. But there were also some people there who disagreed with them and declared their allegiance to Christ alone.

The second reason is that the Corinthians were beginning to find pleasure in eloquence and worldly philosophy, with the result that although they were nominally Christian, they were imbued with notions which were contrary to the faith. The third reason is that they were puffed up with anger, because Paul had not been to visit them. The fourth reason concerned someone who was guilty of fornication, whom they were allowing to remain in their midst. The fifth reason was Paul's need to remind the Corinthians of a previous letter which he had written before the one which we call the first.

The sixth reason is that the Corinthians were behaving unlawfully and fraudulently toward one another, and preferred to seek re-

dress in the pagan courts. The seventh reason is that, although Paul was allowed to accept financial support, he refused to do so, so as not to set a precedent for rapacious pseudo-apostles. The eighth reason was the need for Paul to respond to the Corinthians' letter, for they were beginning to be thrown into confusion by heretics on the subject of marriage. The ninth reason was his assertion that everyone should remain steadfast in what he has believed. The tenth reason concerned virgins, about whom Paul had been given no instructions. And there are other reasons as well, which will become apparent in the body of the text.

1 Corinthians 1

[1]Paul, called by the will of God to be an apostle of Christ Jesus, and our brother Sosthenes,

Paul begins his epistle to the Romans differently, because his subject matter is different. He writes to the Corinthians that he is an apostle of Jesus Christ by the will of God, because everything which he has done, he has done by the will of the Son of God, who said to him: *Depart, for I will send you far away to the Gentiles.*[1] In these words he is also alluding to those [false apostles] who had not been sent by Christ and whose teaching was not true. He often uses the names *God* and *Christ* in order to show that Christ is God but not the Father, or that Christ is the Son although the Father is also God, and that they are not identical, be-

---

[1]Acts 22:21.

cause it is clear that the Son is being spoken of [as a distinct person]. There were many sects which had emerged and which preached Christ according to their own whims. They broke up churches, and some of their dried-up branches are still with us today. For this reason, Paul sets out everything which is opposed to the heresies and asserts that he is a true preacher because he has been sent by Christ, according to God's will.

Paul commends Sosthenes by associating him with himself.

2To the church of God which is at Corinth, to those sanctified in Christ Jesus, called to be saints together with all those who in every place call on the name of our Lord Jesus Christ, both their Lord and ours:

Paul writes to the church as a whole, because at that time leaders had not yet been appointed for individual churches. He censures them for many things, but in spite of that he still says *to those sanctified in Christ Jesus*. This is because they have been born again in Christ and are therefore sanctified. However, they later began to behave badly, so that although the whole church was sanctified in Christ, some members of it had been deflected from the truth by the wicked teaching of the false apostles.

The Corinthians were called to be saints, which means that they could not deviate from the narrow path of sanctification. Paul linked them, as Gentiles, with the true Jews, because salvation is of the Jews, so that wherever there are Gentiles who call on the name of the Lord Jesus Christ, and wherever there are true Jews, both are united in him. But the false apostles, who preached the name of Christ in accordance with the wisdom of this world, criticized the law and the prophets. Like Marcion and Mani, they maintained that Christ was not really crucified, but that it merely appeared

that he had been. For this reason, the apostle says: *but we preach Christ crucified.*[1] Neither did they believe in the resurrection of the body, which the prophet Isaiah proclaims when he says: *The dead shall live, their bodies shall rise.*[2]

3Grace to you and peace from God our Father and the Lord Jesus Christ.

In order not to appear to have said nothing about the name of the Father and his gift, because he had said *Whoever invokes the name of our Lord Jesus Christ*, and in order not to give any accidental pretext for believing that there is no difference between them, Paul teaches that Christ should be invoked in prayer, but that all grace comes from the Father. In this way he shows that the two are one in their divinity, but primacy belongs to the authority of the Father.

4I give thanks to God always for you because of the grace of God which was given you in Christ Jesus,

Although Paul is writing to everybody in the church, he nevertheless indicates, whenever he rebukes or praises anyone, that each person should realize what is being said both for and against him. Paul is writing to two different groups inside the one fellowship of the church. When he is casting blame, he wants those who are behaving badly to recognize that these remarks are intended for them. Likewise, when he is awarding praise, he wants those who are doing the right thing to know that he has them in mind. This is why he says: *I give thanks to God always for you in Christ Jesus.* He says that grace is given by God in Christ Jesus, because God has decreed that a person who believes in Christ can be saved without works; by faith alone he receives the forgiveness of his sins.

---

[1]1 Cor 1:23. [2]Is 26:19.

⁵*that in every way you were enriched in him with all speech and all knowledge—*

This means that the Corinthians have remained steadfast in the grace which they have received and in the preaching of the doctrine of truth, because they have acquired spiritual knowledge. Paul therefore gives thanks to God for these things.

⁶*even as the testimony to Christ was confirmed among you—*

The testimony of Christ has been confirmed in them because they have been strengthened by their faith and had come to put no trust in man. Rather, all their hope was in Christ, for they were ensnared neither by pleasure nor by the enticements of pleasure.

⁷*so that you are not lacking in any spiritual gift, as you wait for the revealing of our Lord Jesus Christ;*

It is clear that Paul was a circumspect man who was full of anxiety as he awaited the day of judgment. He says that on that day the Lord Jesus Christ will be revealed both to believers and to unbelievers, so that the latter will realize that what they did not want to believe is in fact true, and the former will rejoice, finding that what they believed in is more wonderful than they had imagined.

⁸*who will sustain you to the end, guiltless in the day of our Lord Jesus Christ.*

Trusting in his keen intelligence, Paul is confident that the Corinthians will persevere in righteousness until the day of judgment. People who could not be shaken in spite of so many turmoils and disagreements proved that they would remain faithful to the end. In praising them, Paul is also challenging those who had been corrupted by the errors of the false apostles, for in proclaiming the faith of the former, he is calling the latter to repentance.

⁹*God is faithful, by whom you were called into the fellowship of his Son, Jesus Christ our Lord.*

Who can doubt the promises and faithfulness of God? It will happen exactly as he said it would, that believers in Christ will be his adopted children. He gives us this assurance: because we believe that Christ is the Son of God, we become his adopted children and are destined to remain in that exalted position just as Christ himself does, the man whom we believe is the Son of God. Fellowship is brotherhood, and just as Paul declares God's unfailing faithfulness toward us in this regard, so we must not be found to be faithless and treacherous with respect to our adoption, but rather we must remain faithful in it.

¹⁰*I appeal to you, brethren, by the name of our Lord Jesus Christ, that all of you agree and that there be no dissensions among you, but that you be united in the same mind and the same judgment.*

Paul prays that the Corinthians will all think one thing, namely, that those who have been born again are children of God. He addresses the whole church, so that those who have started to turn away may return to their earlier faith, which those who had persevered in it would therefore glorify all the more. He wants them to be perfectly united in the teaching which he had given them, and challenges them to think this way and to defend his teaching, following the example of those whom he praised earlier.

¹¹*For it has been reported to me by Chloe's people that there is quarreling among you, my brethren.*

Although they have been corrupted, Paul still calls the Corinthians his brothers, just as in Isaiah God tells the prophet's followers to say to those who had trusted in false prophets: *You are our brothers.*[1] The reason for this was that they should not quarrel with them because of their fraternal relationship.

As for "Chloe's people" some commentators think that they are those who remain faithful and bear fruit in the faith of Christ. Others think that Chloe is a place, as if one were to say "Antioch's people," for example. But others think that she was a woman devoted to God, in whose company there were many faithful worshipers whose trustworthiness was not questioned when they reported from Corinth that *there are disputes among you.* They said that there were disputes among them in order to show that they were divided about the Lord's teaching. The nature of this disagreement is stated next.

[12]What I mean is that each one of you says, "I belong to Paul," or "I belong to Apollos," or "I belong to Cephas," or "I belong to Christ."

Paul exposes their error without mentioning the names of the people responsible, who did not stay put but wandered about trying to confuse simple people. The men whom he names here were undoubtedly all good teachers, but by alluding to them in this way he is really getting at the false apostles. For if the Corinthians were not to boast of their devotion to any of these men, how much more would this be true in the case of false teachers, whose corrupt doctrine he refers to next? Note however that Paul also mentions that there were steadfast people among them, who said that they were of Christ, and not of any man, and these people are praised earlier on.

[13]Is Christ divided? Was Paul crucified for you? Or were you baptized in the name of Paul?

By believing different things about Christ, the people have divided him. One person thought that Christ was a mere man, another that he was only God. One says that he was foretold by the prophets, while another denies it. Since only Christ is both God and man, these people divide him by each claiming something different about him. Because they hold many church meetings in his own name, Paul adds: *Was Paul crucified for you?* He starts with himself, so that nobody will think that he is disparaging the status of others in order to commend his own. If Christ died for us, argues Paul, how can we attribute his grace and blessing to men, thereby doing him a grave injustice?

[14]I am thankful that I baptized none of you except Crispus and Gaius; [15]lest any one should say that you were baptized in my name. [16](I did baptize also the household of Stephanas. Beyond that, I do not know whether I baptized any one else.)

Paul thanks God that he has not baptized many of the Corinthians because he did not want an erroneous opinion like this to be associated with his name. He is arguing here against both the baptizers and the baptized, who were insulting their Savior by attributing the grace of his baptism to men in order to glorify those liars.

These Corinthians were like the Novatianists and the Donatists of today, who claim baptism for themselves and do not recognize anybody else's. Those who are so baptized glory in the names of Novatian and Donatus, having been deprived of the name of Christ. Crispus and Gaius are called as witnesses, because although they were baptized by Paul, they never suggested that he should be given

---

[1]Cf. Is 66:5.

any glory because of it. The household of Stephanas are the *firstfruits of Achaia*, as he says toward the end of the letter, where he testifies that they have consecrated themselves to the service of the saints.[1]

¹⁷*For Christ did not send me to baptize but to preach the gospel, and not with eloquent wisdom, lest the cross of Christ be emptied of its power.*

Because it is a greater thing to preach the gospel than to baptize, Paul says that he was sent to do the former, not the latter. The dignity of all ordinations belongs to a bishop, because he is the head of the other limbs. In this way, Paul also humbles those whom the Corinthians were honoring simply because they had been baptized by them. He tells them that it is no great thing to baptize, because not everyone who baptizes is competent to preach the gospel. After all, the words used at baptism are an established formula. When Cornelius became a believer, the apostle Peter gave orders that he should be baptized along with his household, but he did not bother to do it himself when he had his assistants standing by. He would only have done it himself if they had not been there and there was no other choice. Paul thus shows how much better he was than the people whom the Corinthians were honoring, but he does not allow this conclusion to be drawn by referring to himself, knowing full well how dangerous it is to arrogate the glory of God to the name of a mere man. In its own way, that is idolatry!

It was because Christian preaching does not need elaborate refinement of verbal expression that fishermen, who were uneducated, were chosen to preach the gospel. In that way the truth of the message would be its own recommendation, witnessed to by its own inner power. It would not depend on the cleverness or ingenuity of human wisdom, like those disciplines which are human inventions, where verbal dexterity has replaced the search for logic and virtue. Anyone who tries to commend the Christian faith in this way is seeking his own glory, because his splendid rhetoric obscures the truth and brings praise to the speaker, not to the faith he is supposedly proclaiming. The false apostles were doing just that, preaching according to the wisdom of this world so as not to appear foolish to the worldly-wise. They were cultivating their rhetorical brilliance and at the same time omitting things which the world does not believe, like the virgin birth of Christ and his resurrection from the dead. It was for this reason that Paul said that he was not preaching according to human wisdom, because he did not want to nullify the power of the cross of Christ. Anyone who proclaims Christ in that way denies the truth of Paul's preaching, as I have already said.

¹⁸*For the word of the cross is folly to those who are perishing, but to us who are being saved it is the power of God.*

It is clear that those who think the cross of Christ is foolish are lost, because they have not been rescued from the death of hell. But there is nothing unclear to those who believe that the cross is the power of God. They believe that the cross of Christ is not weakness but power, because they understand that in the cross death has been conquered. Those who have the sign of the cross are saved, because death cannot hold them captive.

¹⁹*For it is written,*
  "*I will destroy the wisdom of the wise,*
  ** *and the cleverness of the clever I will***
  **   *thwart.*"**

God destroys the wisdom of the wise by doing

---

[1] 1 Cor 16:15.

what the wise say cannot be done, and he rejects the cleverness of the clever when he shows that a supposedly uncaring Deity has drawn near to things which they regard as foolish. For example, the Son of God became man of a virgin and was crucified for the salvation of the human race. This action truly speaks louder than words.

20Where is the wise man? Where is the scribe? Where is the debater of this age? Has not God made foolish the wisdom of the world?

Here Paul attacks the Jews as much as the Gentiles, because their scribes and doctors of the law think that it is foolish to believe that God has a son. Gentiles also laugh at this, but the Jews' unbelief is based on the fact that the matter is not openly stated in the law, whereas the Gentiles think it is silly because the reasoning of the world does not accept it, claiming that nothing can be made without sexual union. The debater of this age is a man who thinks that the world is governed by the conjunction of the stars and that births and deaths are brought about by the twelve signs of the zodiac.

The wisdom of this world is made foolish, because the world, which thinks that it is wise, turns out to have been exactly the opposite. What the world thought was impossible, because it imagined that God was totally uncaring, is shown to be possible. Is there anything more foolish than the belief that the creator does not care about the world he has made? What would be the point of making it in that case? It is because they see some people enjoying life and others not, because they see the righteous suffering while the wicked boast, that they have come to believe that God does not care. But to say this is to say that God is malevolent and unjust. Either he will judge the world, or else he is unjust,

playing tricks with good men and allowing evil to spread unchecked. If they can think straight and lay aside their hatred for God's law, they will see that the question is not finally decided by us. We are simply waiting for God's judgment, when those who have been violently oppressed will be honored and the violent will be humbled, *for God shows no respect of persons.*[1]

21For since, in the wisdom of God, the world did not know God through wisdom, it pleased God through the folly of what we preach to save those who believe.

The world has not recognized God, but has attributed divine majesty to his creatures and to the elemental powers of the universe, thinking that visible things ought to be worshiped. God has therefore chosen a form of preaching which will seem foolish to such people, so that those who reject what they believe may be saved while they themselves are condemned. This is how the false is condemned by the true according to the mind of God.

22For Jews demand signs and Greeks seek wisdom,

The Jews seek signs because they do not reject the possibility that things like this can happen. What they want to know is whether it has actually occurred, like Aaron's rod which sprouted and bore fruit,[2] and Jonah who spent three days and nights in the belly of the whale before being spewed out alive.[3] What they really want is to see something like what Moses saw: God in the burning [bush].[4] This is why they say: *we know that God spoke to Moses,*[5] even though the fact that Lazarus emerged alive from the tomb, after being dead and even rotting for four days, was a much greater miracle. But the Greeks seek wisdom, refusing

---

[1]Rom 2:11. [2]Cf. Num 17:8. [3]Cf. Jon 2:1-10. [4]Cf. Ex 3:2. [5]Jn 9:29.

to believe anything which does not accord with human reason.

²³but we preach Christ crucified, a stumbling block to Jews and folly to Gentiles,

It is a stumbling block to the Jews when they hear Christ calling himself the Son of God yet not observing the sabbath, and it is foolishness to the Gentiles because they hear things like the virgin birth and the resurrection being preached, although they are irrational.

²⁴but to those who are called, both Jews and Greeks, Christ the power of God and the wisdom of God.

With a power which is stronger than words, Jews who believe in Christ understand that he is the power of God, and when Greeks believe in him, they understand that he is the wisdom of God and that the worldly wisdom which they previously had regarded as sensible is in fact the greatest foolishness. Christ is God's power because the Father does everything through him, and he is God's wisdom, because God is known through him. It would not be possible for God to be known through anyone who was not from him in the first place, because *no one has seen the Father except the Son, and whomever the Son has chosen to reveal him to.*[1]

²⁵For the foolishness of God is wiser than men, and the weakness of God is stronger than men.

Paul talks about *the foolishness of God*, not because God is foolish, but because his reasoning is spiritual and not in accordance with the reasoning of his world. It is wiser than men, because spiritual things are wiser than carnal ones. Spiritual things do not exist through carnal ones, but the other way round, and there-

fore carnal things are subordinate to spiritual ones. Similarly, heavenly things are stronger than earthly ones, so the weakness of God is not really weak at all, because the weakness of Christ is a great victory. He conquers just when he appears to be defeated, as he says in Psalm 49: *You shall conquer when you are judged.*[2] When he was killed, he emerged as the victor, and turned the accusation back on his persecutors.

²⁶For consider your call, brethren; not many of you were wise according to worldly standards, not many were powerful, not many were of noble birth;

It is obvious that those who are puffed up by the knowledge of this world, rather than truly learned, that is to say, those who observe and divine the motions of the stars, are few in number. In worldly terms, these people are wise and therefore powerful. They can assert that the suffering of Christ on the cross is a sign of his weakness, because for the time being, wickedness appears to be powerful and victorious. The same people are also noble, because they claim that their superstitions are of ancient origin, and look down on us as parvenus. But God is not elitist in his choice of believers.

²⁷but God chose what is foolish in the world to shame the wise, God chose what is weak in the world to shame the strong,

The foolish things of the world are the virgin birth of Christ and his resurrection from the dead, because they are the things that the worldly-wise regard as foolish. The wise are confounded because they see that what a few of them deny, the many profess to be true. There is no doubt that the opinions of the many take precedence over those of a small

---

[1]Mt 11:27. [2]Cf. Ps 50:6 in English versions. The translation is not accurate.

number. Likewise, those few who are wise in this world think our faith is weak, but they are put to shame by the vast numbers of people who, to their embarrassment, assert that it is the power [of God]. They see the so-called weak things of Christ overturning demons and performing miracles. To the world the injuries and sufferings of the Savior are weak things, because the world does not understand that these make for power, because Christ submitted to suffering in order to overcome death. To suffer unjustly and to be able to resist is glory for the sufferer and damnation for the killer.

28God chose what is low and despised in the world, even things that are not, to bring to nothing things that are,

God chose ignoble and contemptible things (not that they are really ignoble and contemptible; this is how the world sees them) because by believing in Christ they have despised worldly reasoning. God did this in order to destroy things which are really ignoble and contemptible, because those who judge are more deserving of judgment and condemnation. Their teaching is asserted in words but not demonstrated in power, and so it is destroyed, but our teaching is proved true not only by words, but by power as its witness as well.

29so that no human being might boast in the presence of God.

The wisdom of the flesh should blush at its error, under the judgment of God. For the opinion of the flesh rejects the belief that a virgin conceived by the power of God, and so on. The reasoning of this world, which is related to the flesh, cannot accept such things.

30He is the source of your life in Christ Jesus, whom God made our wisdom, our righteous-

ness and sanctification and redemption;

In the faith of Christ we belong to God, the Almighty. It was God's plan that we should learn of his truth and mercy through Christ. His truth is the mystery of the Trinity, and his mercy is seen in the fact that he redeemed us from our captivity. Christ did what he did in order to strengthen believers. We are to know that we have learned wisdom, and have been sanctified, justified and redeemed by God through Christ, for no one can redeem something which did not originally belong to him. Therefore, whether it is because we have been redeemed or because we have been sanctified (i.e., purged from the works of the flesh and the filthiness of idols), or because we have been justified (for it is just to worship the creator and spurn everything else), or because we are wise, having learned that worldly people are unwise—all this is a gift of God through Christ. But this is our redemption—when the devil desires it, Christ offers himself to the devil so that he may cancel sin and rescue the devil's captives.

31therefore, as it is written, "Let him who boasts, boast of the Lord."[1]

What Jeremiah says is commendable, because the person who glories in the Lord will not be confounded. God's workmanship and magnificence are apparent in his acts, which is why he says [in effect]: Let those who worship idols, which do not send rain and have not made heaven and earth, be confounded, along with those who glory in men whom they know to be powerless, as Scripture says: *Hope in man is vain.*[2]

1 Corinthians 2

1When I came to you, brethren, I did not come

---

[1]Cf. Jer 9:24. [2]Cf. Jer 17:5.

proclaiming to you the testimony of God in lofty words or wisdom. [2]For I decided to know nothing among you except Jesus Christ and him crucified.

Earlier in the letter, Paul gradually showed us the shape of our faith, but now he demonstrates that he preaches it to others in no other way than the one he has just used with the Corinthians, because he has spoken to them about the mystery of Christ in speech that was humble and in preaching that was "foolish" in the world's terms. What Paul calls the mystery here is that which was incarnate, what had been hidden from all ages with God, is God the Word. Heretics played fast and loose with these things and preached their wicked doctrine with great eloquence. Following the wisdom of the world they emptied Christ's cross of its power. They did not preach that Christ was born of a virgin, nor that he was truly crucified, because it seemed foolish to say such things. The apostle John also refers to such people when he says: *Whoever denies that Christ has come in the flesh is antichrist, and whoever denies the Son, denies the Father also.*[1] These heretics claimed that the Father was himself called the Son as well, and Marcion got his error from them. He preached secret doctrines, not revealing what they really meant, but wanting them to be understood according to the wisdom of the world, which is hostile to true faith. Paul wants us to figure out the things he was attacking from the judgment he passes on them. He shows that everything the world laughs at as foolish in our faith could be found in the Corinthian church. He refers to the body because the function of each of its members can be worked out by considering the whole. These things were clear enough to the Corinthians, of course, because they were not unaware of what they were being censured for.

[3]And I was with you in weakness and in much fear and trembling;

By preaching Christ in what appeared to be folly to human wisdom, Paul provoked hatred and persecution against himself, because he appeared to be proclaiming something which was nonsensical and hostile to Jews and Gentiles alike.

[4]and my speech and my message were not in plausible words of wisdom, but in demonstration of the Spirit and of power,

Paul shows that he had no desire to flatter human wisdom or cultivate the art of rhetoric merely to gain the approval of men. Rather he has been faithful to his Master, who wanted his teaching to gain acceptance, not by the appeal of human tradition or by the clamor of words, but by the deeds themselves, because deeds speak louder than words. The deeds may be phrased in words which seem weak when put alongside power, and perhaps they seem foolish to the wise of this world, but God did not want his gospel to be preached by the witness of mere words. He wanted it to go out in power, so that what people think is the foolishness of the Word may show by its actions that it is wisdom founded on the reasoning of the Spirit.

[5]that your faith might not rest in the wisdom of men but in the power of God.
[6]Yet among the mature we do impart wisdom, although it is not a wisdom of this age or of the rulers of this age, who are doomed to pass away.

The mature are those who preach the cross as wisdom because of the witness of Christ's power at work. They know that actions speak louder than words. Their wisdom is not of this

---

[1]Cf. 1 Jn 2:22-23.

age, but of the age to come, when the truth of God will be manifested to those who now deny it. The present age does not accept this way of thinking because worldly thought is weak. It is obvious that this wisdom does not belong to the princes of this world, who are being destroyed by it. Christianity roots out and destroys the errors which they have sown— idolatry, greed and other vices, to quote the apostle John: *The Son of God came to undo the works of the devil.*[1]

[7]But we impart a secret and hidden wisdom of God, which God decreed before the ages for our glorification.

Paul testifies that he has been sent to reveal a secret wisdom which the princes of this world do not know and the world has not heard, and which is therefore thought to be stupid. But the evidence of its power shows that it is rational and has the power to save; every effort of human reasoning falls back before its might. The wisdom of God is hidden because it is not in words but in power. It is impossible in human terms, but can be believed by the power of the Spirit. Wisdom is so far said to have been always present in God that Paul claims it was foreordained before the beginning of time, for the glory of us who believe. God foresaw the future sins of the world he was about to create and therefore decreed this in order to confound those who would turn his wisdom into their own stupidity, and also to glorify us, who would believe it.

[8]None of the rulers of this age understood this; for if they had, they would not have crucified the Lord of glory.

The rulers of this age are not only those who were great among the Jews and the Romans, but every spiritual power referred to above, to whom this saying applies and against whom we struggle: *The spiritual powers of evil in the heavenly places.*[2] It was by their decision and their will that Christ was crucified. After the temptations which the devil dared to inflict on our Lord, *he departed*, says the Evangelist, *until the time* [should come].[3] The Lord himself says: *The prince of this world has come and found nothing in me.*[4] The rulers of this world crucified the Lord of glory through their ignorance. The Jewish rulers cannot be called rulers of this age because they were subject to the Romans. Nor did the Romans crucify Jesus, because Pilate himself said: *I find no reason to put him to death,*[5] and as a result washed his hands, telling the Jews: *I am innocent of the blood of this man; see to it yourselves.*[6] These are the ones who crucified him, over whom he triumphed in his own person. They crucified him, even though Mark the Evangelist says that *they knew that Jesus was the Christ.*[7] They certainly did know that he was the one who was promised in the Law, but they did not know his secret, which was that he was the Son of God. Peter the apostle said this to the Jews as well: *I know, brothers, that you did this evil thing through ignorance, as did your rulers*, though he did not add the words *of this age.*[8] But even if the servants killed their master through ignorance and so ought not to pay the price for their sin, they still should not be allowed to continue in their ignorance. They may not have known that he was their master, but they still knew that they were doing something wrong. The crucified one is called the Lord of glory because he does not know what death is. Death is ascribed to him because the Word has been made flesh, in other words, the Son of God has become a man, and of course the Jews were not merely persecuting the flesh, but the one who was functioning in the flesh. Therefore, although the Lord of glory does

---

[1]Cf. 1 Jn 3:8. [2]Eph 6:12. [3]Lk 4:13. [4]Jn 14:30. [5]Lk 23:22. [6]Mt 27:24. [7]Mk 1:41 (variant). [8]Acts 3:17.

not know what death is, so far as the avowed intention of the Jews is concerned, as well as that of the rulers of this world, they killed the Lord in the flesh.

⁹But, as it is written,
"What no eye has seen, nor ear heard,
nor the heart of man conceived,
what God has prepared for those who love
him,"[1]

These words were expressed somewhat differently by Isaiah, and they are also found in the apocryphal *Apocalypse of Elijah*. Paul uses them to refer to the incarnation of Christ, which not only goes against human perception but is beyond the understanding of heavenly powers as well. Paul wanted to underline what he had already said, namely, that if the rulers of this world have not understood that the Lord has become a man, how much more have other men failed to understand this! But if expressing this doctrine in words caused scandal, this was no reason to deny the faith, given its power and its wonderful signs. Its power should have been rated more highly than human weakness and ignorance, and what seemed impossible to human reason should have been believed. God has prepared this gift for those who love him—in other words, for believers.

¹⁰God has revealed to us through the Spirit. For the Spirit searches everything, even the depths of God.

Because the rulers of this world were ignorant of this, God revealed these things through his Spirit to believers, for the things of God cannot be understood without the Spirit of God. Paul says that he is declaring that the holy revelation was given not only to human beings, but also to the rulers and powers of the heavenly realms who crucified the Lord, so that those who dwell in the created heavens and live below the elements of the firmament may be taught by his preaching of these things on earth. The apostle's uniqueness is such that he alone has received the grace to expound the doctrine of the Trinity in the way he did, and for this reason he has often been called the divinely chosen vessel.[2]

The Holy Spirit is of God, and therefore knows everything about him. Paul talks about *the deep things of God* because he knows God's power and foreknowledge, which nothing in his creation is capable of.

¹¹For what person knows a man's thoughts except the spirit of the man which is in him? So also no one comprehends the thoughts of God except the Spirit of God.

It is obvious that only our rational soul, which Paul calls our *spirit*, knows what our thoughts are. In his Gospel, Luke says, among other things: *And her spirit returned to her.*[3] Likewise only the Spirit of God knows what is in God. The Spirit of God has taught us what he knows by nature, not what he has been taught himself. Furthermore he has taught us about the mystery of Christ, because he is not just the Spirit of God, but the Spirit of Christ as well.

¹²Now we have received not the spirit of the world, but the Spirit which is from God, that we might understand the gifts bestowed on us by God.

We know that we have received the Spirit of God because the spirit of this world cannot know the things which God has revealed to us. The *spirit of the world* is the one by which godless madmen are possessed. Of all the worldly spirits which exist, the most power-

---

[1]Is 64:4; 65:17. [2]Cf. Acts 9:15. [3]Lk 8:55.

ful is called Python, because it is he who guesses what will happen in the world. He deceives people by illusions which appear to be real, and has spoken through the Sibyl, using the reasoning common among our people and striving for a place among the heavenly beings.[1] It is because we have been given the Spirit of God that we understand what we have received from him. We could not have understood this if we had only the spirit of the world, because the spirit of the world cannot know such things. No one knows the mind of God except the Spirit of God who comes from him. Inferior beings cannot know the mind of superior ones, nor can a creature discern the will of his creator.

[13]And we impart this in words not taught by human wisdom but taught by the Spirit, interpreting spiritual truths to those who possess the Spirit.

It will be clear that we know what we have been given by God because we talk to other people about these things, so that they may learn through this spiritual teaching. Inward understanding was given by God to preachers, that is to say, to apostles, which they could then share with their people, so that the rulers of this world might learn what evil they had lost control of.

The words of human wisdom do not convey this understanding, nor can it be acquired through studying literature. It can only be obtained by spiritual reasoning, as Isaiah the prophet says: *Unless you have believed, you will not understand.*[2] It is more easily learned through the law of nature than by studying the movement of the stars and calculating the constellations which can be discerned in the firmament. Finally, believers realize that their beliefs do not depend on human words but cohere with the nature of the beliefs

themselves, because the artifact recognizes its maker. Thus the gospel speaks spiritual things to our souls, encouraging them to recognize their creator.

Imparting spiritual things to those who are spiritual. That is, conveying the spiritual efficacy contained in the mystery of faith by means of those things which confound the wisdom of this world, in order to bring light to the minds of men of good will. It is those who believe the things which this world's wisdom calls foolish who are truly spiritual.

[14]The unspiritual man does not receive the gifts of the Spirit of God, for they are folly to him, and he is not able to understand them because they are spiritually discerned.

Like cattle, the unspiritual man has his awareness focused downward, toward the earth. He does not go after anything beyond what he can see and thinks that sexual intercourse is the be all and end all of everything. When he hears that God has begotten a Son and that a virgin has given birth, he just laughs, as he does when he hears that bodies which have decomposed have been called back to life, even though God is more greatly glorified by the belief that he has done these things, which cannot be scientifically analyzed, because only God can do them. Human weakness thinks that anything which science cannot demonstrate must be foolish, whereas it ought to be more skeptical of the powers of science, and reckon it wise to think that these things cannot be understood because they are acts of God.

When the human race rejected belief in one God and preferred to follow their own ideas instead, the spiritual effect was that they were puffed up by the reasoning of the flesh and imagined that these things were impossible. Marked out as reprobates because of this, they were spiritually condemned.

---

[1]The so-called *Sibylline Oracles* were prophecies which supposedly foretold the fate of Rome. [2]Cf. Is 7:9.

[15]*The spiritual man judges all things, but is himself to be judged by no one.*

The reasoning of spiritual people, that is believers, is true, and therefore they can judge all things. Unbelief will be judged by their example, but no one will judge them. For who can condemn a man who tells the truth? When such a person states that all the enemies of the faith regard falsehoods as true, their accusations are reduced to nothing because they are condemned by the judgment of the truth. *He who has not believed has already been judged.*[1]

[16]*"For who has known the mind of the Lord so as to instruct him?"*[2] *But we have the mind of Christ.*

The mind of God orders things to be done spiritually, and so the world is judged foolish when it says that none of the wonders that have happened could have taken place. No one who understands this rejects it, so as to presume to correct the mind of God. Rather, whoever recognizes this truth praises the power of God, whereas whoever denies that he is almighty does not even believe that he made the world. Why should it be a problem for him to make something out of himself, if you accept that he has made everything that exists out of nothing? The Savior himself said: *With God, all things are possible.*[3]

But we have the mind of Christ. Paul says this because believers are partakers of that mind, which is the divine wisdom.

1 Corinthians 3

[1]*But I, brethren, could not address you as spiritual men, but as men of the flesh, as babes in Christ.*

Paul is speaking to people who were carnal because they were still slaves to the desires of the present age. Although they had been baptized and had received the Holy Spirit, they were carnal because after their baptism they had returned to their old selves, which they had renounced. The Holy Spirit stays in a person into whom he has poured himself if that person stays firm in the conviction of his new birth. Otherwise he departs, but only provisionally. If that person repents, the Spirit will return, for he is always ready for what is good, being a lover of repentance.

[2]*I fed you with milk, not solid food; for you were not ready for it; and even yet you are not ready,*

Although they had been born again in Christ, they were not yet fit to receive spiritual things. Although they had received the faith which is the seed of the Spirit, they had produced no fruit worthy of God, but like babies, they were eager for the sensations of imperfection. But Paul, who was a man of God and a spiritual physician, gave to each of them according to his strength, so that no one should suffer scandal where spiritual matters were concerned because of imperfection or inexperience. He makes it quite clear that those people were not fit to hear the things which have to be said to those who have been confirmed. Paul is also arguing strongly against those who were complaining that they had not heard anything spiritual for a long time, when in fact they were not worthy to hear it. The false apostles conveyed their message indiscriminately to anyone who would listen, but it is generally agreed that our Lord and Master spoke one way in public and another way to his disciples in private, and that even among the latter a distinction was made, for he displayed his glory on the mountain to only three disciples and told them to say nothing about what had

[1]Jn 3:18. [2]Is 40:13. [3]Mt 19:26.

happened until he should rise again from the dead.

3for you are still of the flesh. For while there is jealousy and strife among you, are you not of the flesh, and behaving like ordinary men?

Paul is here explaining precisely why they were unworthy. Whoever hopes for help from other people is carnal, but whoever puts his hope in God is spiritual, because *God is a spirit.*[1]

4For when one says, "I belong to Paul," and another, "I belong to Apollos," are you not merely men?

People who glory in God and put all their hope in him are called *gods*, because they have been adopted by God. Likewise, people who glory in men are called *men* and *carnal*. This is demonstrated by the judgment of God, who says: *You are gods, but you will die like men.*[2] Paul uses himself as an example, so as not to be thought to be maligning those he is referring to through ill will, and he shows that it is a great mistake and an insult to God when the glory which belongs to him is given to men instead. It is pure paganism when people put their hope in mere men.

5What then is Apollos? What is Paul? Servants through whom you believed, as the Lord assigned to each.

Because these men are only servants, hope is not to be found in them but in the Lord, whose servants they are. Thanks are to be given to the person who owns the property which we receive as gifts; these men are slaves who are obliged to bring us gifts whether they want to or not. Was not Moses forced to go to Pharaoh, and was not Jonah sent against his wishes to preach to the people of Nineveh?

Even Ananias was sent to lay hands on Paul, in spite of his protests.

As the Lord assigned to each. God has handed out the responsibilities of ministry to each person as he has wished and intended.

6I planted, Apollos watered, but God gave the growth.

To plant is to evangelize and to bring to faith, to water is to baptize with the approved form of words. To forgive sins, however, and to give the Spirit belongs to God alone. Therefore, if it is God who puts salvation into effect, none of the glory connected with this belongs to any man. We know that the Holy Spirit is given by God without the laying on of hands, and it has happened that an unbaptized person has received the forgiveness of his sins. Was such a person invisibly baptized, considering that he received the gift which belongs to baptism?

7So neither he who plants nor he who waters is anything, but only God who gives the growth.

It is normal for things which have been planted to die and for things which have been watered to fail to mature to the point of bearing fruit if God does not give them life. As far as God's honor is concerned, man is nothing. As far as the ministry is concerned, a man may be honored in the way that a slave is honored, on the understanding that nothing can be expected from him, since that would be an insult to God.

8He who plants and he who waters are equal, and each shall receive his wages according to his labor.

They are equal because they are both wage earners, although their duties are different.

---

[1]Jn 4:24. [2]Ps 82:6-7.

But even though they are equal, the one who preaches the gospel is still greater than the one who baptizes, and will receive a bigger reward. Here Paul is referring not only to this distinction, but also to the purity of the teaching. Whoever conveys perfect doctrine deserves his wage.

⁹For we are God's fellow workers; you are God's field, God's building.

This refers to the part played by the apostles, who, everyone agrees, are God's helpers because they are his agents.

¹⁰According to the grace of God given to me, like a skilled master builder I laid a foundation, and another man is building upon it. Let each man take care how he builds upon it.

Paul says that grace was given to him in order to make him worthy to preach the gospel. Wanting to make it clear that this also belongs to God, not man, Paul says that it is in accordance with this grace that he has laid a foundation like a wise master builder. The wise master builder is one who preaches the same gospel as that which was preached by the Savior. Afterward, other people build on the foundation, sometimes well and sometimes badly. We need to pay attention to make sure that what we build coheres with the foundation, because if it is crooked or lightweight it will collapse, though the foundation itself will remain intact. Even when people have taught badly, the name of Christ endures, because it is the foundation, although the bad teaching will perish. As the Lord says: *Every plant which my heavenly Father has not planted will be uprooted.*[1]

¹¹For no other foundation can any one lay than that which is laid, which is Jesus Christ.

Nobody can lay another foundation, because even if some people are heretics, they do not teach except in the name of Christ. They cannot commend the inventions of their error in any other way, so that the dignity of his name may make contradictory and absurd ideas acceptable.

¹²Now if any one builds on the foundation with gold, silver, precious stones, wood, hay, straw—

He gave as his examples three excellent materials and used them as illustrations of good teaching. He then listed three other kinds of material, flimsy ones this time, in order to point out how different the corrupt and empty teaching signified by them actually was.

¹³each man's work will become manifest; for the Day will disclose it, because it will be revealed with fire, and the fire will test what sort of work each one has done.

In the fire, bad teaching will become clear to everyone, though for the moment it is deceiving some people. Because the testing will take place by fire, if it finds nothing to burn, then the person concerned will be proved to have been a good teacher. Bad and corrupt teaching is indicated by wood, hay and straw, which shows that it is ready made for the fire.

¹⁴If the work which any man has built on the foundation survives, he will receive a reward.

If none of the impurity of bad teaching is found in him and he turns out to be pure gold, he will be just like the three brothers in the fiery furnace,[2] destined to receive as his wage heavenly life with glory. The good teacher will remain incorruptible, just like gold, silver and the precious stones which fire cannot destroy.

---

[1] Mt 15:13. [2] Dan 3:25.

[15]If any man's work is burned up, he will suffer loss, though he himself will be saved, but only as through fire.

The work which is said to catch fire is bad teaching, which will perish. All bad things will pass away, like the way of the unjust, because it is not just the deed but the assertions behind them which are perverted. To suffer loss is to endure punishment. For what person, when subjected to punishment, does not lose something thereby? The man himself will be saved, because his substance will not perish in the same way that his bad teaching will. The teaching is not essential to his being. Note that when Paul said that the man would be saved through fire he did not mean that the man tested by the fire would escape burning on his own merit and be saved. What he meant was that he will suffer punishments of fire and be saved only by being purged. Unlike complete unbelievers, he will not be tortured in eternal fire, and so to some extent it will be worth his while to have believed in Christ. It is always necessary for a person who has defended a lie instead of the truth to blush with shame at having done so. A person will always have God's faith if he has followed the truth, having thrown away falsehood, and surrendered to godliness, having jettisoned everything ungodly. For whatever is outside the catholic faith is contrary to it.

[16]Do you not know that you are God's temple and that God's Spirit dwells in you?

He says that we are God's temple so that we may know that God lives in us, for God has to live in his own temple. Note that because he says that the Spirit of God lives in us, the word God must be taken to refer to the Holy Spirit in this verse.

[17]If any one destroys God's temple, God will destroy him. For God's temple is holy, and that temple you are.

Paul says this in order to prick the consciences of those who have corrupted their bodies through evil living, especially the man who was having an affair with his father's wife, so that he would become a defendant before his case burst out into the open. When he judges the man's case, he speaks in a similar way, indeed in exactly the same way, when he says: *Do you not know that your body is the temple of the Holy Spirit, which you have from God?*[1] Earlier on, he talked about the temple of God, and now it is the temple of the Holy Spirit. On the strength of this, who can doubt that the Holy Spirit is God?

[18]Let no one deceive himself. If any one among you thinks that he is wise in this age, let him become a fool that he may become wise.

Let no one think that he can do himself any good by his own, human way of thinking. Here Paul is returning to what he said in the first chapter. He says this because, if anyone understands the promised salvation and the mystery of the incarnation of our Lord Jesus Christ, he becomes *foolish*, in other words, he runs away from the wisdom of the world, which will therefore think he is foolish. In fact, he will then be wise, because the man who is foolish according to the world's wisdom is wise in the sight of God, because he believes that God has done things which the world's reasoning cannot accept, as I have said above. But false apostles, wanting to appear wise in terms of this world, were preaching that God did not have a son, that the incarnation never happened, and that the resurrection of the body was impossible.

---

[1] 1 Cor 6:19.

¹⁹*For the wisdom of this world is folly with God. For it is written, "He catches the wise in their craftiness,"*¹

The wisdom of this world is foolishness with God in the sense that God proves the world's wisdom to be foolish by doing things which the world says cannot be done. Since the worldly-wise say that there are many gods, but faith shows that there is only one, with his power as its witness, the "wise" will be confounded in their folly.

²⁰*and again, "The Lord knows that the thoughts of the wise are futile."*²

This is from Psalm 93,³ and the sense is basically the same. Knowing that their thoughts are vain, God rebukes their wisdom in order to prove that they are foolish, showing that what they thought was false is true and vice versa.

²¹*So let no one boast of men. For all things are yours,*

Human reasoning is unwise and weak, so one should not glory in man, but in God, whose word cannot be altered. Whatever human beings think apart from God is foolishness.

²²*whether Paul or Apollos or Cephas or the world or life or death or the present or the future, all are yours;* ²³*and you are Christ's; and Christ is God's.*

Paul talks about this same thing elsewhere, when he says: *But we are your slaves because of Jesus.*⁴ He uses the word *slaves* instead of *servants* so that they should not defend particular individuals, but make use of all of them equally. Even the Lord says: *I am in the midst of you, not to be served but to serve.*⁵ The whole world belongs to us, as long as we accept that

we must approach it in accordance with God's will and recognize the laws of nature to be subject to that. Our present life is also given to us, but only on condition that we live modestly and glorify God.

We are Christ's because we were made by him, both physically and spiritually. Paul mentions death, in order that we should be glad to die for Christ, in the hope of the promise of a future life. We ought to use present things in a way which will not give offense. Believing in future things, we make ourselves worthy to receive them, all the more because they are better things. Just as these things are granted and placed at our discretion, so we are subject to Christ, given that it was in him that we began to exist, both in human and in spiritual terms. Christ is the only Son of God his Father, doing the Father's will so that we may do his. If we are Christ's servants, why should we put our trust in other people, to his detriment?

1 Corinthians 4

¹*This is how one should regard us, as servants of Christ and stewards of the mysteries of God.*

Paul says this because some of the Corinthians thought less of him. But in order for others to have the same opinion of him as God had, who had chosen him, Paul says: *servants of Christ and stewards of the mysteries of God.* Since he was trying to be understood not through the strife of words or through human wisdom, it was his duty to dispense the sacrament of Christ, in which it was not words but power which shone forth, and thus it was not man but God who would appear in glory. The fishermen's colleague did not preach anything different from what they did. By calling himself a servant of Christ and a steward of the mysteries of God, Paul points out who the false apostles are and denies that what they preach

---

¹Job 5:13. ²Ps 94:11. ³Ps 94 in English versions. ⁴2 Cor 4:5. ⁵Lk 22:27.

is of Christ, because it is not in accordance with apostolic tradition.

[2]Moreover it is required of stewards that they be found trustworthy.

What Paul says refers not only to the character of the false apostles, but also to all those who occupy some office in the church but who hesitate to argue against bad ideas or morals because of modesty, fear or a desire to look good in the eyes of others. Paul himself was so straight that he would sacrifice even his own life for the right to carry out his duties faithfully.

[3]But with me it is a very small thing that I should be judged by you or by any human court. I do not even judge myself.

Paul is saying that it is disgraceful that he is being judged by people whom he is condemning for their great wickedness, when in fact he should not be judged even by the righteous. He ought not to be judged even by the world's laws, because, having gone beyond human justice, he was anxiously awaiting the justice of heaven. As the Lord says: *Unless your righteousness exceeds that of the scribes and Pharisees, you will not enter the kingdom of God.*[1] In referring to a human court, he is pointing also to the divine court, where Christ will pass judgment.[2] Just as the judges and the pontiffs, whom they call priests, have laid down the court days on which they will pass judgment, so the [court] day of the Lord is fixed, when he will judge the world.

[4]I am not aware of anything against myself, but I am not thereby acquitted. It is the Lord who judges me.

It is obvious that Paul was not worried about himself because he had a clear conscience. But he humbles himself and speaks like a man who can incur guilt without being aware of it. In saying that God is his judge he is telling the truth. Even though he has already humbled himself, he still pays great tribute to the Lord Jesus Christ, who when judging the secrets [of the heart], brings to light things which are hidden to human eyes. Here Paul is not acting like a defendant, but is merely being prudent. Although he is a man whom it is impossible [to accuse of anything], unless there is something hidden from him [of which he is unaware], there are still times when we think that something is beneficial to us when it is not. Nor do we have all the parts or dimensions of human behavior laid out before us. We are clearly forbidden from committing crimes which are serious, but there are still cases which often deceive us when they arise from certain sets of circumstances, making us think that harmful things might be beneficial. This is less serious of course [because it is accidental].

[5]Therefore do not pronounce judgment before the time, before the Lord comes, who will bring to light the things now hidden in darkness and will disclose the purposes of the heart. Then every man will receive his commendation from God.

Paul advises the Corinthians not to pass judgment because they too will be judged and incur a double penalty, as the Lord says: *Judge not, that you be not judged.*[3]

Instead they should wait for God's judgment day, on the assumption that they have been faithful and good. A judge is insulted if one of his servants presumes to pronounce a verdict or a sentence before he makes his decision known.

Paul says these things because on the day of judgment, nothing which has been said or

---

[1]Mt 5:20. [2]Ambrosiaster reads the word *court* as "day," but this can be corrected without altering the meaning. [3]Mt 7:1.

thought will be hidden. Both sincerity and hypocrisy will come to light on that day, with the result that the one who was despised may appear worthy after all, and the one who was honored may be found to have been false all along. On the day of judgment, everything will be revealed. Then there will be praise for the person whose thoughts and deeds are good. But it is unlikely that someone who is praised on earth will turn out to be worthy, for as Paul says elsewhere: *It is not the one who commends himself who is approved, but the one whom the Lord commends, from whom nothing is hidden.*[1]

[6]I have applied all this to myself and Apollos for your benefit, brethren, that you may learn by us not to go beyond what is written, that none of you may be puffed up in favor of one against another.

Paul has used himself and Apollos as examples in order to nullify the boasting and the perverse teachings of the false apostles under the cover of his own person and that of Apollos. He refers to them as a group, not as individuals, perhaps in order to prevent some major dissension from arising in the congregation. No one who hears himself or someone he supports being attacked by name will be prepared to stay silent. Any listener who thinks that what is being said applies to him will try to hide the fact, as long as his name is not mentioned openly. It was with the same intention that Paul nullified their pretensions when he said: *I planted, Apollos watered.*[2] By this means, he wanted the Corinthians to learn not to attribute anything to men.

[7]For who sees anything different in you? What have you that you did not receive? If then you received it, why do you boast as if it were not a gift?

There are some people who are particularly blessed in their baptism or in the teaching they have received and therefore claim that others are less well off. Paul wrote this to those who thought that it was better to be baptized by some people than by others who had been led astray by their eloquence and who by some trick believed that perverse teachings were right. There was such great discord among the people that they had split into many factions, each with its own party line. So the apostle aimed his remarks at everyone without mentioning particular names. In this way, when the letter was read, each faction took what was said to refer to itself, hearing what it realized was directed at the cause of strife. Paul says that his hearers had not received anything from anyone else, beyond what they had received from the apostle. He only appears to be speaking to one person because he is addressing one section of the congregation.

One of the things Paul's accusers used to do, through their own incompetence, was to boast of the things he had given them as if they were not gifts at all, thereby rendering him of no account. They would boast about their authority as teachers and, by means of their powerful eloquence, would deflect the glory of their admired preaching to themselves. Paul, by contrast, was willing to appear contemptible, as long as he could make God's glory more acceptable.

[8]Already you are filled! Already you have become rich! Without us you have become kings! And would that you did reign, so that we might share the rule with you!

This is pure irony. These are the words of an angry man, not of someone trying to bring comfort. He is saying that the people whom he is upbraiding for such serious faults are acting

---

[1]2 Cor 10:18. [2]1 Cor 3:6.

like kings, for that is how they were thinking when they were boasting about the teachings of the false apostles. Like a devoted father, Paul wishes his children well even when they are ungrateful. They could hardly have become kings, he says, had it not been for the apostles! For whatever the apostles had not taught was full of error. The flow of words here should really have been: *Would that you were reigning with us*, but as he had already remarked that they had become kings, he could do no other than say *so that we might share the rule with you*. To be a king is to trust in the hope and promises of Christ, and to rejoice in adversities which occur because of his name, because they bring gain, not loss. This is why, in another place, he says: *When I am weak, then am I strong.*[1]

[9]For I think that God has exhibited us apostles as last of all, like men sentenced to death; because we have become a spectacle to the world, to angels and to men.

Paul applies this to his own person because he was always in trouble, suffering persecutions and afflictions more than others, just as Enoch and Elijah will suffer them when they return as apostles at the end of time. For they have to be sent ahead of Christ to prepare the people of God and to fortify all the churches to resist the antichrist. A text from the book of Revelation bears witness that they will suffer persecution and be killed.[2] The apostle compares that time with his own life, using the words *like men sentenced to death*. Death awaited them all in the end.

Enoch and Elijah will be such a spectacle that their bodies will be thrown out in the sight of all the unbelievers, and in a similar way, the apostles have been made a spectacle, because they were jeered at in public, when they were exposed to injuries and the death

which they were to suffer. He mentions angels because there are wicked angels as well, as David says in Psalm 77: *He let loose on them a company of destroying angels.*[3] And bad men are unbelievers, of course. To them the injuries done to the apostles are a source of pleasure. Unbelief is described as *the world* because it pursues things which are visible.

[10]We are fools for Christ's sake, but you are wise in Christ. We are weak, but you are strong. You are held in honor, but we in disrepute.

Those who love Christ are fools as far as the world is concerned, but whoever is judged *wise in Christ* by the unfaithful does not defend Christ's cause in the right way. For example, Marcion, who denies that there is a Son of God, or that God can become flesh, is wise in the world's eyes, and so is Photinus, because he does not accept that Christ is God on the ground that he was born. People who were preaching Christ without pretentiousness, and (as it seemed to worldly people) with a degree of foolishness, were regarded as weak and subjected to injuries. The Corinthians, on the other hand, were *strong* because they confessed Christ in such a way as not to offend anybody, and so they were protected. Because Christ was promised to Abraham and was prophesied from the beginning, whoever does not confess him is *noble* because he attributes the ancient origin of the promised Christ to others. But whoever confesses the Christ who existed from the beginning is *ignoble* in the world's eyes, because the world denies this.

Everything which Paul appears to be denying here he is in fact asserting, and conversely, he is negating everything which he states in a positive manner. These are the words of an angry man, who inverts his speech in order to make his point.

---

[1]2 Cor 12:10. [2]Rev 11:7-8. [3]Ps 78:49 in English versions. The interpretation is mistaken.

[11]To the present hour we hunger and thirst, we are ill-clad and buffeted and homeless,

Preaching Christ freely and in accordance with the true faith, without any pretentiousness, and rebuking the fruits of evil living, the apostles were unpopular with men and were *buffeted*, that is to say, attacked. They had no fixed abode because they were constantly being forced to flee, so that they would not remain in one place and teach more people.

[12]and we labor, working with our own hands. When reviled, we bless; when persecuted, we endure;

They also worked with their hands, not only because they were unpopular, but also because it was not right for them to receive anything from the supporters of error. As David says in Psalm 140: *The oil of a sinner will not anoint my head.*[1] The reason for this is that if he were to allow such a thing, he would lose his freedom to rebuke the man, and the person who receives this kind of anointing commits a sin, because he is going out of his way not to be attacked.

The apostles used to encourage those who attacked them to do good instead. They suffered persecution and endured because they did not put up resistance to those who persecuted them.

[13]when slandered, we try to conciliate; we have become, and are now, as the refuse of the world, the off-scouring of all things.

The apostles used to ask those who slandered them to let them explain their position. By not resisting anyone or returning evil for evil, but by always humbling himself in order to provoke people to good by his patience, he became contemptible and despised [in the eyes of others]. Even among the Corinthians, for whom he has suffered the attacks he refers to above, he has been despised—and is still being despised! When he realized that his humility was doing him no good in their eyes, he complained, moved to regret that his great self-abasement and the injuries he has received have borne no fruit, but rather have proved to be detrimental—which is much worse.

[14]I do not write this to make you ashamed, but to admonish you as my beloved children.

I am not writing to you to make you blush, but to put you straight. Paul is still making himself a suppliant, in order to prevent the Corinthians from rejecting his advice after being rebuked by him and stirred to anger. Paul is acting here like a good physician who alleviates the pain caused by his operation to remove the disease, so that the sick person will let himself be cured.

[15]For though you have countless guides in Christ, you do not have many fathers. For I became your father in Christ Jesus through the gospel.

Paul is telling the Corinthians that nobody else will ever love them the way he does. Who would love other people's children more than his own? Because of this, they ought not to spurn the advice of someone who has suffered so much on their behalf.

[16]I urge you, then, be imitators of me.

Oh, the benevolence of the holy apostle, who implores his children to imitate their father, who asks the sick to take their medicine voluntarily! Paul wants them to be imitators of him in these things, so that just as he has

---

[1]Ps 141:5 in English versions.

endured many hardships from unbelievers for their salvation and is still doing so as long as he preaches the free gift of God's grace day and night, so they too ought to remain in his faith and doctrine and not accept the evil teachings of the false apostles. Instead, they should resist them, despising abuse and slander, in order to protect their feelings for their spiritual father.

**17*Therefore I sent to you Timothy, my beloved and faithful child in the Lord, to remind you of my ways in Christ, as I teach them everywhere in every church.*

Paul urges the Corinthians by using Timothy, whom he describes as his dearest and most faithful son in the Lord. He wants them to learn from Timothy where they were sinning, because in giving Timothy this recommendation, he is in fact rebuking the Corinthians.

Through this man, whom he affirms as his faithful son in the Lord, Paul urges them to return to the rule of the truth, conveyed by himself, so that warned by his words and the example of his deeds, they should be brought back to their senses and recognize that, when they learned that all the churches held the same beliefs, they had not been so badly taught by the apostle after all.

**18*Some are arrogant, as though I were not coming to you.*

Some of the Corinthians were angry that Paul had not come to them, not because they wanted him to but because they were proud and imagined that Paul thought they were unworthy of a visit. In fact, Paul wanted to go but had more important things to do.

**19*But I will come to you soon, if the Lord wills, and I will find out not the talk of these arrogant people but their power.*

Paul couches his promise to come in the will of God, because God knows more than man. If there were some advantage in Paul's going to Corinth, God would make it known, and if he did not turn up, the Corinthians would know that the Lord had not wanted him to, probably because they were unworthy.

**20*For the kingdom of God does not consist in talk but in power.*

Just as the kingdom of God is not commended by splendid words, the Corinthians should show that they are worthy of a visit from the apostle, not by words alone but by the power of their spiritual works.

**21*What do you wish? Shall I come to you with a rod, or with love in a spirit of gentleness?*

Paul introduces these words of terror, so that those who had been puffed up might be humbled by suffering shame, and if they really wanted the apostle to come to see them, they might prepare themselves to receive him. In other words, they should wash themselves of every stain of wrongdoing, so that when Paul came to them, he would enjoy the happiness of being reunited with his most beloved children.

1 Corinthians 5

**1*It is actually reported that there is immorality among you, and of a kind that is not found even among pagans; for a man is living with his father's wife.*

To show how serious this crime is, Paul says that even those who do not know God do not commit it. He wants to show precisely what penalty a man charged with such a heinous crime would have to pay under both secular and divine law. He reveals the nature of the charge, of which he has been informed in advance, not only to make the man liable to the death penalty, but also to make it clear that those who associated with him were not innocent either. The very fact that it is a difficult sin to commit makes him all the more liable to be charged.

²And you are arrogant! Ought you not rather to mourn? Let him who has done this be removed from among you.

Paul humbles their pride, but in such a way that instead of making them angry he makes them willing to cooperate with him. They were accomplices because they permitted a man charged with so enormous a crime to attend their meetings without hindrance. What they ought to do is decide unanimously to throw him out, unless he mended his ways. Of course, if someone has no power to throw a man out when he knows that he is guilty of such a crime, or cannot produce proof of it, he is innocent, nor is it the role of a judge to condemn someone without a prosecutor. Even the Lord refused to cast out Judas, although he was a thief, because he had not been prosecuted.

³For though absent in body I am present in spirit, and as if present, I have already pronounced judgment

Paul means that he is absent in physical terms, but present by the authority of the Spirit, who is everywhere.

⁴in the name of the Lord Jesus on the man who has done such a thing. When you are assembled, and my spirit is present, with the power of our Lord Jesus, ⁵you are to deliver this man to Satan for the destruction of the flesh, that his spirit may be saved in the day of the Lord Jesus.

Since all carnal pleasure comes from the devil, it is to be understood that when he is sent back to his pleasures he is in fact being handed over to Satan. The flesh is mortal by nature, so when the soul is attracted by the desires of the flesh, it cancels out its spiritual power and suffers death along with the flesh. So, if this man arrested for the debauchery that he has committed feels any shame at having been thrown out, he will not perish if he then repents. For it was decreed that he should be thrown out of the church not only by the common consent of the congregation and in their presence, but also by the power of the Lord Jesus, that is to say, by the sentence of the one on whose mission the apostle is engaged. Although every sin shows a man to be carnal, it is the desire of the flesh, more than anything else, which hands over a soul stained with filth to hell. This is because the soul, once captured, becomes flesh through the lust of the flesh, just as a body which is well controlled becomes "spiritual." It is the will which either makes the entire man carnal (if it is defeated by temptation), or, if it retains the strength of its natural state, is superior to the flesh and is thus called "spiritual."

This corrupt man is being handed over to Satan so that the Holy Spirit can be preserved in the members of the congregation on the day of judgment. He was deserting them because of this contamination, and [if that continued], on the day of the Lord they would be found naked and would hear the Lord their judge say to them: *Depart from me, for I never knew you.*[1] Similarly, Paul says to the Romans: *Whoever does not have the spirit of Christ does not belong to him,*[2] and in another epistle he writes: *Do not grieve the Holy Spirit of God.*[3] For if the Holy Spirit is grieved he will depart and is not protected. Of course, he is not unprotected from his own standpoint, since he is incapable of suffering, but he is unprotected as far as we are concerned, who need him to prove that we

---

[1]Mt 7:23. [2]Rom 8:9. [3]Eph 4:30.

are children of God. Something which is lost is not protected, not from its own point of view, but from the standpoint of the person who loses it.

⁶Your boasting is not good. Do you not know that a little leaven leavens the whole lump?

Boasting is bad. The Corinthians were happy when they should have been appalled on account of their brother, who was committing such a terrible sin, just as Samuel was upset by the sins of Saul.[1] Faced with his crime, the bad teachers of Corinth either made excuses or failed to rebuke him, just as Eli did not rebuke his sons when they sinned against God in order not to fall out with them.[2]

The sin of one person contaminates many if it is not dealt with once it is known, and so does the sin of the many who know what is happening and either do not turn away from it or pretend that they have not noticed it. Sin does not look like sin if it is not corrected or avoided by anybody.

⁷Cleanse out the old leaven that you may be a new lump, as you really are unleavened. For Christ, our paschal lamb, has been sacrificed.

The old leaven has a double meaning here. On the one hand, it refers to false teaching, just as Jesus warned his disciples to beware the leaven of the Pharisees.[3] On the other hand, it also refers to the sin of fornication being dealt with here. Paul is referring both to the need to watch out for bad teaching and to the present case at issue—the old leaven would be thrown out when the corrupt man was dealt with. The new lump is the teaching of Christ.

Unleavened bread is so called because of the unleavened flour which was used when the children of Israel were expelled from Egypt.

Because of this, "leaven" was associated with what was old, and "unleavened" with what was new. Once the Israelites had thrown away the errors of the Egyptians, they were led into the new law. In the same way, the Corinthians, after being delivered from the errors of the pagans, were led into the gospel of Christ. Therefore Paul is exhorting them to live as recipients of the new life which they have gotten from the apostle in Christ's name. This is what it means to be *unleavened*.

Following the law, Paul teaches that the new state of affairs comes about because of the meaning of the Passover. Christ was put to death so that the new preaching would produce a new kind of life. It is because we accept the meaning of this Passover that we do not cling to the old life. The Passover is a sacrifice, not just a "passing over," as some people think. The sacrifice comes first, well before the example of the Savior and the sign of salvation, for it was not such a sign before the cross. The children of Israel performed the Passover in Egypt by sacrificing a lamb in the evening and painting their doorposts with its blood, so that when the angel passed by at night he would not touch a place which had been smeared with the blood of the lamb.[4]

⁸Let us, therefore, celebrate the festival, not with the old leaven, the leaven of malice and evil, but with the unleavened bread of sincerity and truth.

Celebrating the joy of being born again, let us turn away from our old ways, casting out all uncleanness from among us, because it is corrupt. Just as a little leaven leavens the whole lump, an evil life corrupts the whole man. Therefore, Paul wants us to avoid not only evil acts but all interest in sin. This is why he adds: *not with the leaven of malice and evil, but with the unleavened bread of sincerity and truth*, so

---

[1]1 Sam 15:35. [2]1 Sam 2:12-17, 22-25. [3]Mt 16:6. [4]Ex 12:21-27.

that sincerity may cleanse our lives and truth may exclude all deception.

⁹I wrote to you in my letter not to associate with immoral men;

Paul tells us here that he has already written to the Corinthians once and told them not to associate with debauchees. Because they failed to take action then, he is now writing a second time to explain what he meant.

¹⁰not at all meaning the immoral of this world, or the greedy and robbers, or idolaters, since then you would need to go out of the world.

Paul did not mean that Christians had to avoid the company of immoral people who belong to this world, but only that they must shun brothers of this kind. He therefore refuted the interpretation of those who had perhaps concluded that he had forbidden any association at all with debauched, avaricious, greedy or idolatrous unbelievers, but not with brothers like this one, and that for that reason they were tolerating the presence in their midst of someone who was having an affair with his father's wife. Paul says that it would be better to die than to mix with brethren who sin like the fornicator in question, because death would put an end to it sooner rather than later.

¹¹But rather I wrote to you not to associate with any one who bears the name of brother if he is guilty of immorality or greed, or is an idolater, reviler, drunkard, or robber—not even to eat with such a one.

Paul does not forbid the Corinthians from eating with unbelievers, since he says: *If an unbeliever invites you to dinner and you want to go, eat whatever is put before you.*[1]

¹²For what have I to do with judging outsiders? Is it not those inside the church whom you are to judge?

A bishop cannot do anything about unbelievers. But a brother who is caught doing such things he can bar not only from the sacraments but also from common intercourse with his fellows, so that when he is avoided by them he may feel ashamed and repent.

Whenever you decide what brother you will associate with, whom you will rebuke and whom you will shun altogether, you are passing judgment.

¹³God judges those outside. "Drive out the wicked person from among you."

Earlier on, Paul said: *Do not judge before the right time,*[2] but here he does not forbid judging. In the earlier passage he forbade judgment on the basis of suspicion only, before the matters involved had been investigated, particularly when these concerned their leader. The reason for this is that it was for God alone to judge things which are hidden. Here, by way of contrast, he goes so far as to order brother to examine brother, just as elsewhere he says: *Test yourselves, to see whether you are in the faith. Examine yourselves.*[3] Outsiders will be condemned on the day of judgment, because the Lord has said: *Whoever does not believe has been judged already.*[4] There is no hope here; such a person is to be considered dead already.

In telling them to drive the wicked out, Paul is once again warning the Corinthians that they should be separated from both evil deeds and evil people.

1 Corinthians 6

¹When one of you has a grievance against a brother, does he dare go to law before the un-

---

[1]1 Cor 10:27. [2]1 Cor 4:5. [3]2 Cor 13:5. [4]Jn 3:18.

righteous instead of the saints?

The Corinthians were wrong in two ways. First, they were unfaithful, and second, they were expounding God's laws with a show of respect but in reality attributing their authority to idols. This is why they were wrong. Justice is more likely to be found in the church, where the Lord of the law is feared, and it is for this reason that Paul says that it is better to be tried before God's servants, who are more likely to give a true verdict because they fear God.

²Do you not know that the saints will judge the world? And if the world is to be judged by you, are you incompetent to try trivial cases?

There is nothing superfluous in what the apostle says here. He speaks of *this world* in order to indicate that there is another one as well.[1] The apostle John also says: *Do not love this world*,[2] and in the Gospel the Lord says: *God so loved this world*.[3] Therefore it is this world which has gone wrong, not the one above, in whose likeness this one has been made, with the result that man is placed on earth, made in the image of God, so that just as everything in the world above has its origin in God, everyone here below descends from a single man.

This explains what Moses says in Deuteronomy: *When the Most High divided the peoples according to the way in which he scattered the children of Adam, he determined the boundaries of the peoples according to the number of the angels of God*.[4] What clearer explanation could there be of why this world is created in the image of the one above? There is a Jerusalem below and one above, which the apostle calls our mother.[5] There is a paradise below, in which man received the command to work and protect it, and there is one above, where the

apostle heard mysterious words in a trance.[6] The saints will judge this world because the unbelief of the world will be condemned by the example of their faith. Furthermore, this world will be judged in us if the work of unbelievers is not found in us. Those who are called to judge the world are in no way unworthy to judge the things which belong to the world.

³Do you not know that we are to judge angels? How much more, matters pertaining to this life!

Paul adds something more by saying that we shall judge angels, that is to say, the spiritual powers which (as he says elsewhere)[7] live in the heavenly places. Angels are to be judged by us in the same way as the world is to be judged.

⁴If then you have such cases, why do you lay them before those who are least esteemed by the church?

Secular court cases are those which relate to the body or to things belonging to the body. Paul uses the term *secular* because he has mentioned a case, though he has not specified what it might be. For there are also divine cases, as when he says: *The helper of my case*.[8] The Corinthians might think that because Paul had forbidden the hearing of secular cases before unbelievers, that the same cases could be heard and decided in church before anyone at all. For this reason, and to embarrass them, he says: *appoint as judges those who are despised in the church*. For the church too has its wooden vessels! But because this ought not to happen, he goes on to add what follows.

⁵I say this to your shame. Can it be that there is no man among you wise enough to decide between members of the brotherhood,

---

[1]Ambrosiaster reads "this world" instead of "the world," a translation which is not demanded by the Greek either here or in either of the verses he cites from John. [2]1 Jn 2:15. [3]Jn 3:16. [4]Deut 32:8 (LXX). [5]Gal 4:26. [6]Cf. 2 Cor 12:4. [7]Eph 6:12. [8]Rom 16:3.

Paul meant that they were so unmanageable and thoughtless that they might choose inexperienced brethren as judges. Here he spoke from experience, for he knew how unenthusiastic and thoughtless they had been in other matters. There must, he said, be some people in the church wise enough to judge such cases, and they should be allowed to do so. The world would be amazed at their decisions! It is, after all, a great shame if there is no one in the church who is capable of examining a case according to the law of the gospel. He said this, incidentally, because at that time no official leader had been appointed in their church.

6but brother goes to law against brother, and that before unbelievers?

Paul means that when brother goes to court against brother, they should be helped to come to agreement, like the blood brothers they are supposed to be, because our faith yearns for peace.

7To have lawsuits at all with one another is defeat for you. Why not rather suffer wrong? Why not rather be defrauded?

A Christian ought not to engage in litigation at all, but if the matter is too serious to be disregarded he should bring the case to the church, so as not to incur an immediate penalty and personal ruin.

8But you yourselves wrong and defraud, and that even your own brethren.

Paul is rebuking the people whose wrongful behavior has started the quarrels, because not only are they liable to be charged for the fraud which they have committed but they also share in the fault of those who, compelled by their injurious or fraudulent actions, call upon unbelievers to pass judgment. Also, whereas they should not pursue cases of fraud and injuries

inflicted, not only do they seek revenge, but they even commit fraud and injuries themselves, and so give their brothers a wonderful excuse for punishing them. And what do you suppose they must be doing to outsiders, If this is the way they treat their own brothers?

9Do you not know that the unrighteous will not inherit the kingdom of God? Do not be deceived; neither the immoral, nor idolaters, nor adulterers, nor sexual perverts,

Paul indicates that they are not sinning unknowingly, and so it is that much harder to excuse them. For if the unmerciful are guilty before God, how much more so are the wicked!

10nor thieves, nor the greedy, nor drunkards, nor revilers, nor robbers will inherit the kingdom of God.

Paul did not say this because the Corinthians did not know it already—after all, he had spent a year and a half among them, teaching God's Word—but in order to revive their reverence for the law and their means of deserving the kingdom of heaven.

11And such were some of you. But you were washed, you were sanctified, you were justified in the name of the Lord Jesus Christ and in the Spirit of our God.

Paul said *some of you* in order not to appear to be including everyone, nor (on the other hand) to be excusing them all, which he would have done if he had said nothing about it. The way it appeared, it seemed as though he had forbidden their crimes, rather than revealed them! He added *but you were washed* so that after having been convicted of their guilt, they could breath a sigh of relief. Some people habitually put up with embarrassment and amend their ways when they hear good things spoken of them.

The Corinthians had received all the benefits of purity in their baptism, which is the foundation of the truth of the gospel. In baptism the believer is washed clean from all sins and is made righteous in the name of the Lord, and through the Spirit of God he is adopted as God's child. With these words, Paul is reminding them how great and how special is the grace which they have received in the true tradition. But afterward, by thinking which is contrary to this rule of faith, they had stripped themselves of these benefits. For this reason he is trying to bring them back to their original way of thinking, so that they can recover what they had once received.

12"All things are lawful for me," but not all things are helpful. "All things are lawful for me," but I will not be enslaved by anything.

By *all things* Paul presumably meant those things which are contained in the natural law and which were also lawful for his fellow apostles. It would not refer to the law of Moses, because Moses forbade many things owing to the hardness of heart of an unbelieving and stiff-necked people.[1] But if you look more closely, you will see that there was something else in the apostle's mind which caused him to say these things. He is really introducing the matter before dealing with it in detail, just as he introduced the case of the man committing incest with a preliminary remark indicating what he was going to treat later on. Then he gets right back to his earlier train of thought, once he has brought the matter up. The reason he said this was because he was permitted to receive payment from them, but because he knew that the false apostles were looking for any excuse to be paid, he did not accept anything for fear that, out of a desire to satisfy the stomach, the power of the truth of the gospel would become slack. If Paul were to receive payment from the people whom he was rebuking for such serious sins, he would undermine the magisterial authority which the Lord had granted him. You cannot go on rebuking people who are paying you, especially if they pay up quickly in order to shut you up. This is why Paul adds that he will not be enslaved by anything.

Some people think that it was on the basis of the freedom to take decisions which had been given to him that the apostle Paul said this. In other words, it might be all right for him to indulge in sexual immorality, but it was not helpful for him to do so! But how can what is forbidden ever be lawful? Of course, if everything is lawful, nothing can be called unlawful in principle. But it is lawful without being helpful—they whisper this rather than assert it openly, because they are either forgetful [of the law] or negligent [in complying with it]. As John the Baptist said to Herod: *It is forbidden for you to take your brother's wife.*[2] Can it be that John, inspired though he was in the womb, lacked human eloquence, because if this line of reasoning is correct, what he should have said was: *You can do it but it is not helpful.* Similarly, the Lord said to the Canaanite woman: *It is not lawful to take the children's bread and give it to the dogs.*[3] And he also said to the Jews: *Have you not read what David did when he was hungry, how he went into the house of God and took the loaves of the presence, which it was not lawful for him to take?*[4] Everything therefore, which is forbidden, is unlawful, and everything which is not forbidden is permitted, but there are times when, for some other reason, it is not helpful.

13"Food is meant for the stomach and the stomach for food"—and God will destroy both one and the other. The body is not meant for immorality, but for the Lord, and the Lord for the body.

---

[1]Cf. Mt 19:8. [2]Cf. Mt 14:3-4. [3]Mt 15:26. [4]Mk 2:25-26.

The destruction of the body comes about when the function of eating ceases; the destruction of eating will take place when giving birth has come to an end. But the false apostles, who traveled about not for the sake of godliness but for pure gain, did not want to treat sinners harshly.

After this he goes back to what he was saying before. The question *What does the Lord have to do with the body?* is implied, and the answer is that he will give it immortality at the resurrection. The body, being dedicated to God, will be rewarded with a spiritual reward for the merit of its ruler, which is the rational soul.

¹⁴And God raised the Lord and will also raise us up by his power.

The meaning here is the same. Paul merely wanted to confirm it by using the precedent of the Lord's resurrection. Christ is the power of God, by which he will raise us up. He said this because the Lord raised up his own body, just as he also said: *Destroy this temple and in three days I will raise it up. But he was speaking about the temple of his body.*[1]

¹⁵Do you not know that your bodies are members of Christ? Shall I therefore take the members of Christ and make them members of a prostitute? Never!

Our bodies are limbs of Christ, but they belong to the new man, made according to God's image, because he himself is the head of the church. He says *never!* because members who join with a prostitute cease to be members of Christ.

¹⁶Do you not know that he who joins himself to a prostitute becomes one body with her? For, as it is written, "The two shall become one flesh."[2]

Paul says this because the person who involves himself in contamination is united with the person with whom he involves himself. Sexual immorality makes them both one, in nature as well as in sin.

¹⁷But he who is united to the Lord becomes one spirit with him.

In the case of those who behave well, the Spirit of God is shared between God and human beings.

¹⁸Shun immorality. Every other sin which a man commits is outside the body; but the immoral man sins against his own body.

Paul is right to warn us to flee from fornication, because through it the sons of God become sons of the devil. He is demonstrating here that fornication is the most serious sin of all, because when it is committed the whole body perishes, whereas with other sins, only a part of the body dies. A man and a woman form one whole body, because the woman is a portion of the man. Whoever commits another sin sins outside himself, but a fornicator sins against his own flesh.

If someone hangs himself or kills himself with a dagger, he does not sin against his body but against his soul, on which he inflicts violence. But to fornicate is a sin of the body which touches both the body and the soul. It is not without the desire of the flesh, because the flesh also has its motives, for the soul feels a desire to sin against the flesh, even though the latter can do nothing without the soul. By committing a sin against his flesh, which is made out of his very self (for he has returned it to its origin), the fornicator is said to sin against his body. This is why he ought to stop what he is doing and spare himself, so to speak.

---

[1]Jn 2:19, 21. [2]Gen 2:24.

According to Novatian, however, a fornicator sins not against his own body but against Christ's. He also expresses this in a different way, saying that the fornicator sins against the Holy Spirit, because he is cut off from the church. This cannot be stated with any logic. The body of Christ is not one or two Christians, but all of them—individuals are simply limbs. How is it then that a fornicator sins against the body of Christ, when in fact he does not corrupt them all? If Novatian were right, every other sin would be outside God, and only fornication would be a sin against God. An idolater would not be sinning against God, nor the man who recants under persecution, because as far as Novatian is concerned, whatever other sin a man commits is outside the body of Christ.

But if he wants to express this in a different way, saying that there is no sin outside the body of Christ, he will then be forced to say that anyone who has committed any sin whatsoever has sinned against God and the Holy Spirit. By this reasoning, a thief, a perjurer and a liar are all said to sin against the Holy Spirit. How does that square with what the Lord says: *All sins and blasphemies will be forgiven men, but he who sins against the Holy Spirit will not be forgiven, either now or in eternity.*[1]

At least it is clear that there exists a distinct sin that excludes others, which is called the sin against the Holy Spirit. In some people's opinion, a fornicator is said to sin against his own body simply because he is a member of the church, and by corrupting himself he sins against the church, whose member he is. In that case, we would have to say to someone who is committing fornication that he is not sinning against himself, but against the church. But the apostle goes on to say that a fornicator sins against his own body because he is failing a part of himself.

[19]Do you not know that your body is a temple of the Holy Spirit within you, which you have from God? You are not your own;

Earlier Paul spoke of the *temple of God*,[2] and here he speaks of the *temple of the Holy Spirit*, because in essence the Spirit is what God is. He said this with the intention that we should keep our bodies uncontaminated, so that the Holy Spirit may dwell in them.

[20]you were bought with a price. So glorify God in your body.

It is clear that someone who has been bought does not have the power to make decisions, but the person who bought him does, with the result that he does not do his own will but rather that of his master. And because we were bought for a very high price, we ought to serve our master all the more, so that the offense from which he has bought our release may not turn us over to death.

To glorify God in the body is to walk according to his law, for he is seen in his law. To carry God is to display the likeness of God by doing good deeds.

1 Corinthians 7

[1]Now concerning the matters about which you wrote. It is well for a man not to touch a woman.

Stirred up by the depraved minds of the false apostles, who in their hypocrisy were teaching that marriage ought to be rejected in order that they might appear to be holier than others, the Corinthians wrote to Paul to ask him about these things. Because they were unhappy about this teaching, they ignored everything else and concentrated exclusively on this. Paul replied to them that it was a good thing not to

---

[1]Mt 12:31. [2]1 Cor 3:16.

touch a woman, although this was not something which [the false apostles] stated anything like as clearly as that.

²But because of the temptation to immorality, each man should have his own wife and each woman her own husband.

In other words, no offense should be committed against the law while what is not against the law is being avoided. Those who look for a shortcut usually end up getting lost. How could men involved in such serious vices abstain from sexual intercourse with their wives? Paul therefore does not give them license to indulge in immoral behavior while abstaining from lawful things, as the Manichees do.

³The husband should give to his wife her conjugal rights, and likewise the wife to her husband.

Paul orders husband and wife to submit to one another in this matter, since the two of them are one flesh and one will, according to the law of nature.

⁴For the wife does not rule over her own body, but the husband does; likewise the husband does not rule over his own body, but the wife does.

Paul says this because neither the man nor the woman has any right to give his or her body to others. The two are indebted to each other in this respect, so that no opportunity for sin should be allowed.

⁵Do not refuse one another except perhaps by agreement for a season, that you may devote yourselves to prayer; but then come together again, lest Satan tempt you through lack of self-control.

Paul says this in order to encourage them to come to some agreement in their marriage relationship and not let disagreement lead to fornication. They may abstain for a while, particularly before the Eucharist, so that they can devote themselves to prayer. Although one should *pray without ceasing*[1] in the sense that this act of meditation should be practiced every day, nevertheless Paul teaches that people should devote special times to prayer every once in a while, in order to concentrate particularly on it and in this way satisfy the demands of God. If God is to show mercy, he must be supplicated in a state of special cleanliness. Even though marriages are clean, one should nevertheless abstain from things which are permitted within it, so that one's prayers may be all the more effective. Even under the law, those who wanted to be sanctified practiced temperance at the Lord's command, giving up wine (among other things) in order to become more holy.[2] The Lord makes it clear that when a person gives up things which are permitted, he is willing to receive the prayer which is being made.

Since he is giving advice to married couples —that men should turn again to the Lord, abstaining from intercourse with their wives, so that they may receive the body of the Lord more worthily—he adds that after the days of prayer are over, they should return to their natural habits. He warns them to abstain for limited periods only, in order not to give the devil any opportunity. The apostle Peter says: *Look, the devil goes about like a roaring lion, seeking whom he may devour.*[3] If one marries for the sake of having children, it seems that there is not much time available for this, because there are so many feast days, processional days and so on. The very way in which conception and childbirth happen makes it clear that a man ought to abstain at those times.[4]

---

[1]1 Thess 5:17. [2]Cf. Num 6:4. [3]1 Pet 5:8. [4]Cf. Lev 18:19.

⁶I say this by way of concession, not of command.

It is clear that in giving this advice, Paul's intention is to avoid fornication, not to put hindrances in the way of those seeking a better way of life.

⁷I wish that all were as I myself am. But each has his own special gift from God, one of one kind and one of another.

Paul was a benevolent and troubled teacher, and in his concern for the Corinthians, he wanted them all to be like himself, if at all possible. But everyone has a gift from God which corresponds with the object of his prayer. So, with the consent of God himself, Paul limits himself to wishing for what is possible. No one should be forced to do something unlawful on the ground that he is forbidden to do what is lawful. It is up to each person to choose which path he will follow.

⁸To the unmarried and the widows I say that it is well for them to remain single as I do.

Paul would not say these things if he were not pure in his own body. If he had had a wife and had told them to be like him, he would hardly be encouraging them to remain virgins. How absurd! Paul had been so fervent in his devotion since childhood that he had never had any desire for sex, since the grace of God had gotten hold of him when he was still a child. Having said that everyone has his own gift from God, he goes on to show which inclination is superior, because in this matter, everyone is helped to obtain the obvious desires of his mind.

⁹But if they cannot exercise self-control, they should marry. For it is better to marry than to be aflame with passion.

Paul wants the Corinthians to compete with one another in the struggle for self-control. But if they find that the impulse of the flesh is too strong for them to be able to continue the fight, then in that case, because they are not sufficiently prepared to receive God's help—for God helps those whom he sees are striving with all their might—they may marry, if they are afraid of being burned. Perhaps they will be able to achieve their aim later, for once a hindrance has been disposed of, the will recovers and becomes even stronger than before.

Paul did not say that it is a good thing to be aflame with passion, and better still to marry. He was just using ordinary idiom here to express himself. We often say that it is better to make a profit than a loss, for example. To burn is to be driven or overpowered by desire. When the will gives in to the heat of the body, it is burned. To suffer desire and not to be conquered is the mark of a distinguished and perfect man.

¹⁰To the married I give charge, not I but the Lord, that the wife should not separate from her husband

After speaking to the unmarried and the widowed, he speaks as if from God himself to those who are joined in marriage.

¹¹(but if she does, let her remain single or else be reconciled to her husband)—and that the husband should not divorce his wife.

The apostle's advice is as follows: If a woman has left her husband because of his bad behavior, she should remain unmarried or be reconciled to him. If she cannot control herself, because she is unwilling to struggle against the flesh, then let her be reconciled to her husband. A woman may not marry if she has left her husband because of his fornication or apostasy, or because, impelled by lust, he wishes to have sexual relations with her in an illicit way. This is so because the inferior party does not have the same rights under the law as the stronger one has. But if the husband turns away from the faith or desires to have perverted sexual relations, the wife may neither marry another nor return to him. The husband should not divorce his wife, though one should add the clause *except for fornication.* The reason why Paul does not add, as he does in the case of the woman, *But if she departs, he should remain as he is* is because a man is allowed to remarry if he has divorced a sinful wife. The husband is not restricted by the law as a woman is, *for the head of the woman is her husband.*[1]

[12]To the rest I say, not the Lord, that if any brother has a wife who is an unbeliever, and she consents to live with him, he should not divorce her.

Paul says this in order to distinguish what the Lord has said directly from what he has entrusted to Paul's authority, for the Lord speaks through him also. As Paul says: *Are you looking for proof that Christ speaks in me?*[2]

[13]If any woman has a husband who is an unbeliever, and he consents to live with her, she should not divorce him.

Paul says this in the case of two Gentiles, one of whom has become a believer. Normally, a pagan detests Christianity and a new Christian does not want to be contaminated by his pagan past, which is why Paul says that if the pagan party is happy to stay together, the Christian one should reciprocate.

[14]For the unbelieving husband is consecrated through his wife, and the unbelieving wife is consecrated through her husband. Otherwise, your children would be unclean, but as it is they are holy.

Paul says that these unbelievers have the benefit of good will, because they do not detest the name of Christ. The fact that the sign of the cross, by which death was conquered, is made [in their household] serves to protect it, for this is their sanctification. Their children would be unclean if they were to send them away against their will, and also if they were to cohabit with others. In that case, they would be adulterers and their children would be illegitimate, and therefore unclean. Instead the children are holy because they have been born of a lawful marriage and because they have been born subject, on the more important side [of the family], to the worship of the Creator. Just as everything sacrificed to idols is unclean, so everything dedicated to God the Creator and done out of belief in him is holy.

[15]But if the unbelieving partner desires to separate, let it be so; in such a case the brother or sister is not bound. For God has called us to peace.

Paul maintains the religious principle that Christians should not desert their marriage partners. But if the unbeliever leaves out of hatred, the believer is not to be blamed for having dissolved the marriage, for the claim of God is greater than that of the marriage.

Marital respect is not owed to a partner who abominates the Maker of marriage. A marriage contracted without devotion to God is not binding, and for that reason it is not a sin if it is abandoned because of God. But the unbelieving partner sins both against God and against the marriage, because he or she is unwilling to live in a marriage relationship dedicated to God.

If Ezra could insist that believers must divorce their unbelieving spouses so that God might show favor to his people and not be of-

---

[1] 1 Cor 11:3. [2] 2 Cor 13:3.

fended by them if they were to take other wives from their own people[1]—for they were not told that, after having divorced such wives, they must never marry anyone else—how much more, if an unbeliever has deserted his wife, should she be free to remarry (if she wishes) a husband of her own faith, for what has been done outside the law of God ought not to be considered matrimony. (However, if he later repents and reforms, and is sorry for having sinned, he ought to be forgiven.) But if both parties are believers, they confirm their marriage through their acknowledgment of God.

It is not right to go to court over an unbelieving man who leaves his marriage, because he is doing this out of hatred for God, and for this reason he is not to be considered worthy [of such attention].

[16]*Wife, how do you know whether you will save your husband? Husband, how do you know whether you will save your wife?*

Paul says this because it is always possible that the unbelieving partner will come to believe if he or she does not detest the name of Christ.

[17]*Only, let every one lead the life which the Lord has assigned to him, and in which God has called him. This is my rule in all the churches.*

God has assigned to each person the time of his salvation, that is, the time when he might believe, and he will keep that person until then. Here too Paul teaches that these people are to be waited for and that no scandal should be caused on their account, because we ought to maintain our hope for them. If they themselves depart, this approach must be concealed from them. If a person who believes is joined in marriage [to an unbeliever], he or she should not desert, but should remain in the marriage,

whether Jew or Greek. By way of persuasion, Paul says that this is his general rule, so that when they hear that others are expected to follow it, they will be more willing to do so themselves. It is always easier to do something when you see others doing the same.

[18]*Was any one at the time of his call already circumcised? Let him not seek to remove the marks of circumcision. Was any one at the time of his call uncircumcised? Let him not seek circumcision.*

Paul says this because he does not want a Jewish convert to think that he is somehow unworthy because he has no foreskin, as if that mattered. Likewise the Gentile who has been called should not think that he must be circumcised because he has heard that the sons of Abraham are given precedence. They are not given precedence because of their circumcision, but because of the merit of Abraham, whose sons they are in two respects, if they believe. But if they do not believe, they are worse than the Gentiles, for it is worse to have once been something and to be that something no longer, than never to have been it at all.

[19]*For neither circumcision counts for anything nor uncircumcision, but keeping the commandments of God.*

It is clear that it is neither an advantage nor a disadvantage. It is faith, backed up by good works, which makes God favorable toward us.

[20]*Every one should remain in the state in which he was called.*

Here Paul is confirming what he has already said above.

[21]*Were you a slave when called? Never mind.*

---

[1]Ezra 9–10.

But if you can gain your freedom, avail yourself of the opportunity.

Paul encourages slaves to serve their earthy masters in the fear of God, so that they may appear to them to deserve their freedom. Perhaps Paul says this because he is afraid that a converted slave might become more negligent in doing good works for his earthly master and give the teaching of Christ a bad name. Such a person would not find favor with God, whereas if he performs his duties well in earthly matters, he lays up merit with God as an investment for himself, for the Lord has said: *He who is faithful in little is faithful also in much.*[1]

[22]For he who was called in the Lord as a slave is a freedman of the Lord. Likewise he who was free when called is a slave of Christ.

Whoever has been delivered from sins, which are the true mark of slavery, becomes a freedman of the Lord. The ancients used to say that anyone who acts unwisely is a slave. They called all wise men free, and the unwise were slaves as far as they were concerned. This is why Solomon says: *free men shall serve a slave who is wise.*[2] Therefore the man who believes, even if he is a slave for a time, becomes a freedman of the Lord, because by believing in Christ, he is doing a wise thing. For if sins create slaves, as Ham, the son of Noah, was made a slave because of his sin and lack of prudence, [Christ can set him free], for when he receives the forgiveness of sins, he becomes a freedman. In any case, even a free person becomes a slave of Christ, for previously he was free from God, which is the biggest sin of all. Having lost his bitter and perverted "liberty," he has received a status which is beneficial to him, as the Lord said: *Take my yoke upon you, because it is easy, and my burden, because it is light.*[3] In this way Paul has cut down pride and created a new

unity, so that no slave would consider himself despised, nor would a free man, puffed up with proud thoughts, put himself above the slave.

[23]You were bought with a price; do not become slaves of men.

It is true that we have been bought at so high a price that only Christ, who owns everything, is able to pay it. Therefore whoever is bought with a price ought to serve all the more, in an effort to pay back the buyer. Having been bought by God, we must not become slaves of men. Slaves of men are those who accept human superstitions. The apostle is here recalling what he censured at the beginning of his letter, because people were saying *I am of Paul, I am of Apollos, I am of Cephas,* or *I am of Christ.* He has added the clause *do not become slaves of men* so that Christ should be acknowledged as God, since he indicates that the servants of Christ may not be called servants of men.

[24]So, brethren, in whatever state each was called, there let him remain with God.

Paul repeats what he said above in order to underline its importance.

[25]Now concerning the unmarried, I have no command of the Lord, but I give my opinion as one who by the Lord's mercy is trustworthy.

Paul is replying to what the Corinthians have written, in line with what he has already said above: *About the things of which you have written to me,* et cetera. He says that he has not received any instructions about virgins, because the Author of marriage could not order anything which goes against marriage without bringing down recrimination on his ancient decree. Paul says that he is giving advice, not because it is unwelcome or tinged with flattery,

---

[1]Lk 16:10. [2]Sir 10:25. [3]Mt 11:29-30.

but because he has received the grace needed for his advice to be useful.

²⁶I think that in view of the present¹ distress it is well for a person to remain as he is.

Here Paul teaches that virginity is better, not just because it is more pleasing to God, but also because it is the more sensible course to follow in the present circumstances. Between the "good" and the "best," it will be understood that there is nothing so fine and so advantageous as virginity, because Paul teaches that it is the more commendable state, not only before God but also for present-day life, when we do not know what stresses of the times a marriage might be called upon to withstand, or what circumstances might arise which would involve the grievous loss of children, or their being made orphans. In order to encourage people to aspire to virginity, he teaches those who are happy with it to profit from the distress of the present time of difficulty. In this way they will not only learn to look at it as the better status before God, but also seek after it with all their might in the present life. It is one thing for virginity to labor to conquer the desire of the flesh when it is free in other respects [but quite another for it to do this when bound by the circumstances of the present age]. Because the flesh is fundamental to our origin and nature, it appears to us to be sweet and pleasant to look at, so that to overcome it is a real triumph.

²⁷Are you bound to a wife? Do not seek to be free. Are you free from a wife? Do not seek marriage.

Here Paul's advice is essentially remedial. He says that no one should be divorced from his wife except in a case of fornication. It often happens that men who divorce their wives

because they want to live a sex-free life end up seducing others when their resolve has weakened. If such a man wants to live better while staying married to his wife, he should try to persuade her to live without scandal in a purer manner. A man who knows that this is more acceptable to God without being a matter of obligation should not go looking for a wife, but only if he abstains from sexual relations with other women. If he does not, what advantage is there in repressing [the lusts of] the flesh? Why reject something which is lawful only to subject oneself to unlawful relations?

²⁸But if you marry, you do not sin, and if a girl marries she does not sin. Yet those who marry will have worldly troubles, and I would spare you that.

The man who marries does not sin, because he is doing something which is permitted. But if he refuses to do it, he earns merit and a crown in heaven, for it takes great self-control to avoid doing something which is not expressly forbidden.

A virgin who marries is not sinning, because before God this is a matter of free choice. But even though they are free from sin, they will suffer troubles in this world: pains of the womb, the raising of children, making a living, finding somewhere to live, dowries, sickness, household maintenance, the duty of staying closely bound to a wife, the domination of a husband.

Paul is trying to spare them all this when he encourages them to opt for a life which excludes the troubles of the flesh and the above-mentioned anxieties. He is also sparing them in a different way in allowing those who desire what he says is burdensome to have what they want, and not standing in their way.

²⁹I mean, brethren, the appointed time has

---

¹A footnote in the RSV text adds, "Or *impending*."

grown very short; from now on, let those who have wives live as though they had none,

Paul meant by this that the end of the world was coming soon, though he knew that it would not come just yet. However, it is not true to say that he should have written differently, because there will be those who will read these things when there really will be only a very short time left. They should not be led into thinking that the day of judgment is far off, and so be unafraid of it and think the whole thing to be false. What is being talked about may still be some way off, but it is a very useful threat. It scares people into leading a better life! Just think how anxious people are in this life to bring a case before the judges when they know that the day of the trial is imminent. What Paul is saying here sounds very much like what he says elsewhere: *Deceiving, yet truthful.*[1]

Because the end of the world is near, believers should not worry about having children and instead should dedicate themselves more fully to the service of God. If they can become careful students of the law, they will be able to put up a fight in the [spiritual] battle which is imminent. For there will be many unprecedented pressures on them, and many will fall into the devil's trap. No one among us who has a proper fear of the pressures which the Savior predicted will want to be caught like that.[2] Let us therefore be as concerned for the interests of others as we are for our own, and abstain from begetting numerous children, while devoting ourselves more to prayer and to the service of God. Let us look ahead to the day of judgment and not be caught unprepared because of the burdens of everyday life, and may we not bring on ourselves the things we are most afraid of. Paul wants believers to exercise temperance even with regard to lawful things, so that they may not only be innocent, but glorious as well. To refrain from things which are allowed is the mark of great valor, and next to it is the ability not to desire things which are forbidden.

[30]and those who mourn as though they were not mourning, and those who rejoice as though they were not rejoicing, and those who buy as though they had no goods,

Those who know that the end of the world is near and that it will be a great consolation to those who are being oppressed for the sake of God's righteousness should comfort each other with this hope. Those who rejoice in the present must realize that grief will soon overtake them, that is, those who rejoice in the world and doubt the coming judgment of God.

Those who buy things ought to believe that little time is left for the world and should not behave in such a way as to devote their whole attention to something which will soon pass away. Instead they should take care of their soul, which they know to be eternal.

[31]and those who deal with the world as though they had no dealings with it. For the form of this world is passing away.

Those who deal with the world should not take its availability for granted, because it will disappear as soon as the world falls to ruin. For the form of this world is passing away. Note that Paul says that the form of this world is passing away, not the substance of it. Therefore if the form of the world is going to perish there is no doubt that everything in the world will vanish. It will all pass away, because every day the world gets older.

[32]I want you to be free from anxieties. The unmarried man is anxious about the affairs of the Lord, how to please the Lord;

[1] 2 Cor 6:8.   [2] Cf. Mt 24:19-31.

Someone who is less anxious about the present age will be more watchful where the things of God are concerned. Paul indicates how we can be free of anxiety by saying that the man who has no wife can be thinking about the Lord's business. Once the anxiety of relations with a wife is disposed of—an anxiety which surpasses any other in the world—the soul can be trained to act worthily in the presence of God. However, this is only true if the hope is to give greater service to God as the soul strips itself of its burdens.

[33]but the married man is anxious about worldly affairs, how to please his wife,

Looking after a wife and family is a worldly thing. Sometimes, just to keep them happy, it even leads to doing things which ought to be punished, as Zerubbabel, one of the three chamberlains of Artaxerxes, relates in the book of Ezra.[1] A disagreeable wife is a great source of bitterness in the home.

[34]and his interests are divided. And the unmarried woman or girl is anxious about the affairs of the Lord, how to be holy in body and spirit; but the married woman is anxious about worldly affairs, how to please her husband.

The man's interests are divided because he cannot put equal effort into God's affairs and into doing the will of his wife.

Women and virgins are distinct, not by nature but by activity, for we read in Numbers of women who are described as virgins.[2] The concerns of a woman are one thing; those of a virgin are another. But when a *woman* is mentioned it is not clear what the word means, unless it is explained. *Virgin*, on the other hand, is perfectly clear. The apostle here placed *virgin* after *woman* so as to indicate

that in this context a *woman* is not a *virgin*. He wanted to show that a virgin is free from the annoyances and labors which a married woman has to endure.

As long as an unmarried woman does not take on the anxiety of a husband and children, she thinks about the Lord's business and how she may keep up her resolve to devote herself entirely to God, asking only how her soul may strive within her pure body for heavenly things, casting away the things of this world. The soul is the thing which either sanctifies or corrupts the body. If anyone tries to have a pure body but a corrupt soul, he will soon have to choose between them. Either the soul must be honored or the body must be condemned.

A married woman is constrained by the law of marriage and has to think about how to fulfill her conjugal duties, while being constantly subject to the necessities of this world.

[35]I say this for your own benefit, not to lay any restraint upon you, but to promote good order and to secure your undivided devotion to the Lord.

Since the better and more advantageous course seems harsh and burdensome to some people, who are rooted in secular habits and attitudes, Paul states the reasons for his approach and argues as straightforwardly and as kindly as he can that what he advocates is for the best. Virginity is honorable because it is holy and clean. It is advantageous because it is dignified in the presence of God and of no account in the present age. What are we saying? If virgins think about God and married women think about the world, what hope is there for those who marry before God? If this is really the case, surely their salvation must be in doubt.

In fact, we see virgins thinking about the

---

[1]1 Esdras 4:25-27. [2]Num 31:18.

world and married women eagerly engaged in the works of the Lord. God will not regard such virgins as holy, and he will reward these married couples, for tied as they are by the bonds of the world and the flesh, they have nevertheless made an effort to earn something of their immortal reward in the future. As for those virgins, not only will they gain nothing from their virginity, they will be punished. Under the pretense of a better hope, they have spent their lives and activities in worldly concerns and anxieties and have been slack in doing the works of God. As the prophet Jeremiah says: *Cursed is he who performs the works of the Lord negligently.*[1]

These are the people whom Paul describes in another epistle as *having an appearance of godliness but denying its power.*[2] The apostle is talking to those people who want to obey the teachings of heaven with pure devotion. He is showing them and teaching them a shortcut by which they can approach God more quickly. Someone who wants to remain a virgin in order to gain God's favor, knowing what the rewards for this are, someone who abstains from what is lawful in order to become a better person, also despises all the hindrances of the flesh, aware that these things hamper the steps of a runner as if his legs were shackled.

[36]If any one thinks that he is not behaving properly toward his betrothed, if his passions are strong, and it has to be, let him do as he wishes: let them marry—it is no sin.

Earlier on, Paul argued that virginity and continence are the things to aim for, and supported his case with reasons which might make it seem that, in comparison with virginity, marriage is useless and to be rejected. But so as not to appear to have a negative attitude toward marriage, Paul now says that a virgin is not sinning if she marries. Nevertheless, she is embarking on a highly laborious business, which if it will not be punished, will not be rewarded by God either. Paul always wants the best out of Christians. If someone really wants to get married, then it is better to marry publicly according to the permission given than to behave badly and be ashamed in private.

[37]But whoever is firmly established in his heart, being under no necessity but having his desire under control, and has determined this in his heart, to keep her as his betrothed, he will do well.

Paul is saying that if a man has a virgin who has no inclination toward marriage, he should keep her in that state and not try to kindle a desire for marriage in a woman who has no leanings in that direction. If one has an obligation to do good deeds, how much more are we obliged not to put an end to them.

[38]So that he who marries his betrothed does well; and he who refrains from marriage will do better.

The man who marries his betrothed is acting well because what he is doing is lawful. The one who refrains from marriage does better because he earns merit for her with God and delivers her from the cares of this world.

[39]A wife is bound to her husband as long as he lives. If the husband dies, she is free to be married to whom she wishes, only in the Lord.

Paul writes this in order to make it clear that a woman who has been rejected by her husband is not free to marry again. If he should die, then she may remarry, but these words merely reinforce what was said previously. They show how blessed a virgin woman is, since she is

---

[1]Jer 48:10.　[2]2 Tim 3:5.

subject to nobody except God. In this way she wins a victory over natural subjection, since what has been made low by nature is raised up [by grace]. A woman may, however, marry a man she thinks suitable for herself, because marriages entered into against the will of one of the parties usually have bad results. She must, however, marry only in the Lord, which means without any suspicion of wrongdoing and within the bounds of her faith.

⁴⁰*But in my judgment she is happier if she remains as she is. And I think that I have the Spirit of God.*

When Paul says *Let her marry*, he is speaking from the standpoint of natural law, although first marriages are from God, while second ones are merely permitted. In other words, first marriages are celebrated in heaven with God's blessing, whereas second marriages, even in the present world, lack glory. They are permitted because some people have no self-control and because women often claim the privileges of widowhood at too young an age.[1] For these reasons, Paul makes allowance for second marriages, but because it is better for a woman to remain continent in order to have greater merit in the future, he gives the advice which in spiritual terms is most important, that she should exercise self-control.

Paul adds that he has the Spirit of God in order to show that his advice is correct. He commends it with deep feeling by the humility of his expression.

1 Corinthians 8

¹*Now concerning food offered to idols: we know that "all of us possess knowledge." "Knowledge" puffs up, but love builds up.*

Paul now goes on to speak about knowledge.

He does not say what this is, at least not straightaway, but in the words below he makes it clear when he says *that an idol is nothing.*[2] Knowledge is "puffed up" because it is obvious that someone who has it glories in the fact, if not publicly (because he is prudent) then at home. This is the sort of knowledge which glories it itself.

Knowledge is great and even useful to itself if it is humbled by love, in order that it might then grow larger. It is then diluted by kind feelings and not strong enough to inebriate the knowledgeable person, so that he gets above himself. Just as wine, unmixed with water, puts a man out of his mind, so wisdom makes one proud if it is not moderated. Everything on its own is unpalatable and harmful. On its own, bread tastes awful, and other foods are equally disagreeable if they are not mixed with something else. In this way, *love builds up.* Although love is expressed by a single word, it is made up of many things. It cannot exist without repentance, or without humility, or without straightforward honesty.

At Corinth there were people who were puffed up by the knowledge that an idol is nothing. To the harm of their more ignorant brothers, they would eat the meat of animals which had been sacrificed to idols, knowing perfectly well that this was lawful and that the eater would not be contaminated by it, because an idol is nothing. These people caused scandal among the brotherhood because they did not put love first, and for them it was a more serious thing to refuse the meat than it was to cause scandal to a brother. Their knowledge was doing damage to the minds of unlearned brothers, who thought that there was some beneficial grace inherent in the idol when they saw more educated brothers eating the meat without any compunction. This is why Paul says that *love builds up.* He wanted these people not to take advantage of the laws

---

[1] Cf. 1 Tim 5:3-16. [2] 1 Cor 8:4.

of knowledge where this matter was concerned, and not to cause scandal, out of concern for the salvation of their brothers.

2If any one imagines that he knows something, he does not yet know as he ought to know.

Paul is making it clear that those who boast in their knowledge have not come to understanding in the way that they should. As long as they were uninterested in love, which is the mother of all good things, they would not know anything in the right way. If knowledge is ever to bear fruit, it must be subject to love.

3But if one loves God, one is known by him.

The person who loves God is the one who tempers his knowledge for the sake of love, in order to be of some use to his brother, *for whom Christ died.*[1]

4Hence, as to the eating of food offered to idols, we know that "an idol has no real existence," and that "there is no God but one."

Paul now develops his argument in detail in order to show that knowledge without love is both useless and harmful. On the basic point at issue, it is true that an idol is nothing, for among Christians there is only one God.

5For although there may be so-called gods in heaven or on earth—as indeed there are many "gods" and many "lords"—

The sun, the moon and the stars are all called heavenly "gods" by pagans, and Apollo, Aesculapius, Hercules and Minerva are their earthly counterparts.

6yet for us there is one God, the Father, from whom are all things and for whom we exist,

and one Lord, Jesus Christ, through whom are all things and through whom we exist.

Everything that exists comes from God, but when Paul says that we are *in him*, he is distinguishing us from other beings which, though they are indeed "out of" him, are not "in him" because they do not yet believe. Everything has been created by the Father through the Son. In recognizing God we have been remade by him who created us. This is because, having been made by him along with other beings, we have by him come to see, after a period of mental dullness and ignorance, the mystery of the one God. Paul spoke of one God, the Father, and one Lord Jesus, his Son, but because it is impossible for God not to be Lord as well, *Lord* must be understood to mean God too. He showed that God and Lord were one and the same thing by restricting the creation to a single originating principle.

7However, not all possess this knowledge. But some, through being hitherto accustomed to idols, eat food as really offered to an idol; and their conscience, being weak, is defiled.

Not all believers have come to understand the mystery of the one God. Therefore some of those who believe think that there is something numinous in idols. Some of the common people, out of their previous veneration for idols, would eat meat sacrificed to them believing that there was some divine power present in it. A conscience is defiled if it is weak concerning the doctrine of the one God.

8Food will not commend us to God. We are no worse off if we do not eat, and no better off if we do.

It is true that we will not please God merely by eating anything and everything, nor will

---

[1]Rom 14:15; 1 Cor 8:11.

we offend him by abstaining from certain things. We can easily refuse to eat meat sacrificed to idols, since there will still be plenty of other things to have. Even if we eat it, it will not be enough to sustain us and we shall still require something more. For this reason, it is to be rejected, because we can easily live without it and to eat it causes scandal to some of the brothers.

9Only take care lest this liberty of yours somehow become a stumbling block to the weak.

In other words, if you say you can eat meat sacrificed to idols because you know that idols do not exist, see to it that you do not thereby cause offense to brothers who do not yet know that an idol is nothing.

10For if any one sees you, a man of knowledge, at table in an idol's temple, might he not be encouraged, if his conscience is weak, to eat food offered to idols?

Paul said this because someone seeing an educated brother reclining, by invitation, in a pagan temple and eating meat from the sacrifices, may think that there is some beneficial grace there and be tempted to eat meat sacrificed to idols, not because he also possesses the knowledge that there is no such thing as an idol, but because he thinks that there is some spiritual power in such food, because he sees his brother eating it without any qualms.

11And so by your knowledge this weak man is destroyed, the brother for whom Christ died.

The weak man will perish if he eats food which has been sacrificed to idols, because to him it goes against faith in one God. These are the words of an angry man, who is pointing out what harm can come from knowledge

if it is not tempered with love. Your education is killing him, because he sees you doing something which he interprets in a different way, and so you become the cause of your brother's death when Christ allowed himself to be crucified in order to redeem him. By this, Paul teaches us, for the sake of love, to pretend not to be learned, because without doubt a brother's salvation is more important than food, which is permitted but not helpful. To think like Paul is to *have knowledge as one ought to know.*[1]

12Thus, sinning against your brethren and wounding their conscience when it is weak, you sin against Christ.

Since they are not competing in the love with which Christ set us free, they are sinning in Christ. They are not sinning against Christ, because to sin against Christ is to deny him. Rather they are sinning in Christ, because to sin in Christ is to sin against things which belong to him. Someone who is under the law is said to sin "in the law," and in this sense, those who are under Christ are also said to sin "in him."

13Therefore, if food is a cause of my brother's falling, I will never eat meat, lest I cause my brother to fall.

Paul teaches that we should be so concerned for love that we should even regard things which are permitted in principle to be forbidden if they might otherwise stand in a brother's way. There is so much evil in sinning through things which are permitted, while not sinning through things which are forbidden, that the law should be kept in the case of things which are forbidden, but ignored with respect to permitted things as long as food is being eaten irresponsibly. The law permits

---

[1] 1 Cor 8:2.

what it grants, with the proviso that there are limits which people should stick to. It is all right to have a wife, but if she commits adultery she is to be rejected. Likewise it is all right to eat meat, but if it has been sacrificed to idols it is to be refused.

1 Corinthians 9

¹Am I not free? Am I not an apostle? Have I not seen Jesus our Lord? Are not you my workmanship in the Lord?

Paul's questions appear to be negative, but in reality they are affirmative; he is speaking in anger. His assurance of being an apostle was confirmed when the Lord sent him to the Gentiles: Go, *I will send you far away to the Gentiles.*[1] His evidence that he is a free man is based on the fact that he never desired anyone's property or preached to them in a flattering way. He even saw the Lord Jesus when he was praying in the temple at Jerusalem.[2] The Corinthians were Paul's workmanship, because he had grounded them in the Lord by preaching the gospel to them for eighteen months.

²If to others I am not an apostle, at least I am to you; for you are the seal of my apostleship in the Lord.

Those Jewish believers who nevertheless continued to observe the law of Moses denied that Paul was an apostle because he taught that it was no longer necessary to be circumcised or to observe the sabbath. Even the other apostles thought that he was teaching something different because of this, and they denied that he was an apostle. But to the Corinthians Paul was an apostle, because they had seen the signs of God's power in him. By his preaching they

had been converted from idols to faith in the one God.

³This is my defense to those who would examine me.

Here Paul begins to develop the argument which he set out above, namely, *All things are lawful for me, but I will not be enslaved by anything. Food is for the stomach and the stomach for food.*[3] This is how he begins his defense.

⁴Do we not have the right to our food and drink?

This is what Paul meant when he said that all things were lawful to him.

⁵Do we not have the right to be accompanied by a wife,[4] as the other apostles and the brothers of the Lord and Cephas?

Women followed the apostles and gave them money and helped because they wanted the Lord's teaching and a virtuous life. Similarly, women followed the Savior himself, ministering to him out of their own means.[5] Paul adds Cephas (that is, Simon Peter) because, although he was the chief of the apostles, he did not refuse offerings of money.

⁶Or is it only Barnabas and I who have no right to refrain from working for a living?

Paul means by this that he and Barnabas do have this right, but they do not want to exercise it. He says *working* instead of *receiving* in order to express himself more honorably. To confirm this he adds what follows.

⁷Who serves as a soldier at his own expense? Who plants a vineyard without eating any of

---

[1]Acts 22:21. [2]Acts 22:17-21. [3]1 Cor 6:12-13. [4]Ambrosiaster read "women" instead of "a wife," a reading which is found in other church fathers, though in very few biblical manuscripts. [5]Lk 8:3.

its fruit? Who tends a flock without getting some of the milk?

⁸Do I say this on human authority? Does not the law say the same?

By *human authority* Paul simply means common sense. He teaches here that his position corresponds to the teaching of Scripture, which he illustrates with many examples of give and take.

⁹For it is written in the law of Moses, "You shall not muzzle an ox when it is treading out the grain."¹ Is it for oxen that God is concerned?

Let us consider this for a moment. In the prophet Jonah it is written: *Shall I not spare a city in which more that a hundred and twenty thousand people live, as well as many cattle?*² And the psalmist says: *You O Lord, will save both man and beast.*³ How can we say then that God does not care about cattle and flocks? Of course he does not care about them for their own sake, but because of us, for whose benefit they were created. He cares about us more than he cares about them.

*¹⁰Does he not speak entirely for our sake? It was written for our sake, because the plowman should plow in hope and the thresher thresh in hope of a share in the crop.*⁴

The whole of Scripture applies to us by way of analogy. It is true that a man labors in the hope that there will be a crop to be harvested.

¹¹If we have sown spiritual good among you, is it too much if we reap your material benefits?

Paul says that it does not matter very much if those who preach the gospel of the kingdom of God and nourish the church on heavenly food take food for their own bodies and receive temporal things in exchange for heavenly ones.

¹²If others share this rightful claim upon you, do not we still more?

Nevertheless, we have not made use of this right, but we endure anything rather than put an obstacle in the way of the gospel of Christ.

What Paul is saying is that if people who are not their fathers in the gospel and do not have the same emotional attachment to the Corinthians can receive payment from them, how much more entitled to it is he? The plural here seems to imply the inclusion of Barnabas, who was also an apostle.

Paul has here brought out into the open an idea which had been hidden for a long time. He is making it clear that the reason he did not accept payment, despite his entitlement to it, is that he was afraid that his evangelistic zeal would cool off. The false apostles who were after money used to flatter sinners so that those who sat under them would not be aware of their sinfulness. But because this went against the demands of the gospel, Paul would not accept payment. That left him free to argue that he was not one of the false apostles. He outlawed things which in themselves were permissible in order to maintain Christian discipline, because the false apostles had caused offense through their bad behavior.

¹³Do you not know that those who are employed in the temple service get their food from the temple, and those who serve at the altar share in the sacrificial offerings?

Here the *temple* refers to the law of the Gentiles and the *altar* to the law of the Jews.⁵ The

---

¹Deut 25:14. ²Jon 4:11. ³Perhaps a misquote of Ps 28:9. ⁴Ambrosiaster reads this as: "since he who ploughs in hope also threshes the corn, it is right that he should see the fruit of his hope." ⁵Ambrosiaster evidently read the word *temple* as referring to pagan shrines.

Lord decreed through Moses that the priests were entitled to a portion of the offerings.[1]

14In the same way, the Lord commanded that those who proclaim the gospel should get their living by the gospel.

It was not by the law of Moses that God followed the practice of the Gentiles, but natural reason itself decrees that a person should live from his labor. By adding these words at the end of his argument, Paul makes his case stronger, showing thereby that the practice which he recommends is not a frivolous and pointless one. But he does not want to profit from this himself, so as not to compromise his freedom to rebuke them.

15But I have made no use of any of these rights, nor am I writing this to secure any such provision. For I would rather die than have any one deprive me of my ground for boasting.

After having shown by several examples that it is all right to receive payment, Paul goes on to add that it is not good for him to do so, because he would be compromised if he accepted anything from sinners, as I pointed out above. He says that his integrity depends on keeping the cutting edge of the gospel intact. He says that he would rather die than violate the laws of the gospel, because he knew that that would be better from the standpoint of his future salvation. He refused to take what was due to him in order not to appear to approve their sinful behavior.

16For if I preach the gospel, that gives me no ground for boasting. For necessity is laid upon me. Woe to me if I do not preach the gospel!

As the Lord says: *When you have done all that is commanded, say "We are unworthy servants;*

we have only done what is our duty."[2] The servant sent by the Lord does what he has to do even if he is not willing, because if he does not do it he will suffer for it. Moses preached to Pharaoh even though he did not want to,[3] and Jonah was forced to preach to the Ninevites.[4]

17For if I do this of my own will, I have a reward; but if not of my own will, I am entrusted with a commission.

It is obvious that no one gets a reward for something he does unwillingly. If he does it voluntarily, he is worthy of payment because he consents to his master's will and because, if it is done voluntarily, it is done better.

There is nothing unclear about this. Someone who acts unconscientiously is not acting voluntarily, but out of necessity. He is not in charge of his actions, but is merely following orders against his will.

18What then is my reward? Just this: that in my preaching I may make the gospel free of charge, not making full use of my right in the gospel.

Paul avoids commending himself openly, but he is nevertheless boasting, and wants the Corinthians to understand what a great reward he deserves precisely because he has not taken advantage of his power in the gospel. Instead he has rejected payment offered to him so as not to compromise the power of his preaching. There was nothing wrong with being paid, but it was not helpful for the salvation of the brothers, who needed to be corrected. Paul wanted to be a model for others, so that they too would not take advantage of practices which are in principle allowable if they see that it would not be helpful to do so. Failure to behave in that way would make them guilty of abusing allowable practices, because they

---

[1]Deut 18:1-5. [2]Lk 17:10. [3]Ex 3:10–4:21. [4]Jon 1:2-3.

would be taking money in a way which had a detrimental effect.

¹⁹For though I am free from all men, I have made myself a slave to all, that I might win the more.

Paul is free from all men because he preached the gospel without getting any praise for it and never wanted anything from anyone except their salvation. He has not accepted large sums of money to spend on himself, which would have been sheer hypocrisy. He says that he has acted as *a slave to all* in order to show by his humility that he was not unlike anyone who is weak in his thinking. Paul wanted to strengthen them by patience for their future salvation by showing his great concern for those who were sinning or who were being slow to follow the commands of their faith. All along, his main aim was that they should not feel bitter resentment at being rebuked.

²⁰To the Jews I became as a Jew, in order to win Jews; to those under the law I became as one under the law—though not being myself under the law—that I might win those under the law.

Did Paul merely pretend to be all things to all men, in the way that flatterers do? No. He was a man of God and a doctor of the spirit who could diagnose every pain, and with great diligence he tended them and sympathized with them. We have something or other in common with everyone, and this is what Paul brought out in dealing with particular people. He became a Jew to the Jews in that he circumcised Timothy,¹ because that was a scandal to them, and when he went to the temple he practiced the rite of purification,² so that the Jews would not be given an opportunity to blaspheme on

his account. He performed an action which by its nature should have been obsolete, but he acted in accordance with the law. He agreed with the Jews that the law and the prophets were from God, and on that basis he showed them that Christ was the promised one. He agreed with them, in other words, in order to get them to accept his teaching.

²¹To those outside the law I became as one outside the law—not being without law toward God but under the law of Christ—that I might win those outside the law.

People who are under the law are known as Samaritans, because being of Persian and Assyrian origin, they accept only the Law, that is, the five books of Moses. The Assyrian king settled them in the region of Samaria after he had deported the children of Israel.³ This is why they also worship fire in the way the Persians do. It was for these people that Paul put himself under the law and did not deny that the law was of God. Instead he taught them as gently as he could that the law speaks about Christ [hoping that they would be converted], as was the Samaritan woman, who said to the Lord: *I know that the Messiah is coming*, having been taught this by the law.⁴ To be under the law of Christ is to be under the law of God, because everything which is of God is of Christ: *Everything that is mine is yours and yours is mine.*⁵

In agreeing with the Gentiles that the world and everything in it was made by God in accordance with natural laws, and that the soul is immortal and that we have our origin from God—for Paul says so in Acts: *As some of you have said, "We are also his offspring."*⁶—he put himself outside the law, and thus indirectly managed to get them to accept the notion that Christ is the one who was predestined to judge

---

¹Acts 16:3. ²Acts 21:24. ³2 Kings 17:24-34. ⁴Jn 4:25. Ambrosiaster's interpretation of this verse as applying to Samaritans is completely wrong. ⁵Jn 17:10. ⁶Acts 17:28.

the world, and that it is through him that God made all things.

22To the weak I became weak, that I might win the weak. I have become all things to all men, that I might by all means save some.

Paul became weak by abstaining from things which would scandalize the weak. Here he shows the true marks of a wise and spiritual man, because having become all things to all men, he nevertheless did not transgress the bounds of his faith. When he made allowances, he did so in order to do good, but he never did anything other than what the law commanded.

23I do it all for the sake of the gospel, that I may share in its blessings.

Paul did all these things in order to share in God's plan for the salvation of the human race.

24Do you not know that in a race all the runners compete, but only one receives the prize? So run that you may obtain it.

Paul now wants to illustrate something else. He takes this example to show how useful the law of Christ is, because the prize is promised not merely to one, but to all. He wants us to run carefully toward the promised reward, because it is a great one.

25Every athlete exercises self-control in all things. They do it to receive a perishable wreath, but we an imperishable.

Athletes abstain from things as demanded by their training because they know that only one of them will win the crown. How much more should we do the same, because we know that salvation is promised to us all. Our gift is of an altogether higher order, and for this reason we ought to be more diligent because

of the spiritual crown which is in store for us, adorned not with fading earthly flowers, but with everlasting jewels, like a royal diadem.

26Well, I do not run aimlessly, I do not box as one beating the air;

Paul means that he is running with great hope, taking his promised reward as certain. He is struggling not merely with his words, but with his deeds.

27but I pommel my body and subdue it, lest after preaching to others I myself should be disqualified.

To pommel the body is to fast and to avoid any kind of luxury. Paul subdues it when he does the will of the Spirit and not his own will. He shows that he disciplines his own body so that he will not miss out on the reward about which he preaches to others. He is afraid that, when others are cured, he may be left nursing his wounds. He therefore says that the hope of his preaching is assured when he shows by his deeds that he practices what he preaches. Someone who fails to do this makes his hearers distrustful, and so they end up doubting that what he promises them is true. By his own example, Paul is demanding that we should act on our beliefs and not merely talk about them.

1 Corinthians 10

1I want you to know, brethren, that our fathers were all under the cloud, and all passed through the sea, 2and all were baptized into Moses in the cloud and in the sea,

Paul wants us to be upset by the example of the Jews, who offended God by their waywardness. He says that they were under the cloud in order to point out that everything which happened to them is meant to be understood as a picture of the truth which has been revealed to us. Under the cloud they were protected from their enemies until they were delivered from death,[1] which is called baptism. For when they passed through the Red Sea under the guidance of Moses they were delivered from the Egyptians who died in it, and this prefigured our baptism. Their past sins were not counted against them, but after they were cleansed by the sea and by the cloud, they were made ready to receive that law and the pattern of our future sacrament.

³and all ate the same supernatural food ⁴and all drank the same supernatural drink. For they drank from the supernatural Rock which followed them, and the Rock was Christ.

The manna and the water which flowed from the rock are called spiritual because they were not formed according to the law of nature, but by the power of God working independently of the natural elements. They were created for a time as figures of what we now eat and drink in remembrance of Christ the Lord. The manna was called the "bread of angels" because it was created by the power which gives angels their being and intimates that the one who would give us spiritual nourishment would come down from heaven. Manna also came from heaven on the Lord's day, in order to satisfy the people. The rock which followed them is said to be Christ, because at times when human help was lacking, Christ was present with them. He followed them precisely in order to be able to come to them in such circumstances. Nor was it a rock which gave water, but Christ himself.

⁵Nevertheless with most of them God was not pleased; for they were overthrown in the wilderness.

Paul said this because the Corinthians did not appreciate the benefits which they had received. It is only right that someone who has received great things but does not believe in smaller ones should not only not receive the latter but should lose the former as well. Earlier on, Paul has given a command and said that he is doing all he can to run toward the promised reward in a worthy manner. Now, in order to correct them and persuade them by scaring them with the example of the ancient Jews, he says that they had also been given God's gift, just as we have been.

⁶Now these things are warnings for us, not to desire evil as they did.

Here the meaning and the argument are what I have indicated above.

⁷Do not be idolaters as some of them were; as it is written, "The people sat down to eat and drink and rose up to dance."

Here Paul is talking about those Christians who thought there was nothing wrong in going to dinner in a pagan shrine. The dancing was in front of a pagan idol, of course, and those who dine in pagan shrines are not immune from blame. It was when Moses was up the mountain that the people did all this, after setting up an image of a calf and sacrificing to it. This is the kind of self-indulgence in which people who are unfaithful to the things of God have always taken delight.

⁸We must not indulge in immorality as some of them did, and twenty-three thousand fell in a single day.[2]

This was the Israelites' punishment for having defiled themselves with Midianite women. The anger of God was aroused against them and

---

[1]Cf. Ex 14:19-31. [2]Num 25:1-13.

was placated only by the zeal of Phineas the priest, who was loyal to God, with the result that no more died.

⁹We must not put the Lord to the test, as some of them did and were destroyed by serpents;¹

The Jews were putting Christ to the test, because it was he who spoke to Moses. Paul is warning us here against being handed over to the devil, who is symbolized by the snakes, so that we may not suffer the same fate as they did.

¹⁰nor grumble, as some of them did and were destroyed by the Destroyer.

To grumble is to complain falsely to one another about prominent people and leaders, though as far as untruthfulness is concerned, it should be said that complaints often arise for good reason.² Those who were destroyed prefigured Judas, who betrayed Christ and was eliminated from the number of the apostles by the judgment of God. By these examples Paul summons us to a more upright life, so that we may earn a reward by listening to his warnings and obey them, or else incur a heavier punishment if we are disobedient. There can be no doubt that sinners who have been warned of the punishment awaiting them if they continue to sin will be much more likely to suffer torments if they do not listen.

¹¹Now these things happened to them as a warning, but they were written down for our instruction, upon whom the end of the ages has come.

We are in the end times because it is clear that these acts of retribution toward those people were done as an example to us, who in the last age would be disciples of Christ. They were done for our benefit, so that if we are scared by what happened to them and so remain in the fear of God, we may receive the glory which was promised to them. Otherwise, their punishments will be doubled in our case, because greater awareness of the law brings greater guilt with it.

¹²Therefore let any one who thinks that he stands take heed lest he fall.

Paul says this to those who, relying on their knowledge that it was lawful to eat anything, were a cause of scandal to their weaker brethren. Thinking that they had risen to a higher level, they in fact declined, because of the teaching of the false apostles, and condemned Paul, when they were the guilty ones. Because of this, Paul strips away their pride, so that they will not be tempted and perish as a result.

¹³No temptation has overtaken you that is not common to man. God is faithful, and he will not let you be tempted beyond your strength, but with the temptation will also provide the way of escape, that you may be able to endure it.

Those who were criticizing the apostle are regarded as being a trial to the Lord because those who criticized Moses and doubted him were also said to be a trial to God.³ Paul therefore scares the Corinthians and warns them that this trial must at all costs be avoided. By contrast, he also warns them that human trials may overtake them. A human challenge is to be distrustful of man because of hope in God—for hope in man is vain—so that in times of need and hardship we may not give up on God and turn to other people for help, as the Jews did when they despaired of the Lord

---

¹Num 21:5-6. ²The text is unclear but this seems to be the sense of it. ³Ex 17:2. Note that in Greek and Latin, the words for "temptation" and "trial" are the same here.

and sought the assistance of idols instead. This is "human help" because the gods of the pagans are merely earthly, and it was human error which invented them. To endure suffering for Christ's sake is a "human trial" by which we gain favor in God's eyes.

Paul says that God is faithful and will not allow us to be tempted beyond what we can bear because he has promised the heavenly kingdoms to those who love him. It is inevitable that he should make this gift, because he is faithful. For this reason, he will stand by those who suffer for his sake and will not allow the affliction to be so great that it cannot be borne. Either he will cause the trial to end quickly, or if it is prolonged, he will give us the strength to endure it. Otherwise, if someone who suffers should be overcome by it, God would not be giving what he has promised.

Because God is faithful, he comes to our aid and fulfills his promises. The Lord says that the days have been shortened so that the elect can be saved and obtain the kingdom of God.[1] But how does God help us if we are only allowed to be tempted to the limits of our ability to resist? Clearly we are helped by not having too much piled onto us, so (for example), we may not be allowed to suffer for four days if God knows that we cannot endure for more than three.

14Therefore, my beloved, shun the worship of idols.

Paul is still exhorting the Corinthians to avoid any connection with idolatry, so that not only their bodies but their minds as well might be separated from it in order to kill any form of temptation. For anyone involved in idolatry will expect something out of it. Remember how Saul abandoned God because God was angry with him for having sinned, and went off after idols in the hope of getting something out of them.[2] For him, this was both a hindrance in the present and a warning that hell, the avenger, lay in the future.

15I speak as to sensible men; judge for yourselves what I say.

Paul gives examples in order to persuade people more easily, because those who are not convinced by words often find examples more compelling.

16The cup of blessing which we bless, is it not a participation in the blood of Christ? The bread which we break, is it not a participation in the body of Christ? 17Because there is one bread, we who are many are one body, for we all partake of the one bread.

Because we are one, Paul says that we ought to think alike, so that our faith may look and be the same.

18Consider the people of Israel;[3] are not those who eat the sacrifices partners in the altar?

Paul is saying, *Look and learn, you people who see God, what carnal things are like and what idolatry is.*[4] Just as we, who share one bread and one cup, are partakers of the Lord's body, so those who eat pagan sacrifices are partakers of the altar of error.

19What do I imply then? That food offered to idols is anything, or that an idol is anything?

Not that an idol is anything, but they are offering sacrifices to demons and not to God.[5]

---

[1]Mt 24:22. [2]Cf. 1 Sam 15:10-31; 28:6-8. The reference is not exact. [3]The RSV add a note here, which says, "Greek *Israel according to the flesh.*" [4]Ambrosiaster has misread the text here, taking "Israel" as a vocative. The result is that he understands Paul to be saying *Consider, Israel, what the flesh is like.* [5]Cf. Deut 32:17.

An idol is nothing in itself, because it is only an image of something dead. But under cover of such images the devil is worshiped. Paul shows the Corinthians that there is more to an idol than what is merely seen on the surface.

20No, I imply that what pagans sacrifice they offer to demons and not to God. I do not want you to be partners with demons.

Paul is saying that beneath the surface of the idol there is a demonic power which is out to corrupt faith in the one God. For this reason the apostle John writes: *the Son of God came in order to destroy the works of the devil.*[1]

21You cannot drink the cup of the Lord and the cup of demons. You cannot partake of the table of the Lord and the table of demons.

As the Lord says: *You cannot serve God and mammon.*[2] Anyone who drinks the cup of demons insults the cup of Christ, and anyone who eats at the table of demons revolts against the table of Christ, that is to say, the altar of the Lord, and crucifies his body again. Christ was crucified in order to destroy the works of the devil, so someone who sacrifices to him is fighting against Christ.

22Shall we provoke the Lord to jealousy? Are we stronger than he?

Ordinary people hardly ever want to take on powerful ones, because they know that they lack the wherewithal to compete with them. Their rivalries are directed toward their peers, more or less. Therefore the apostle said that people would not compete with the Lord Jesus because they know that he is Lord; otherwise he whose lordship they enviously begrudge would not seem to them to be worthy of the name. Satan invented idolatry out of envy so that people would worship imaginary gods and goddesses while denying the Lord God.

23"All things are lawful," but not all things are helpful. "All things are lawful," but not all things build up.[3]

Paul is saying that in natural terms everything is lawful, because everything is by nature clean. Here the issue is food, particularly meat which had been offered to idols. How can it be said that things which are prohibited and forbidden are sometimes permitted, when Paul shows that even things which are allowable are occasionally not helpful? The policy to adopt in all such cases is the one which follows the advice of the apostle Peter, who says: *If this is the case with a husband and wife, it is not good for them to marry.*[4]

Everything may be eaten in principle, but it is not helpful to eat food which has been sacrificed to idols, because that scandalizes one's brother, as has already been said. For this reason, one should sometimes refrain from doing certain things which are in themselves lawful, because to do them would not be beneficial to anyone. This is why Paul refused to accept payment from the Corinthians, even though he knew that it was all right to do so.

24Let no one seek his own good, but the good of his neighbor.

It is true that anyone who dines in a pagan temple is pleasing himself and placing scandals in the way of the weaker brother's conscience. This is why we ought to be quick to forbid doing what we want to do, for the love of our Lord Jesus Christ and for the salvation of our neighbors. As Paul, the chosen vessel and spiritual doctor, says elsewhere: *Not seeking my own advantage, but that of many.*[5]

---

[1] Jn 3:8. [2] Mt 6:24. [3] Cf. 1 Cor 6:12. [4] Mt 19:10. The text gives this as the opinion of all the disciples, not just of Peter. [5] 1 Cor 10:33.

25*Eat whatever is sold in the meat market without raising any question on the ground of conscience. 26For "the earth is the Lord's, and everything in it."1*

Paul backs up his statement that nothing is unclean of itself by quoting the precedent of Psalm 23,2 for nothing which belongs to the Lord can be unclean. And since he has just said that all kinds of food are allowed, he follows this up with the command to eat whatever is sold in the market. He adds this in order to make sure that our consciences are clear. If something happens to have been polluted by having been sacrificed to idols, for example, but the buyer does not know this, there is no reason for him to hesitate, and he is quite blameless in God's eyes.

27*If one of the unbelievers invites you to dinner and you are disposed to go, eat whatever is set before you without raising any question on the ground of conscience.*

Eat what is set before you without asking where it comes from.

28*(But if some one says to you, "This has been offered in sacrifice," then out of consideration for the man who informed you, and for conscience' sake—29I mean his conscience, not yours—do not eat it.) For why should my liberty be determined by another man's scruples?*

Paul is speaking to mature people who are able to eat meat which has been sacrificed to idols while at the same time despising idolatry, knowing that it means nothing. They understand that the Creator cannot corrupt anything which is eaten in his name. But it is because someone else, who is an idolater, will be delighted at seeing you eating the sacrificial meat, because to him you will be venerating

idols, that it is wrong to do this. The idolater, of course, will be happy to go along with you if he sees you helping yourself to what has been sacrificed to idols.

Paul says that his liberty should not be judged by someone else's scruples because, since his own conscience is clear when it comes to idolatry, why should anyone think that by eating sacrifices he is somehow worshiping idols? He is being judged as no different from an idolater merely because he is not put off by something which has been offered to an idol.

30*If I partake with thankfulness, why am I denounced because of that for which I give thanks?*

Paul means this: if I partake of the grace of God, because I eat in his name, why should anyone think that I am an idolater, just because I am not put off by something which has been offered to an idol? The idolater denounces me, and rejoices in his idol. As long as he thinks that I am participating in his behavior, he has some excuse for remaining in his error, and sets a bad example to the brothers. For if the law teaches that groves, altars, inscriptions and the idols themselves should be broken down,3 ask yourself whether it is not a sin to abstain from this sort of thing on the one hand, and yet take part in feasts of this kind on the other. For all these reasons it is not very helpful to eat sacrificial offerings.

31*So, whether you eat or drink, or whatever you do, do all to the glory of God.*

Paul is saying that to eat in a pagan temple, even if one's conscience allows it, is an act of hostility toward God, because these feasts are dedicated to the devil and are insulting to the one God. For to eat and drink to God's glory is to eat and drink modestly, after giving thanks

---

1Ps 24:1. 2Ps 24 in English versions. 3Cf. Deut 7:5.

to the Creator. Something is done to the glory of God when God is praised through the acts and behavior of a Christian, or when the birth of children is hoped for from God.

32Give no offense to Jews or to Greeks or to the church of God,

Paul is saying that one's behavior should be controlled in such a way as not to give offense by it. Offense is given to the Jews when they see that a Christian, who claims the inheritance of the law and the prophets, is not afraid of idols, which they detest. Offense is given to the Greeks, that is to the Gentiles, if their sin of idolatry is not only not contested but actually encouraged by people in the church who fail to reject things sacrificed to idols. The church of God is scandalized when some of its members do things which are hostile to God.

33just as I try to please all men in everything I do, not seeking my own advantage, but that of many, that they may be saved.

For someone to please everybody in all things is to act in a way which does not cause scandal to anyone, and to further what is in their interest, so that it may be advantageous both to them and to him.

1 Corinthians 11

1Be imitators of me, as I am of Christ.

It is normal that we should imitate those whom God has set over us as teachers. For if they imitate God, why should we not imitate them? For just as God the Father sent Christ as the teacher and author of life, so Christ sent the apostles to be our teachers, so that we should imitate them, for we are unable to imi-

tate him directly. The Lord says to his Father: *Just as you have sent me into the world, so I send them into the world.*[1] And because they were destined to be worthy imitators, he added: *And for their sake I sanctify myself.*[2]

2I commend you because you remember me in everything and maintain the traditions even as I have delivered them to you.

Having attacked their morals and behavior, Paul now goes on to correct their traditions. He is not supporting them but is angry with them, because although he was their apostle, they had forgotten what he had taught them and had not learned anything so far. Instead, they were copying the example of other churches, which is why he repeats his teaching as if he were saying it for the first time, as follows.

3But I want you to understand that the head of every man is Christ, the head of a woman is her husband, and the head of Christ is God.

Paul was talking in the context of authority, because everyone has his being from God, albeit through Christ. A woman also has her being through Christ, but as she was made from man, she is subordinate to her husband. The Father is rightly called the head of Christ because he begat him, but Christ is head of a man in one way, a man is head of a woman in another, and God is the head of Christ in yet another. God is the head of Christ because Christ was begotten of him, Christ is the head of the man because he created him, and the man is the head of the woman because she was taken from his side. Christ is the head of a man because Adam was created by him out of nothing. Thus one expression has different meanings, according to the difference of person and substance.

[1]Jn 17:18.. [2]Jn 17:19.

[4]*Any man who prays or prophesies with his head covered dishonors his head,*

To pray is to make intercession, and to prophesy is to proclaim the future coming of the Lord in symbolic terms, after prayer.

[5]*but any woman who prays or prophesies with her head unveiled dishonors her head—it is the same as if her head were shaven.* [6]*For if a woman will not veil herself, then she should cut off her hair; but if it is disgraceful for a woman to be shorn or shaven, let her wear a veil.* [7]*For a man ought not to cover his head, since he is the image and glory of God; but woman is the glory of man.*

Although man and woman are of the same substance, the man has priority because he is the head of the woman. He is greater than she is by cause and order, not by substance. The woman is inferior to the man because she is part of him, for her origin is in the man. She was created out of him, and for that reason a woman is under obligation to her husband and is subject to his control. Paul says that the honor and dignity of a man makes it wrong for him to cover his head, because the image of God should not be hidden. Indeed, it ought not to be hidden, for the glory of God is seen in the man.

There is an enormous distance between the glory of God and the glory of a man, for a man is formed in the likeness of God and a woman is not. She is the likeness of God because of the man. God created only one human being, so that just as all things come from the one God, all human beings come from the one man. The result is that one man bears on earth the likeness of the one invisible God, so that the one God would see the authority of the single originating principle being maintained. This would be to the consternation of the devil, who wanted to claim lordship and divinity for himself, to the detriment of the one God. The prophet Ezekiel alludes to this, as does the apostle, when he says: *So that he sits in the temple of God, flaunting himself as if he were God.*[1]

[8]*(For man was not made from woman, but woman from man.* [9]*Neither was man created for woman, but woman for man.)* [10]*That is why a woman ought to have a veil on her head, because of the angels.*

The veil signifies power, and the angels are bishops, as it says in the Revelation of John,[2] where, because they are men, they are criticized for not rebuking the people, though good behavior on their part is also praised. A woman therefore ought to cover her head, because she is not the likeness of God but is under subjection. Because transgression began with her, she ought to indicate this by covering her head in church out of reverence for the bishop. Nor should she speak, because the bishop takes the place of Christ. In front of him, and because he is the representative of Christ, she ought to appear as she would before a judge, as one under subjection, because of the way the sin of which we are guilty originated.

[11]*(Nevertheless, in the Lord woman is not independent of man nor man of woman; . . .)*

They are both in the Lord because God has made them out of one, to be both two and one at the same time. They are one flesh and one body in the Lord, that is to say, in accordance with the purpose for which the Lord created them. Those people who do not believe that woman originated from man think that mankind came into being without the Lord, and not in line with God's purposes.

---

[1]2 Thess 2:4; cf. Ezek 28:1-10. [2]Cf. Rev 2:1, 8, 12, 18; 3:1, 7, 14.

12(. . . for as woman was made from man, so man is now born of woman. And all things are from God.)

This confirms what I have already said, that both are one in nature because the origin of woman is man, and in Genesis we read that he was made by the Lord the Creator.

After expounding particular details step by step, Paul adds that all things are from God, in order that everything might be subject to him and that the notion of a single first principle may be kept in mind. His purpose here is twofold: that the woman will not be upset because of her state of subjection, and that the man will not be proud, imagining that he has some exalted position.

13Judge for yourselves; is it proper for a woman to pray to God with her head uncovered?

Now we see why Paul censured the Corinthians with irony back at the beginning of this chapter. It was the church's tradition for women to be veiled, but since the Corinthians were ignoring it, Paul made his appeal not to the authority of tradition, which they had disregarded, but to the argument from nature, and what he says is right.

14Does not nature itself teach you that for a man to wear long hair is degrading to him,

This is in line with Leviticus,[1] which prohibits a man from having long hair.

15but if a woman has long hair, it is her pride? For her hair is given to her for a covering.

Naturally Paul means that it is honorable, and practically compulsory, for a woman to be veiled when making amends and giving thanks to God. Long hair is a symbol of veiling, which

appears as a voluntary addition to nature. No unveiled woman ever obtains any authority.

16If any one is disposed to be contentious, we recognize no other practice, nor do the churches of God.

After giving reasons to refute dissenters, Paul lays down his authority, claiming that Jewish custom knew nothing of unveiled women, so neither Moses nor the Savior handed down such a tradition. This is why he says that neither he nor the churches of God [recognize any other practice].

17But in the following instructions I do not commend you, because when you come together it is not for the better but for the worse.

In the same way as he corrects their behavior by rebuking it, Paul also corrects their traditions by censuring rather than by praising them.

18For, in the first place, when you assemble as a church, I hear that there are divisions among you; and I partly believe it, 19for there must be factions among you in order that those who are genuine among you may be recognized.

Paul starts by showing the nature of the sin which brought about the errors which he is correcting. Where there is dissension, nothing is right. It is because he knew that some people had been corrupted in their thinking by the devil's cunning that he says that there must be heresies. Paul did not want heresies or choose them, but the Lord had also said: *Causes of stumbling must come,*[2] and *The Son of Man must suffer,*[3] knowing as he did that Judas would be a traitor. When Paul adds that the purpose is that the genuine believers might be recognized, he is referring to those who,

---

[1]Lev 19:27.　[2]Cf. Mt 18:7.　[3]Cf. Lk 9:22.

by holding fast to received tradition, were an example of the proven quality of the gospel discipline, to the condemnation of others. These are the same people he refers to at the beginning of the letter, who said *But we are of Christ*, when others were saying, *I am of Paul, I am of Apollos.*[1]

20*When you meet together, it is not the Lord's supper that you eat.* 21*For in eating, each one goes ahead with his own meal, and one is hungry and another is drunk.* 22*What! Do you not have houses to eat and drink in? Or do you despise the church of God and humiliate those who have nothing? What shall I say to you? Shall I commend you in this? No, I will not.*

Paul is here criticizing people who used to gather in church in such a way that when the presbyters came in—for this was in the days before rectors were appointed everywhere—they would offer their gifts and then help themselves to what they had offered, because of schism. For the false apostles had sown divisions among them and made them possessive of their offerings, even though they were all blessed with one and the same prayer. The result was that those who had not offered, of whom there were always some, or who had nothing to offer were covered with shame at not receiving a share. Furthermore, it all happened so quickly that those who came later found nothing left to eat. Therefore, says Paul, if you meet in such a way that people merely eat what they have brought with them, you should do this at home, and not in church, where we gather together for the sake of unity and the mystery [of the Eucharist], not for quarreling and gluttony. Once a gift is offered it becomes the property of the whole congregation, who are all included in the one bread. It is because we are one that we should all share in the one bread.

It is clear that once their wrongdoing has been pointed out and rebuked, the Corinthians should put it right and accept the truth of what Paul had already taught them, at the very beginning. He repeats the pattern given by the Savior with reference to this sort of situation, when he says what follows next.

23*For I received from the Lord what I also delivered to you, that the Lord Jesus on the night when he was betrayed took bread,* 24*and when he had given thanks, he broke it, and said, "This is my body which is for you. Do this in remembrance of me."* 25*In the same way also the cup, after supper, saying, "This cup is the new covenant in my blood. Do this, as often as you drink it, in remembrance of me."*

Paul shows here that the mystery of the Eucharist which was celebrated in the course of a meal was not in itself a meal, for it is spiritual medicine which purifies the person who receives it in faith and with reverence. It is the memorial of our redemption, whose purpose is that we should remember our Redeemer and so deserve to receive greater things from him.

26*For as often as you eat this bread and drink the cup, you proclaim the Lord's death until he comes.*

Because we have been set free by the Lord's death, we are indicating that we are the new covenant when we remember this fact in eating and drinking the body and blood, which were given for us. It is in this way that we have received the new law, which brings the person who is obedient to it straight to the courts of heaven.

Moses also collected the blood of a calf in a dish and sprinkled the children of Israel with it, saying: *This is the covenant which God has made with you.*[2] This act was symbolic of the

---

[1] 1 Cor 1:12. [2] Ex 24:8.

covenant which the Lord, by his prophet, called *new*, thereby making the covenant introduced by Moses *old*. The covenant was made in blood in order to indicate the loving kindness of God. In the symbolism of this, we perceive that the mystical cup is for the protection of our bodies and souls, because the blood of the Lord has redeemed our blood, that is to say, it has saved the whole human being. The flesh of the Savior is given for the health of our body, but his blood was shed for our soul, as Moses symbolized. For Moses had said: *Flesh is offered for the body, but blood is for the soul*, and therefore it was wrong to eat blood.[1] Thus if the ancients possessed a symbol of the truth, which has now appeared and been made manifest in the coming of the Savior, how is it that heretics imagine that the old covenant is contrary to the new, when in fact each bears witness to the other?

[27]Whoever, therefore, eats the bread or drinks the cup of the Lord in an unworthy manner will be guilty of profaning the body and blood of the Lord.

Paul is saying here that whoever celebrates the mystery in a way different from the one handed down by him is unworthy of the Lord. Anyone who presumes to act in a way different from that prescribed by the Author cannot be a follower of his. Therefore Paul is warning us that the mind of a person who approaches the Eucharist should be dedicated to the traditional pattern, because a trial is coming, at which everyone must give an account of himself, according to the way in which he has approached the Eucharist. Those who approach it without self-discipline are guilty of the body and blood of the Lord. What does it mean to be guilty, other than to be liable to pay the penalty for the Lord's death? For Christ was put to death for the sake of these people, who are making light of his mercy.

[28]Let a man examine himself, and so eat of the bread and drink of the cup. [29]For any one who eats and drinks without discerning the body eats and drinks judgment upon himself.

Paul teaches that one should come to communion with a reverent mind and with fear, so that the mind will understand that it must revere the one whose body it is coming to consume. We ought to judge this inwardly, because it is the Lord's blood we are drinking in the mystery, and he bears witness to the mercy of God. If we receive him in a self-disciplined manner, we will not be unworthy of the body and blood of the Lord, for it will appear that we are giving thanks to the Redeemer.

[30]That is why many of you are weak and ill, and some have died.

In order to prove that there will be a testing of those who receive the Lord's body, Paul now presents a picture of those who had done so thoughtlessly, while they were in the grip of fever and sickness, and many were dying. He wants others to learn from these people and be put right out of fear at what happened to these few. They should be made aware that one does not receive the body of the Lord negligently without being punished, and that a person whom God has temporarily passed over for punishment will be treated all the more severely because he has disregarded the example given to him.

[31]But if we judged ourselves truly, we should not be judged. [32]But when we are judged by the Lord, we are chastened so that we may not be condemned along with the world.

Paul says this because, if we were correcting our own faults, we would not come under the Lord's judgment. The fact that we are being

---

[1]Cf. Lev 17:10-14.

chastised is for our benefit, however. Its purpose is that we should be corrected by our fear, for the correction of everyone is based on the evidence of a few cases. The person who comes to the Lord's table irreverently is no better than an unbeliever.

33So then, my brethren, when you come together to eat, wait for one another—34 if any one is hungry, let him eat at home—lest you come together to be condemned. About the other things I will give directions when I come.

Paul tells them to wait for one another so that they may make their offering together and serve one another. If anyone cannot wait, then he should stay home and eat there. We should not celebrate the mystery in a reprehensible way which causes offense.

Paul has already said that the high point of our salvation should be celebrated in an orderly manner, and he has already given instructions about what behavior is fitting for both sexes with respect to the church. If there has been wrongdoing in this, it is not a trivial matter. As for his other concerns about building up the church, he promises that he will put these right when he comes to them in person.

1 Corinthians 12

1Now concerning spiritual gifts, brethren, I do not want you to be uninformed. 2You know that when you were heathen, you were led astray to dumb idols, however you may have been moved.

Now that he is about to give them spiritual teaching, Paul recalls their former way of life. His intention is that, just as they have been worshipers of idols in the shape of statues and used to be led about by the will of demons, so now, as worshipers of God, they may walk according to the model of the law, so as to be pleasing to God. For the shape of each law can

be seen in the declared faith and behavior of the worshiper. The visible form and outward manifestation of God's law is the person whose faith and behavior reflects the truth of the gospel.

3Therefore I want you to understand that no one speaking by the Spirit of God ever says "Jesus be cursed!" and no one can say "Jesus is Lord" except by the Holy Spirit.

People who did not understand how spiritual things work were giving glory, through their individual spiritual gifts, to men rather than to God, not having received from the Holy Spirit the power to control this gift, and the person who calls Jesus Lord does not say this without the Holy Spirit. Such a person has grace by the very fact of his faith, because of the glory of the name of Christ. For to say that Jesus is Lord is not [possible] without the gift of God. By this, Paul shows the Corinthians that in everything praise and thanks belong to God. Just as the likeness of idols is seen in their priests, who correspond in particular degree to their respective ranks, even though the whole thing is a human invention, so also in the law of the Lord there are rankings of spiritual gifts. They are granted to the office bearers in the church not according to human merit but in and of themselves, as is the case with offices of human origin also, since they are meant to contribute to the building up of the church. After all, it is the honor attached to the school that glorifies its graduate, and not his own reputation.

Paul says, therefore, that no one can say "Jesus be cursed" in the Spirit, because any voice which says that is the fruit of human error. Whatever is false comes from man. Similarly, no one can say "Jesus is Lord" except in the Holy Spirit, because this saying is uttered not out of the flattery of men, as happens when idols are called gods, but in the truth of the Holy Spirit. Any truth spoken by anyone is spoken by the Holy Spirit.

In the case of idols, men created them so that someone who is not a god might be called one, and for this reason, their temple priests are in a state of bondage. To prevent people from thinking that the approval of other people played a part in the Christian way of life and to stop them from being therefore totally unwilling to accept criticism, Paul told them that there was no human merit in a statement proclaiming Jesus as Lord, but rather this was a gift of God, who has deigned to reveal his mystery to mankind. Indeed, the mere fact of professing [faith] brings about the forgiveness of sins, just as devotion to idols increases them.

Paul therefore teaches that people who say that Jesus is Lord are not doing their religion a kindness, but are receiving kindness from God. He wants them to realize that the approval of other people plays no part in the law of the Lord, which is certainly not the case with idols, when someone is called a god when he is not one. Finally, those who did not understand that faith brings with it a gift of God used to attach themselves to particular men, saying *I am of Paul, I am of Apollos,* et cetera.[1] Paul shatters their pride, so that they may be prepared to accept criticism.

[4]***Now there are varieties of gifts, but the same Spirit;***

Paul does not want the variety of gifts to be attributed to human merit, as I have already said, but to the grace of God, so that his name might be honored. For just as the person who says Jesus is lord does so in the Holy Spirit, whatever kind of person he may be otherwise, so also someone who is an office holder in the church has a grace which is certainly not his own, but is given to the office through the agency of the Holy Spirit. This is why he said earlier in the letter: *Neither he who plants is*

anything, nor he who waters, but God gives the increase.[2]

[5]***and there are varieties of service, but the same Lord;***

Paul is saying that the different gifts are given by the same Spirit. In saying this, he links Christ with the Holy Spirit.

[6]***and there are varieties of working, but it is the same God who inspires them all in every one.***

Paul is so emphatic in asserting that this is not to be attributed to men as if it were their own that he goes as far as to say that the gift of the Holy Spirit and the grace of the Lord Jesus are the work of one and the same God. The grace and the gift cannot be divided according to the persons of the Father, Son and Holy Spirit, but must be understood as constituting the one work of the undivided unity and nature of the Three. In this way Paul is able to attribute all power and glory to the one God. The diversities of graces are assigned to offices held in the church, not to particular people.

If the Holy Spirit is Lord and the same Lord is God, the three are one God. Since the glory and power of the Holy Spirit and the Lord Jesus is divine by nature, the Holy Spirit and the Lord Jesus and, of course, the Father as well all constitute one God. They are all individually God, and the one God is three. Finally, all three are involved when one of them is at work, and so the mystery of the Trinity is contained in the incomprehensible nature and power of the one God.

[7]***To each is given the manifestation of the Spirit for the common good.***

Each person receives a gift so that, governing

---

[1] 1 Cor 1:12. [2] 1 Cor 3:7.

his life by divine constraints, he may be useful both to himself and to other people, while presenting an example of good behavior.

8To one is given through the Spirit the utterance of wisdom, and to another the utterance of knowledge according to the same Spirit,

In other words, he is given knowledge not by book learning, but by the enlightenment of the Holy Spirit, with the result that he has a heart that is enlightened and prudent, able to distinguish between things which must be avoided and things which must be pursued. In the Spirit, he has knowledge of divine matters.

9to another faith by the same Spirit, to another gifts of healing by the one Spirit,

Paul says this to encourage the person concerned to suppress his shyness and receive the ability to profess and lay claim to faith. By the gift of healing, Paul means the casting out of demons.

10to another the working of miracles, to another prophecy, to another the ability to distinguish between spirits, to another various kinds of tongues, to another the interpretation of tongues.

Power is given to some to perform miraculous signs. Prophecy refers to speaking of future events when filled with the Spirit. The discernment of spirits means the ability to understand and determine whether what is being said comes from the Holy Spirit or from one of the spirits of this world. To interpret is to interpret faithfully by God's gift the sayings of those who speak in tongues, or in writing.

11All these are inspired by one and the same Spirit, who apportions to each one individually as he wills.

Paul is here attributing to the Holy Spirit what he earlier attributed to all three persons. Because they are of one nature and power, the three do what the one does. There is only one God, whose grace is distributed to individuals as he wishes, not according to the merits of any particular person, but for the upbuilding of his church. All those things which the world wants to imitate but cannot, because it is carnal, may be seen in the church, which is the house of God, where they are granted by the gift and instruction of the Holy Spirit. They are seen in the ministries of particular individuals, so that people who are contemptible in the world's eyes may become vehicles for demonstrating the truth.

12For just as the body is one and has many members, and all the members of the body, though many, are one body, so it is with Christ. 13For by one Spirit we were all baptized into one body—Jews or Greeks, slaves or free—and all were made to drink of one Spirit.

By these words Paul is teaching that we should not treat anyone with contempt, nor should we regard anyone as perfect. For it is one and the same God who is glorious in everyone. We all share the same baptism and all have the same Holy Spirit. Paul says this because, as we have already mentioned, the Corinthians were glorying in some people but despising others.

14For the body does not consist of one member but of many.

In saying this, Paul shows that the different kinds of gifts have an inner unity, and that their diversity does not contradict the oneness of God's power. The unity of the body does not consist in being a single thing, but is seen in its many members, which supply the things which the other parts lack.

15If the foot should say, "Because I am not a hand, I do not belong to the body," that would

not make it any less a part of the body.

This means that a weak brother cannot say that he is not a part of the body simply because he is not strong.

¹⁶And if the ear should say, "Because I am not an eye, I do not belong to the body," that would not make it any less a part of the body.

Paul is saying that the person who is slightly inferior should not for that reason think that he is unnecessary to the body.

¹⁷If the whole body were an eye, where would be the hearing? If the whole body were an ear, where would be the sense of smell?

If everyone had a single function and a single task, how would the body's other needs be met, since we all agree that many functions are necessary in governing the body.

¹⁸But as it is, God arranged the organs in the body, each one of them, as he chose.

Paul is saying that the will of God, which is farsighted and rational, has attached different members to the body so that it will lack nothing but may be complete in its many parts.

¹⁹If all were a single organ, where would the body be?

If everyone in the church were the same, there would be no body, because a body is governed by the different functions of its members. They could not all be alike but are there precisely because they are different from one another in function.

²⁰As it is, there are many parts, yet one body.

Paul says this because the members need each

other and are therefore not discordant in their nature. Diverse though they are, this diversity in the members of the body unites for the purpose of ensuring that the body fulfills its potential. Likewise, those elements of which the earth consists, diverse though they are not just in their functions but in their natures, nevertheless have the beneficial effect of making the one world complete, and from them there arises a certain regulated diversity in their fruits, which is beneficial to mankind.

²¹The eye cannot say to the hand, "I have no need of you," nor again the head to the feet, "I have no need of you."

A more powerful person cannot say to an inferior, "I do not need you." It is through the eyes that seeing takes place, but it is the hands which carry out the work. The person who is greater in rank or dignity cannot do without those who are lower. For there are things which a humbler person can do which an exalted one cannot, just as iron can do things which gold cannot. Because of this, the feet perform an honorable function for the head.

²²On the contrary, the parts of the body which seem to be weaker are indispensable,

It is clear that no matter how elevated a person may be, if he has no one under him, his rank is contemptible. It is through service, after all, that rank acquires its meaning. Think what would happen if an emperor had no army. The greatest emperor still thinks that an army is necessary because it is a member of his body, with tribunes, generals and commanders out in front. Below them come the foot soldiers, who are even more essential. They are like those parts of the body which appear to be inferior but which in fact are more useful. Work is done by the hands without the eyes, and walking enables us to look for food.

23and those parts of the body which we think less honorable we invest with the greater honor, and our unpresentable parts are treated with greater modesty,

The meaning here is similar. We find something to praise in people who appear to have no rank, just as happens with those parts of the body which Paul calls less *honorable*, because we find greater pleasure in them than in the others. How worthy of honor are our hands, because with them we can grasp whatever we want! Or the feet, because with them we can go wherever we wish! For this reason, we give them honor. Because our feet are lowly and lacking in dignity, we adorn them with shoes. It is clear that our private parts, which are thought to be shameful, cover themselves with respectability by avoiding public display, so as not to obtrude irreverently. Likewise some of the brothers who are poor and unseemly in their dress are nevertheless not without grace, because they are members of our body. They go about in dirty little garments and barefoot, but although they may look contemptible, they are more to be honored because they usually lead a cleaner life. What men find despicable, God may find quite beautiful.

24which our more presentable parts do not require. But God has so composed the body, giving the greater honor to the inferior part,

It is obvious that the head does not need any further adornment, nor does the face or the hand. Thus we do not have to add anything to those brethren whose eagerness for expertise and respectability is obvious—the honor due to them is given already. But an exhortation is necessary regarding the despised and lowly to ensure that some honor is given to them, so that they may become useful. Otherwise, if these people are despised, they will become more negligent about themselves.

25that there may be no discord in the body, but that the members may have the same care for one another.

Paul is saying that the human body is so organized that all its members are necessary, and because of this, all are concerned for one another. One cannot exist without the other, and parts which are thought to be inferior are usually more necessary. No one ought to be despised as useless.

26If one member suffers, all suffer together; if one member is honored, all rejoice together.

It is undoubtedly true that if any part of our physical body is in pain because of illness, the whole body suffers along with it. In this way, Paul is teaching us to share pain with our brothers if we have to. It is obvious that the head is happy if the feet or other limbs are well looked after and healthy. So we ought to feel glad if we see some brother become better behaved and more respectable in his demeanor—healthy by intention, so to speak!

27Now you are the body of Christ and individually members of it.

Paul states openly that he has been talking about us when developing the logic of the limbs of the body. We cannot all do the same things, but each of us has a gift granted to us in proportion to the quality of our faith.

28And God has appointed in the church first apostles, second prophets, third teachers, then workers of miracles, then healers, helpers, administrators, speakers in various kinds of tongues.

Paul has placed the apostles at the head of the church. They are the ambassadors of Christ, as the same apostle says: *On behalf of whom* we carry out our task as ambassadors.[1] They may be identified with bishops, as Peter said of Judas: *Let another take his bishopric.*[2] There are two types of prophets, those who predict the future and those who interpret the Scriptures. The apostles are also prophets, because the top rank has all the others subordinated to it. Even a wicked man like Caiaphas uttered prophecies on the strength of his rank,[3] not for any virtue he might have possessed. However, prophets were specifically both interpreters of the Scriptures and predictors of the future. For example, there was Agabus, who predicted disaster and imprisonment for the apostle at Jerusalem[4] and foretold a famine which happened in the reign of Claudius.[5] Therefore, even if an apostle is a greater man, he still sometimes needs prophets. Because everything comes from the one God, the Father, he has decreed that individual bishops should take charge of individual churches.

Teachers are those who instructed boys in the synagogue in reading and writing, a practice which has come down to us in the church as well. It is also possible for someone who is not a bishop to be a faith healer. In fifth place Paul puts the gift of the intellect, since these are the people who give assistance and do the administrative work. Paul wants common sense to play its part in religious affairs, but in such a way that when such a person cannot complete a task by himself, he may get what he lacks from someone else, since not everything can be given to a single individual. The existence of administrators shows people that there are spiritual bonds [which unite us].

It may be one's gift from God to be able to speak many languages. The grace of God may also give people the ability to translate from one language to another.

[29]Are all apostles? Are all prophets? Are all teachers? Do all work miracles?

A church has only one bishop, and prophecy is not given to everybody. A teacher is a person to whom this gift has been granted. A man who is able by God's grace to cast out demons can be said to work miracles.

[30]Do all possess gifts of healing? Do all speak with tongues? Do all interpret?

It is obviously impossible for everyone to have the gift of healing. Equally obviously, not everybody can speak in tongues, but only a person who receives the gift of doing this. Furthermore only a person who is given the gift can interpret tongues.

Paul has explained and accounted for the fact that everybody has a different gift and that no one person has them all. This is exemplified by the members of our body, by means of which Paul indirectly expounds the nature of our spiritual body. Therefore God is to be praised, and we must glory in the name of the one who has given us this grace. We find the same order of things in nature. Gold is nobler than silver, but silver is more widely used. Bronze is necessary, but iron more so, for almost nothing is done without iron, inferior though it is.[6]

[31]But earnestly desire the higher gifts. And I will show you a still more excellent way.

Paul goes on to point out a better way in what follows. He moves the Corinthians on to higher things, showing them that all the aforementioned graces of the Lord which are seen in men do not relate to the merit of the individual, but to the honoring of God. It is because these things do not always relate to

---

[1]2 Cor 5:20. [2]Acts 1:20. [3]Jn 11:49-52. [4]Acts 21:10-11. [5]Acts 11:28. [6]This paragraph is detached from the commentary and represents an early recension of Ambrosiaster's text.

merit that the Savior says: *many will say on that day: "Lord, Lord, have we not prophesied in your name and cast out demons and done many mighty works?"*[1] Because there is no connection with merit, and these are works of the church, the Lord says to them, to the utter bewilderment of the Gentiles and in order to bear witness to the honor due to God alone: *Depart from me, you workers of evil. I do not know you.*[2] Being complacent because the work of God was apparent in them, these people were neglecting themselves. Now the Savior also says to the seventy-two disciples, when they are rejoicing because the demons have been subjected to them: *Do not rejoice in the fact that the demons have been made subject to you, but in the fact that your names have been written in heaven.*[3] Why is this, other than because they were subjected to the name of God and not to the merit of these particular individuals? Why is it that people today do not have the grace of God in this way? These things had to happen at the beginning, in order to give the faith a sure foundation. But now it is not necessary, because people are bringing each other to the faith when they see good works and hear straightforward preaching.

1 Corinthians 13

[1]*If I speak in the tongues of men and of angels, but have not love, I am a noisy gong or a clanging cymbal.*

It is a great gift to be able to speak in different languages. To speak with the tongues of angels is even greater. But in order to show that none of this can be ascribed to merit and that every tongue is subject to the glory of God, Paul adds that a man without love is like a noisy gong or a clanging cymbal.

For just as a bronze vessel resounds and a cymbal tinkles when somebody else strikes it, so the man who speaks in tongues receives the working of the Holy Spirit, which gives him the ability to speak. As the Savior says elsewhere: *It is not you who are speaking but the Spirit of your father who is speaking in you.*[4]

Balaam the son of Beor had an ass which spoke a human language in order to demonstrate the majesty of God,[5] and children sang the praises of Christ, in order to confound the Jews.[6] In fact the Savior went further and declared that even stones could cry out to condemn unbelievers and give glory to God.[7] Furthermore, in the early days, those being baptized would speak in tongues, thereby proclaiming their faith.

[2]*And if I have prophetic powers, and understand all mysteries and all knowledge, and if I have all faith, so as to remove mountains, but have not love, I am nothing.*

I get nothing out of it, because prophesying is done for the glory of God, as David the prophet says: *Not to us, Lord, not to us, but to your name give glory.*[8] Balaam prophesied even though he was not a prophet, and Caiaphas also prophesied, not because he deserved to, but on the strength of his priestly office.[9] So did Saul when, because of his disobedience, he was filled with an evil spirit. He did nothing to deserve this honor, but prophesied in the interests of God's cause, so that he could not capture David, whom he wanted to kill.[10] Judas accompanied the other disciples and understood all the mysteries and knowledge given to them, but he got nothing out of it, because as an enemy of love he betrayed the Savior. The prophet Ezekiel indicates that the devil too knows the mysteries of heaven, when he shouts out that he was in God's paradise

---

[1]Mt 7:22. [2]Mt 7:23. [3]Lk 10:20. [4]Mt 10:20. [5]Num 22:28. [6]Cf. Mt 21:15-16. [7]Lk 19:40. [8]Ps 115:1-2. [9]Jn 11:49-52. [10]1 Sam 19:23-24.

and testifies that he possessed precious stones, which our apostle took to mean the mysteries of divine teaching.[1] It was of no benefit to him though, because he fell headlong into arrogance, with no thought of love.

Knowledge is no good if love is absent. Both Tertullian and Novatian were men of no small learning, but because of their pride they lost the fellowship of love and, falling into schism, devised heresies, to their own damnation. Finally, it did the scribes and Pharisees no good. As the Savior says: *You have the key of knowledge and you neither enter in yourselves nor allow others to enter.*[2] By spoiling love through their meanness, they reduced their knowledge of God to nothing.

It is God's power and glory at work when mighty works are done or demons are cast out by faith. Even this is worthless though, unless the person who does these things has been determined to behave well, as I said above.

[3] *If I give away all I have, and if I deliver my body to be burned, but have not love, I gain nothing.*

It is clear that even if we give away everything we own, it does us no good if we have no love. Love is the very head of religion, and someone who has no head is dead. Without love nothing is of any benefit to us, for love is the foundation of faith. Anything which lacks it is sure to collapse.

[4] *Love is patient and kind; love is not jealous or boastful; [5] it is not arrogant or rude. Love does not insist on its own way; it is not irritable or resentful; [6] it does not rejoice at wrong, but rejoices in the right. [7] Love bears all things, believes all things, hopes all things, endures all things.*

Love plays such an important part in Paul's

teaching that it is given precedence over all the other virtues, and not without reason. People who obey other commandments but ignore the requirement of love are striving in vain. The reason why the apostle John says *God is love*[3] is to show that whoever does not have love does not have God either. In another letter, the apostle Paul says: *God, who is rich in mercy, pitied us because of his great love.*[4] Thus a person who has no love is being ungrateful to the mercy of God. He does not love because he has been saved [but because God has shown him mercy and has loved him first]. Therefore the Corinthians ought to realize that the people who were putting food ahead of brotherly love were sinning greatly, because it is brotherly love which is beneficial in the present age and which remains with God forever.

[8] *Love never ends; as for prophecies, they will pass away; as for tongues, they will cease; as for knowledge, it will pass away. [9] For our knowledge is imperfect and our prophecy is imperfect; [10] but when the perfect comes, the imperfect will pass away.*

Paul said that the gift of all the graces would be canceled out because none of them can contain the fullness of the truth. How indeed can the human tongue possibly speak of everything that belongs to God? For this reason, our inadequacies will be destroyed. What is true will not be canceled out, but the process by which the missing elements are added to [perfect] what is inadequate, that inadequacy will be destroyed. For when the inadequate is made perfect, it is destroyed in the process.

[11] *When I was a child, I spoke like a child, I thought like a child, I reasoned like a child; when I became a man, I gave up childish ways.*

Paul says this because it is certain that the

---

[1]Cf. Ezek 28:13; 1 Cor 3:12-15. [2]Lk 11:52. [3]1 Jn 4:8. [4]Eph 2:4.

saints leaving this world will find more than they can now imagine. As the apostle John says: *Then we shall see him as he is.*[1] In this life we are children, compared with what we shall become in the next life. For everything in this life is imperfect, including knowledge.

12For now we see in a mirror dimly, but then face to face. Now I know in part; then I shall understand fully, even as I have been fully understood.

It is clear that what we now see are images of things, through faith, but then we shall see the things themselves. Paul's desire is to see the things which have been promised, just as he is seen by them. In other words, he wants to be in the presence of God, where Christ is.

13So faith, hope, love abide, these three; but the greatest of these is love.

Love is the greatest because while faith is preached and hope pertains to the future life, love reigns. As 1 John says: *By this we know his love, that he laid down his life for us.* Love is therefore the greatest of the three, because by it the human race has been renewed.

1 Corinthians 14

1Make love your aim, and earnestly desire the spiritual gifts, especially that you may prophesy.

Paul says that next to love the most important thing to be concerned about is prophecy, because however important the other gifts he mentions are, this one is greater because it is to the benefit and advantage of the church, since by it everybody learns the principles of God's law. Whoever devotes his attention to this receives a gift for doing so. As Solomon

says: *To know the law is the best thinking.*[2] Knowledge resting on love is not puffed up, but gentle, contributing to everyone's well-being.

2For one who speaks in a tongue speaks not to men but to God; for no one understands him, but he utters mysteries in the Spirit.

Paul is saying that someone who speaks in tongues is speaking to God because God understands everything. Human beings, however, do not have this knowledge and so get nothing out of it. Moreover, such a person is speaking in the Spirit and not with his mind, because he has no idea what he is saying.

3On the other hand, he who prophesies speaks to men for their upbuilding and encouragement and consolation.

A person is built up when he finds out the answer to disputed points. He is encouraged to persevere in his desire to be a prophet and is consoled by having a reason to be hopeful when he is confronted with [those who show only] contempt for his calling. Knowledge of the law strengthens souls and encourages them to hope for greater success.

4He who speaks in a tongue edifies himself, but he who prophesies edifies the church.

Because he is probably the only person who understands what he is saying, the person who speaks in tongues edifies himself alone, but a person who prophesies edifies everyone, because everyone understands what he is saying. Paul is saying that prophets are interpreters of the Scriptures. Just as a prophet speaks of unknown things to come, so a person who clarifies the meaning of the Scriptures, which are obscure to many, is also said to prophesy.

---

[1] Jn 3:2. [2] 1 Jn 3:16. [3] Cf. Prov 28:7.

⁵Now I want you all to speak in tongues, but even more to prophesy. He who prophesies is greater than he who speaks in tongues, unless some one interprets, so that the church may be edified.

Paul could not forbid speaking in tongues, because this is a gift of the Holy Spirit, but the pursuit of prophecy is more acceptable because it is more useful. A person who interprets will be just as great, because he is edifying the church. What benefits everyone is greater. The person who speaks in tongues and then interprets does so by God's gift, like the renowned Twelve in the Acts of the Apostles.

⁶Now, brethren, if I come to you speaking in tongues, how shall I benefit you unless I bring you some revelation or knowledge or prophecy or teaching?

All this means just one thing: no one will be able to teach unless he is understood.

⁷If even lifeless instruments, such as the flute or the harp, do not give distinct notes, how will any one know what is played? ⁸And if the bugle gives an indistinct sound, who will get ready for battle?

Because examples speak louder than mere words, Paul gives examples, so that the Corinthians will more readily understand that they should not speak in church in tongues which cannot be interpreted. What is the point of saying something which nobody can understand?

⁹So with yourselves; if you in a tongue utter speech that is not intelligible, how will any one know what is said? For you will be speaking into the air.

In other words, you will achieve nothing.

¹⁰There are doubtless many different languages in the world, and none is without meaning;

There are many kinds of tongues, says Paul, but they give their own meanings to particular sounds, and in that way they can be understood.

¹¹but if I do not know the meaning of the language, I shall be a foreigner to the speaker and the speaker a foreigner to me.

Paul is saying that people should not appear as strangers to one another by using unknown tongues, but in the search for harmony should rejoice with a shared joy in a common understanding.

¹²So with yourselves; since you are eager for manifestations of the Spirit, strive to excel in building up the church.

The soul is stirred and rejoices when it learns something about the Scriptures, and the more it tends in this direction, the more it abandons vices. It is for these reasons that Paul advises that one should make efforts in this direction.

¹³Therefore, he who speaks in a tongue should pray for the power to interpret.

A person who speaks in tongues should pray for the gift of interpretation, so that his desire may be of benefit to others.

¹⁴For if I pray in a tongue, my spirit prays but my mind is unfruitful.

It is clear that our soul does not understand if it speaks in an unknown tongue. Latin-speakers sing in Greek and enjoy the sound of the words but do not understand what they are singing. The Spirit which is given in baptism knows what the soul is praying when it speaks or prays in an unknown tongue, but the mind, which is the rational soul, gets nothing out of it. What can a person achieve if he does not know what he is saying?

15What am I to do? I will pray with the spirit and I will pray with the mind also; I will sing with the spirit and I will sing with the mind also.

Paul says this because when a person speaks in a language which he knows, he prays as much in mind as in spirit. Not only his spirit, which was given in baptism, but his rational mind also knows what is being prayed. Nor is it ignorant of what is sung.

16Otherwise, if you bless with the spirit, how can any one in the position of an outsider say the "Amen" to your thanksgiving when he does not know what you are saying?

The inexperienced person, hearing something he does not understand, does not know when the prayer comes to an end and therefore does not respond "Amen" to it. The confirmation of the prayer comes about when people say "Amen." The words spoken are confirmed in the minds of the hearers by the confession of truth.

17For you may give thanks well enough, but the other man is not edified.

Paul is speaking here of God, who understands what a person is saying even when the person himself does not. But if you come together for the edification of the church, you ought to speak in a way that your hearers can understand you. What is the point of someone speaking in a tongue known only to him, when the listener gets nothing out of it? Such people should be silent in church and let others who

have something useful to say do the talking.

18I thank God that I speak in tongues more than you all;

Because Paul has already said that speaking in tongues is a gift of the Holy Spirit, he here attributes to God the fact that he speaks in the language of them all. To avoid any suggestion that he might have been saying this out of a spirit of partisanship or malice, he makes it clear that he can speak everybody's language, but that this does not do much for anyone.

19nevertheless, in church I would rather speak five words with my mind, in order to instruct others, than ten thousand words in a tongue.

Paul says that it is better to say a few things clearly than to make a great speech which nobody can understand. These people were descendants of Jews who used either Aramaic or Hebrew in their books and sacrificial rites, hoping to be admired for it. They gloried in the name of Hebrews because of the merit of Abraham, which our apostle Paul discounted completely, saying: *Far be it from me to glory, except in the cross of our Lord Jesus Christ.*[1] In imitation of these people, [there were some in the Corinthian church who] preferred to address the congregation in an unknown tongue, just as some Latin-speakers prefer blessings to be in Greek.

20Brethren, do not be children in your thinking; be babes in evil, but in thinking be mature.

Paul wants them to be perfect so that they will know what is needed for the upbuilding of the church, and thus leave behind malice and errors, striving instead for the things which are conducive to the good of the brotherhood. A perfect person is one who acts in a way which

---

[1]Gal 6:14.

will benefit someone else, especially a brother in Christ.

21In the law it is written, "By men of strange tongues and by the lips of foreigners will I speak to this people, and even then they will not listen to me, says the Lord."[1]

The Lord said this about those whom he knew in advance would not believe in the Savior. For to speak in other tongues and with other lips is to preach the new covenant. As the prophet Jeremiah says: *Behold, the days are coming, says the Lord, when I shall make a new covenant with the house of Israel and the house of Judah, not the same as the one which I made with their fathers.*[2] In the new covenant, God speaks in a different way from the old law. The people were constantly hearing that now the sabbath was abolished, the new-moon celebrations were canceled, circumcision was abandoned, and sacrifices were being altered. They were being told that it was all right to eat things which had long been forbidden, and it was being preached that Christ was God from God. All this really was speaking with other lips and in other tongues! Unbelievers, of course, had no desire to obey God in any of these things.

Another possible interpretation is that because many of the Jews were hostile and therefore it was not advisable to preach the gospel to them openly Paul ought to speak to them in parables instead. The Jews therefore ought to prepare themselves to hear the words of God explained to them and realize that they were not getting his revelation because they were wicked and were not correcting themselves. This is why the disciples said to the Lord: *Lord, why are you speaking to them in parables?* And the Lord replied: *Because it has been given to you to know the mystery of the kingdom of God, but not to them, so that seeing, they may not see, and hearing, they may not*

understand.[3] This was said because unworthy people cannot obtain salvation. They did not want to please God by punishing what they had done, in order to further the advance of goodness in themselves, nor did they want to become changed people in this way.

22Thus, tongues are a sign not for believers but for unbelievers, while prophecy is not for unbelievers but for believers.

The utterances of God are hidden beneath the veil of an unknown tongue, so that they should not be seen by unbelievers. When unknown tongues were being used, they were a sign which merely confirmed unbelievers in their lack of faith. Paul was saying that tongues are useful for hiding ideas from unbelievers. It is not right for believers to hear things which they cannot understand, but this is fine for unbelievers, as the prophet Isaiah said: *Go and say to this people: "You will hear with your ear and not understand,"* et cetera.[4]

23If, therefore, the whole church assembles and all speak in tongues, and outsiders or unbelievers enter, will they not say that you are mad?

It is clear that if everybody is speaking in a different language, the result will be a disorderly tumult of people who appear to have gone mad.

24But if all prophesy, and an unbeliever or outsider enters, he is convicted by all, he is called to account by all, 25the secrets of his heart are disclosed; and so, falling on his face, he will worship God and declare that God is really among you.

When he sees that God is being praised and that Christ is being adored, and that nothing is disguised or being done in secret, as happens among pagans, whose eyes are blinded

1Cf. Is 28:11-12. 2Jer 31:31-32. 3Cf. Mt 13:10-17. 4Is 6:9.

so that they cannot get a clear picture of what they call sacred and understand that they are being deluded by various pretenses, he will understand clearly that this is a true religion. All imposters try to conceal things and present falsehoods as if they were true. Therefore among us nothing should be done in an underhanded way, nothing hidden behind a veil. Rather let the one God, from whom all things come, be praised with simplicity, and likewise the one Lord Jesus, through whom all things have come to be. For if there is nobody an unbeliever can understand, or who is able to refute him, he can argue that our faith is some kind of deceit and empty pretense, which would be disgraceful if the truth about it were known.

26What then, brethren? When you come together, each one has a hymn, a lesson, a revelation, a tongue, or an interpretation. Let all things be done for edification.

Some people praise God through singing. Others can explain the meaning of things because they have received spiritual wisdom. Some can prophesy about hidden things and so touch the minds of everyone by the grace of the Holy Spirit. Paul allowed people who spoke in tongues to do so, so as not to upset them, but only if an interpretation followed. This is why he adds that a time would be allowed for speaking in tongues if an interpreter were present. He sums up by saying that nothing should be done in church if it has no purpose. Particular effort should be made to ensure that unlearned people will benefit. Nothing should be done to hide things from them because of their lack of learning. Therefore Paul wants everyone to come together with their different gifts, so that they may be kept expectant with their minds awake, and by encouraging each other, may aspire to the higher gifts and thus bring understanding to their brothers.

27If any speak in a tongue, let there be only two or at most three, and each in turn; and let one interpret.

Two or three people may speak in tongues, but not more, and each one must speak in turn, so as not to appear to be mad. In limiting the number to three at the most, Paul is saying that he does not want these people to take up the whole day and leave insufficient time for prophets, who are the sources of illumination for the whole church, to expound the Scriptures.

28But if there is no one to interpret, let each of them keep silence in church and speak to himself and to God.

He should pray silently inside himself and speak to God, who hears everything that is silent to us. A person who speaks in church ought to do so to the benefit of everyone.

29Let two or three prophets speak, and let the others weigh what is said.

Paul adopted the same reasoning here as in the previous case, allowing two or three to speak, one at a time. But he allowed others to ask questions about ambiguous matters, so that they might be elucidated by clearer discussion.

30If a revelation is made to another sitting by, let the first be silent.

In particular, the higher ranking person should give way to the lower and not be upset that the gift can be given to somebody of lower rank and not to him. It is simply not the case that everything can be granted to one individual, nor one can it be that anyone, however low in the hierarchy, should have nothing given to him. No one is without the grace of God.

31For you can all prophesy one by one, so that

all may learn and all be encouraged;

It is a tradition of the synagogue which Paul is asking us to follow, whereby the people dispute while seated in chairs, on benches or on the floor, according to their rank. Paul says that if a revelation has been given to someone sitting on the floor he should be allowed to speak and not be despised because of his low rank.

³²and the spirits of prophets are subject to prophets.

There is only one Spirit who speaks through those prophets who reveal the future and those who expound the Scriptures, giving them both their train of thought and the nature of their subject matter. Paul said that he is made subject to the prophets in order to encourage minds with the hope that the Spirit would support their best efforts. The Spirit comes to the aid of the best desires, and helps people to speak the things of God, so that they may perfect what they have undertaken to do. The same thing was said of the Savior: *They drank from the spiritual rock that followed, and the rock was Christ.*[1] He followed in order to be on hand to bring help when human efforts failed. The Spirit is said to be subject so that he may facilitate the good efforts which he prompts. "To be subject" is the same thing as "to follow." The Spirit appears to be subject because he brings the labors of others to completion.

³³For God is not a God of confusion but of peace.
    As in all the churches of the saints,

It is a matter of peace, as the Savior said: *My peace I give to you, my peace I leave with you.*[2] No one should stop anybody else from speaking, and in order not to foment discord in the body, no one ought to object to someone who is

speaking either. Those who are called in peace ought to aim for patience, so that the laws of peace are not broken. In saying this, Paul is exhorting the Corinthians to act according to his teaching, which he says he gives to all the churches equally.

³⁴the women should keep silence in the churches. For they are not permitted to speak, but should be subordinate, as even the law says.

Here Paul is conveying teaching which he had forgotten to mention earlier, when he gave instructions that women should be veiled in church.[3] Now he makes it clear that they should also be quiet and modest, so that their veiling will be worthwhile. For if it is the man who is the image of God and not the woman, and if she is subjected to the man by the law of nature, how much more ought the woman to be in subjection when she is in church, as a sign of respect for the man who is the ambassador of the One who is his head.[4]

What does the law say? *Your desire shall be toward your husband and he shall have lordship over you.*[5] This law is for women only. Because of it, Sarah called her husband Abraham her lord.[6] Women are told to remain silent so that the force of the above-mentioned law will not be compromised. Although she and her husband are "one flesh," she is told to be subject to him for two reasons: because she is "out of the man" and because it was through her that sin entered the human race.

³⁵If there is anything they desire to know, let them ask their husbands at home. For it is shameful for a woman to speak in church.

It is shameful because it is contrary to discipline for them to presume to speak about the law in the house of God, who has taught that they

---

[1] 1 Cor 10:4. [2] Jn 14:27. [3] 1 Cor 11:5-16. [4] Cf. 1 Cor 11:3, 7. [5] Gen 3:16. [6] Cf. Gen 18:12; 1 Pet 3:6.

are subject to their husbands, when they know that men have the primacy there and that for them it is more fitting to be free to pray while holding their tongues, and to open their ears to hear how the mercy of God, through Christ, conquered death, whose reign began through Eve. If they dare to speak in church it is a disgrace, because they are veiled in order to appear humble. Moreover, women like this show that they are immodest, which is a disgrace to their husbands too. For when women are insolent, their husbands receive the blame as well.

36What! Did the word of God originate with you, or are you the only ones it has reached?

These are words of rebuke. The Corinthians were so puffed up with the belief that salvation had been promised to them, and that it would only be through them that other Gentiles would be called to the faith, that they imagined that no one would believe if the apostles were the preachers! This is why Paul says: *Did the word of God originate with you?* Anyone who wants to buy something which he knows is not in demand approaches the seller with a certain pride, thinking that he is doing him a favor. Paul issued the Corinthians with this reproof because they were so elated with vanity. The suggestion was that if they did not obey the words of the faith, there would be no one who would believe. Similarly, Paul says to the Jews: *It was your due that I should speak the words of this life to you first, but since you have rejected them, making yourselves unworthy of eternal life, see, we are turning to the Gentiles.*[1]

37If any one thinks that he is a prophet, or spiritual, he should acknowledge that what I am writing to you is a command of the Lord.

Paul is alluding to the false apostles mentioned above, by whom they had been depraved, and who were teaching things which people wanted to hear, but which were not of God. By saying that he was handing on nothing of his own, Paul was trying to indicate that what he was saying came from God and not from men. He therefore preaches consistently, with a clear conscience, because he does not desire to please men but God. He is not urging people to grow in sin, but to desist from it.

38If any one does not recognize this, he is not recognized.

Anyone who does not recognize that what the apostle says is from God will not be recognized on the day of judgment, when the Lord will say: *Truly I say to you, I do not know you.*[2]

39So, my brethren, earnestly desire to prophesy, and do not forbid speaking in tongues;

Although Paul is rebuking them and in many respects finding fault with them and chastising them because they had ignored his teaching, he nevertheless refers to them as brothers, because the prophet Isaiah says to the Lord's people: *Say to them who do not walk rightly in my ways, "You are my brothers."*[3] Therefore, in order to console them after all his rebukes, Paul calls them brethren and encourages them to have a desire to prophesy, so that by frequent discussion and exposition of the divine law they may become better equipped to be able to learn that what the false apostles were teaching was perverse.

People should not be stopped from speaking in tongues, again out of a spirit of loving kindness. If they can speak in tongues and there is someone there to interpret, fine. Paul's aim is to avoid dissension.

40but all things should be done decently and in order.

---

[1]Cf. Acts 13:46. [2]Mt 25:12. [3]Cf. Is 66:5.

In other words, they should be done as outlined above. Something is done decently when it is done peacefully and with discipline.

1 Corinthians 15

¹Now I would remind you, brethren, in what terms I preached to you the gospel, which you received, in which you stand, ²by which you are saved, if you hold it fast—unless you believed in vain.

Paul is showing the Corinthians that if they have been led away from his teaching, especially from belief in the resurrection of the dead on which it is based, they will lose everything they have believed. Paul was talking to those who were firm in their faith on this point. He is addressing a mixed audience, hoping that those who are steadfast in their faith will rejoice and that those who are faltering will be upset at being censured and mend their ways.

³For I delivered to you as of first importance what I also received, that Christ died for our sins in accordance with the scriptures,

Paul is referring to the Old Testament Scriptures, which sang of the future passion of the Lord. The prophet Isaiah said: *He was led like a sheep to the slaughter,*[1] and *Since his life shall be removed from the earth, he has been led to death by the wickednesses of my people.*[2] Everyone accepts that these things were fulfilled by Christ. It is no contradiction that the text speaks in the past tense, because with God, who has foreknowledge of everything, there is no such thing as the future. This is why he can speak of what to us is in the future as if it had already happened. In the Revelation of John he says: *The Lamb that has been slain from before the foundation of the world.*[3] It is because this

will not happen in any other way than the one which God already knows, that it is spoken of as if it had already happened. From our point of view it is still in the future, but this is not true of God, for whom there is no future. In a psalm he says: *The Lord has reigned from a tree,*[4] and Moses alluded to the cross when he said: *At that time you will see your life hanging before your eyes, yet you will not believe.*[5] The reason why God sometimes expresses himself in the future tense is to prevent the wicked from claiming that it does not apply to Christ, which would happen if he referred to everything as being past.

⁴that he was buried, that he was raised on the third day in accordance with the scriptures,

There is no doubt that Jesus was buried when he was dead. As the prophet Isaiah says: *And I shall give bad men for his burial.*[6] Faith covers everything, past, present and future. Therefore the future resurrection of the Lord on the third day was described with particular reference to the Lord's people. The prophet Hosea says: *After two days he will make us well, and on the third day we shall rise again and live in his sight.*[7] No believer would deny that in Christ we have all risen again, just as we all died in Adam. Similarly, a psalm where the reference seems to be to a man makes allusion to Christ as well, saying: *You have put everything in subjection under his feet; you have crowned him with glory and honor.*[8]

⁵and that he appeared to Cephas, then to the twelve.

Cleopas and his companion testify in Luke's Gospel that Christ appeared to Peter on his own. The fact that he later appeared to the others is also contained in the Gospel.[9]

---

[1]Is 53:7. [2]Cf. Is 53:5. [3]Rev 13:8. [4]No such verse exists in any known psalm. [5]Cf. Deut 28:66. [6]Cf. Is 53:9 (LXX). [7]Hos 6:2.
[8]Ps 8:5-6. [9]Lk 24:35-36. Ambrosiaster is assuming that Cleopas and his companion were Luke's informants.

⁶Then he appeared to more than five hundred brethren at one time, most of whom are still alive, though some have fallen asleep.

This is not recorded in the Gospels, but Paul knew it independently of them. He says that many of them were still living at the time of writing this letter.

⁷Then he appeared to James, then to all the apostles.

Jesus appeared to James on his own, as he did to Peter. I think he did this so that by appearing in a variety of different ways, he would strengthen belief in his resurrection. It was the second time that he was seen by all the apostles *On a mountain, where Jesus had assembled them*, as Matthew puts it.[1] It was earlier in Jerusalem, on the eighth day after his resurrection, that is, on the Lord's day, that he appeared to his disciples in order to strengthen the faith of Thomas, as the apostle John tells us.[2] It is generally agreed that it was on the mountain that Jesus gave them their orders.

⁸Last of all, as to one untimely born, he appeared also to me.

Jesus appeared to Paul first in the sky,[3] and later when he was praying in the temple.[4] By *untimely* Paul means that he was born again outside time, because he received his apostleship from Christ after the latter had ascended into heaven.

⁹For I am the least of the apostles, unfit to be called an apostle, because I persecuted the church of God.

Paul is being modest and recording the flow of events as they applied to himself. He was the least because he was the last in time, not because he was inferior in any way to the others. But because he had also been a persecutor [of the church], he humbles himself, saying: *who am not worthy to be called an apostle, because I persecuted the church of God.*

¹⁰But by the grace of God I am what I am, and his grace toward me was not in vain. On the contrary, I worked harder than any of them, though it was not I, but the grace of God which is with me.

Paul gives glory to God, who chose him, and does not defend his office, saying instead that he is unworthy. In this way he earns a greater reward, knowing that the Lord has said: *He who exalts himself shall be abased.*[5] He says this because he did not receive any less grace, having been a persecutor. He makes the further point that not only is he not inferior to the others, but he was subjected to more suffering than they were because of the determination with which he maintained his faith in Christ and grew in dignity through his patient endurance. Afraid that he might be accused of boasting about himself, he immediately humbles himself again and ascribes everything to the grace of God, rather than to himself. His intention is always to ascribe all the glory to God, from whom his right to be honored derives.

¹¹Whether then it was I or they, so we preach and so you believed.

Here Paul repeats what he said above, that the grace which he has received in his mission has not been less than that given to the other apostles, but entirely equal to it. For this reason he rebukes the Corinthians even more, because although the belief he has been talking about has been clearly preached in all the churches, they had drawn back from faith and hope in it, as he goes on to say.

---

[1]Mt 28:16-20. [2]Jn 20:26-29. [3]Acts 9:4. [4]Acts 22:17-21. [5]Lk 14:11.

12Now if Christ is preached as raised from the dead, how can some of you say that there is no resurrection of the dead? 13But if there is no resurrection of the dead, then Christ has not been raised; 14if Christ has not been raised, then our preaching is in vain and your faith is in vain.

These things were taught by the false apostles, who said that Christ was neither born, nor suffered in the body, nor was raised from the dead. The apostle John reproaches them as well, because they denied that Christ had come in the flesh. Thus he says: *he who denies that Christ has come in the flesh is antichrist, and he who denies the Son does not have the Father either.*[1] These people were going around subverting the faith of some members of the church, playing on their fear of being mocked by the worldly-wise, who think the resurrection of the dead is nonsense. But as Paul says, if Christ has not risen from the dead, he and the other apostles are false preachers, and their faith is worthless. For when the apostle preached it, they believed that the dead would rise again, and it was in this hope that they were attracted to the faith. He says that they will be harmed if they believed the truth first and then turned away from it, but helped if they believed something which is not going to happen [and have now been put right].

He makes them feel ashamed and tells them that their struggles are useless if what they have heard from the false apostles is true—that the dead will not rise again—something which nobody allows anyone to say about himself. Paul wanted them to return to their earlier faith, because their departure from it was really a reaction against him.

15We are even found to be misrepresenting God, because we testified of God that he raised Christ, whom he did not raise if it is true that the dead are not raised.

Someone who claims that Christ was raised from the dead is a false witness if this is not true. But someone who attributes such a wonderful thing to the power of God is proclaiming that power and not acting out of hostility to God. If it is true that God raised Christ from the dead, what shall we say to somebody who bears false witness against God and claims that his work is nonsense?

16For if the dead are not raised, then Christ has not been raised. 17If Christ has not been raised, your faith is futile and you are still in your sins. 18Then those also who have fallen asleep in Christ have perished.

Paul strikes fear into the Corinthians in order to make them regret having started to believe something which goes against them, because nobody wants evil for himself. Who would not want to hear that his sins have been forgiven? He adds that those who have fallen asleep in Christ have perished in order to frighten them, because they do not want to think of the death of their loved ones as annihilation. For those who have departed this life in hope, or who have risked being killed because they believed that the dead rise again, as Christ did, have perished forever if this is not true. Paul says something to them which they do not want to hear, because they love their departed ones too much. His intention is to scrape away something which, in their error, they once wanted to hear.

19If for this life only we have hoped in Christ, we are of all men most to be pitied.

It is clear that we hope in Christ both for this life and for the next one. Christ does not abandon his servants but gives them grace, and in the future they will dwell in eternal glory. If there were no hope of a future life, we would

---

[1] A free rendering of 1 Jn 2:22-23.

be the most pitiable people of all. What would be the point of fasts, vigils, martyrdoms, clean living, justice and mercy if these things carry no future reward? In that case, it would be unbelievers who would reap a reward—from this present life.

20But in fact Christ has been raised from the dead, the first fruits of those who have fallen asleep. 21For as by a man came death, by a man has come also the resurrection of the dead.

Paul says this in order to get at the false prophets who claimed that Christ was never born, and thus cannot have risen again, because someone who was never born cannot have died either. The resurrection from the dead proves that Christ was a man, and therefore able to merit by his righteousness the resurrection of the dead. The end result of this is that, because death was brought about by a man's sin, the righteousness of Christ has earned the resurrection of the dead.

22For as in Adam all die, so also in Christ shall all be made alive.

Paul says this because just as Adam brought death into the world because he sinned, and that death has held all his descendants in its grip and caused them to be destroyed, so Christ, who was without sin, overcame death, in that death comes from sin, and won life (that is, resurrection) for all Adam's descendants. Although Paul has admitted that everyone, the righteous and the unrighteous alike, dies in Adam, and everyone, believers and unbelievers alike, will also be raised in Christ, he also says that unbelievers will be handed over for punishment. Even so, they will appear to have been raised from the dead, because they will receive their bodies back again in order to suffer eternal punishment in those bodies for their unbelief.

23But each in his own order: Christ the first fruits, then at his coming those who belong to Christ.

Here Paul wants to explain the many stages of the resurrection, so that the Corinthians would not think it was all a myth, seeing that in the case of people other than Christ it has not yet happened. He therefore reveals the stages and times when the resurrection has happened, and when it will yet happen. In the Acts of the Apostles it says that it is written in [the law of] Moses that *Christ must suffer, and that he would be the first to rise from the dead*, et cetera.[1] So Christ rose first in order to become a model for those who believe in him.

Those who belong to Christ will rise at his coming. This must be understood in two ways. When he comes again, the saints will rise according to their faith, as the Revelation of John bears witness, just as at his first coming, that is to say, at his resurrection, many bodies of saints rose again as a witness to the overthrow and destruction of death.[2] Paul refers to the two comings of the Lord by using the one expression.

24Then comes the end, when he delivers the kingdom to God the Father after destroying every rule and every authority and power. 25For he must reign until he has put all his enemies under his feet. 26The last enemy to be destroyed is death. 27"For God has put all things in subjection under his feet."[3]

Paul says this because when the kingdom is handed over, the end of the world will come, since the resurrection will have been brought to its conclusion. Some people are terrified by this and reject the literal meaning of the

---

[1]Acts 26:23. [2]Mt 27:51-53. [3]Ps 8:6.

expression because, as they say, they want to think higher thoughts. They are shocked when they hear the sound of the expression *When he shall have handed over the kingdom to [his] God and Father*, because they think that if you take it literally, it means that Christ will be left without anything for himself. They suppose that if he hands something over, then he will no longer have it, as if the Father had made himself destitute when he gave everything to the Son [in the first place]. For the Lord himself says: *All things have been handed over to me by my Father.*[1] Later he adds: *This is eternal life, that they should recognize that you alone are the true God and he whom you have sent, Jesus Christ.*[2] You see from this that while the Son is ruling, the Father is ruling also. How could anyone believe that when the Son hands everything back to the Father, he is thereby leaving himself with nothing, when the angel said to Mary: *And the Lord God shall give to him the throne of his father David, and he will reign in the house of Jacob forever and there shall be no end of his kingdom?*[3]

Daniel also describes the same kingdom: *The God of heaven shall summon up another kingdom, which shall never be destroyed, and this kingdom will last forever.*[4] No one should doubt, therefore, that the Son will reign with his Father forever. This is the standard teaching about the kingdom, that once all things have been made subject to the Son and they have worshiped him as God, and once death has been destroyed, then Christ will make it clear to them that he is not the ultimate source of all things, but that it is only through him that all things exist. To hand over the kingdom to God the Father will be to show that the Father is the one *from whom all fatherhood in heaven and on earth is named.*[5] Then the end will come. Finally, the resurrection of the dead is the destruction of death.

But when it says, "All things are put in subjection under him," it is plain that he is excepted who put all things under him. [28]*When all things are subjected to him, then the Son himself will also be subjected to him who put all things under him, that God may be everything to every one.*

Paul is here expounding the same idea as before, wanting to make clear what it means for the Son to hand the kingdom over to his God and Father. It does, however, add this to the sense: the Father, in handing the kingdom over to the Son, has not thereby subjected himself to the Son in the way that the Son has subjected himself to the Father.

The Father has subjected everything to the Son in order for the Son to be honored in a way similar to that in which the Father is honored. Therefore, when everything has confessed that Christ is God and been subjected beneath his feet, Christ the Lord will also be made subject to God the Father, so that God may be all in all. What Paul is saying is that when the pride of all rulers and powers and dominions has been put down and they have all worshiped Christ as God, then even Christ, because of the Father's unique authority, will show that although he is God, he is also from God, so that the sublime and ineffable authority of the single originating principle may be preserved.

The subjection of Christ to the Father means that every creature will learn that he is subject to Christ, who in turn is subject to the Father, and will thus confess that there is only one God, from whom all things derive. For this to be the case is for all creation to share the same opinion and for every utterance of every thing, celestial, terrestrial and infernal, to confess with a single voice that there is only one God, from whom all things have come. If Paul had said, *So that God may*

---

[1]Jn 13:3. [2]Jn 17:3. [3]Lk 1:32-33. [4]Dan 2:44. [5]Eph 3:15.

be in all things, it would be understood that he is in everything, but this is so because of a disposition of the mind or a shared understanding, not because these things derive from him directly. But when Paul said *all in all*, he meant that all things are from God himself and exist in themselves. They are from himself because they have been created by him, and in themselves, because in the confessed opinion of them all, there will be only one God. However, the Son is not subject to the Father in the same way as the creation is subject to the Son.

29Otherwise, what do people mean by being baptized on behalf of the dead? If the dead are not raised at all, why are people baptized on their behalf?

Paul is so eager to defend the resurrection of the dead as signed, sealed and delivered that he cites the example of people who were so convinced of the coming resurrection that they had themselves baptized on behalf of the dead—if death had accidentally overtaken someone. It seems that people were baptized for the dead because they were afraid that someone who was not baptized would either not rise at all or else rise merely in order to be condemned. A living person would therefore be immersed on behalf of a dead one, and Paul asks: *Why are people baptized on their behalf?*

In citing this example, Paul is not showing approval of their behavior, but merely illustrating what a firm faith in the resurrection had led to in their case. Remember that Jephthah too was found faithful, even though it was in a matter which, according to the account which has come down to us, is unbearable— he sacrificed his daughter in order to keep his vow that he had foolishly sworn.[1] It is not the action, therefore, that Paul approves of, but the perseverance in faith which it bears witness to.

30Why am I in peril every hour? 31I protest, brethren, by my pride in you which I have in Christ Jesus our Lord, I die every day!

Paul made a distinction between different types of people, making it clear that those who were baptized on behalf of the dead were not orthodox. What he said was *Why were* they *being baptized on behalf of the dead?* not *Why are we being baptized on their behalf?* But when he talks about the dangers and toils faced by preachers, he says: *Why are we running risks*, et cetera. The subtext here is that unless there is such a thing as the resurrection of the dead, all this is pointless, something which he did not mention earlier. Confident that after this death true life will follow, the preachers are not afraid of the dangers they face at the hands of unbelievers because of their zeal. They have arrived at faith and are therefore upset at these people's self-destruction. Paul thus revealed the concern which he had for their salvation, because of the glory which the Lord had promised. As it says in the law: *Raise your voice like a trumpet. If they hear you, you will profit their souls.*[2] The apostle hastens to do this, always eager for an increase of the glory before God which comes to him from the salvation gained by many people.

32What do I gain if, humanly speaking, I fought with beasts at Ephesus? If the dead are not raised, "Let us eat and drink, for tomorrow we die."[3]

According to the human way of thinking, which does not believe that there will be a resurrection of the dead, because it is not natural for the flesh, once it has been destroyed, to be restored to life again, there is no point in offering myself to wild beasts, because I shall not get anything out of it. This is not so, however, and being certain of the promised life to

---

[1]Judg 11:30-40. [2]Cf. Is 58:1-14. [3]Is 22:13.

come, Paul has not only been unafraid, he has even been glad to let himself be offered up to wild beasts. In the same way, Paul says in the Acts of the Apostles: *I am prepared not only to be put in bonds, but even to die at Jerusalem, for the name of the Lord Jesus Christ.*[1]

It is the prophet Isaiah who says: *let us eat and drink, for tomorrow we die.*[2] He said it because there were people who thought that there was nothing to come after death, and so cared only for the lusts of the stomach, in the way that cattle do. The people who were corrupting the Corinthians were just the same.

[33]Do not be deceived: "Bad company ruins good morals."[3]

Paul meant that good intentions could be ruined by the idle gossip of bad people. The habit of evil conversation depraves the mind, and for that reason, one should beware of these people. For whoever wants to keep the faith which he has received should above all avoid noisy agitators from the start. This is the way to carry out what one has determined ought to be done for the general good.

[34]Come to your right mind, and sin no more. For some have no knowledge of God. I say this to your shame.

Paul warns the Corinthians that they must be watchful so that they will not be trapped by the deception of evil thinking, led away from the faith and corrupted by not believing in the resurrection of the dead. He tells them to be just, because he wants them to act in accordance not only with earthly justice but with heavenly justice as well, since earthly justice is not meritorious any more than it produces guilt. How can it be a great achievement not to steal somebody else's property, if the reason for not doing so is purely fear? On the other hand, it is a great achievement to be generous with one's goods toward someone in need, for that is true justice. According to this line of reasoning, what Paul wanted the Corinthians to understand was that he was not commanding them to respect temporal justice, but divine justice. For a person who practices divine justice is undoubtedly made perfect in this present age.

It was because they were ignorant of the purposes of God that these people among them had undergone a change of heart and were saying that it was foolish to believe that the dead would rise again. Therefore he strikes shame into them, saying that they are unwise, because they were putting their trust in men who had no knowledge of God and were teaching things which went against his law.

[35]But some one will ask, "How are the dead raised? With what kind of body do they come?"

This statement is an expression of the corrupt thinking of those people who had no knowledge of God. He answers them as follows.

[36]You foolish man! What you sow does not come to life unless it dies.

Paul deals with the unspiritual man not by quoting the authority of the law, as if to persuade him through its precedents—though of course he would not be wrong to do so if the unbeliever was prepared to accept the force of these—but by the logic of natural science, on which he is priding himself in not believing that dead bodies which have dissolved can ever rise again. Paul demonstrates from nature that things are in fact restored to life and multiplied, and in doing so he refutes this human error.

[37]And what you sow is not the body which is to

---

[1]Acts 21:13. [2]Is 22:13. [3]Menander, *Thais.*

be, but a bare kernel, perhaps of wheat or of some other grain. ³⁸*But God gives it a body as he has chosen, and to each kind of seed its own body.*

If a bare seed died and by God's grace, with a little help from the elements, comes back again fully clothed, with so much additional benefit to the human race, why is it incredible that a human body should rise again, by the power of God, with an equally improved substance, which is not multiplied in number? What is the unbeliever looking for, when there are so many evidences for this faith in resurrection in a better state which involves no loss of substance? After all, according to the examples quoted above, it is his own body which he will get back, the body in which he was created as a human being.

³⁹*For not all flesh is alike, but there is one kind for men, another for animals, another for birds, and another for fish.*

Since all flesh comes ultimately from the same matter, how does it come about that there is so much diversity among these beings, and that one basic material makes so many different species? Let the Sophists of the world and the astrologers explain this if they can understand things outside themselves, while being totally ignorant of what is inside them! The philosophers of this world are unwilling to submit their minds to the law of God in order to believe in him, and instead they confound one another with diverse and mutually contradictory theories, none of which can be proved. God, on the other hand, does not argue. Instead, he demonstrates his power, which no words can resist.

So, just as the flesh of living creatures is diverse, even though it is made from the same basic material, human beings will differ in

dignity at the resurrection, even though they are all of the same flesh. Everyone will appear in the manner befitting his merit, so that here too we can see a diversity of bodies.

⁴⁰*There are celestial bodies and there are terrestrial bodies; but the glory of the celestial is one, and the glory of the terrestrial is another.*

Heavenly bodies are those of people who rise again, but all bodies are earthly before they die or rise. It is because Christ is heavenly [to begin with] that heavenly bodies are called after him, whereas earthly bodies are called after Adam, who is earthly.

⁴¹*There is one glory of the sun, and another glory of the moon, and another glory of the stars; for star differs from star in glory.*

Paul compares different items of a single nature in order to present a logical discussion of a single category of being. The sun, moon and stars are of one nature, but they differ in their brightness, and in the same way, human beings, although they are of one species, will differ in glory according to what they deserve. The honor of those bearing the number one hundred, who have aimed for the highest rank in an effort to become perfect, will be equal to that of the sun.[1] It has been said of them: *Then the righteous shall shine forth like the sun in the kingdom of their Father.*[2]

Those whose good works have earned them the number sixty will be comparable to the brightness of the moon, and have merit of the second rank. The merits of those who have sought to achieve the number thirty by their righteous endeavors will be compared with the brighter stars. Sinful men, who have not been able to acquire any of the three ranks, are to be likened to the remaining stars, which are halfway between the bright and

---

[1]The number is a reference to the hundred-fold increase mentioned in Mt 13:23.   [2]Mt 13:43.

the semidarkened ones. The resurrection of unbelievers is like the flickering stars, the last ones of all, because in following error they are like stars which lead people astray, as Jude the apostle says in his letter.[1] Unbelief cannot have a bright resurrection, because just as charcoal is darkened when it is covered with its own ash, so these people will lack light, being surrounded by the shadows of error as a result of their unbelief.

42So is it with the resurrection of the dead. What is sown is perishable, what is raised is imperishable.

Paul illustrates this point so that, once his reasoning is accepted, there will be no further doubts about the resurrection of the dead. *To sow* is to bury, so that decay may take place. *To rise* again in incorruption is for that which has been raised up not to be subject to further decay, but to have the splendor of immortality.

43It is sown in dishonor, it is raised in glory. It is sown in weakness, it is raised in power.

It is sown in dishonor because it is placed in a coffin where it rots and is eaten by worms. But when it rises again it will do so in glory, and all trace of this dishonor will vanish. It is sown in weakness because it is motionless and inert; it rises in power because then it will be alive and vigorous.

44It is sown a physical body, it is raised a spiritual body. If there is a physical body, there is also a spiritual body.

The body is "natural" as long as it needs food in order to stay alive; it will be "spiritual" when it no longer needs anything, because it will have changed into a new kind of life. Every-

thing which has been said up to now is summarized in this expression. For there has been nothing in the preceding utterances other than that the natural body dies and that a spiritual one, which does not eat or drink or suffer infirmity, and is not stinking or loathsome in nature, rises in its place.

45Thus it is written, "The first man Adam became a living being";[2] the last Adam became a life-giving spirit.

It is written in Genesis that when man received his spirit from the breath of God he became a living soul.[3] It is the spirit's function to animate the body, though the body will not go on living unless it relies on the assistance of food and drink.

46But it is not the spiritual which is first but the physical, and then the spiritual.

The man who was once alive in natural terms but later became spiritually alive through the resurrection can no longer die, because he will be made fully alive.

47The first man was from the earth, a man of dust; the second man is from heaven.

The first man, Adam, was from the earth, subject to the passage of time and the coming of death. The second man, Christ, is from heaven. Rising again from the dead, he does not know death.

48As was the man of dust, so are those who are of the dust; and as is the man of heaven, so are those who are of heaven.

Because Adam was mortal, earthly people are also mortal. By sinning, Adam brought death [into the world], with the result that everyone

---

[3]Jude 13. [2]Gen 2:7. [3]Gen 2:7.

who descends from him will also die.

But because Christ did not sin and is heavenly, conquering death, those who believe in him do the same. Admittedly, unbelievers are also going to be "spiritual," but like the *spiritual powers of wickedness*,[1] they will also be obscured in darkness. Here, however, Paul is talking about the saints, who will rise again in glory. Just as those who do not believe have already been judged, so those who believe are already called heavenly.

[49]*Just as we have borne the image of the man of dust, we shall also bear the image of the man of heaven.*

This means that just as we have borne the corruptible body of the earthly Adam, having been made slaves to sin, so we shall in future bear an incorruptible body, through the righteousness of the Savior. We shall become slaves of righteousness, not the world's righteousness, but God's, and do those deeds which are worthy of immortality.

[50]*I tell you this, brethren: flesh and blood cannot inherit the kingdom of God, nor does the perishable inherit the imperishable.*

By *flesh* Paul means disobedience, and by *blood* he means an evil and wicked life, because lust is generated by a heating of the blood. Paul wants to show that it is not only the unbeliever whose resurrection will be lacking in honor, but also the person who is a slave to the desires and vices of the flesh. He is both warning and instructing the Corinthians as to how we may deserve to attain the kingdom of heaven.

Paul is saying that a corrupt and lecherous life must be punished. He uses the word *perishable* to stand for lust. It is clear that he

cannot have been referring to death, because everyone agrees that in the resurrection everyone will be immortal.

[51]*Lo! I tell you a mystery. We shall not all sleep, but we shall all be changed,*[2]

Both believers and unbelievers will rise together. Here Paul is referring to the merit of each individual at the resurrection, and how that event is to be tailored to each individual person.

[52]*in a moment, in the twinkling of an eye, at the last trumpet. For the trumpet will sound, and the dead will be raised imperishable, and we shall be changed.*

This will happen very quickly, without any delay. The last trumpet refers to the last war which will be waged against demons, princes and powers, as well as against the devil himself. This will happen after a thousand years, when the antichrist has been destroyed and the Savior has reigned, Satan will be released from his prison in order to lead astray the nations of Gog and Magog, who are demons, in order that they might attack the fortresses of the saints. Time-bound men will not be able to win out against eternal beings. For the apostle John also says: *I saw Michael and his angels fighting in heaven against the dragon and his angels, he being the devil and Satan.*[3] The reason Paul says the last trumpet is that it is not just once that war has been waged against the devil. He has already been defeated over the antichrist and over the false prophet who performed signs and wonders in his presence.[4] In this context, God will be fighting against him for the last time, before he is sent down to hell. The Savior also says, among other things: *Now the prince of this world shall*

---

[1]Eph 6:12. [2]Ambrosiaster read this as "we shall NOT all be changed," a variant reading which is found in some manuscripts. [3]Rev 12:7-9. [4]Cf. Rev 19:20.

be sent down below.[1] He has therefore been defeated on many different occasions. So it is too that Isaiah the prophet says: *How Lucifer has fallen from heaven, who used to rise in the morning.*[2]

At the resurrection of the sinful and impious, the saints will be changed into a state of brightness and their flesh will become spiritual and glorious, as if lead had been changed into gold. The saints will rise when the Lord comes, as is said above: *Christ the first beginning, and then those who are of Christ, at his coming.* Sinners are not of Christ, for the Lord will tell them: *I do not know you.*[3] *For those who are of Christ have crucified the flesh with its vices and lusts.*[4] In the first Psalm it is written: *Therefore the ungodly will not rise in the judgment, nor sinners in the council of the righteous.*[5] Nothing will be expected from the ungodly. They will rise again only to perish, since what they have been unwilling to believe is true. "To perish" is to be cut off from God. As Paul says to the Romans: *Those who have sinned outside the law will perish outside the law, and those who have sinned within the law will be judged by the law.*[6] Sinners will be judged for this reason, because they are unworthy to rise with the saints. As [the psalmist] says: *Nor sinners in the council of the righteous.*[7]

53For this perishable nature must put on the imperishable, and this mortal nature must put on immortality.

Paul says again what he has said above, that the dead will rise again uncorrupted, that is to say, immortal, though not incapable of feeling. The people of whom he is speaking will suffer punishments according to the nature of their sins, so that they may go out with their debt fully paid. But the ungodly will be tormented with everlasting punishment, for the Lord

says: *He who has not believed has been judged already.*[8] Hence the prophet Isaiah says: *Their fire shall not be extinguished and their worm shall not die.*[9]

At the coming of the Lord the saints will also rise again, and those who are still alive [on earth] will be caught up into the air to meet the Lord in a state resembling that of sleep.[10] In this rapture death and resurrection will occur simultaneously, as Paul says to the Thessalonians. In the time of the antichrist, the rest of the Gentiles will be either apostates, or guilty, or in hiding, or enduring punishment already, and the Lord Jesus *will slay* them, along with their ruler, the antichrist, *with the breath of his mouth.*[11] That is to say, at his command they will be burnt up by the angels of his power.

54When the perishable puts on the imperishable, and the mortal puts on immortality, then shall come to pass the saying that is written:
   "Death is swallowed up in victory."[12]
   55"O death, where is thy victory?
   O death, where is thy sting?"[13]

After the resurrection of the ungodly and sinful, death will be swallowed up in victory. These are the words of someone who is reviling a fallen enemy. The resurrection of the dead is victory over death, which has been conquered. *Death* refers to the devil, who is the one being insulted. He is described as prone to making a challenge, because in his arrogance he used to put up resistance, even though he was unequal to God in strength. The fact that he is being trampled on in victory and his spoils are being taken from him shows how angry God is with him for having fought against him.

56The sting of death is sin, and the power of sin is the law.

---

[1]Cf. Jn 12:31. The Greek *exō* (out) has been read as *katō* (down). [2]Is 14:12. [3]Mt 7:23. [4]Gal 5:24. [5]Ps 1:5. [6]Rom 2:12. [7]Ps 1:5. [8]Jn 3:18. [9]Cf. Is 66:24. [10]1 Thess 4:16-17. [11]2 Thess 2:8. [12]Is 25:8. [13]Hos 13:14.

By *sting* Paul means authority, because death received authority through sin. If sin did not exist, the devil would have atrophied and there would be no death.

The reason why the power of sin is the law is that *if the law did not exist, sin would not be called into account.*[1]

[57]But thanks be to God, who gives us the victory through our Lord Jesus Christ.

Paul is saying that the Savior's triumph has been for our benefit. Christ did not win the victory for himself, but for us, so his victory is ours. For when he became a man he remained God, and by overcoming the devil, he who never sinned gained the victory for us, who were bound in death because of sin. The death of Christ, who had not sinned, defeated the devil, who then lost control over all those whom he was holding captive because of sin. In trampling down the human race, the devil incurred guilt. So the death sentence passed on the human race has been canceled. Souls have been rescued and taken up to heaven, so that it was not by violence that they were raised up, but by God's justice at work in our Lord Jesus Christ.

[58]Therefore, my beloved brethren, be steadfast, immovable, always abounding in the work of the Lord, knowing that in the Lord your labor is not in vain.

Now that he has expounded everything necessary for establishing the church's doctrine, making clear what should be sought after and what should be avoided, Paul exhorts them to hold fast to what is good and to do works which are profitable in God's sight, to be wide awake at all times and generous. Those who persevere in a life of faith and good works know that they will be accepted by God and

receive their reward, and they will not be led astray by wicked arguments.

1 Corinthians 16

[1]Now concerning the contribution for the saints: as I directed the churches of Galatia, so you also are to do. [2]On the first day of every week, each of you is to put something aside and store it up, as he may prosper, so that contributions need not be made when I come.

Paul was giving instructions for a collection to be made on the Lord's day as he had also done for the other churches. On the day the Lord rose again, his people should be gathered together for the praise and glory of God, to celebrate the defeat of death. At the same time, funds should also be collected in order to help those saints who were suffering persecution for the name of the Lord, because of the zealotry of Gentiles or Jews who were not letting them preach the grace of God through the name of Christ. The reason for this is that they ought to get relief from those people on whose behalf they were being persecuted.

On each Lord's day, Paul ordered the congregation to assemble, and told each of them to make a voluntary contribution toward the gifts of God. They should each keep this with them as in a treasure store, so that when the apostle came, it would be available for the purposes for which it was needed. Paul's logic is that what is gradually accumulated is not a burden, and turns out to be quite enough in the end.

[3]And when I arrive, I will send those whom you accredit by letter to carry your gift to Jerusalem.

This collection was doubly beneficial, because it helped the saints mentioned above and

---

[1]Rom 5:13.

also the poor people who were in the church, because it helped the elderly and the poor. Paul says that he will accredit those whom the Corinthians appoint as suitable guardians of the money. The letters will provide a testimonial for the emissaries, so that they will be graciously received.

4If it seems advisable that I should go also, they will accompany me.

Paul is saying that if the collection is generous, he can go too. For if a bishop is going, he ought to take a large amount with him for the relief of the saints.

This is what Paul means when he says to the Romans: *If the Gentiles have shared in their spiritual things they ought also to minister to them in bodily things.*[1] The people at Jerusalem who were greatly hated by Jewish unbelievers were themselves Jews, about whom the Lord says: *Salvation is from the Jews.*[2]

5I will visit you after passing through Macedonia, for I intend to pass through Macedonia, 6and perhaps I will stay with you or even spend the winter, so that you may speed me on my journey, wherever I go.

After all his instruction, Paul keeps them happy by promising to come to them. By saying this, he is further strengthening the admonitions by which he is putting them right. For someone who knows that the one from whom he has heard the law is coming will be all the more anxious not to be ashamed when he arrives.

7For I do not want to see you now just in passing; I hope to spend some time with you, if the Lord permits.

Knowing that he has a lot to do in Corinth,

Paul does not want to pass through on his way somewhere else, but to spend time with them when he comes. The Lord will allow him to stay with them only if they show themselves worthy, by putting right the wrongs for which he has rebuked them.

8But I will stay in Ephesus until Pentecost, 9for a wide door for effective work has opened to me, and there are many adversaries.

Paul made it clear that he was staying at Ephesus because he had found hearts there who were thirsting for the grace of God, and in them he could quickly instill the mystery of Christ. But because the devil is always restless, and hostile to those who long for God, he adds that his enemies are many. For the more they sought after the faith, the more adversaries there were who contradicted them and fought against the teaching of the Lord.

10When Timothy comes, see that you put him at ease among you, for he is doing the work of the Lord, as I am.

Although Timothy was preaching what he had learned from Paul and was a gifted evangelist, the apostle commends him because he did not have the same intrinsic authority. He was afraid that Timothy might not be received as he deserved by dissidents in the church, that they would create a fuss, that Timothy would be afraid and that his coming would do nothing for their salvation.

11So let no one despise him. Speed him on his way in peace, that he may return to me; for I am expecting him with the brethren.

The Gentiles could be roused to revolt by the congregation's disorder, seizing the opportunity to attack Timothy. Therefore Paul

---

[1]Rom 15:27. [2]Jn 4:22.

says that he should be received as one with apostolic authority, because he was also a bishop. Paul mentions Timothy's great merit in order to teach them not only that he should be treated with honor in their company, but that once he had made preparations to leave he should be sent on his way with deference, because he was an apostle of the Lord. He made it clear that Timothy was such a close colleague that he was waiting for him himself, along with the other brothers, because of the gospel of Christ.

12As for our brother Apollos, I strongly urged him to visit you with the other brethren, but it was not at all his will to come now. He will come when he has opportunity.

In saying this, Paul made it clear, by outlining his own strong desire to the Corinthians, that he had given an adequate response to their wish and request. He excused Apollos when he declared that he had been unable to go to them, though not totally, because Apollos's visit was only postponed. It is also implicit that, in this reference to Apollos, Paul is hinting that he did not want to go to Corinth because the church there was divided, in the hope that when they heard this they would be eager to make peace. It is also to be understood that he would have said, with reference to Timothy, *see to it that he may be in peace among you*, because some of the people who had been sent had not been well received. They should also know that Apollos would come when the church reached agreement.

13Be watchful, stand firm in your faith, be courageous, be strong. 14Let all that you do be done in love.

They were to be watchful in case they were secretly attacked in their faith. They were to stand firm, being bold in confessing what they had been taught, not like children who do not know which way to turn. They were to be strong in both word and deed, because it is the right combination of these which makes people perfect.

All these things should be done in love, because things done in love reflect the fear of God and zeal for him. Whatever causes harm to a brother is unfruitful. Some people need to be encouraged to do good, and not discouraged, [which might happen], for example, if you perform an act of mercy and in the process harm someone else, or if you are kind in a way which entails disparagement of another person, or if by eating something you trample on the feelings of someone who abstains from it and cause him distress. Everything should be done in a way which promotes improvement, and not bad feeling; then there is peace. This is why the Lord says: *By this you shall know if you are my disciples, if you love one another.*[1]

Where there is strife and dissension there is no love.

15Now, brethren, you know that the household of Stephanas were the first converts in Achaia, and they have devoted themselves to the service of the saints; 16I urge you to be subject to such men and to every fellow worker and laborer.

The Corinthians are Achaians, and so he is speaking to them about people of their own number, whom he is using in order to encourage them to do this kind of work. It is a great thing for Christians when greed is put down and people are generous to those in need of their labors. By doing this, they become imitators of God the Father, *who is rich in mercy.*[2] But when he tells them they should humble themselves before people like this, he is really saying that once they have become imitators

---

[1]Cf. Jn 13:35. [2]Eph 2:4.

themselves, they should not look down on others as if they were somehow inferior.

17I rejoice at the coming of Stephanas and Fortunatus and Achaicus, because they have made up for your absence; 18for they refreshed my spirit as well as yours. Give recognition to such men.

It is one thing to make a collection for the saints, and another to pay the ministers of the gospel a stipend for their services. As the Lord says: *The laborer is worthy of his hire.*[1] Paul is intimating that the household of Stephanas has been good in both respects, by collecting money for the saints and also helping people who were ministering to the churches. They were thus benefiting not only the apostle, along with the brothers Fortunatus and Achaius, but also their followers. Thus he says that they have refreshed *both my spirit and yours.*

He is also shaming the Corinthians here, and on a later occasion he will say that he will not take any payment from them. As he will put it: *This boasting in the regions of Achaia will not be broken in me.*[2] How can he then say that they have refreshed both his spirit and theirs? I believe that his spirit was refreshed with respect to those whom he had helped. Paul is saying that what helps those whom he wants to help helps him also. Therefore he urges the Corinthians to respect such people and to imitate them.

19The churches of Asia send greetings. Aquila and Prisca, together with the church in their house, send you hearty greetings in the Lord.

By this salutation, Paul is urging the Corinthians to become like those others who belong to

the single province [of Asia]. Paul refers to two kinds of church: public and domestic. One in which everyone assembles he calls public. The other, in which people gather together through friendship, he calls domestic. Any place where a presbyter celebrates the solemn rites is called a church.

20All the brethren send greetings. Greet one another with a holy kiss.

He is easing their minds when he makes it clear that all the brethren remember them. The holy kiss is the sign of peace, teaching the people to stick together and doing away with discord.

21I, Paul, write this greeting with my own hand.

Paul makes it clear that he has written the subscript with his own hand, and he then adds the words of the subscript themselves, as follows.

22If any one has no love for the Lord, let him be accursed. Our Lord, come!

The interpretation of this is that if there is anyone who does not love the Lord Jesus, who has already come, he should be cut off. The word *maranatha* means "the Lord has come."[3] Paul is referring to the Jews, who were accursed by the Lord who has already come, because they denied that.

23The grace of the Lord Jesus be with you. 24My love be with you all in Christ Jesus. Amen.

Paul put in this subscript because of those

---

[1]Lk 10:7. [2]2 Cor 11:10. This is a mistranslation, because the Latin made a mistaken etymological connection between the Greek word *phrassō* (silence) and the Latin *frango* (break). [3]The choice here is between *maran atha* ("our Lord has come") and *marana tha* ("our Lord, come!").

people who were promoting dissension. They did not love the Lord Jesus, because they said things like *I am of Paul, I am of Apollos*, and *I am of Cephas*.[1] Someone who loves Christ does not give glory to mere human beings. It is because there is no hope in mankind that Paul says: *the grace of the Lord Jesus Christ be with you*, and the implication is that the *you* refers to those who love the Lord Jesus.

Because the Corinthians did not love one another, Paul gives them this teaching from himself, when he says: *My love [be] with all of you in Christ Jesus*, in order that they might learn to love each other with the same love with which they were loved by the apostle, not with carnal emotion, but in Christ Jesus.

---

[1] 1 Cor 1:12.

AMBROSIASTER
Commentary on 2 Corinthians

Preface

Paul was aware of the beneficial effect of the first letter which he had sent to Corinth on account of their various errors and now writes a second letter to urge them to obey his teaching. In this letter he focuses on the stubbornness of those who were incorrigible. But he was greatly relieved to hear that the problems concerning the organization of the church had been put right, and he was sure that the faults of the people would gradually be corrected, since most of them had become obedient to his teaching. The reason he writes to them in haste is so that, after having been grieved by his rebuke, they may have consolation and the fruits of repentance may grow within them. Once the Corinthians saw that they were pleasing Paul they would become all the more eager to do good deeds. For what is repentance other than ceasing from error when grief of mind intrudes? So in order to show them that he was well disposed toward them, he writes to them as follows.

2 Corinthians 1

¹*Paul, an apostle of Christ Jesus by the will of God, and Timothy our brother.*

To the church of God which is at Corinth, with all the saints who are in the whole of Achaia:

Freed from all anxiety about the Corinthians, Paul confidently declares that he is an apostle of the Lord. In the first letter he said that he was *called an apostle*, though he was not approved of by those who had been lured away from his teaching. In order to affirm that his apostleship has been ratified, he adds that he has been made an apostle by the will of God. For this is how the Lord spoke to the Jews: *Since I always do the things which are pleasing to him*, that is, to God the Father.[1] He writes in association with Timothy, the man by whom he sent his first letter and from whom he has heard the good news of the changes which have taken place at Corinth, and he associates the people there with believers in other churches, in order to confirm to them that they have made progress.

²*Grace to you and peace from God our Father and the Lord Jesus Christ.*

Since the gift of God and of Christ is one and the same, Paul wants them to be partakers in the grace of God, that is, in the grace of Jesus Christ.

³*Blessed be the God and Father of our Lord Jesus Christ, the Father of mercies and God of all comfort,*

Throughout the letter, Paul always conveys the mystery in this way when he wants to talk about God the Father and his gift, and about the Lord Jesus Christ, indicating that two persons are named and assumed to exist individually, even though they are of one substance.

---

[1]Jn 8:29.

Thus the vain assertion of Sabellius has no impact.

Paul starts his argument with God himself. Here he is giving much relief to people who had been grieved by his rebuke, for when they hear that God is not just the Father of creation, but the Father of mercies as well, they will have hope and be assured that they have been rebuked so that they may find the mercy of God, once they have mended their ways. Why did he say *the Father of mercies*, if not in order to recognize that through repentance they were being born again and made anew, which was not just a pardon but a restoration of their previous state of existence. He puts *mercies* in the plural because of their many sins, his aim being to console those who have been grieved on account of their faults.

4who comforts us in all our affliction, so that we may be able to comfort those who are in any affliction, with the comfort with which we ourselves are comforted by God.

Paul mentions two kinds of consolation. One is the sort by which people who are suffering distress unjustly on account of the name of Christ find consolation in being set free from that. The other is the consolation of those who, when they are grieved because of sins, receive consolation from the fact that hope is promised to them when they mend their ways, by those who have received consolation from God and been rescued from distress.

5For as we share abundantly in Christ's sufferings, so through Christ we share abundantly in comfort too.

It is clear that Christ himself, for whose sake we are suffering, is present with us, consoling us and rescuing us from trouble by his divine intervention.

6If we are afflicted, it is for your comfort and salvation; and if we are comforted, it is for your comfort, which you experience when you patiently endure the same sufferings that we suffer. 7Our hope for you is unshaken; for we know that as you share in our sufferings, you will also share in our comfort.

Paul is speaking in general terms to the effect that because they were suffering persecutions from unbelievers for the sake of believers, they would be set free by God's help, as a consolation to believers, so that they would not desert their faith because of a stumbling block like that. The injuries suffered by the apostles were a temptation to believers [to abandon their faith]. As it is written in the prophet Zechariah: *I shall strike the shepherd and the sheep of the flock shall be scattered.*[1] However much they said they believed in the things to come, they became a stumbling block to new Christians when trouble arose, because when they saw preachers overcome by force they were inclined to think that the promise of Christ was an empty one. But if a believer is steadfast, he will suffer along with his master, trusting in his hope for the future and being consoled by Christ, along with whom he is suffering.

8For we do not want you to be ignorant, brethren, of the affliction we experienced in Asia; for we were so utterly, unbearably crushed that we despaired of life itself.

Paul listed the sufferings which were inflicted on him until he nearly died, because he wanted the Corinthians to know the evils he was enduring for the sake of their salvation. That way, they would not take it too badly if their own errors were rebuked by people who were enduring such harsh treatment for their sake.

---

[1]Zech 13:7.

What doctor would fail to upbraid a patient who was not looking after himself properly on the ground that if he took care of himself, the doctor's medicine would not have its desired effect?

⁹*Why, we felt that we had received the sentence of death; but that was to make us rely not on ourselves but on God who raises the dead;*

Paul means that there was such a violent upsurge of evil against preachers of the faith that death was staring them in the face. Having been rescued from this affliction, they are saying that they have been restored to life, because they had been in such trouble that they had despaired of their present lives. But God does not refuse his protection to people in extreme danger, especially when they belong to him, and he rescued them when they were in deep despair. Their affliction was so great that they would not have withstood it if God had not been with them.

¹⁰*he delivered us from so deadly a peril, and he will deliver us; on him we have set our hope that he will deliver us again. ¹¹You also must help us by prayer, so that many will give thanks on our behalf for the blessing granted us in answer to many prayers.*

Paul is saying that the grace of God had consoled the apostles because of the many people, indeed all believers in fact, for whose sake the afflictions had come upon them. For this reason they should all thank God when a time of trial comes to an end, and when it starts again they should all turn to prayer.

¹²*For our boast is this, the testimony of our conscience that we have behaved in the world, and still more toward you, with holiness and godly sincerity, not by earthly wisdom but by*

the grace of God.

Paul says this because they assumed that his conscience was totally free of pretense, and for this reason they believed that God would help them. The boast of Paul's conscience was simplicity and sincerity, qualities which belong to God's teaching. It was because of this that he added the words *not by earthly wisdom but by the grace of God.* In this way he made it clear that he has demonstrated that his conscience was clear, not in order to boast of human wisdom but in order to preach the gospel. In fact, he is returning to a familiar theme from the past. In his first letter Paul had criticized teaching based on earthly wisdom, and he alludes to that again here. He accused preachers of that kind both because they preached according to the wisdom of the world and because they were doing it in order to make money. For that reason, Paul was unwilling to receive any payment from the Corinthians, because he did not want to give them any opportunity [to criticize him] by being like them in this way. This is why he says: *we acted with simplicity*[1] *all the more abundantly so towards you,* because although he accepted payment from others, he would not take anything from them, so as not to lose his authority to rebuke them.

¹³*For we write you nothing but what you can read and understand; I hope you will understand fully,*

Paul is saying that he is writing things which they can see, not only on paper, but also in his actions. He wants to affirm that what he says is backed up by his actions, and it is through actions that we learn what a person really thinks.

¹⁴*as you have understood in part, that you can*

---

[1]Where the RSV text reads "holiness and godly sincerity," Ambrosiaster's text reads "simplicity."

be proud of us as we can be of you, on the day of the Lord Jesus.

Paul hopes that the Corinthians are growing in their faith, because now they have begun to improve by recognizing the fatherly feeling which he had for them and were beginning to boast of him in the way that children boast of their father. Hence he asserts that his boasting over his obedient children is noticed, and that this will be to their advantage on the day of judgment. Saying this, he urges them to persevere.

[15]*Because I was sure of this, I wanted to come to you first, so that you might have a double pleasure;* [16]*I wanted to visit you on my way to Macedonia, and to come back to you from Macedonia and have you send me on my way to Judea.*

This is proof that the Corinthians have mended their ways, because earlier on Paul did not want to see them at all. Now they would have every reason to be grateful when he came, because a letter is a picture, but personal presence is the reality. That Paul had wanted to go to see them but did not actually go is therefore not an irrelevance; he wanted them to understand that he did not do what he wanted to because of the behavior of some people in their midst, hoping that they would set to work and clean things up.

[17]*Was I vacillating when I wanted to do this? Do I make my plans like a worldly man, ready to say Yes and No at once?*

It is because he had said *I want to come to you* and did not go that Paul asks this question, because someone who says one thing and then does another appears to be vacillating. In order that no one should be able to accuse him of

this, Paul dismisses the charge that he cannot be trusted by telling the Corinthians that he did not change his mind lightly. He had good reasons for not doing what he had originally planned. He says: *Do I make my plans like a worldly man?* When people who think this way do not carry out their intentions, it is usually because they are deferring to someone of higher rank, or else have succumbed to bribery and flattery. The apostle never behaved like that.

When a spiritually minded person does not do what he intends to it is because he has in mind something more providential for the salvation of someone's soul. The apostle did not carry out his original plan in order that the Corinthians might become better men and women. He delayed his coming specifically because there were some among them who had not purified themselves, and he was waiting for that to happen first. He says in effect that the decision *Yes, yes* and *No, no* rests ultimately with him. This means that he has not done anything other than what he knew had to be done, because a profitable outcome has to be preferred over his own personal wishes. This is spiritual thinking. Carnal thinking, by contrast, makes changes of plan in order to suit personal desires, not in order to do what is beneficial.

[18]*As surely as God is faithful, our word to you has not been Yes and No.*

This is what Paul says to the Galatians too: *If I build things which are the same as those I have destroyed, I make myself a transgressor.*[1] Paul is saying that God's preaching through him has been faithful. Flatterers, on the other hand, frequently fail to mention things which are true in order not to offend people.

[19]*For the Son of God, Jesus Christ, whom we*

---

[1]Gal 2:18.

preached among you, Silvanus and Timothy and I, was not Yes and No; but in him it is always Yes. ²⁰*For all the promises of God find their Yes in him. That is why we utter the Amen through him, to the glory of God.*

As far as competent preachers are concerned, they ought to be clear about what they say and do nothing which is not beneficial. Given that our human will often tends in the opposite direction, Paul is insistent that he is not acting according to his will, but according to what he knows will be helpful. In Christ, of course, this problem does not exist, because he always wills what is beneficial. Furthermore, his will never changes and he is never unwilling, as a human being might be, to do what is useful. Nor is he ever uncertain about some things or does he change his mind.

²¹*But it is God who establishes us with you in Christ, and has commissioned us;* ²²*he has put his seal upon us and given us his Spirit in our hearts as a guarantee.*

Paul is saying that Christ confirms the Gentiles in the faith promised to the Jews, because he has made us both one.[1] He has joined the circumcision and the uncircumcision, *making peace in one new human being.*[2] This is why he says that the Lord establishes us and has commissioned us by giving us the anointing that belongs to royalty. The apostle Peter also says: *We are a royal race*[3] because of this spiritual anointing, which was symbolically prefigured in the anointing of the ancient Jewish kings.

God has set his seal upon us by giving us his Spirit as a pledge, so that we will have assurance of his promises. If he has already entrusted his Spirit to mortal beings, there can be no doubt that he will add to their glory when they become immortal.

Paul is also saying that the work of the

Father and the Son is one, because he says that it is both Christ who establishes and God. For whomever the Son establishes, the Father establishes too, because the Holy Spirit comes from both of them. Paul says the same thing to the Romans: *If anyone does not have the Spirit of Christ, he is not his.*[4] He mentions the Trinity here because he has been speaking about the perfecting of mankind, and the whole sum of perfection is found in the Trinity.

²³*But I call God to witness against me—it was to spare you that I refrained from coming to Corinth.*

Now Paul is explaining why he had postponed his visit to Corinth, even though he had wanted to go earlier, since now he would find that almost all of them had finally mended their ways. Paul is addressing people who apparently wanted to reform but were not making much of an effort in that direction. Because he had to rebuke them, he changed his plans and went elsewhere, so as not to upset many of them. This was *to spare them.* In order to get them to take him seriously, he calls on God as his witness. Paul did not want them to think that he despised them as unworthy. Once they realized that, they would mend their ways, and then the apostle would come to visit them.

²⁴*Not that we lord it over your faith; we work with you for your joy, for you stand firm in your faith.*

Paul says this because faith is not a matter of compulsion but of free will. The exercise of a master's power is a form of compulsion, but he worked with them for joy. In other words, just as there is grief in a bad action, so there is joy in mending one's ways. *We work with you for your joy* he says, because they were admon-

---

[1]Eph 2:14. [2]Eph 2:15. [3]1 Pet 2:9. He actually says: *We are a royal priesthood.* [4]Rom 8:9.

ishing those who wanted to mend their ways, so that they could bring their new desires to fulfillment.

2 Corinthians 2

[1] For I made up my mind not to make you another painful visit.

It is clear that Paul was unwilling to go to Corinth because he was afraid that if he rebuked a few he would cause pain to many. For all the members of a body suffer when one of them is in pain.

[2] For if I cause you pain, who is there to make me glad but the one whom I have pained?

Paul did not want to hurt the Corinthians, but because they had been wallowing in their sins, he saw that as inevitable. It was against his own wishes, except in the sense that once they had become obedient they would become a delight to those who had been upset in their company. Paul would therefore rejoice in those whom he had rebuked and hurt, as long as they mended their ways.

[3] And I wrote as I did, so that when I came I might not suffer pain from those who should have made me rejoice, for I felt sure of all of you, that my joy would be the joy of you all.

Paul is saying that he has written these things so that when he eventually comes to them there should be no reason for him to be upset. By then, their sins would have been wiped out and he would rejoice in their company, as if he were with his most beloved children. Unbelievers had caused him grief, but at least the believers would be a cause of rejoicing. The purification of the people is the apostle's joy. He is glad because he would then have no rebuking to be done among people in whom he ought to be rejoicing.

[4] For I wrote you out of much affliction and anguish of heart and with many tears, not to cause you pain but to let you know the abundant love that I have for you.

It is obvious that when someone rebukes another and in the process suffers more grief over it than the person being rebuked, he is not doing this in order to cause grief to someone else, but in order to show what deep love he has for him. Someone who rebukes another without feeling this way merely tramples on his feelings.

[5] But if any one has caused pain, he has caused it not to me, but in some measure—not to put it too severely—to you all.

By *you all* Paul means the saints among the Corinthians. For, as I noted in my commentary on the first letter, they were divided into those who were saints and those who were not, but it is the former he is addressing here. They have been upset at the error of a brother, just as he has been. In saying this, Paul is putting pressure on anyone who was sinning or who had been sinning. A person becomes even more guilty when many others suffer because of his sin. What comes next is the logical consequence of this.

[6] For such a one this punishment by the majority is enough;

A person who sees that his wrongdoing is offensive to many people will undoubtedly suffer pain.

[7] so you should rather turn to forgive and comfort him, or he may be overwhelmed by excessive sorrow.

Paul is teaching that we should help a person who is afflicted on account of his sins. This is because repentance bears immediate fruit if it really comes from the soul, that is, if a person who is rebuked immediately feels pain in his soul. Even David had his wrongdoing wiped out after he recognized that he had sinned in his behavior toward Uriah the Hittite.[1] Finally, it says in 1 Kings that Ahab received instant pardon when he was upset by the rebuke of a prophet.[2]

The apostle also wanted the man who had committed incest by having an affair with his father's wife to be called back, since he had been upset by his rebuke and rejection. Paul did not want this man to despair at seeing himself shunned [by the church] when he was consumed with regret, and thus surrender his soul to this world, as if he had no place in the presence of God. A person who is swallowed up in too much affliction will turn in desperation to committing sins. True repentance, on the other hand, is a turning away from sin. If this person does that, he will prove that he is sorry for what he has done.

[8]*So I beg you to reaffirm your love for him.*
[9]*For this is why I wrote, that I might test you and know whether you are obedient in everything.*

As far as anyone can tell, Paul was commending the Corinthians for their obedience in other respects. They had already put matters right in their church administration, and now he was asking them to be obedient in this matter as well, and thereby strengthen their brother by receiving him lovingly into their fellowship.

[10]*Any one whom you forgive, I also forgive. What I have forgiven, if I have forgiven anything, has been for your sake in the presence of Christ,*

Paul is obviously practicing what he preaches.

He has the right to give orders, but he cannot refuse to do himself what he is asking others to do. In the first letter he condemned this man's crime, in the hope that everyone would loathe him for it, but now he wants him to be received back and prays that they will no longer show any anger toward him and thus find it hard to have fellowship with him. The Corinthians evidently did not have the apostle's wisdom and did not understand that this ought to be done immediately, at least in the case of this man. Therefore Paul prays that they will restore him, implying that God has forgiven him, because the apostle did nothing without the Spirit of God.

By talking of his own forgiveness, Paul is bearing down on the Corinthians, because if a teacher has listened to his pupils' request and forgiven the sin of someone on whose behalf they have interceded, how much more should the pupils then obey the master's teaching. In order to show that God approved of this, Paul says that he has forgiven what he has forgiven in the presence of Christ. This means that because it was agreed that Christ, whose envoy Paul was, had taken away the sin, the apostle's act of forgiving was the act of Christ himself. As he said: *Whatever sins you remit on earth, they shall be remitted in heaven.*[3] If Christ, through the apostle, has forgiven the man for whom the Corinthians had interceded, how much more had forgiveness already been granted to the one to whom Paul himself is urging them to grant it?

[11]*to keep Satan from gaining the advantage over us; for we are not ignorant of his designs.*

Paul says what I have referred to above because consolation ought to be given to relieve the brother who was repenting his offense. He did not want this brother, being filled with sor-

---

[1]2 Sam 12:1-14. This sentence and the following have been rearranged, because the manuscript has them in the wrong chronological order. [2]1 Kings 21:27-29. [3]Mt 18:18.

row and being contemptuously excluded from the love of the church, to despair of himself, because the devil, who is always subtle in his tricks, would then see that this man's mind was an easy prey, approach him and suggest that at least he should enjoy the things of the present, given that he has been denied any hope of future reward. Thus the brother would perish, being possessed by the devil, even though an opportunity for repentance had been given to him, enabling him to change and be reformed as the Lord says through Ezekiel the prophet: *I do not wish the death of a dying person, so much as that he may turn around and live.*[1] And again: *Let them be converted and I shall replant them.*[2]

[12]When I came to Troas to preach the gospel of Christ, a door was opened for me in the Lord; [13]but my mind could not rest because I did not find my brother Titus there. So I took leave of them and went on to Macedonia.

Paul means that when he got to Troas to preach the gospel of Christ, there were people who received the message. But without the consolation of Titus's presence he found the work unbearable, because there was so much opposition to him. For although some people had opened their hearts and accepted the word of God, there were many unbelievers who reacted with impudent hostility, and one person could not teach the new believers and fend off these attacks at the same time. Therefore Paul said goodbye to those who had received him and left for Macedonia.

[14]But thanks be to God, who in Christ always leads us in triumph, and through us spreads the fragrance of the knowledge of him everywhere.

For God to lead us in triumph in Christ is to make us victors in the faith of Christ, so that when unbelief has been trodden underfoot, faith may have its trophy. All this time people are being changed from unbelievers to believers, and the wicked do not succeed in their persecution of the faithful.

[15]For we are the aroma of Christ to God among those who are being saved and among those who are perishing,

The aroma of the knowledge of God is in Christ and through Christ. The reason why Paul said *aroma* was because, just as some things are recognized by their smell even though they are invisible, God also, who is invisible, wished to be understood through Christ, so that the preaching of Christ, which reaches our ears just as an aroma reaches our nostrils, might bring God and his only-begotten Son into the midst of his creation. Thus, in accordance with what the Lord said to God, the Son to the Father: *Just as you have sent me into this world, so I send them into this world,*[3] the apostles, who were engaged on a mission for this cause, would manifest the aroma of Christ and God through their signs and wonders. Their preaching about God and Christ is proved to be true by the evidence of its power. This is implied in the word *aroma*, because although God is not seen, he is understood by the works which he carries out invisibly through the agency of the apostles, with the intention that the truth of their teaching may be made clear.

Furthermore a person who speaks the truth about Christ is a good aroma from God, worthy of praise from the one who believes, and not to be maligned by unbelievers. But a person who makes wrong assertions about Christ is a bad smell to believers and unbelievers alike, as far as God is concerned, and guilty in the eyes of both. For the unbeliever does not believe be-

---

[1]Ezek 18:23. [2]Cf. Ezek 17:22. [3]Jn 17:18. As in 1 Cor 6:2, Ambrosiaster reads the Greek article "the" as "this."

cause what he hears is perverse, and the believer believes in a way which is not correct.

Thus the apostle spoke in line with the law. Just as in the law, someone who offered sacrifice with a good prayer was a good aroma to the Lord and acceptable to him, so too the power of preaching gives off a fragrance of teaching which smells acceptable to God. For this reason, God assured by his interventions on their behalf that his apostles were protected and enabled to pour words of knowledge into open ears, both of Jews and of Gentiles. In addition to these there was also the sacramental fact of the incarnation of the Lord Jesus, which happened in accordance with the will of his God and Father, in the unity of a saving faith, for the salvation of believers and the destruction of unbelievers.

¹⁶to one a fragrance from death to death, to the other a fragrance from life to life. Who is sufficient for these things?

Paul says this because to unbelievers the preaching of the cross is the smell of death. On hearing the word of God they receive it as if it were a plague from which death arises, and what then happens is necessarily in accordance with their belief.

But to others it is the fragrance of life. To believers the word of God is a messenger of eternal life, and it affects them in accordance with their faith. Therefore, both in the case of those who are perishing and of those who are being saved, the apostles were a good aroma for God, because they preached sincerely and without flattery. Unbelievers were putting a noose around their own necks, while the apostles remained untouched. As the Lord said to the prophet Ezekiel: *Preach your message. If they hear you, you will be benefiting their souls; if not, let them look out for themselves. But you will escape from their destruction.*[1]

¹⁷For we are not, like so many, peddlers of God's word; but as men of sincerity, as commissioned by God, in the sight of God we speak in Christ.

Paul is alluding to various false apostles who used to corrupt the word of God through bad interpretation. Some of them were so zealous for Jewish tradition that they did not teach properly about Christ. He therefore says that they are incompetent, whereas the apostles preached sincerely what they had received from God himself. They spoke in Christ, who was himself their witness, and did not seek their own glory, but God's. To speak in Christ is to preach his honor and power.

2 Corinthians 3

¹Are we beginning to commend ourselves again? Or do we need, as some do, letters of recommendation to you, or from you?

Paul is finding fault with the false apostles, describing their teaching as wrong and claiming, in contrast to them, that he is a true preacher. In doing this, it appears that he is boasting, as in his first letter. In order to make it clear that he is not doing this as a way of tricking people into honoring him, Paul goes on to ask whether he needs letters of recommendation at all. In saying this, he is removing any hint of self-interest from his own thinking, yet still finding fault with the false apostles. He is pointing out that they are still going around the churches in order to get honor and reward for themselves and to do away with salvation, not to grant it.

Among them were those to whom the Lord says: *You devour the houses of widows and orphans, delivering long speeches. Because of this you will get heavier judgment.*[2] The false teachers were claiming both their good and their

---

[1] Cf. Ezek 33:9. [2] Mt 23:14. The authenticity of this verse is doubtful, since it occurs in only a few biblical manuscripts.

souls; the apostle, by contrast, did not touch their property and saved their souls by the truth of his teaching.

2You yourselves are our letter of recommendation, written on your hearts, to be known and read by all men;

Evidence of salvation is an epistle in itself. Paul was therefore speaking correctly, because the salvation of the Corinthians was in his heart and in the hearts of those who were with him, for he was always thinking about it. So because they are in the heart of the apostle and his companions, they are a letter written on their hearts. When one person keeps thinking about another one, that second person is written into his thinking.

3and you show that you are a letter from Christ delivered by us, written not with ink but with the Spirit of the living God, not on tablets of stone but on tablets of human hearts.

It is clear that because they are called Christians, they are the letter of Christ, revealing the salvation which God has given to everyone in him, while the apostle did the writing. For while the [apostles] are teaching, they are also writing. The things which are promised are eternal and are therefore said to be written with the Spirit of God, unlike temporal things written in ink, which fades and loses its power to record anything.

Here Paul attacks the old law, which was given first on stone tablets and abolished by Moses when he broke the tablets at the bottom of the mountain.[1] The new law is written on the rational soul, that is to say, on the heart, not by a pen but by the Spirit. Because faith is something eternal, it is written by the Spirit so that it may last. The old teachings will die out as the world fades away. Just as the one law

is different from the other, so too the guardians of the ancient law are different from the guardians of the law of faith.

4Such is the confidence that we have through Christ toward God.

Paul is making clear how great the inherent authority of the apostles was when he says this. His purpose was to show that the ancient prophets did not have this position of trust in God's eyes, because theirs was a lesser ministry.

5Not that we are competent of ourselves to claim anything as coming from us; our competence is from God, 6who has made us competent to be ministers of a new covenant, not in a written code but in the Spirit; for the written code kills, but the Spirit gives life.

Although Paul is proclaiming his dignity as an apostle, he nevertheless bursts out with praise to God for this and does not claim that it rests on his human merits. For the sake of human life, the grace of God condescended to embark on a saving mission, whose purpose was to bring salvation to those whom the old law regarded as guilty, by means of the forgiveness of sins granted through Christ our Lord.

The written commands of Moses were given in order to kill those who flouted the law. But the Spirit, who is the law of faith which is not written, but which is contained in the rational soul, is life-giving, drawing to himself those who are guilty of mortal sin, so that they may be made righteous and cease altogether from sinning. The law had been given in [a spirit of] rectitude, so that people would be afraid to sin. But because the human race is weak, the mercy of God was given to the apostles so that believers in

---

[1]Ex 32:19.

Christ might escape death by having their sins forgiven. This is the message of the new covenant, which God promised through his prophets.

⁷Now if the dispensation of death, carved in letters on stone, came with such splendor that the Israelites could not look at Moses' face because of its brightness, fading as this was, ⁸will not the dispensation of the Spirit be attended with greater splendor?

It is obvious that the grace of the law of faith is greater than that of the law of Moses. For although the law of Moses was intended to be beneficial, it became the law of death because it was flouted. Then, because there was no way it could make provision for sinners to be saved, there came the law of faith, which not only forgives sinners but also makes them righteous. There is therefore a great deal of difference between one law and the other. In ancient times people who were stained with sin could not look on the face of Moses when he came down from the mountain with the law which he had received on tablets. Because his face had become glorious, sinners who deserved to die could not look at him. This glory is now fading away because of the law of the Spirit. Now that forgiveness of sins has been received, sinners have been justified and are able to look on the glory of God, just as Peter, James and John saw the glory of Christ on the mountain.[1]

⁹For if there was splendor in the dispensation of condemnation, the dispensation of righteousness must far exceed it in splendor.

Paul says this because the gift of God's righteousness through the faith of Christ is richer than that of the old law; there is more glory in salvation than there is in death. However justly a judge may condemn someone, he earns more honor if he shows mercy, so that the guilty party is given an opportunity to mend his ways.

¹⁰Indeed, in this case, what once had splendor has come to have no splendor at all, because of the splendor that surpasses it.

The law of Moses was not made glorious because of the splendor on his face. That splendor was of no benefit to anyone and did not have the reward of glory. It was rather a hindrance, not through its own fault but through the fault of sinners. In that case there was no glory, but in our case there is a glory which abounds in grace, so that now that darkness has been wiped away by the gift of God, people who have been made clean can see the glory of Christ.

¹¹For if what faded away came with splendor, what is permanent must have much more splendor.

Paul does not deny that there was splendor in the law and on the face of Moses, but it did not endure because in his case it was a symbol and not a reality. The difference between the face of Moses and the glory of Christ is the same as the difference between the picture and the person whom it portrays. It is for this reason that Paul said *because of the splendor which surpasses it* in the last verse. The former glory was only as great as the kind of glory which should be entrusted to a slave, but the present glory is as great as that of the Father, because *the Lord Jesus is in the glory of God the Father.*[2] For just as stars are glorious in the evening but their brightness fades away when the sun comes up, so the glory of Moses vanishes when the glory of Christ appears.

¹²Since we have such a hope, we are very bold,

---

[1]Mt 17:1-8; Mk 9:2-8; Lk 9:28-36; 2 Pet 1:18. [2]Phil 2:11.

Paul is saying that we have a hope of seeing glory, not the kind that was on the face of Moses, but the kind which the three apostles saw on the mountain when the Lord revealed himself. It is on that basis that we ought to judge how much the divine mercy has bestowed on us and how much it has deigned to enrich us with the gift of a grace superior to that given to the Jews. For even though the glory of Moses' face was a lesser glory, the Jews were still not able to look at it, whereas we believe that we shall see not the inferior glory of Moses but the surpassing glory of the Savior. So whereas the Jews did not earn the right to see the glory of a servant, we shall see the glory of the Master we have in common. Therefore we ought to repay the love of God as far as we can by being more fervent in our love for him, who by cleansing us from our sins has given us this confidence. Now our confidence ought to increase, because what we eventually see will be in proportion to what we now believe.

13not like Moses, who put a veil over his face so that the Israelites might not see the end of the fading splendor.

Paul says this because we have been made worthy by the grace of God to see the glory of Christ. Moses put a veil on because the sinful Israelites could not bear to look at the splendor of his face, but once our sin is taken away, we are given power to see the glory of God right to the very end. It is not revealed as long as they are not converted to the grace of faith, and so it comes to nothing. For once merit comes to them through faith, their unworthiness disappears.

14But their minds were hardened; for to this day, when they read the old covenant, that same veil remains unlifted, because only through Christ is it taken away.

Paul is saying that their minds have been hard-ened as long as they do not believe. This hard-ness is the result of unbelief. Therefore the perception of the mind is sharpened in people who have been converted to the faith, so that they may see the splendor of the divine light. Their minds were hardened through unbelief, and this will not change until they convert and believe in Christ. When their wrongdoing is removed they will begin to see what they could not see before, because their sin was getting in the way.

15Yes, to this day whenever Moses is read a veil lies over their minds;

It is clear that when this part of the law is read the thinking of those who are under the law is being recalled.

16but when a man turns to the Lord the veil is removed.

To be converted to the Lord is to believe in Christ, so that in recognizing the Lord [for who he is], a person may deserve to receive forgiveness. To remove the veil is for the thinking by which he was judged guilty under the law to disappear.

17Now the Lord is the Spirit, and where the Spirit of the Lord is, there is freedom.

Because God is Spirit, he has given through Christ the law of the Spirit, which persuades us to believe in invisible things which our reasoning understands spiritually. This law gives liberty because it demands only faith, and because it believes what it does not see we earn the right to be rescued from our condition.

18And we all, with unveiled face, beholding the glory of the Lord, are being changed into his likeness from one degree of glory to another; for this comes from the Lord who is the Spirit.

Paul is saying that all of us who have obtained freedom by the gift of God's grace reflect the Lord's glory through faith and are transformed into the likeness of what we hope for. That is, we are so transformed that after this life is over we shall look like the appearance of Christ's glory, as the apostle John says: *We know that when he appears we shall be like him.*[1]

We shall be raised up by the goodness of God from the glory of Moses, which we could not look at because of our sinfulness, and be transformed into a glory which we believe has been given to us by the Spirit of the Lord. The greatness of the coming glory will be proportionate to what it is fitting for God to give us through his Spirit. The glory of Moses was neither as great as this nor was it eternal. He received glory in a form which corresponded to the law. So too, glory will be given to believers in a way which corresponds to the law of faith, in which the Spirit of God is present. For God has granted his Spirit to his faithful people as a gift and pledge of the glory which he has promised them.

2 Corinthians 4

[1]Therefore, having this ministry by the mercy of God, we do not lose heart.

Paul says that the hope inherent in his ministerial task is such that he is not discouraged by his troubles, but strengthened by faith in the things it promises. This is why, earlier, on, he said: *we are very bold.*[2] Trusting in what has been promised, they are enduring every reverse they face. He attributes his perseverance not to human merit but to the mercy of God, which first cleanses a person, then makes him righteous, adopts him as a son of God and endows him with a glory like the glory of God's own Son.

[2]We have renounced disgraceful, underhanded ways; we refuse to practice cunning or to tamper with God's word, but by the open statement of the truth we would commend ourselves to every man's conscience in the sight of God.

Paul is teaching that in order for us to be made worthy of the glory [promised to us], everything shameful and corrupt which can happen or be thought about must be eradicated, not only from what we do but from what we think as well. These words are really an invitation. Under cover of speaking about himself and his associates, Paul is exhorting the Corinthians to lead a better life. He does this because of the vices mentioned above, which he often finds in them. The *underhanded ways* he mentions may also be ideas, conceived as a result of bad thinking, for preaching with deceitful intent. This is why he adds what comes next.

Whoever dreams up teaching in order to deceive the hearts of simple people is disgraced and disfigured as a result, for he will be found guilty on the day of judgment. The craftiness of an evil mind, trying to achieve its own willful intention, corrupts the words of God and makes them mean the opposite of what they say. To tamper with God's word is to want to exclude its true meaning and substitute a false one instead.

Paul says that he is commending himself because in the course of his preaching the gospel he has not made himself suspect in anyone's eyes. Furthermore, when he says *in the sight of God* he is affirming that this fact is abundantly clear, not only to other people but to God as well, from whom nothing is hidden. He is calling God to witness that even in his sight, Paul is trustworthy, because his preaching agrees with what his Master had given to him. God bears witness to him by performing signs and wonders through him.

---

[1] Jn 3:2. [2] Cor 3:12.

[3]And even if our gospel is veiled, it is veiled only to those who are perishing.

It is true that unbelievers do not see this, because unbelief throws darkness over the splendor of the power of God. There is a veil over their heart and a dulled perception, especially in the case of the Jews.

[4]In their case the god of this world has blinded the minds of the unbelievers, to keep them from seeing the light of the gospel of the glory of Christ, who is the likeness of God.

Paul is saying that God dims the sight of worldly people because they are hostile to the faith of Christ, and he does not want them to see the truth of the gospel of Christ's majesty. He is giving them what they want, since it is because people are hostile and tell lies that they are helped toward not being able to believe what they do not want to believe. They claim that Christ is a mere man, although he is the image of God, and leaving aside his claims, they talk only about his flesh. Isaiah said of such people: *He has blinded their eyes, so that right until now they cannot see with their eyes or hear with their ears.*[1]

[5]For what we preach is not ourselves, but Jesus Christ as Lord, with ourselves as your servants for Jesus' sake.

Paul means by this that they are not proclaiming their own glory. No one should say that they are preaching the gospel for their own sake, with some short-term benefit in view. On the contrary, they are proclaiming Jesus the Lord, submitting themselves to his power and majesty. Since they are not striking terror into anyone or coming down hard on anyone, and are professing that Christ is our Lord, why should they be considered arrogant or self-

interested in their preaching, as if they were trying to earn praise for themselves?

Paul represents himself as a slave of Christ, because it is at Christ's command that he is these people's servant, and so it is to their advantage to be subordinate to him during the preaching of the gospel. In expressing himself humbly, Paul spoke in a way which was designed to show that he was not preaching the gospel for his own advantage, but for the glory of the Lord Christ, to whom he is obedient and whose service he is performing, in accordance with what the Lord himself says: *I am in the midst of you, not to be served but to serve.*[2] Paul spoke like this not because the people he was serving deserved it but because the Lord commanded him to.

[6]For it is the God who said, "Let light shine out of darkness,"[3] who has shone in our hearts to give the light of the knowledge of the glory of God in the face of Christ.

Paul says this because it is by God's mercy that we who were unbelievers in ignorance and darkness [were brought into the knowledge and light of his glorious truth] so that through us God might give light to the other Gentiles as well. How very humble he still is with regard to himself, in order to promote the glory of God alone and of Christ. They have been enlightened in order to have knowledge of the glory of God through Christ. Paul speaks of *the knowledge of the glory of God*, that is, not of God alone but of Christ too, who is his glory. His intention is to demonstrate that it is not only God who comes to be known, but also his works, his mercy and his providence, by which he both founded and saved the human race. He is revealed in Christ through the glory of his power.

[7]But we have this treasure in earthen vessels,

---

[1]Cf. Is 6:10.　[2]Cf. Lk 22:27.　[3]Gen 1:3.

to show that the transcendent power belongs to God and not to us.

By treasure, Paul meant the sacrament of God in Christ, which is made manifest to believers but which has been concealed from unbelievers with a veil, because just as a treasure is put in a hidden place, the sacrament of God is hidden within a person, in his heart. He is saying that this treasure is in the soul and body, a gift conferred by God, so that the preeminence of his power may become apparent, if only through human preachers. The intention is that every tongue may be reconciled to its creator, not for the greater glory of human beings but for the glory of God, who manifests himself through people who may be lowly and unskilled, but who nevertheless have received power from God, both to speak and to do great things.

The reference to earthen vessels is an allusion to the weakness of human nature, which can do nothing unless it has received power from God. God may proclaim himself through them in their weakness so that glory may be given to him and not to human beings, who are made out of clay.

[8]We are afflicted in every way, but not crushed; perplexed, but not driven to despair;

Paul is making it clear that they were suitable preachers because God was always with them in adversity. God never allowed them to be oppressed to the point where they gave way.

[9]persecuted, but not forsaken; struck down, but not destroyed;

God was with them, like a shepherd, when they were in need. He looked after their interests so that their enemies would not get the better of them. They were beaten to the ground but not killed, because God prevented it. They may have been imprisoned or chained up, but they kept on escaping from the hands of their enemies with God's help. Finally, when Paul and Silas were imprisoned after having been beaten, and their hands were tied with rope, they would cheerfully sing a hymn to God, because they had become braver than those who had not been beaten.

[10]always carrying in the body the death of Jesus, so that the life of Jesus may also be manifested in our bodies.

It is a fact that in the martyrdoms of believers Christ himself is put to death, that their sufferings are his sufferings and that consequently his life is made manifest in their bodies. Sufferings are evidence of the fact that one deserves the life to come which Christ has promised. Thus Paul says elsewhere: *When I am weak, then I am strong,*[1] and again *It is through tribulations that we must enter the kingdom of God.*[2]

[11]For while we live we are always being given up to death for Jesus' sake, so that the life of Jesus may be manifested in our mortal flesh.

What Paul is saying is clear. We have the power to go on living, but we do not object to being handed over to death for Jesus' sake, so that the life by which Christ rose from the dead may be granted to this mortal flesh of ours. We are not afraid to die because we have the promise of resurrection.

[12]So death is at work in us, but life in you.

Paul is saying this because he and Timothy were being subjected to death for their sakes. By preaching to the Gentiles, they were stirring up hatred against themselves both from Jews and Gentiles, risking even death.

---

[1] 2 Cor 12:10. [2] Acts 14:22.

---

¹³*Since we have the same spirit of faith as he had who wrote, "I believed, and so I spoke,"*[1] *we too believe, and so we speak,*

Paul says that he shares their spirit, by which faith is strengthened. He and his companions were suffering such evils on behalf of the Corinthians that they were bound together in faith.

Paul quoted from Psalm 115[2] in order to show that he was prepared to endure anything, because he believed in the resurrection to come. Because he was confident of the future life, he was not concerned about the present one, because he believed that if this life is despised, the one to come may be hoped for instead.

¹⁴*knowing that he who raised the Lord Jesus will raise us also with Jesus and bring us with you into his presence.*

Paul says that in the midst of their troubles they have this hope because of their faith. The example of the resurrection of the Lord Jesus has taught us what will become of believers. For *Just as in Adam all die, so in Christ shall all be made alive.*[3] Adam is the image of death because of his sin, but Christ is the image of life because of his righteousness. For *he did not commit sin, nor was falsehood found in his mouth.*[4] Because he has said that they share a common faith, he also says that Jesus will establish him and his companions along with the Corinthians after the resurrection. In that way those who share the same faith will dwell in the same house of peace. Once the Corinthians understand that Paul and his companions are suffering disasters for their sake, and are upset by their sufferings as if they were sharing them too, they will immediately be partakers of the promised life. Having sunk to the depths of despair together, they will have joy together also.

¹⁵*For it is all for your sake, so that as grace extends to more and more people it may increase thanksgiving, to the glory of God.*

God does not want anyone to be excluded from his gift. But because not everyone had received the word of faith, God's apostle, who knew his will, was not afraid to suffer persecutions and perils as long as he could preach to everyone faithfully, so that more people might believe. His intention was that God's abundant gift should not be diminished because so few people offered thanks—that would be an insult to God. Rather, God's gift should benefit many through the thanksgiving of many, and this would be to God's glory. What great honor Paul deserves! He has always put his life in mortal danger so that the gift of God might not turn out in the end very different from what was originally intended. Is it not a great insult to someone if he prepares a rich banquet and invites many guests and then hardly anybody turns up?

¹⁶*So we do not lose heart. Though our outer nature is wasting away, our inner nature is being renewed every day.*

This obviously refers back to the thought expressed above. To show that his devotion is still very keen where the things of God are concerned, Paul adds these words, in which he says that he is not at all giving up his effort to fulfill what is pleasing to God. Rather, he is confident about the promised resurrection. The flesh is damaged by persecution, beatings, hunger, thirst, cold and nakedness, but the soul is restored by its hope of a reward to come, because it is cleansed by these constant troubles. In times of persecution the soul advances; every day it adds something more to its merit. Even the damage done to the body is conducive to immortality through the merit of the soul.

---

[1] Ps 116:10. [2] Ps 116 in English versions. [3] 1 Cor 15:22. [4] 1 Pet 2:22.

[17]*For this slight momentary affliction is preparing for us an eternal weight of glory beyond all comparison,*

Paul is saying that our present afflictions are light because they are happening within time and space. In return for this light tribulation, we shall gain a degree of glory beyond measure.

[18]*because we look not to the things that are seen but to the things that are unseen; for the things that are seen are transient, but the things that are unseen are eternal.*

Paul is saying that people who long for heavenly things despise the things of this world, because in comparison with what they want, they are nothing. Present things relate to eternal things as an image relates to the reality. An image perishes, but the reality remains. Because of this, the righteous are not afraid to leave this present age, but rather they are glad to do so.

2 Corinthians 5

[1]*For we know that if the earthly tent we live in is destroyed, we have a building from God, a house not made with hands, eternal in the heavens.*

Paul is saying that, on the strength of this faith, we should not be afraid of being separated from this body by the violence of unbelievers or by some chance circumstance of life, because in heaven there is an eternal habitation for us, so that when we are expelled from our time-bound, earthly home, we shall be received into one that is eternal. Indeed, we should be looking forward to this as much as we can. But we should not overdo this, because then another person might perish because of the way we are rejoicing. But if it does happen, we should endure it willingly. Paul says that our present body is our earthly home because it is mortal, and that when we are released from our present home, we shall find an eternal one in heaven. This second home is our immortal body, which we shall dwell in forever once we have risen from the dead, and whose shape is already clear in our Lord's heavenly body.

[2]*Here indeed we groan, and long to put on our heavenly dwelling,* [3]*so that by putting it on we may not be found naked.*

Paul is saying that people are yearning that when they rise again they may be clothed in the promised heavenly glory. They are earnest in their prayers that they should not be excluded from the glory which is promised. This is what being found naked means. For when the soul is clothed in a body it must also be clothed with the glory which is its transformation into brightness.

Death comes from the earth but resurrection from the heavens, as long as there is a change into glory. There will be, but only if on departing out of this body we are clothed in Christ, because everyone who is baptized in Christ puts him on like a garment.[1] So if we have remained in the form and faith of our baptism, we shall be found with our body stripped, but not naked, because Christ dwells in our inner selves, and when we are clothed (or when the Holy Spirit has been given to us), we shall be worthy of being clothed in the promised glory of heaven. The promised brightness will fall on the person whom he sees as having the sign of adoption.

[4]*For while we are still in this tent, we sigh with anxiety; not that we would be unclothed, but that we would be further clothed, so that what is mortal may be swallowed up by life.*

---

[1]Cf. Gal 3:27.

Here the meaning is the same again. Paul is saying that when we are oppressed by bodily sufferings and the storms of this world, pleas are addressed to God that this body may not be taken away from us by being defeated and made unworthy, but that, if death occurs, we may be found by the Holy Spirit (who is Christ in substance) persevering in our faith. We shall be able to be clothed on top when the Holy Spirit has taken us out of this body but not deprived us of it completely. What is mortal will be *swallowed up by life*, so that at the resurrection we shall be gloriously clothed on top by immortality, so that our body may no longer die or suffer. A person who rises from the dead only to suffer punishment is not *swallowed up by life*.

[5]He who has prepared us for this very thing is God, who has given us the Spirit as a guarantee.

What we are pleading for in our groaning is not to be left naked, but to be found worthy of being clothed on top [of our mortal bodies]. In line with the thought expressed previously, Paul is saying that God brings this to completion on the day of judgment, because he has made a promise and is faithful, giving the Spirit as a pledge that he will fulfill this, for he is the sign of our adoption.

[6]So we are always of good courage; we know that while we are at home in the body we are away from the Lord, [7]for we walk by faith, not by sight.

It is clear that we are with the Lord in faith, not by being present in body with him. For this reason, we are traveling not in faith but by sight. Why is it that this same man says in the Acts of the Apostles: *In him we live and move and have our being*[1] but here says that we are

traveling apart from the Lord? If God is everywhere, how can this be? It is undoubtedly true that God is everywhere, or rather that everything is in him, but because his throne is in heaven and is always to be seen there, we who are placed here, where he is not seen, are said to be traveling apart from him. Since we do not see him, even though he is present, we are said to be absent from him.

[8]We are of good courage, and we would rather be away from the body and at home with the Lord.

Paul is right to be of good courage, because relying on the promise of God and knowing that it is much better to be in that other place than it is to remain in this world, they are willing to leave the body and rest until the day of resurrection under the throne of God.

[9]So whether we are at home or away, we make it our aim to please him.

Paul is saying that we must do this and put our energy into good works in order to please God, whether we remain in this life or go to stand before the judgment seat of Christ. If we keep up our self-discipline, we will be pleasing both here and there, because someone who is pleasing here will hardly be displeasing there.

[10]For we must all appear before the judgment seat of Christ, so that each one may receive good or evil, according to what he has done in the body.

If, on the day of Christ's judgment, we are going to receive what we have done in the body, it is clear that we shall not be judged without a body, good or bad. Paul does not say *in the flesh* because the deeds of the flesh always

---

[1]Acts 17:28.

deserve punishment, but *in the body*, because sometimes the body acts spiritually and sometimes it acts carnally.

[11]Therefore, knowing the fear of the Lord, we persuade men; but what we are is known to God, and I hope it is known also to your conscience.

Since the judgment of God, when the deeds of every individual will be judged, will take place through Christ, the apostle says that he uses persuasion to get people to think sensibly and live rightly. He wants his hearers to be free from anxiety about the punishment to come, and he exults in possessing them as a reward for his labors. Because doubt is being cast on the day of God's judgment by the wicked talk of certain people—for *bad conversations corrupt good morals*[1]—he says that he persuades people with the intention that they may believe and be prudent, so as not to wait until the day of judgment and repent then, when it is too late. Paul and his companions were preaching what God had told them to, and he knows what is good. At the end, God will say to evildoers: *I do not know you.*[2]

Their purity was clear to the Corinthians because they had never been caught in the act of flattery, their preaching had not been displeasing to the saints, and they had not tried, as people often do, to extract payment of any kind from them. They did not want to appear to be outwardly sincere in public but hypocrites within. Therefore he is prodding their consciences so that they might be witnesses to their genuineness.

[12]We are not commending ourselves to you again but giving you cause to be proud of us, so that you may be able to answer those who pride themselves on a man's position and not on his heart.

Since earlier on Paul appeared to be praising himself by saying that his preaching was true, he now makes the same point, that he is not saying this in order to praise himself, but for their glory, so that they may rejoice at the fact that, having these men as their missionaries, they have received true teaching.

Paul is saying this because many people used to get above themselves and take a personal pride in the apostles, making it known that they had been taught by men who had always been with the Lord.

Therefore Paul is also saying that he is giving them a reason why they might glory in opposition to them, which is that they had been instructed by an apostle too. This is why he says elsewhere: *I have done nothing less than those who are assuredly apostles.*[3] Paul is forced to say this, because he is afraid that silence on his part might be harmful to them. Someone who glories in his heart has suppressed pride, because *God gives grace to the humble but resists the proud.*[4] The mind of proud people does not bring any worthwhile benefit in God's eyes.

[13]For if we are beside ourselves, it is for God; if we are in our right mind, it is for you.

Paul says this because, if he is thought to have spoken over-enthusiastically, or out of pride—as he has appeared to be praising himself while speaking the truth—this is something which must be referred to God. But if he is understood to have been speaking not out of pride but for the glory of his hearers, he says that it is beneficial to the Corinthians. What he has said is sane from his hearers' point of view, as long as it is understood in the sense in which it was uttered, but if it is thought to have been spoken out of boastfulness, it is insane. For all pride is a kind of insanity.

[14]For the love of Christ controls us, because we

---

[1] Cor 15:33. [2] Mt 25:12. [3] 2 Cor 12:11. [4] Prov 3:34; cf. Jas 4:6; 1 Pet 5:5.

are convinced that one has died for all; therefore all have died.

Since Christ gave himself up to death out of love for the human race, in order to redeem them, the apostles, wanting to give him something back in return, are exhorting people, as much as they can, to be obedient to him. In order to do this, the apostles have to insist that their teaching is true and that what others are teaching is wrong. If they want bad teachers to be punished, they cannot be silent about their own credentials. They were not doing this out of pride, but in order that the gift of Christ might be understood by everyone and that those who were faithful in their devotion should thank him in return.

Because of the love of Christ the apostles were not silent about the gifts from him with which those who loved him were surrounded. They were not boasting about them, but inviting their hearers to become Christ's disciples. This was in order that the death of Christ would not seem pointless, not so that the reputation of the apostles would be enhanced. It is through the worth and renown of the apostles that Christ's grace and God's blessings are recognized.

[15]*And he died for all, that those who live might live no longer for themselves but for him who for their sake died and was raised.*

Because everyone must die as a result of Adam's sin, Christ died for everyone, in order to set them free from a second death. Therefore those who live in the body who know that Christ died for them should be subject to him, proclaiming him as their Lord. Christ's resurrection testifies that his death is beneficial to them. Therefore a person who does the Lord's will does not live for himself.

[16]*From now on, therefore, we regard no one from a human point of view; even though we once regarded Christ from a human point of view, we regard him thus no longer.*

Now that Christ has risen from the dead, birth according to the flesh loses its importance, bodily weakness ceases to count, and the sufferings of death no longer matter either. [This is the case, certainly not for Christ's sake, because the fate of human weakness did not touch him, but for our sake, to whom this example has been given, so that if we follow in the footsteps of the one who died for us, we shall also rise again at the promised time, after we have departed this life, and all weakness and corruption will cease. The reason why Paul says this is because, in the resurrection of Christ, a model for incorruption and splendor was given, so that it might be recognized as being beneficial to everyone who obeys Christ.][1] Right up until the cross there was a suspicion that Christ was weak, but once he rose from the dead, all that vanished, and what was previously doubted came to be believed, just as he himself said: *When you have raised the Son of Man on high, you will know that I am.*[2] The apostle is therefore recalling this in order to show the devotion with which Christ should be submitted to. For he deigned not only to be born as a man for the salvation of mankind but also to be treated with unjust violence and to die, so that those who know how precious his death is may serve him all the more willingly, rendering him his due not as to a man but as to God, because the acts of deference showered upon him must correspond to his person and his merits.

[17]*Therefore, if any one is in Christ, he is a new creation; the old has passed away, behold, the new has come.*

---

[1]The section in brackets occurs in only one of the surviving manuscripts. [2]Jn 8:28.

It is clear that all things have been made new by Christ if they recognize his dignity. He becomes "new" to them in the sense that whereas previously they had thought of him only as a man, now they realize that he is God. As a result, their weakness ceases, his divinity receives recognition, and the old error which had led the human race away from faith in the one true God into polytheism comes to an end, as everyone returns to the proclamation of unity, worshiping the one God in Trinity.

18All this is from God, who through Christ reconciled us to himself and gave us the ministry of reconciliation; 19that is, in Christ God was reconciling the world to himself, not counting their trespasses against them, and entrusting to us the message of reconciliation. 20So we are ambassadors for Christ, God making his appeal through us. We beseech you on behalf of Christ, be reconciled to God. 21For our sake he made him to be sin who knew no sin, so that in him we might become the righteousness of God.

Although Christ has redeemed us, all things come from God, because all fatherhood comes from him. Therefore precedence must be given to the person of the Father.

Almighty God, the Father of Christ—for all the things which he had made through Christ became mortal because of the sin which caused them to forget their creator—thought it right that Christ our Lord should come from his holy dwelling place to the people of this world. He became flesh and appeared as a man, with the intention of offering the human race a model of how God, its creator, could be reconciled to it. The Son is God the Father's envoy, in accordance with their nature. Jesus says that *The Father is in me and I am in the Father,*[1] which means that the Father is in the Son because they have the same substance. Where there is unity there is no differentiation and they are interchangeable, because both their appearance and their likeness is identical. Thus he who has seen the Son is said to have seen the Father also. As the Lord himself says: *He who has seen me has seen the Father also.*[2]

Therefore it is correct to say that God was in Christ, that is to say, the Father was in the Son, reconciling the world to himself, not counting their sins against them. Creation sinned against God and did not repent, so God, who did not want his work to perish, sent his Son in order to preach through him the forgiveness of sins and thus reconcile them to himself through the very one by whom he had created us. God exhorts his people, whether through his Son or through his servants, because all things must be attributed to him, by whose will and providence Christ was made incarnate and obtained the salvation of the human race by ransoming it. When it was his will to return to the Father, he gave his disciples the stewardship which he had received from the Father.

Paul is saying that the Father made his Son Christ a "sin," although he knew no sin, that is to say, he had never sinned himself. It was the one who was made flesh, not inherently changed but made incarnate, who became a "sin." In the same way, a person who becomes a senior officer does not lose his previous standing but takes on the status of being someone he previously was not. Christ did not have to be born as a man, but he became man because of sin. It was only because all flesh was subject to sin that he was made sin for us. In view of the fact that he was made an offering for sins, it is not wrong for him to be said to have been made "sin," because in the law the sacrifice which was offered for sins used to be called a "sin."[3]

He who did not know sin—in the words of Isaiah: *He who did not know sin, neither*

[1]Jn 14:10. [2]Jn 14:9. [3]Lev 4:1-12.

was treachery found on his lips[1]—was killed as a sinner, so that in Christ sinners might be made righteous before God. For Satan fell victim to jealousy toward the savior when he saw him teaching people how to make God show his favor toward them by renouncing the devil. Because of this, Satan killed him, not realizing that Christ would soon turn against him. For after his death on the cross Christ descended to hell, because it was death, working through sin, which gave hell its power. Christ defeated death by his death, and brought such benefit to sinners that now death cannot hold those who are marked with the sign of the cross.

2 Corinthians 6

[1]*Working together with him, then, we entreat you not to accept the grace of God in vain.*

Paul is trying to show his concern for the salvation of mankind in two ways, both by his devotion to God's providence and by his belief that it is his duty to love the whole human race.

[2]*For he says,*
   "At the acceptable time I have listened to you,
   and helped you on the day of salvation."[2]
Behold, now is the acceptable time; behold, now is the day of salvation.

Paul is teaching that God's grace in Christ was predestined. God decreed that his mercy would be poured out in this way, that help would be lavished on those who called for it in the name of Christ.

[3]*We put no obstacle in any one's way, so that no fault may be found with our ministry,*

Paul is saying that the time has come when sinners may obtain forgiveness, when a cure has been found for human sicknesses. This is why he is also concerned for the health of the sick, in case the gracious gift of medicine happens not to have the result which his good will intends it to have. By his faith and vigilance, Paul is cutting away everything which might cause the negligent to stumble, out of fear that their sluggishness might present his disciples with a cause for stumbling. They are also saying by this that they are freemen, because they are preaching in all sincerity and with great persistence. This is why he adds the words: *so that no fault may be found with our ministry.* Fault would have been found with their ministry if they did not exemplify in their deeds the things they were teaching.

[4]*but as servants of God we commend ourselves in every way: through great endurance, in afflictions, hardships, calamities,*

Servants of God teach without flattery, so that they might please him whose servants they are, unlike the false apostles, who know that they have not been sent by God and are concerned only with their immediate advantage.

Endurance saves people. If Paul had not endured, how would he have saved the Corinthians, whom he had found, even after he had visited them, deeply involved in serious moral vices and heretical errors, and whom, by his endurance, he was gradually bringing back to the true faith.

Paul has endured afflictions, knowing what God has promised as a reward for them. It was a hardship for him to teach, even when he was subject to affliction, but he did so because he had been sent by the Lord. Even when he was deprived of future hope by the opposition of unbelievers, he did not give up.[3]

---

[1]Cf. Is 53:9. [2]Is 49:8. [3]Ambrosiaster interpreted the word "calamities" as "deprivations."

[5]beatings, imprisonments, tumults, labors, watching, hunger;

Even after frequent beatings by both Jews and Gentiles, Paul did not keep silent about the grace of Christ. Though often in prison, he continued to preach God's gift, without any thought for his own safety. He was so devoted to God that even riotous tumults did not lessen the trust which he placed in him. He did not stop laboring with his hands so as not to be a burden on anyone, knowing for sure that this would win God's approval. He was so anxious about the responsibility assigned to him that he stayed awake even at night. He endured times of hunger, sometimes voluntarily and sometimes because he was too poor to buy food, and then he thanked God who was feeding him spiritually for being content with this. He would not be deflected from his purpose merely for the sake of his stomach.

[6]by purity, knowledge, forbearance, kindness, the Holy Spirit, genuine love,

By claiming purity, both in his body and in his preaching of the gospel, Paul made many enemies. By asserting that knowledge of the law and the gospel did not lie in human wisdom or in pretense, he showed God that he was a faithful steward of Christ. He was forbearing in supporting the weaknesses of the brothers and in being contemptuous of this world. As he says elsewhere: *From my point of view the world has been crucified, and so have I been from the world's point of view.*[1] Paul was kind because although he certainly rebuked people, it was also his practice to comfort them and to console them after the rebuke by means of gentle encouragement. *The Holy Spirit will flee falsehood.*[2] By teaching them with sincerity, he was conveying the gift of God in the Holy Spirit. Love which is feigned reveals itself in people who desert their brothers when they get into difficulty. Paul was always sincere in his love, making his brothers' difficulties his own. He shared everyone's sufferings, as he says elsewhere: *Who is caused to stumble and I do not burn?*[3] This is genuine love, when a person stops thinking about himself and looks after someone whom he claims to love, and this is what the apostle always did.

[7]truthful speech, and the power of God; with the weapons of righteousness for the right hand and for the left;

The word of truth was in Paul's teaching, because he conveyed no message other than the one which he had received from the Lord. The power in him was of God; through signs and wonders it showed that he was fit to be a servant of God. He has also been a balance for weighing believers and unbelievers.[4] By the weapons of righteousness he has destroyed wickedness.

[8]in honor and dishonor, in ill repute and good repute. We are treated as impostors, and yet are true;

Paul is saying that he was recognized as a sincere and faithful preacher by those who believed that the gospel was the glory of God. Even to those who thought that the gospel was wretched and vile, he presented himself as a faithful servant of God and was not afraid to say things which they would have been scandalized to hear.

He also showed that he was a true steward of God to those who were developing a good opinion of the faith as well as to those who were turning away from it. He was never upset by this but kept on preaching the message re-

---

[1]Gal 6:14. [2]Wis 1:5. [3]2 Cor 11:29. [4]Ambrosiaster seems to have interpreted the word for "weapons" in the broader sense of "instruments," which included a scale of weights.

gardless. Unbelievers used to call the apostles impostors, but believers would regard them as truthful and sincere. Paul did not yield to this hatred and disguise the truth because of it.

⁹as unknown, and yet well known; as dying, and behold we live; as punished, and yet not killed;

To the wicked the apostles were unknown, but to the good people they were well known, because they were recognized as having the truth in them. Those who hated the apostles thought that they were paying the price for their wickedness every day of their lives, but because they were preaching with God's approval, they kept being rescued from death by the help of Christ.

The apostles looked like people who were being punished when they were treated in such a way that they seemed to be failing. Because they were not defeated, they were not killed. The person who is not steadfast in the faith is handed over to death—not the death of this world, but the death of the world to come. [It can also be understood as referring to the death of this world though, because God was allowing them to be punished, so that they would grow in merit through their difficulties, but he would not let them be killed.][1]

¹⁰as sorrowful, yet always rejoicing; as poor, yet making many rich; as having nothing, and yet possessing everything.

This sadness brings about rejoicing, and so those who were causing it were in fact increasing the apostles' joy. In the present life the apostles appeared to be poor, but in fact they were lavishing spiritual riches on those who believed. They were needy in this world but rich in heaven. It was the glory of the apostles that without the anxiety or title of possession

they owned not only the things which belonged to believers, but the believers themselves. It was inevitable that everything would be laid at their feet because of their miraculous powers, as we read in the Acts of the Apostles.[2]

¹¹Our mouth is open to you, Corinthians; our heart is wide.

Paul is saying this because of the freedom he enjoyed in a pure conscience. A mind with a bad conscience is afraid to speak, loses its train of thought and makes verbal slips. People whose hearts are enlarged are happy with themselves because they are confident that they have behaved well. They are not crushed by tribulation because they are hopeful of a future reward. Just as in this life, payment will not be made for work which has not been done, so in God's world, reward will not come if there has been no suffering beforehand.

¹²You are not restricted by us, but you are restricted in your own affections.

Paul is saying that it did not reflect badly on teachers if their pupils disregarded the power of their teaching and turned out badly. Everyone will be rewarded according to his works, because they have not been silent about their masters' instruction. As the Lord says to the prophet Ezekiel: *raise your voice and speak to the people. If they hear you, you will be profitable to them, but if not, you will save your own soul.*[3]

¹³In return—I speak as to children—widen your hearts also.
¹⁴Do not be mismated with unbelievers. For what partnership have righteousness and iniquity? Or what fellowship has light with darkness?

Paul is exhorting them to good behavior and to

---

[1]This sentence is missing from one manuscript and may be a later addition to the commentary. [2]Acts 4:34-35. [3]Cf. Ezek 33:7-9.

hope. They must have faith and cleanse their consciences, being happy with themselves and having the confidence of a pure mind, like their teachers. They must separate themselves from association with unbelievers who engage in evil activities. Paul therefore wants them to broaden their thinking by behaving well and hoping for what is still to come. Someone who is struggling and has no belief in the future is mentally crushed by despair, like an unbeliever.

It is obvious that Paul is talking here about things which are diametrically opposed to one another. He is teaching that we should flee from the second of them because the Lord said: *No one can serve two masters.*[1] The law preaches righteousness, that we should flee from evildoing. The light which is truth makes it clear that we should abandon the ignorance which is darkness.

[15] *What accord has Christ with Belial? Or what has a believer in common with an unbeliever?*

Christ, in the mystery of God, proclaims that we should escape from the devil, who wants to pretend that he is God. He promises believers eternal life, and so we should leave aside all treachery and the wrongdoing of unbelievers.

[16] *What agreement has the temple of God with idols? For we are the temple of the living God; as God said,*
"I will live in them and move among them,
and I will be their God,
and they shall be my people."[2]

He has forbidden the worship of idols because they are incompatible with the temple of God. We are temples of the living God, and there is nothing more damaging to us than idols, because they force us to depart from our faith in the one true God.

Let us explain the meaning of the first thing quoted and make it clear who the speaker is. These are the words of Christ, for this is what Jeremiah bore witness to when he said, among other things: *After these things he was seen on earth and kept company among men.*[3] Christ dwelt among us, as the apostle John says: *the Word was made flesh and dwelt among us.*[4] Because he is our God, Jeremiah says on another occasion: *This is our God.*[5]

[17] *"Therefore come out from them,*
and be separate from them, says the Lord,
and touch nothing unclean;[6]
then I will welcome you,
[18] *and I will be a father to you,*
and you shall be my sons and daughters,
says the Lord Almighty."[7]

God wants us to be set apart from all contamination so that he can receive us as his children, as he says: *My little children, I am with you for yet a little while.*[8] I do not think the identification with Christ should be disputed on the ground that the speaker is "the Lord Almighty," for if, as he says, the Son does whatever the Father does, then the Son can do whatever the Father can do; if there is anything which the Father cannot do, the Son will not be able to do it either. But the Son is able and says of the Father: *With God all things are possible.*[9] By this testimony Paul exhorts us to a pure life and shows that our Lord Jesus Christ was already our Lord in ancient times and was predestined to receive us in the fondness of his love.

2 Corinthians 7

[1] *Since we have these promises, beloved, let us cleanse ourselves from every defilement of body and spirit, and make holiness perfect in the fear of God.*

[1]Mt 6:24. [2]Lev 26:12. [3]Bar 3:38. [4]Jn 1:14. [5]Bar 3:36. [6]Cf. Is 52:11. [7]Cf. Hos 1:10. [8]Jn 13:33. [9]Mt 19:26.

What Paul is saying is clear, but *defilement of the flesh* is to be interpreted in a complex way. Notice that he did not say *from defilement of the flesh* but *from* every *defilement of the flesh*, in order to encourage us to flee from all carnal vices—for everything which the law prohibits is carnal—so that we might perfect holiness of the Spirit in the fear of God. We do this by pursuing the things which are right in the fear of God and which are therefore holy, abstaining from sins in the name of Christ. People who restrain themselves from vices without professing Christ are sanctified according to the world, but not according to the Spirit of God, because according to God it is believers who are clean, and others, whatever they may be like, are unclean. As Paul says to Titus: *Where unbelievers are concerned, nothing is clean; their mind is defiled as is their conscience.*[1]

²Open your hearts to us; we have wronged no one, we have corrupted no one, we have taken advantage of no one.

Paul wants the Corinthians to give thought to what he is saying, so that when they have taken it to heart they may conclude that what he is saying is true and turn away from the people he is talking about, transferring their whole attention to men whom they see love them with true feeling. It was the false apostles who were doing them harm, corrupting their ideas and being a charge on their purses by deception of a serpentine ingenuity.

³I do not say this to condemn you, for I said before that you are in our hearts, to die together and to live together.

Paul is not rejecting the Corinthians, but he warns them they must reform. A person who is condemning someone else does not grant

him remission at the same time. Paul wants them to realize in what frame of mind he is speaking to them. He is certainly not rejecting people whom he wants to have as sharers with him, both in the present sufferings in Christ and in the life to come, but he is exhorting them to make themselves worthy of this sharing.

⁴I have great confidence in you; I have great pride in you; I am filled with comfort. With all our affliction, I am overjoyed.

Paul is confident because of the way the Corinthians responded to his reproof in the first letter. The fact that they did not take it badly has given him the confidence to admonish them again. He also says that he has been consoled by this to such an extent that in spite of all his affliction he is overflowing with joy. Seeing that there is hope for the people on whose behalf he is enduring hardships, he is rejoicing in spite of his tribulations, being certain that he will receive from God a reward for the fact that they have received salvation.

⁵For even when we came into Macedonia, our bodies had no rest but we were afflicted at every turn—fighting without and fear within.

Paul was referring here to the afflictions and murderous beatings which he was suffering for the sake of believers, in order to move them to love. [Does flesh have feeling, so that it may suffer without the soul? By *flesh* Paul meant the whole person.[2] The Savior too said: *The spirit is willing but the flesh is weak.*[3] Because the Holy Spirit, who is not subject to suffering, was in them, Paul could not say that their spirit had no rest. Rather, it was in comparison with the Spirit that Paul said that the whole human being was *flesh*—just as in comparison to the brightness of the sun,

---

[1]Tit 1:15. [2]In accordance with this, the English translates "flesh" as "bodies." [3]Mt 26:41.

the stars are dark—because the Spirit was joyful, knowing that they would benefit from their tribulations.][1]

Paul says that *our flesh has no rest* in order to win the sympathy of the Corinthians, so that they would give up their lives for the salvation of believers, even if this should mean death. For before one affliction or bodily injury could be absorbed, another would surely come, and there would be no rest for the sufferer. It is also because the flesh is irrational that Paul says that it has no rest from its suffering, but the soul, although it was suffering in the body, did have rest, because of the hope that God would reward them for the tribulations which were being inflicted on them by unbelievers. Even during their afflictions they would still be singing hymns to God.

According to the historical record, they went to Macedonia at the calling of the Lord.[2] Later, after a number of people had become believers and they had found the comforting support of the woman Lydia, who became a believer along with all of her household, it happened that Paul exorcised a spirit called Python, a spirit of divination, from the maidservant of some people, who started a riot against Paul and Silas when they realized that they had lost a considerable source of income which the girl brought in through her prophesying, and hauled them before the magistrates in the forum.[3] They sentenced Paul and Silas to many lashes and put them in the depths of a dungeon, with orders that their feet should be tied with a rope. This was the affliction which they suffered in Macedonia, and it was for this reason that Paul said that their flesh had no rest.

Fightings were inflicted on the body, and fears attacked the soul. Fear occurs where there is understanding, but this fear arose on account of the people who had become believers. Paul was afraid that they might stumble because of his suffering. After all, why would the sufferer feel any fear for himself at this stage, especially as he had said in the Acts of the Apostles, that he was prepared, not only to be bound, but to die for the name of the Lord Jesus Christ?[4] Paul seems to have meant here that the whole man was subjected to affliction in the flesh, with the proviso that he was not at all afflicted in the Spirit, who is given to people so that they might endure such things and who is not himself subject to suffering.

Another possible interpretation is that outside there were "battles," in the sense that these were started by unbelievers against believers, when, full of madness, they resisted the truth. The person who then reported this caused "fears within," in the place where the apostle was staying. After all, who would not be afraid of the problems that might cause? But because he was especially fervent in his devotion to God, Paul overcame this fear with hope.

6But God, who comforts the downcast, comforted us by the coming of Titus,

Because God does not forget his people and always brings them comfort in their suffering, he hastened the arrival of Titus, so that he might be a kind of refreshment to people who were in the heat of battle. It is always a great comfort, when we are suffering, to have someone near us who can share it with us.

7and not only by his coming but also by the comfort with which he was comforted in you, as he told us of your longing, your mourning, your zeal for me, so that I rejoiced still more.

What adds more to Paul's comfort is the fact that he has heard from Titus that the Corinthians are ready and willing to mend their

---

[1]The section in brackets is found in only one manuscript. [2]Acts 16:9-10. [3]Acts 16:14-24. [4]Acts 21:13.

ways, so much so in fact that Titus, who had once been grieved by their disobedience, was now consoled by their repentance. Paul showed what great affection he had for them because he did not take account of the depth of the dungeon, nor of the pain of the lashes, nor of the rope with which his feet were bound, but when he heard that the Corinthians had amended their ways he rejoiced, and forgetting his sufferings, he thanked God for their salvation, reckoning it as a kind of reward for his troubles.

Titus had brought the news that they were eager to mend their ways. On learning what has been promised to those who lead good lives, the Corinthians had been stirred up to desire those things for themselves. When they were rebuked they began to weep, sorrowful that they had sinned, and they had not tried to make excuses for themselves. This is why Paul takes such pride in them. For on learning how much the apostle loved them, they began to defend him against his enemies.

8For even if I made you sorry with my letter, I do not regret it (though I did regret it), for I see that that letter grieved you, though only for a while.

It is clear that Paul has no need to repent of something which has brought results, even though he had rebuked them somewhat severely in his first letter. He was not ashamed of that, because the situation demanded it. To some extent he had regretted grieving them because of his love for them, but even if he had repented, the comfort of joy would have taken its place, because it was beneficial to the Corinthians that he had grieved them.

9As it is, I rejoice, not because you were grieved, but because you were grieved into repenting; for you felt a godly grief, so that you suffered no loss through us.

Paul is saying that the reason he has been rejoicing is that, although they were grieved out of a sense of shame, the Corinthians had not turned to anger. Someone who feels ashamed when rebuked will promise to mend his ways, but someone who is angry shows that he will only get worse in the future. Everything Paul did had an effect on them. Even the fact that he had grieved them was for their benefit.

10For godly grief produces a repentance that leads to salvation and brings no regret, but worldly grief produces death.

It is clear that someone who is grieved because he has sinned is grieved in a godly way, because he is grieved for having done something that God hates. This is directly connected to the enduring quality of his salvation.

Paul is saying this because godly grief brings about life, as the sinner repents and puts his hope in the mercy of God. Worldly grief, on the other hand, brings about death. When the sinner is found out, he is grieved because he is bound to be punished, not having anyone from whom he may expect mercy. Perhaps for the moment there may be nobody who can exact retribution, but he will not be able to escape the judgment of God.

11For see what earnestness this godly grief has produced in you, what eagerness to clear yourselves, what indignation, what alarm, what longing, what zeal, what punishment! At every point you have proved yourselves guiltless in the matter.

It is true that someone who repents is troubled by the fear that he might sin again. The Corinthians did nothing to excuse themselves, because it is not excuses but confession which is the sign of true repentance. Paul is pointing out here the alarm which sin causes, demanding forgiveness because of wrongdoing. A person who knows that he has been deformed by sin longs to reform himself. Someone who realizes that he is being rebuked for his own good starts to experience a zeal for bringing good works to completion. Someone who knows of another person's affection toward him will vindicate that person, and someone who torments himself because of his sin is his own vindicator.[1]

As the Corinthians are taking to heart everything which is perceived to be of use for the advancement of Paul's best hopes for them and are imitating their apostle and teacher in every obligation of human social life, they are doing their best, guided by faith, to be seen as people of integrity.

[12]So although I wrote to you, it was not on account of the one who did the wrong, nor on account of the one who suffered the wrong, but in order that your zeal for us might be revealed to you in the sight of God.

Paul is saying that the man who committed incest had behaved wrongly, and he is also referring to those people whom he mentioned in his first letter as having behaved in a harmful and dishonest way toward the brothers. The people who were badly treated were those who had suffered from these brothers' pernicious activities. Paul is here expressing the same idea that he mentioned at the beginning of the letter, where he says: *If you have forgiven something, so have I.*[2] Paul is making it clear that forgiveness ought to be granted to those who did wrong not mainly for their sake, but for the sake of the church, because when one person does wrong many people suffer, and when one person suffers insult or fraud, many people become indignant, because *if one member suffers, all the members suffer along with it.*[3] By correcting wrongdoers and sanctifying the corrupt, reconciling them to the church, Paul is showing that he

is concerned for the whole church, as I have already said above.

[13]Therefore we are comforted.

And besides our own comfort we rejoiced still more at the joy of Titus, because his mind has been set at rest by you all.

Paul is saying that by this he has both received comfort and is giving it. He has been comforted by the fact that those whom he rebuked wished to mend their ways by reforming themselves through repentance. He gives it when he reconciles them to the church, so that they may not despair of themselves for a long time and in public, and so go astray into a way of life which is deadly.[4]

Hearing that those whom he has rebuked in his first letter now want to mend their ways, Paul has been comforted. But on learning from Titus that they were experiencing pain on account of their error he was consoled even more, and filled with joy, because their resolve had been confirmed by their behavior.

[14]For if I have expressed to him some pride in you, I was not put to shame; but just as everything we said to you was true, so our boasting before Titus has proved true.

Before Titus went to Corinth, he heard from the apostle and his companions that the Corinthians were persevering in their determination to correct their wrongdoings. Because of this, when Titus returned and gave Paul a report about these things, the apostle was not proved wrong but was delighted, because Titus had found that matters in Corinth were no different from what he had heard about them.

The apostle is writing this in a spirit of exultation. He is so happy with them that he approves of their willingness by saying that it is as true [to the faith] as was his preaching

---

[1] Ambrosiaster interprets the word "punishment" as "vindication." [2] 2 Cor 2:10. [3] 1 Cor 12:26. [4] 2 Cor 2:6-11.

to them, at least as far as his rebuking them was concerned. The truthfulness of someone issuing a rebuke is seen clearly if those who receive the rebuke start to mend their ways, for as long as those who are rebuked change, they offer a testimonial to the person who rebukes them.

15And his heart goes out all the more to you, as he remembers the obedience of you all, and the fear and trembling with which you received him.

Paul is saying that Titus's mind and affection is concerned with them, because he has seen their progress, for the mind of a saint is concerned with everything that is good. The Corinthians, knowing that Titus had been sent by the apostle, and aware of how great the vices were for which he had rebuked them, were terrified by his arrival. Because they had begun to cleanse their lives of their faults, they were anxious to obey Paul's teachings, so that when Titus returned to the apostle, he would soften the latter's attitude toward them. Paul is implying here that Titus has praised this, for in their reception of Titus, they treated the apostle himself with reverence.

16I rejoice, because I have perfect confidence in you.

Paul is glad not only because of their good resolve but because of the good actions by which they were correcting their former sinful practices. This is why he has perfect confidence in them.

2 Corinthians 8

1We want you to know, brethren, about the grace of God which has been shown in the churches of Macedonia,

Paul says that they had received the grace

of God because they accepted the word of faith devoutly. Even amid the troubles which afflicted Paul and Silas, which I referred to above, they did not find any cause to stumble, but received it with exultation of mind, being confident of the hope promised to them. In this way they demonstrated that they had passed the test brought on them by these men's sufferings.

2for in a severe test of affliction, their abundance of joy and their extreme poverty have overflowed in a wealth of liberality on their part.

Paul is talking about their devotion, saying that although they were short of material resources their souls were rich, because they ministered to the saints with a pure conscience, trying to please God rather than men.

3For they gave according to their means, as I can testify, and beyond their means, of their own free will,

As far as was right and pleasing to God, who knew what they were capable of, they contributed to the ministry out of their own resources. Because they gave themselves to God wholeheartedly, they wanted to offer more than their strength allowed.

4begging us earnestly for the favor of taking part in the relief of the saints—

Paul is saying that they offered assistance with such sincerity and devotion that it was beyond their strength, and so, although they begged him to accept their offer with tears, by which they hoped to force him to accept something when it did not seem right for him to do so, because it was more than their material resources could sustain, Paul was inclined to refuse their contribution, fearing that hardship would later cause them to repent of their good deed. But because they showed themselves to be of such character that they stood firm, with a pure mind in the confidence of faith, attaching more importance to the promises for the future than to immediate rewards in the present, in the end it seemed right for him to accept their contribution so that he would not lose his reward out of kindness toward them.

⁵and this, not as we expected, but first they gave themselves to the Lord and to us by the will of God.

Therefore, Paul says, it was right to accept their contribution, since by correcting their former errors and the vices of their lifestyle and customs right at the start, they have devoted themselves to God beyond what was expected of them. It was apparent that they were acting in sincerity, and so the person to whom the assistance was offered was not afraid to accept it. They were certainly not trying to buy off their leaders so that the latter would overlook their vices, and were not calculating that gifts blind the eyes and deflect the power of authority.

By giving themselves to God first and correcting their vices, and then by giving themselves to their brethren when they made their offering of money, the Macedonians had no need to be made to feel ashamed, because they had demonstrated their sincere desire to be made perfect almost before they had begun. Paul quoted their example in the hope of persuading the Corinthians to be strengthened by their example and fulfill their undertakings with firm determination.

⁶Accordingly we have urged Titus that as he had already made a beginning, he should also complete among you this gracious work.

Because Paul knew that Titus's feelings about them were sincere, and because they had not disobeyed him, he means that he can quite easily use Titus to persuade them to undertake this work also. Therefore, just as Titus had been rewarded for his previous exhortation, he should also be regarded for this act of grace, making them eager to give assistance to the saints. In this way, those people who were already correcting their faults would have the reward of this generosity. For people who give merely in order not to be rebuked will get nothing in return.

⁷Now as you excel in everything—in faith, in utterance, in knowledge, in all earnestness, and in your love for us—see that you excel in this gracious work also.

Paul is exhorting the Corinthians to take pride in these things in the sight of the other churches, for if they are keen to minister to the saints it is proof that they have mended their ways.

⁸I say this not as a command, but to prove by the earnestness of others that your love also is genuine.

It is clear that Paul is not ordering the Corinthians to send money to those who are suffering want, but encouraging them to do so, demonstrating that they have the right attitude toward God and other people. In return for that they will undoubtedly receive a reward.

⁹For you know the grace of our Lord Jesus Christ, that though he was rich, yet for your sake he became poor, so that by his poverty you might become rich.

Paul is saying that Christ was made poor because God deigned to be born as man, humbling the power of his might so that he might obtain for men the riches of divinity and thus share in the divine nature, as Peter says.[1] He was made man in order to take man into the Godhead. As it is written: *I have said, you are gods.*[2] In this way he is exhorting them to become like poor people, so that their poverty might be beneficial to us. Christ was made poor, not for his sake but for ours, but we are made poor for our own benefit.

[10]*And in this matter I give my advice: it is best for you now to complete what a year ago you began not only to do but to desire,* [11]*so that your readiness in desiring it may be matched by your completing it out of what you have.*

Paul is saying that if their intention is genuine, this should be apparent from their behavior. Subject to their resources, the Corinthians should give as much as they are willing and able to give. That way their conscience would become clear and not be clouded by pretense, pleasing man but not doing anything for God.

[12]*For if the readiness is there, it is acceptable according to what a man has, not according to what he has not.*

Since the Corinthians are being encouraged to perform this work of service, Paul is instructing them to give what they are able but not to overdo it. Perhaps he did not want them to feel that they were acting under compulsion to offer more than they could afford, and that they would come to be resentful because they were not acting voluntarily, and thus would be unlikely to receive any reward from God in the future. The churches of Macedonia made their offerings voluntarily and persistently, proving that they were acting completely willingly in giving more than they could afford, and for this reason their gifts were acceptable. The more generous they were in giving, the more

they would themselves receive. If someone gives as much as he can or wants to, that is accepted, because he is seen to be acting judiciously. Because of this, he should give as much as his mind can and will allow, so that he may be rewarded for his deed.

[13]*I do not mean that others should be eased and you burdened,*

It is true that giving should not cause hardship to the givers. Paul says this in order to persuade people to divide what they have at the time. What is demanded is not more than they ought to keep for themselves, because the Lord says: *You shall love your neighbor as yourself.*[3] On this principle, Zacchaeus says: *See, I give half my goods to the poor.*[4]

[14]*but that as a matter of equality your abundance at the present time should supply their want, so that their abundance may supply your want, that there may be equality.*

What Paul is saying is this. At a time when the saints are suffering want, they should concentrate on study and prayer for the benefit of many, abandoning the things of the world and occupying themselves only in religious activities. Believers who are engaged in crafts or businesses, or who have inherited wealth, should minister to the needs of the saints, so that at some other time, when the saints in that place are rich and the people now being addressed are poor, their assistance may be repaid. As the Lord says: *As long as you have done it for one of the least of these, you have done it for me.*[5]

The equality Paul is speaking of consists in the fact that because they are ministering to the saints at this time they will be repaid by them in the future, for they are making the saints their debtors.

---

[1]2 Pet 1:4. [2]Ps 82:6. [3]Mk 12:31 (Lev 19:18). [4]Lk 19:8. [5]Mt 25:40.

[15]*As it is written, "He who gathered much had nothing over, and he who gathered little had no lack."*[1]

The quotation is from Exodus. The saints, with their hope in the world to come, have more than those who appear to be rich in this world. But both will be made equal, because those who give of their wealth to help the saints now will be helped by them at some future time, when they are in need. For they have not surrendered themselves wholly to God so as to make the people here poor and those over there rich. To the extent that people here are rich and people there are poor, the latter will be enriched by the help of the saints who are here now, but who may be somewhere else on another occasion. There is no merit in ministering to the saints by doing the wrong thing.

[16]*But thanks be to God who puts the same earnest care for you into the heart of Titus.*

God, who is just and who knows that the Corinthians want to make progress, has kindled in Titus the feeling which he has toward them, making him want to bring to fulfillment, by his exhortation, their desire for good action. Seeing their progress, he has rejoiced and been consoled on their account.

[17]*For he not only accepted our appeal, but being himself very earnest he is going to you of his own accord.*

Seeing that the Corinthians are making progress in good works, Titus has become particularly concerned about their attitude and has even volunteered to go to visit them, when earlier on he did not want to because of their vices.

[18]*With him we are sending the brother who is* *famous among all the churches for his preaching of the gospel;* [19]*and not only that, but he has been appointed by the churches to travel with us in this gracious work which we are carrying on, for the glory of the Lord and to show our good will.*

Paul is commending this man, because he was unknown to the Corinthians. He wanted them to be aware of the high regard in which they, to whom such men were being sent, were now held, and to rejoice with them, encouraging them in their faith in God's work, for whose glory they were acting as Christ's deputies, and in this way God, the maker of heaven and earth, would be recognized.

[20]*We intend that no one should blame us about this liberal gift which we are administering,*

Since the matter had to do with administering aid, Paul makes this additional remark in order not to be thought negligent concerning the care of the poor or of the saints if he appeared to be acting rather slowly. For the apostles had agreed to keep the poor in mind, as he makes clear to the Galatians.[2] Since the apostle is completely free from the reproach of being judged negligent in this matter, he means here that he is giving advance warning of this, so that when the work is complete, his carefulness and prudence will be apparent in every respect.

[21]*for we aim at what is honorable not only in the Lord's sight but also in the sight of men.*

Paul is providing goods in the sight of God when he teaches that what God commands concerning the administering of aid to the saints or to the poor ought to be put into practice, but he also provides goods in the sight of men, because he is sending people to urge them to take part in this undertaking. Paul does not

---

[1]Ex 16:18. [2]Gal 2:10.

want his teaching to incur reproach because of improvident assistants.

22 And with them we are sending our brother whom we have often tested and found earnest in many matters, but who is now more earnest than ever because of his great confidence in you. 23 As for Titus, he is my partner and fellow worker in your service; and as for our brethren, they are messengers of the churches, the glory of Christ.

Paul calls Titus his colleague because he was also a bishop to whom he had given a ministry which was well known to all the churches of the province in question. To these he adds a third brother, who was proven in many good works and conscientious. In his account of Titus (with his report about the Corinthians' good intentions) and the other missionaries, whom he calls *the apostles of the churches of Christ's glory*, Paul is making it clear that he has become more eager to see them and to exhort them to give aid to the saints. On hearing that the Corinthians had become better people, he had been encouraged. For this reason, he was not preoccupied with them, because he was sure that they would be obedient.

24 So give proof, before the churches, of your love and of our boasting about you to these men.

Paul is urging the Corinthians to demonstrate their love by the way they treat the men whom he is sending to them. If they received them with honor, they would be demonstrating to all the other churches how far they had progressed, and that the good things which were said about them were true. He is therefore encouraging their resolve, for someone who is well thought of usually shows improvement.

2 Corinthians 9

1 Now it is superfluous for me to write to you about the offering for the saints,

These too are the words of somebody who is well satisfied, for Paul is saying that it is superfluous for him to write about the work of ministering to the saints which is going on, as if he thought well of them for doing so. It is superfluous to make an exhortation to someone when you know that they are about to take action. But in order to demonstrate his diligence, it was necessary for Paul to write like this, so that they would be all the more willing to do what they were asked and demonstrate the truth of what he says about them. For superfluities tend to show greater concern. Our Lord did not doubt Peter's love for him, but even so he asked the apostle three times: *Simon Bar-Jona, do you love me?*[1] This repetition may seem to be superfluous, but it contributed to the perfecting of the admonition, since Peter would learn from it that he must act with great diligence.

2 for I know your readiness, of which I boast about you to the people of Macedonia, saying that Achaia has been ready since last year; and your zeal has stirred up most of them.

Following the Macedonians, Achaia (that is, the churches of the province of Achaia, though not all of them, because the Corinthians were also Achaians) has gotten ready to emulate them in giving aid to the saints. By saying this, Paul is exhorting the Corinthians by pointing out that the others have been ready since the previous year, but that he is waiting for their aid to be distributed according to the need of each individual. He was hoping that the Corinthians would also get ready as they had promised, for then the other churches

---

[1]Jn 21:17.

would copy Corinth; when they heard that a church which had previously been involved in many errors had put them right, they would be moved to good works. For if those who, after accepting the faith and then behaving badly, began to have this desire, how much more ought others, in whom such vices were not present, have it also?

³But I am sending the brethren so that our boasting about you may not prove vain in this case, so that you may be ready, as I said you would be;

The brothers Paul is referring to are those mentioned above, that is, Titus and the helpers accompanying him, so that they might give the Corinthians an even more powerful exhortation to fulfill their promise to give assistance to the saints. Paul's intention was that Titus and the others should convey positive feelings to the Corinthians, not only by letter but also face to face, by frequent admonitions, so that the apostle's exultation, in which he boasted about the splendor of their attitude, should not become an empty sham. By referring to this matter repeatedly, Paul makes it clear that he is anxiously concerned about them and does not want them to come to grief in any way.

⁴lest if some Macedonians come with me and find that you are not ready, we be humiliated—to say nothing of you—for being so confident.

It is obvious that if Paul arrives and finds that the Corinthians are not what they have been cracked up to be, he will be embarrassed and they will feel even more frustrated, not even having made an effort, seeing that the apostle has been their witness, to act in a way which would make the reports come true, in view of the importance of such a great man.

⁵So I thought it necessary to urge the breth-

ren to go on to you before me, and arrange in advance for this gift you have promised, so that it may be ready not as an exaction but as a willing gift.

It was in order to make his anxiety even clearer that Paul said that he had asked this of the brothers. As a result of their admonitions, the Corinthians would fulfill what they had promised but were not in fact carrying out. Since he says earlier that Titus set out voluntarily—that is, pressure was not put on him, but as soon as he heard the news, he was willing to undertake the task, so that it would appear that he had set out voluntarily, because of his hope for them—he does not now mean that he had to ask Titus and his colleagues to go to Corinth, as if they were not willing to do so, but in order to prove his love for them. Titus and his friends wanted to go, and Paul is urging them to do so, so that they would go without delay. This is what they wanted and what Paul was praying for. He was behaving in this way so that they would be faithful and keep their promise. The reason why he implies that he is giving them warning is that he has a high regard for them and not because he was trying to extort money from them. He wanted them to give only as much as would not cause them to have any regrets later on.

⁶The point is this: he who sows sparingly will also reap sparingly, and he who sows bountifully will also reap bountifully.

Paul is referring to misers when he talks about people who sow sparingly. Such people have to be forced to give, because they regret having promised anything. Paul infers that the Corinthians are like this because they have been so slow to do anything. They had promised to act a long time before but were still deliberating. The harvest of someone who sows sparingly is very small, because he sows in doubt, not knowing that what he is doing will be to his advantage. A person who sows bountifully is one who does so willingly, in the hope that he will be rewarded in the future.

[7] Each one must do as he has made up his mind, not reluctantly or under compulsion, for God loves a cheerful giver.

Paul is teaching them that it will be to their advantage in the future if they do this with the right attitude. Of all the people who contribute, God chooses to reward the one who acts from a devout heart, as if he is storing up treasure for himself in the presence of God. Anyone who acts unwillingly, because he is afraid of being put to shame when the other contributors regard him as disgraceful, gets no reward.

[8] And God is able to provide you with every blessing in abundance, so that you may always have enough of everything and may provide in abundance for every good work.

Paul wants the power of God to be present in them so that, just as it has led their hearts to amend their faults and accept the truth of Christian teaching, so it will assist them, once they have begun, to abound in every good work by the grace of God.

He says this and prays that they may always be self-sufficient by God's will, not lacking what they need for their salvation. If they choose to be content only with what they need, they will have plenty left over for the work of God. It is the necessary corollary of keeping what they need for themselves that they should disburse their remaining resources for the use of the saints or of the poor. In this way they will have plenty for every good work.

The question to be asked is not only "How much?" but "From how much?" and "In what spirit?" The famous widow in the Gospel was praised for the small amount she gave, but those who gave much more were not praised.[1] Her small amount was a lot, because she gave more than she could afford, but the rich men's contribution was less, because they could afford so much more. Because of this, that woman's modest sum, which she gave beyond her means, was more valuable than the rich men's large amounts, because they were giving only part of what they had in abundance. Therefore the person who gives as much as he can is acting correctly, but he is still behind that widow, because she gave everything she had.

[9] As it is written,
   "He scatters abroad, he gives to the poor;
   his righteousness endures for ever."[2]

This is written in Psalm 111.[3] Paul is adding the example of care for the poor, so that the Corinthians may abound in all good works. People who are publicly in need are the ones who can be called "the poor." The saints are distinguished from them, because they are the servants of God, devoting themselves to constant prayer and fasting, just as Anna the prophetess did: *Who did not depart from the temple, doing service by repeated fasting and prayer day and night, putting all worldly care behind her.*[4]

This taking of pity is called righteousness because, knowing that God, the giver of all good things, makes his gifts to everyone in common—for his sun rises on everyone, rain falls for everyone and he has given the earth to everyone[5]—the righteous person shares with those who do not have worldly wealth, so that they will not appear to be deprived of God's beneficent gifts. The righteous person is one who does not keep to himself what he knows has been given to all. He is righteous not just for a time but forever, because in the world to come he will have this righteousness with him forever.

---

[1] Lk 21:1-4. [2] Ps 112:9. [3] Ps 112 in English versions. [4] Lk 2:37. [5] Mt 5:45.

10He who supplies seed to the sower and bread for food will supply and multiply your resources and increase the harvest of your righteousness.

All things belong to God; both seeds and young creatures grow and multiply for the use of human beings. God himself, therefore, who gives all these things, also orders that a portion of them should be set aside for those who are in need. Thus it is not possible for someone who has made a charitable contribution in accordance with God's will not to be enriched by things of a kind which have the ability to grow in a way which increases the fruits of righteousness.

11You will be enriched in every way for great generosity, which through us will produce thanksgiving to God;

God increases the resources of the giver, so that he will have more from which to make generous gifts. Righteousness consists of this: the circumstance whereby, because God gives, a human being also bestows gifts on those who are in need. He wants such people to help those who, choosing what is better, despise the wealth of this present age and devote themselves entirely to the things of God.

Because the saints want nothing other than to have enough food and clothing, God has arranged for those who are rich in the goods of this world to look after them, so that someone who has ministered to them well and with simple-heartedness, may be enriched by God's will and have the resources always to be generous. Having riches both for the present and for the future, he reaps two harvests from one sowing, with this proviso—if he is taking into consideration hopes for the future, he will not want to keep the people concerned in a state of subjection to himself, but rather he

will be kindly disposed toward them, because in doing so he will receive a reward from God. If he wants them to be humbled before him in this age, he will lose hope for what is still to come. The person who acts without simple-heartedness will get what he deserves. As the Lord says: *Truly, I say to you, they have received their reward.*[1]

12for the rendering of this service not only supplies the wants of the saints but also overflows in many thanksgivings to God. 13Under the test of this service, you will glorify God by your obedience in acknowledging the gospel of Christ, and by the generosity of your contribution for them and for all others; 14while they long for you and pray for you, because of the surpassing grace of God in you. 15Thanks be to God for his inexpressible gift!

Paul says this because whoever facilitates this work through the stewards of God, as a result of which those who receive the money they need in the name of Christ give thanks to God for it, creates a situation in which those people are no longer subject to beggary but to God, by whose good gifts they know they are nurtured. Moreover, it is not only those who have been delivered from beggary to the service of God who rejoice, but all the brethren who see the want being supplied. Thus it is that those who give a charitable offering to a few are commended to God by the prayers of many. People magnify the Lord in them, giving approval to the intention behind their action. Strengthened by their hope of this, they are obedient to Christ's gospel in submissiveness of mind in such a way that they provide the saints with what they need and have no desire to humiliate them.

To behave like this is to act in simplicity of sharing, commending themselves to the prayers of those people and their desires. For

---

[1]Mt 6:2.

who would not wish to see with his own eyes people submissive for the sake of the name of God, ministering to their own necessities?

Finally, they are called the gifts of God. A person who helps these people is making a gift to God, because he orders it to be done and the fact that it is given is credited to him. It is a gift of God which spurs people on to good works, for the hope that has been promised is the stimulus behind the work of assistance mentioned above.

By this service Paul and his companions are testing the Corinthians' attitude and magnifying the Lord.

2 Corinthians 10

¹I, Paul, myself entreat you, by the meekness and gentleness of Christ—I who am humble when face to face with you, but bold to you when I am away!—

Paul is saying that he is the same kind of person whether he is present or absent. He is not humble when present face to face as if to flatter them or appear to be subservient to them, but is rather the man who was so determined to be consistent that he sometimes restrained himself even from doing things that were allowable so that he would not be distracted. As he says in his other letter: *All things are permitted to me but I shall not be brought under anyone's power. Food is for the stomach and the stomach for food. But God will destroy both the one and the other.*[1]

He refers here to the meekness and gentleness of Christ because he does not want to appear to be harsher in person than in a letter. Those who had not yet mended their ways should soften the apostle's severity toward them by reforming, and then he would rejoice, suppressing his severity as soon as he found them practicing restraint. By *boldness* he meant

the assuredness of severity, which some may have thought he put in his letter but did not show them face to face, because in the first letter he seemed to be too severe and too rigid. He is warning them that he could be severe with them when he comes, which is not what they were hoping for.

²I beg of you that when I am present I may not have to show boldness with such confidence as I count on showing against some who suspect us of acting in worldly fashion.

The idea here is the same. Paul repeats himself in order to make it perfectly clear. He is praying that he might find them so disposed that he will not have to get angry but may be comfortable with them. Here he is making plain something which he has hinted at above and makes even clearer in what follows, that his *boldness* is the same as what he calls here his *confidence* in the power given to him by Christ, whose deputy he is, to punish those who act in the name of Christ but are at the same time disobedient, and thus to correct the faults of which they are guilty. He is speaking of those who do not accept the spiritual things said by the apostle, but who were forming an opinion of him on the assumption that he was expressing carnal ideas which were unacceptable. It is because of this that he refers to *people who think that we walk in accordance with the flesh.*

³For though we live in the world we are not carrying on a worldly war,

This means that although we are living in the body we act in a spiritual way. Anyone who does what is pleasing to God is acting spiritually. A person who wages war according to the flesh is one who obeys the desires of the flesh, for all wrongdoing is called "the flesh." Paul himself, however, is waging war for Christ,

---

[1] 1 Cor 6:12-13.

obeying him in both faith and discipline.

⁴for the weapons of our warfare are not worldly but have divine power to destroy strongholds.

The weapons of our warfare are powerful because they are uncorrupted, for all carnal things are corrupt. They are mighty because they fight against vice, having as their battle standard that of their emperor, who is Christ, the enemy of all vice. For just as the emperor protects his empire by means of his soldiers, so the Savior defends the profession and discipline of faith in the one God by using us.

⁵We destroy arguments and every proud obstacle to the knowledge of God, and take every thought captive to obey Christ,

Spiritual weapons consist of the faith which comes through uncorrupt preaching. By these means God conquers the princes and powers who, as is generally agreed, are raised up against the faith with the intention of usurping its empire and infiltrating the thoughts of human beings with a view to calling them away from the rule of God. The truth of the faith destroys this kind of reasoning. Paul is therefore referring to the princes and powers, *the spiritual principles of wickedness,*[1] as "fortifications" which raise themselves up and arm the rational souls of human beings to contradict Christ. Against them fights the law of God, which throws their plans into disarray.

Paul takes an intellect captive when he conquers it, just as it is contradicting him by its reasonings, and he leads it, humbled and tame, to the Christian faith.

⁶being ready to punish every disobedience, when your obedience is complete.

It is clear that Paul avenges disobedience when he condemns it through obedience, de-stroying it at the same time as he leads to the faith those who resist, in order that unbelief may be condemned by those who used to defend it.

⁷Look at what is before your eyes. If any one is confident that he is Christ's, let him remind himself that as he is Christ's, so are we.

Now Paul wants the Corinthians to consider things which are no secret, that is, to judge what he is about to say because it is clear. Paul is criticizing those whom he is referring to, who in the inflated pride of their own presumption have a lower opinion of him than he deserved and imagine that they had no need of his teaching. He is now warning them that if they were confident in what they believed about themselves, that they were servants of Christ, they ought not to have doubts about the apostle, but to think of him (however unequal to them he might be) as at least comparable, although they certainly ought to regard him, the teacher of the Gentiles, as their superior.

Here he is teaching them with humility, equating himself with them, although he was the *chosen vessel*[2] and the *teacher of the Gentiles in faith and truth.*[3] He therefore wants them to consider this, something which was as clear as daylight itself. Since there was no one among the believers [in Corinth] who did not think more highly of the apostle than of himself, how much more should no one think of him as his inferior? Paul gives this testimony and this teaching in order that they may not lose the deserved reward of a good life through proud thinking. The person who knows that he is something ought to humble himself so that he may become greater.

⁸For even if I boast a little too much of our

---

[1]Eph 6:12.　[2]2cts 9:15.　[3]3 Tim 2:7.

*authority, which the Lord gave for building
you up and not for destroying you, I shall not
be put to shame.*

Now Paul is saying that previously he has
humbled himself when comparing himself with
them, but if he were to exalt himself instead,
he would not be ashamed of doing so. For
he had received from the Lord the power to
preach in order to save those who were obedient, not to destroy them. Therefore, if the
one who has been sent by the Lord humbles
himself and compares himself with his inferiors, how much more should people with no
evidence of their authority not compare themselves, and certainly not prefer themselves, to
people who are greater than they are?

*[⁹I would not seem to be frightening you
with letters.]¹ ¹⁰For they say, "His letters are
weighty and strong, but his bodily presence is
weak, and his speech of no account." ¹¹Let such
people understand that what we say by letter
when absent, we do when present.*

Paul is saying that he is no different when
absent from what he is like when present, and
for this reason he is not an imposter. For he
had received power from the Lord. Someone
to whom power has not been given can be bold
when absent, but when present he is put to
shame. The apostle will not be put to shame
when issuing his rebuke, because he is doing
this in bold reliance on his power. He is saying
this because of people who were preaching in
a flattering manner, even though they had not
been commissioned, because they wanted to
commend themselves.

*¹²Not that we venture to class or compare
ourselves with some of those who commend
themselves. But when they measure themselves
by one another, and compare themselves with*

one another, they are without understanding.

People who commend themselves are those
who wish to dominate, claiming authority for
their own name, even though they have not
received any power. A person who is sent on
a mission lays claim to power, not on his own
behalf but on behalf of the one who sent him.
Here Paul is saying that he has been chosen
as a steward of the Lord. By not presuming
to anything beyond what has been granted to
him, he is not associating himself with those
people who preach without a commission.

*¹³But we will not boast beyond limit, but will
keep to the limits God has apportioned us, to
reach even to you.*

Paul says that he is taking advantage of just
as much power as was granted to him by the
Authorizer, and no more. Therefore, he says,
our glory will not be a matter of boasting,
since it does not go beyond the limit of the
power granted to him. He used the term *glory*
to stand for the authority which he employed
in his habit of rebuking sinners in order to
save them. Yet he says that he is not glorying
in exultation at his authority, but for their
edification. He is putting his power on display,
and if he wants to glory in this, it would not
be anything to be ashamed of, because it was
given to him by the Lord.

But Paul takes advantage of his authority
only to the extent that he glories in the progress of believers, constantly reproving wrongdoers, so that he may glory in their salvation
and so that his power may be conducive to
salvation and not to self-aggrandizement. His
assertion that he is not glorifying himself excessively has two implications. First, he was, as
he said, glorifying himself in a way appropriate
to the power which had been given to him, and
he did not claim any authority in places where

---

¹This verse is omitted in Ambrosiaster's commentary.

his preaching had not been heard. Now he had confidence in the people whom he had himself established in the faith of Christ.

He is saying that God has apportioned to individual missionaries the people to whom his mission should be directed, so that they would all have their own cities in whose faith they could take pride. It was by God's will that this apostle was called to preach to the Macedonians, and he was also prompted by the Lord to bring the gospel to the Corinthians. He therefore speaks boldly to these people, whom he has himself established in the faith and to whom he has journeyed by the will of God. He does not speak to others with the same confidence, because they were under someone else's authority, that is to say, they had been allotted to some other evangelist.

¹⁴*For we are not overextending ourselves, as though we did not reach you; we were the first to come all the way to you with the gospel of Christ.*

It was not as if Paul had made his journey to Corinth without having been sent there on his mission. On the contrary, he had been appointed to go there by God. To be "overextended" was to be extended beyond what was allowed. Paul did not go too far in what he was doing, but stayed within the limits set for his task by God. He makes this explicit here so that the Corinthians will know that God has sent him to them, and so they ought to obey his warnings. Otherwise they might appear to be resisting God, by whom Paul was sent.

¹⁵*We do not boast beyond limit, in other men's labors; but our hope is that as your faith increases, our field among you may be greatly enlarged,*

Here it is very obvious what Paul is saying. He himself had established them in their faith, and it was because of this that he spoke to them with such assurance. They had not been won for the faith by the efforts of anyone else. As he says in the other letter: *For in Christ, through the gospel, I begat you.*[1] Someone who takes a pride in his own work is not being excessively proud of himself. Because he is hoping for a reward for his labor of winning them to the faith, Paul asserts that for this reason he is not acting negligently and not giving way in the face of tiresome and difficult circumstances. His reasoning is that he believes that he is being made great in God's eyes if the number of his pupils is increased. As the Lord says: *Father, just as you have sent me into this world, so I have sent these people into this world and on their behalf I make myself holy.*[2] He says this because the testimonial of a teacher is made up of obedient pupils.

¹⁶*so that we may preach the gospel in lands beyond you, without boasting of work already done in another's field.*

Happy in their faith, Paul now says that he must go on to preach in other places as well, where there had been no preaching before. It is clear that a prudent man does not rely on the labors of others, which is why Paul does not claim any credit for those who have come to faith by the preaching of other evangelists, for fear that he might be appearing to glory in other people's labors. Instead, what Paul wants is to preach the gospel to those to whom the message has not yet been given, so that he will have glory from his own labor.

¹⁷*"Let him who boasts, boast of the Lord."*[3]

By saying this Paul intimates that even his assurance and pride are to be given to the Lord, because it is by his favor that he has them.

---

[1]1 Cor 4:15. [2]Jn 17:18-19. [3]Jer 9:24.

Someone who has confidence in the power of the gospel has confidence in God who is his authority, and thus God reaps the reward for all godly work. A person who has not received power from God cannot glory in the Lord, because he is seeking his own glory.

¹⁸*For it is not the man who commends himself that is accepted, but the man whom the Lord commends.*

It is true that the Lord commends that person, and that the one who is approved is the one whom he considers suitable and sends to preach his gift. God does not commend someone whom he does not send. On the other hand, someone who preaches without a commission commends himself, and therefore he is not suitable but presumptuous and an impostor.

2 Corinthians 11

¹I wish you would bear with me in a little foolishness. Do bear with me!

Paul says that he is being foolish when he starts to talk about himself because it looked as if he was boasting about himself, something which is censured in Scripture as follows: *Let your lips not praise yourself, but rather your neighbors.*¹ But Paul is forced out of sorrow to do so because these people were harboring unworthy thoughts, when they of all people ought to be thinking well of him.

²I feel a divine jealousy for you, for I betrothed you to Christ to present you as a pure bride to her one husband.

Paul is making it clear that what he is about to say he will say out of love for them, so that it may be conducive to their progress as much as to his praise and that they may learn from it

how to do a favor to their father in the gospel. For to speak ill of a father harms the sons, and the praise of sons is a father's glory. He wants them therefore to be virgins in the faith. For this reason he is jealous even for the corrupters of the faith, [because he wants] to hand them over to Christ the judge, undefiled on the day of judgment. This is why we read in the Revelation of John: *These are they who have not defiled themselves with women, for they have remained virgins. These follow the lamb wherever he goes.*² By *women* he means wrongdoing, because wrongdoing began through a woman. Similarly, he speaks of a woman as Jezebel,³ because of the wife of Ahab, who killed the prophets of God out of zeal for Baal,⁴ when what is meant is idolatry, by which morals and the truth of the faith are corrupted. For if you take *women* literally and suppose that they are called virgins because they have kept their bodies undefiled, you will exclude the saints from this glory, because all the apostles except John and Paul had wives. And consider whether it is appropriate to blame the apostle Peter, the chief of the apostles, and therefore even more prominent than the rest of us!

³But I am afraid that as the serpent deceived Eve by his cunning, your thoughts will be led astray from a sincere and pure devotion to Christ.

Paul is clarifying why it is that he is forced to protest the truth about himself. He is saying that glory was given to him, not in order that he should praise himself, but so that he might be able to blame those who, in the name of Christ, were preaching against Christ, and by whom the Corinthians were being seduced. Paul wanted this truth to benefit them and not himself. He is acting in this way so that the seducers, whom he compared to the devil because of their wickedness in trying to entice

---

¹Cf. Prov 27:2. ²Rev 14:4. ³Rev 2:20. ⁴1 Kings 18:4.

the hearts of the faithful away from the truth of Christ, should not get a hearing.

[4]For if some one comes and preaches another Jesus than the one we preached, or if you receive a different spirit from the one you received, or if you accept a different gospel from the one you accepted, you submit to it readily enough.

Why does Paul say, *You would do well to tolerate him*[1] if another Christ had been preached to you or if another Spirit or another gospel had been conveyed to you, whereas he says to the Galatians: *If anyone preaches to you anything other than what you have received, let him be anathema?*[2] If it was wrong for the Galatians to receive something other than what had been conveyed to them by the apostles, why was it right for the Corinthians, if another Christ had been preached to them?

[What is really being said however is: *You would be right to tolerate him* if you have heard anything other than what we have said, or if another Christ is being proclaimed to you who is greater than the one we preach, or a more powerful Spirit is given in the heat of persuasion, with the result that you prefer preachers of this kind to us.][3] But it was in the knowledge that the Christ who was being preached was never anyone other than the one who was crucified, that the apostle says: *You would be right to tolerate him*, if some other, more powerful Christ had been preached by those who came to them.

But to the Galatians he said *anathema* if they heard anything different—not, to be sure, anything greater, but anything contradictory. Furthermore Paul says that if he who is preached by these people is Christ himself, the same one who is proclaimed by us, why should we be considered their inferiors, since nothing of greater importance is being taught

by them? Earlier he was talking about false apostles, corrupters of the faith, but here he is talking about true preachers. This is because the Corinthian congregation was swamped by a variety of errors. Some of them were favoring false apostles, some were listening to the same things they had heard from the apostle, only in more finely crafted words, and others were supporters of the apostles as the Lord's companions, disparaging Paul because he had not seen the Lord in the flesh.

[5]I think that I am not in the least inferior to these superlative apostles.

Paul does not think that the grace of God given to him is inferior to that of the other apostles because he has taught the same things and done the same miracles. They were being regarded as more important because they had begun to teach earlier and had been the Lord's companions, and were therefore thought to have greater authority, even though the choosing of this apostle was a well-attested fact; he has labored more than the others and has seen the Lord and spoken to him while praying in the temple.[4]

[6]Even if I am unskilled in speaking, I am not in knowledge; in every way we have made this plain to you in all things.

This does not refer to the apostles, who were unlettered men of no eloquence, but to the false teachers whose rhetorical skill the Corinthians preferred, in spite of the fact that in religious matters it is power of speech which counts, not pleasantness of sound.

How is it that Paul humbles himself and says that he is a poor speaker, considering that Festus said: *Paul, Paul, your great book-learning is driving you out of your mind.*[5] Paul did not

---

[1]This is how Ambrosiaster read the words *You submit to him readily enough.* [2]Gal 1:8. [3]This passage occurs only in one manuscript, in place of the other material which follows. [4]Acts 22:17-21. [5]Acts 26:24.

mean by this that he did not know how to speak, but that commendation did not depend on mere eloquence.

In spite of this, it is also the case that he said he was unskilled, because this was something he could not be blamed for. He did not say that he was inexpert in something which he ought to have had, and which gains salvation. A person of little eloquence is not guilty before God, but someone who does not know God is liable to be charged with ignorance, because it was a sin to be ignorant of what is conducive to salvation. For this reason the apostle, in rejecting eloquence, was acting to ensure that the faith would be acceptable with power as its message; it was not eloquence which would commend the faith, but power, before which eloquence would have to give way.

He says that he is on display to the Corinthians in all things, because they were aware that he did have that skill in speaking. Knowing this, they favored other people for that reason, not because they were aware that Paul was inferior. He is speaking therefore emotionally, because it was very bad that, although they knew that he was not deficient in anything, they were treating him as if he were inferior to others, although they had seen not only that his preaching was filled with apostolic power but also that signs and wonders were being performed with it.

7Did I commit a sin in abasing myself so that you might be exalted, because I preached God's gospel without cost to you?

Since the Corinthians were puffed up with pride because Paul had refused to accept payment from them and were preferring others to him because of this, he says, *Have I sinned because I humbled myself in considering myself unworthy to receive anything? Why are you angry with me, as if this were a matter of sin and not of glory?* Paul humbled himself when he did not demand what was owed to him. It was his due that he should receive payment from the people to whom he preached the gospel of God, as the Lord decreed when he said: *The workman is deserving of his pay.*[1]

Paul refused [payment] in order to act in their interest. It was for two reasons that he would not accept payment. He would not resemble the false apostles who were preaching for their own advantage and not for the glory of God, nor would he allow the vigor of his message to become sluggish. For the person who accepts payment from sinners loses the authority to be censorious of them. Thus the Corinthians are *exalted* since nothing is being taken from them, the aim in view being that they should be reproved and corrected, raised from death to life.

8I robbed other churches by accepting support from them in order to serve you. 9And when I was with you and was in want, I did not burden any one, for my needs were supplied by the brethren who came from Macedonia. So I refrained and will refrain from burdening you in any way.

Paul is bearing down on them, showing that not only did he not wish to receive anything from them, but that he had even received from others and exercised his ministry toward them. In order to make it clear that it was a large amount that he had received, and not a small one, he says: *I robbed other churches, accepting support from them in order to serve you.* He is therefore intimating that he has expended a considerable amount on them, because when he says *I robbed* he means that they gave and he received a large amount, not that he had extorted anything from them. This is why he adds *accepting support*, for this is what someone on military service receives for his

---

[1]Lk 10:7.

expenses instead of a salary.[1] He therefore gave them good reason to be embarrassed. He certainly did not refuse payment in order to deceive them, because he ministered to them in person [so that they should have no excuse for plundering, for when one person does not receive any payment, another person cannot ask for a large sum][2] in order that they would fulfill the promise of help which they had made, knowing that they were in arrears. The result was that their help would not now be very impressive, but rather a debt they owed, so they would not have any reason to boast on that account.

Paul accepted contributions from the Macedonians because they corrected their faults earlier on. But he refused anything from the Corinthians because they were less ready to correct theirs. It was right for him to accept money from the Macedonians, so that they would not lose the harvest for which they were sowing so well.

Paul says that he will always do this, even if they mend their ways. This was because of the false apostles, who were looking for an excuse to rob them.

10As the truth of Christ is in me, this boast of mine shall not be silenced in the regions of Achaia.

Paul urges the whole of Achaia to give aid to the saints, but at the same time he refuses to take anything for himself from any of them for fear that he would not complete the glorious work which he has begun. It is "glory" to abstain from things which are allowed, particularly if this helps in saving others. *In the regions of Achaia* then, he did not want to take advantage [of the Corinthians, but] in other regions he did. He makes a further promise, saying that, with Christ as his witness, he will stick to this practice and never accept support from the regions of Achaia.

11And why? Because I do not love you? God knows I do!

Having given his side of the story, Paul calls on God's knowledge to witness his love toward them, saying that the reason why he did not want to accept payment was not because he did not love them but because he did. He wanted his love for them to be beneficial, as I have said.

12And what I do I will continue to do, in order to undermine the claim of those who would like to claim that in their boasted mission they work on the same terms as we do.

The glory of the false apostles was in receiving money payments. The apostle's reason for rejecting this practice was so that he would not appear to be like them. If the apostle had not avoided this, the false apostles would have had greater opportunity for receiving, or rather for extorting, money, for they would point out that the apostle had set the example in this respect.

13For such men are false apostles, deceitful workmen, disguising themselves as apostles of Christ.

They are deceitful because they preached Christ out of greed, not out of a religious disposition, and without any commission, usurping the title of *apostles*.

14And no wonder, for even Satan disguises himself as an angel of light.

It is clear that Satan often tricks many people,

---

[1]The word translated "support" is *stipendium* in Latin. [2]The editor of the Latin text has transposed this sentence from earlier in the manuscript to this point.

presenting himself to them as an angel of God in order to deceive them. Thus Peter, in trouble on board the boat, asked Jesus who it was had appeared to him. The apostles in the boat were terrified and thought it was an apparition. So the apostle Peter, when the Lord said: *Do not be afraid; it is I*, said (not finding it easy to believe): *if it is you, command me to come to you over the waters*, on the assumption that if he had placed his foot firmly on the waters, he would know for a fact that he was not seeing an apparition.[1]

[15]*So it is not strange if his servants also disguise themselves as servants of righteousness. Their end will correspond to their deeds.*

The servants of righteousness are the apostles, whose associates these people falsely pretended to be, so as to deceive their hearers. *Their end will correspond to their deeds* no doubt, because people of this kind will be judged according to the wickedness of their intentions. They pretend to be God's servants, not for God's sake, but for the sake of their stomachs. Paul however said that their end would be in accordance with their deeds. Just as activities focused on the stomach and its nourishment will perish, so these people will perish also.

[16]*I repeat, let no one think me foolish; but even if you do, accept me as a fool, so that I too may boast a little.*

Paul returns here to what he said at the beginning of the chapter: *I wish you would tolerate my foolishness for a moment.*[2] He is referring back to this because he always makes a prior announcement of what he will later follow up after some lengthy digressions. What he has set out above he now begins to relate in full. What he is about to say is true, though it may make him appear to be foolish, because these

truths redound to his praise. He says that he will boast *a little*, because his self-glorification is only words and not the thought behind them. Paul is not really boasting but merely wants to show that others who boast have nothing more to show for themselves than he has, so that if they are worthy of praise so is he.

He is saying that it is characteristic of a fool to do something for the sake of self-praise, but he feels constrained to say these things. It upsets him that the Corinthians, who had nothing more important than himself, were treating the false apostles as distinguished men while looking down on him.

[17]*(What I am saying I say not with the Lord's authority but as a fool, in this boastful confidence; . . .)*

Paul is not speaking here with the Lord's authority, because these things have to do with being puffed up with regard to the flesh. God does not approve of boasting, because what counts with him is humility.

Paul says that his boasting is not complete nonsense, but only partly so, because it is the truth. It is because boasting is wrong, even though what he is saying is true, that it is a sort of foolishness for any individual to praise himself, whereas it is utter nonsense if someone praises himself for no reason. The first type of person is proud on the basis of truth, but the second is proud on the basis of falsehood. The *boastful confidence* referred to here is carnality, because the glory referred to will die like the flower of hayseed.[3]

[18]*(. . . since many boast of worldly things, I too will boast.)*

Paul is saying this because some Jewish believers were claiming superiority as children of Is-

---

[1]Mt 14:23-33.　[2]2 Cor 11:1.　[3]Cf. Is 40:6-8.

rael. To glorify oneself according to the flesh is to claim nobility of the flesh. The Jews claimed this because they are the children of Abraham, who believed in God, even though *a soul which has sinned shall die*.[1] If this is glory, says Paul, then he too will boast, because he too is a son of Abraham. But it is faith that saves, not descent from Abraham, so the glory referred to here is the glory of the flesh, as if, for example, someone were to be called a nobleman's son.

[19]*For you gladly bear with fools, being wise yourselves!*

Paul gives the name of fools to those who prided themselves in the circumcision of the flesh. It was because these people were being supported by the Corinthians and looking praiseworthy as a result that Paul wants them to put up with him, recognizing that he too can boast of this. But in accordance with God's will, he does not glorify himself as a result. On the contrary, he points out that such boasting is *according to the flesh* and stupid. He says this in order to cancel the glory out and to teach that he has broken forth into praise of carnal things only because he was forced to do so. He is being ironic here, because how can people who are frequently being rebuked be considered *wise*? The foolishness of the apostle is wiser than their wisdom. The wise man is here putting up with unwise people. He is forbearing in his patience in order that they may make some progress. He also wants to avoid making them worse by provoking and rejecting them, and to ensure that if he has no success with them he will at least preserve his modesty.

The Corinthians had none of these things. How could they have suffered fools gladly if they were wise, if not because the meaning is not to be taken as corresponding to what the words apparently say? It is all a matter of innuendo and tone. The same words will have a different meaning if they are said in a different tone of voice, and so Paul sometimes speaks straightforwardly and sometimes says the opposite of what he really means. These people were imprudent and unwise, which is why they were tolerating false apostles.

[20]*For you bear it if a man makes slaves of you, or preys upon you, or takes advantage of you, or puts on airs, or strikes you in the face.*

It is true that they were being reduced to slavery, not because they were wise but because they were foolish enough to enter the service of false apostles. They were also being preyed on, because they were happy to see their property eaten up by false teachers. To take advantage is to trap someone by trickery, so Paul means that they are being trapped by false teachers and enduring what is not advantageous. Putting on airs is pride. He is therefore alluding to people who were proud, reviling the apostle, and who were [nevertheless] acceptable to the Corinthians.

Someone is struck in the face when an injury is inflicted on that part of the body. Here Paul is referring to some of the race of Abraham who were maltreating them because they were uncircumcised. They were claiming high rank for themselves and humiliating everyone else.

[21]*To my shame, I must say, we were too weak for that!*
But whatever any one dares to boast of—I am speaking as a fool—I also dare to boast of that.

In saying that he was too weak for that, Paul is repeating what he has said above: *I too will glorify myself, according to the flesh*.[2] He is saying that there is no cause for praise in the fact that he was not lacking in the qualifications which were the boast of the people to whom

---

[1]Ezek 18:20. [2]2 Cor 11:18.

he is secretly alluding. This is why he adds: *I also dare to boast of that.* It is clear that he was not lacking in the glorious heritage on which the Jewish believers were priding themselves. The Corinthians were tolerating these people as if their apostle were somehow different from them in this respect, whereas in fact he was also of the seed of Abraham.

Because of this, the Jews were not lacking in the glory of the flesh. But those who had been joined to the race of Abraham were being considered lacking. So, as if they were somehow deficient in the thing on which the others based their claim to higher rank—the fact that they were Israelites—they wanted to humble themselves in this very thing. In order to show them that in this matter they were not different or deficient, Paul, while thinking always of his own situation, also implicitly introduces the example of his colleague Barnabas. This is why he says in his first letter too: *Or do only I and Barnabas not have the power to operate in this way?*[1] They were not inferior in that glory on which the Jews prided themselves, but they did not congratulate themselves because of that.

Finally Paul says that he will boast of whatever it is the others are boasting of, foolish though that is. This is to say that he is not lacking in the glory on which the Israelites prided themselves, but that he is not judging himself wise for that reason. Wise men do not normally claim high rank for themselves. It is as a fool that he is saying that he dares to speak of what the others are boasting about, namely, that they are children of Abraham. In order to nullify their self-glorification, Paul says that he is foolish, since he is afraid that they might otherwise appear to be wise or noble in this respect.

²²*Are they Hebrews? So am I. Are they Israelites? So am I. Are they descendants of Abraham? So am I.*

Paul is making it clear that he is the equal of the men to whom he referred above. His purpose was to show that the disparaging opinions by which they were judging him were false.

²³*Are they servants of Christ? I am a better one—I am talking like a madman—with far greater labors, far more imprisonments, with countless beatings, and often near death.*

Paul calls himself a fool, when in fact he is speaking the truth, because he wants people to realize that it was only under compulsion that he has broken out into self-praise. For someone who mentions his accomplishments without being prompted to do so would not call himself a fool! He is really pointing out why he is a more faithful servant of Christ than these other preachers are. Being given the opportunity, he touches on the personal standing of everyone, including the apostles. He is upset that he has been judged less well-endowed with the grace of God in this respect, although he was carrying out the same tasks as the other apostles and was enduring greater disasters for the sake of the faith. It is because of this that he says in his other letter: *I have labored more than all of them.*[2]

The other apostles labored, but not as much as Paul. He used to earn his living with his own hands, from early morning until about eleven o'clock, and from then until four in the afternoon he would engage in public disputation with such energy that he would usually persuade those who spoke in opposition to him. It is clear that he was sent to prison more often than the others. His beatings were beyond measure, because they went beyond what was appropriate.[3] He was often near death, because it is true that he endured more dangers than the others.

²⁴*Five times I have received at the hands of the*

---

[1] 1 Cor 9:6. [2] 1 Cor 15:10. [3] Ambrosiaster interprets as "beyond measure" the word rendered in the English translation as "countless."

Jews the forty lashes less one.

Paul says this because he was whipped five times by the Jews, in accordance with the law of Moses, receiving thirty-nine lashes as prescribed in the book of Deuteronomy.[1] Here he is briefly recording that this happened on five separate occasions.

[25]*Three times I have been beaten with rods; once I was stoned. Three times I have been shipwrecked; a night and a day I have been adrift at sea;*

Paul suffered the beating with rods at the hands of Gentiles. He was stoned by the Jews in a city of Lycaonia.[2] Someone who sailed as much as he did would easily have been shipwrecked three times. He was adrift at sea on his journey to Rome, when he had appealed to Caesar.[3] At that time he despaired for his life on the high, that is, the open seas, when death stared him in the face. As it is written in that passage: *In such a way that we despaired of living.*[4]

[26]*on frequent journeys, in danger from rivers, danger from robbers, danger from my own people, danger from Gentiles, danger in the city, danger in the wilderness, danger at sea, danger from false brethren;*

Now Paul recalls other dangers in order to show that he suffered bodily afflictions for Christ on both land and sea. But if he is relating dangers from his travels, why is it that he mentions *danger from rivers?* The reason for this is that he was in danger from rivers in winter, when there was constant rain and rivers often overflowed their banks.

When the devil failed to kill him in a city, he would stir up robbers against him on the highway, in spite of the fact that he was carrying nothing that robbers might desire. He also speaks of dangers from the Jews, who were his own people according to the flesh, because they were upset at his conversion to the gospel of Christ and his abandonment of the law. He also suffered persecution from the Gentiles because of the mystery of the incarnation of the Lord Jesus Christ, and his preaching of the one God.

He was in such danger in a city that he escaped through a window from the hands of someone who had him trapped.[5] The danger in the desert was brought about by Jews who wanted to ambush him and kill him on the highway.[6]

Paul has already said: *Three times I suffered shipwreck. I was on the open sea for a night and a day.* What was this other danger at sea? The danger at sea which he is alluding to here was the danger that the soldiers guarding prisoners on board would kill them all rather than risk letting them swim to safety in a shipwreck. The centurion prevented this danger from materializing because he did not want Paul to be killed, but rather to be taken alive to Rome.[7]

The false brethren are the people of whom Paul speaks to the Galatians: *Because of false brothers brought in secretly, who have crept in in order to spy on the freedom which we have in Christ Jesus.*[8] Some of them were Christians and some of them Jews, neither fully mature, who used to stir up ill will against the apostle because of their zeal for the law. This was because Paul was saying that the law was now giving way to Christ, the subject of his preaching. Finally, it was under pressure from these people that he was forced to circumcise Timothy.[9] Only a fake Christian would persecute another Christian out of zeal for the law. This is what a false brother is.

---

[1]Deut 25:3. [2]Acts 14:19. [3]Acts 27:14-44. This cannot have been what Paul meant, because it occurred later in his career. [4]Cf. Acts 27:20. [5]Cf. Acts 9:23-25. [6]Cf. Acts 23:12-22. This cannot have happened before Paul wrote this letter. [7]Acts 27:42-44. [8]Gal 2:4. [9]Acts 16:3.

If they had only been Jews, and Paul was calling them false brethren because of their Judaism, why would he have had to repeat himself? He has already spoken of the danger from his own people. No, in the eyes of the world it is not they who are the false brethren, but those who are not wholeheartedly Christian in the relationship with Christ. There were other false brothers too, like Demas and Hermogenes.[1]

27in toil and hardship, through many a sleepless night, in hunger and thirst, often without food, in cold and exposure.

It is true that toil is sometimes unrelated to hardship, but Paul added the latter word here to show that this kind of toil was pernicious. Some of Paul's sleepless nights were voluntary, but others were forced on him. When he was in dire straits he had to stay awake and seek God's help. Furthermore he taught not only in the daytime but at night as well, as he says in the Acts of the Apostles.[2]

Being frequently forced to flee by the Jews who were persecuting him, he inevitably suffered hunger and thirst because of want. He often fasted, so as to deserve the protection afforded by God's help. Someone who fasts does not have anything to eat and abstains. He was cold and exposed when he was shipwrecked, as he says: *Finally the barbarians on the island of Malta made a fire and gave us refreshment, because of the threatening storm and the cold.*[3]

28And, apart from other things, there is the daily pressure upon me of my anxiety for all the churches.

This anxiety, which he calls daily, happened because Paul adopted the habit of teaching the people entrusted to him on a daily basis. The things to which he refers earlier were brought on him by force of necessity, for daytime is given for work and night for rest. It was because necessity forced him to face all kinds of things that he used to teach at night, for he did not hesitate to put himself out so as not to appear that God had given him nothing to do.

29Who is weak, and I am not weak? Who is made to fall, and I am not indignant?

Paul is saying that he suffers in sympathy with everybody, and that he shares their pain in order to provide medicine for the wound. He presses the point in order to show how carefully he is guarding and ruling the church entrusted to him. In this way he shows that he should not be considered inferior to the other apostles, seeing, as was quite obvious, that he labored more than all of them.

Paul was working in a context of greater hostility from the Jews than the rest of the apostles, because while he was persecuting the church he was suddenly converted and became its defender, testifying and proclaiming that he had heard Christ, whom he had previously regarded as a dead man, speaking to him from heaven. Inevitably, many people accepted what he said, because they knew that there had to be a good reason for him to have changed from being a persecutor to being a defender [of the church]. For this reason, the Jews were angry and always trying to kill him.

In this context, to be *made to fall* is to experience the desires of the flesh. Because people are usually made to stumble by being attracted to the shapeliness or beauty of a body, or by the heat of their own flesh, the apostle, contemplating the inevitability of the human condition, says that he burns. He wants to show his concern for such people, sympathizing with their weakness and not condemning them, but rather urging them in humble terms to resist the stimuli of the

---

[1]2 Tim 1:15; 4:10. [2]Acts 20:31. [3]Acts 28:2.

flesh in the hope of the promised reward. His aim is that none of those who hear him will be overcome by fleshly desire, despairing of themselves and thinking that God would not think it meritorious of them if they were now to reform, and so come to ruin by persisting in those same desires.

30 If I must boast, I will boast of the things that show my weakness.

Paul is saying this because if a Christian must boast he should boast in humility, from which comes growth in God's sight. Thus elsewhere he says: *When I am weak, then I am strong.*[1] That is to say, when I am being humbled for the sake of the brothers, then I am raised up. This is what one should boast about, and not carnal descent, because one is from the seed of Abraham.

31 The God and Father of the Lord Jesus, he who is blessed for ever, knows that I do not lie.

Paul calls God as his witness in order that what he says may be readily believed, for the sake of those, at least, who were not honoring him as a true apostle.

32 At Damascus, the governor under King Aretas guarded the city of Damascus in order to seize me,

The governor of Damascus, seeing that the Jews had set a trap for the apostle, wanted to bring this wicked scheme to pass by a wrongful use of his power. He intended to capture Paul both in order to keep the Jews happy and to demonstrate that he was doing his job properly by killing a person he had heard was a trouble-maker in the interests of keeping the peace. This occurred at the very beginning of Paul's ministry.

33 but I was let down in a basket through a window in the wall, and escaped his hands.

At the same time, when the Lord appeared to Paul on the road to Damascus, the Jews were enraged to discover that the man who had come to lead believers in Christ back to Jerusalem in chains was preaching the doctrine which he had come to condemn. Thus it happened that he was let down in a basket through a window in the city wall by his disciples and escaped.

Some people say that this action was not worthy of Paul, because he was not set free by the help of God. But what need was there for that when he could be delivered by the help of men? The time when God's help is necessary is when human help fails.

2 Corinthians 12

1 I must boast; there is nothing to be gained by it, but I will go on to visions and revelations of the Lord.

Paul says that it is not expedient for him to boast because the joy of this present life is fragile. For if he had not escaped, he would have been put to death. But because it is commanded that in the event of persecution one should flee,[2] Paul fled, using the help he had been given to do so. Nor should anyone wait for a sin to be committed against himself. Therefore he says that it was something to boast about that he had escaped. But it is not expedient to do so because of human pride. Growth comes from humility, and the help of God is given to the meek, not to the proud. Besides, someone who boasts that he has escaped a death inflicted for the sake of the faith implies that it is of no consequence to suffer for Christ. It is therefore not expedient to boast.

Paul is now going to describe how he has

---

[1] 2 Cor 12:10. [2] Cf. Mt 10:23.

been raised up in order that the Corinthians might understand how great and how wonderful the things said to him were, and that they might realize that he is not inferior in any way to the other apostles, as some of them thought he was.

2I know a man in Christ who fourteen years ago was caught up to the third heaven—whether in the body or out of the body I do not know, God knows.

Paul mentions both things because he recognized that either is possible; he could have been caught up in his body or else not in it. It may seem to someone that it is nothing much for a man in Christ to be caught up into the third heaven, since that is where the moon is, but that is not right. What this means is that he was caught up beyond all the stars of the universe into the heaven which is third in the hierarchy of spiritual heavens.

3And I know that this man was caught up into Paradise—whether in the body or out of the body I do not know, God knows—4and he heard things that cannot be told, which man may not utter.

Paul says that he was caught up twice—first into the third heaven and then into Paradise, which is where the Lord said that the thief on the cross would be with him *in the Paradise of the Father.*[1] No wonder it is believed that after the resurrection, the body, which will then be purged of its sin and heaviness, will be in the heavens, if the apostle has no doubt that his own body, while still mortal, had been able to be lifted into the heavens and carried up to the celestial Paradise of God the Father.

5On behalf of this man I will boast, but on my own behalf I will not boast, except of my weaknesses.

He says that he is boasting of such a man, that is, one who is so worthy in God's sight as to have had this experience, and does not want to say openly that he is talking about himself, for fear that he might be thought to be praising himself. The apostle John too, although it is known that he was speaking about himself, says: *This is the disciple whom Jesus loved, who laid back on his breast at supper,*[2] because he did not want to appear to be speaking about himself in a self-glorifying way.

Paul does not boast about himself insofar as he does not make an open assertion about himself. He is saying that he will certainly boast about his weaknesses though. Indeed, giving an account of hardships in sufferings and of weaknesses in dire straits does not seem boastful but pitiable. He says therefore that he is glorying in those things, knowing however that they lead to the attainment of heavenly rewards. For what self-glorification is so great for a Christian contemplating the future as to relate the troubles inflicted upon him for the sake of Christ?

6Though if I wish to boast, I shall not be a fool, for I shall be speaking the truth. But I refrain from it, so that no one may think more of me than he sees in me or hears from me.

Paul says this because if someone proclaims his own worth in God's sight he is not unwise, for what he says is true. So if anyone talks about the things which have been revealed to him he is not foolish, though if he keeps quiet about them he is wise.

Here Paul makes clear why he is not openly boasting. What he is saying is, *For fear that anyone should think I am enlarging my reputation beyond what the limited nature of my merits permits.* He is referring to the people who defamed him, as I have noted above. It is certainly good not to be silent about the rewards

---

[1]Lk 23:43. The text does not include the words *of the Father.* [2]Jn 13:23.

earned, so that believers may be won to the faith.

[7]And to keep me from being too elated by the abundance of revelations, a thorn was given me in the flesh, a messenger of Satan, to harass me, to keep me from being too elated.

Paul is testifying that God makes provision for those who have done well, while at the same time he allows them to be cast down by various trials. This is both so that they shall not be deprived of the fruits of their labors, but also that they may be enriched by their trials so that they may have even greater eternal rewards. This remedy was given to the apostle so that he could not become elated by the greatness of the revelations, being oppressed in mind by the injuries he received, for he thought it was inevitable that a heart at leisure would be elated by the things that he had seen.

[8]Three times I besought the Lord about this, that it should leave me; [9]but he said to me, "My grace is sufficient for you, for my power is made perfect in weakness." I will all the more gladly boast of my weaknesses, that the power of Christ may rest upon me.

These are the goads of the devil, which he uses in order to harm the servants of God by inserting them treacherously into their minds. Paul is saying that although he prayed three times to the Lord, asking that they might leave him, he did not succeed in having his request granted. It is not that he was saying that he had been disregarded, but that he was unwittingly making a plea which was against his own best interests, asking that trials would depart from him when in fact he was being made more perfect by them. Therefore he says to the Romans: *For we do not know what to pray for in a way that is right.*[1]

Hence he says that the answer he received was this: that the grace of God was sufficient for him, either because his powers of endurance were being strengthened, or because the time of his affliction was being shortened. He wanted them to see that his devotion was proved because he was not broken by the weakness which resulted from the affliction which kept coming upon him.

Paul is clearly teaching that the time for boasting is when one is being humiliated by unjust injuries. Christ gives us the power to endure these so that what previously appeared to be painful and loathsome may be accepted with gladness and be soothed by the help of Christ. He is therefore saying that he is glad to receive beatings, as long as he is cured by Christ, knowing that the healing power of Christ contributes more to salvation than his weakness takes away from his health.

[10]For the sake of Christ, then, I am content with weaknesses, insults, hardships, persecutions, and calamities; for when I am weak, then I am strong.

It is true that the time when a Christian is victorious is when he is thought to be losing and that unbelief is the loser at the time when it congratulates itself on having won. Paul therefore applauds when insult is cast upon him, and he rises up when he is oppressed.

[11]I have been a fool! You forced me to it, for I ought to have been commended by you. For I was not at all inferior to these superlative apostles, even though I am nothing.

Paul is saying that he has been forced to disclose the truth of the matter. He is certainly not foolish, having spoken the truth about himself, but is abasing himself in this way in order to make it clear that he is not putting his

---

[1]Rom 8:26.

own merits on display voluntarily.

It is obvious that these people, among whom he founded a church and showed miraculous signs of his apostolic calling, should have given him a testimonial to show to his defamers, and so defended him, the man whom they had as their father in the gospel of Christ, without his having to say anything.

These apostles appeared to be *superlative* to some people, though they were just the same as the apostle Paul was. He is saying this because he was not their inferior in preaching or in miracle-working, but only a later arrival in time. If we have to write at length about precedence in time, John [the Baptist] began to preach before Christ, and it was not Christ who baptized John, but John who baptized Christ.[1] God did not judge the matter this way [in terms of chronological order]. Furthermore, Andrew became a disciple of the Savior before Peter did, and yet it was not Andrew who was the chief apostle but Peter.

Why was it then that Paul appeared to some people not to be an apostle, when by the grace of God he had the power to do the same things as the apostles also did? Paul therefore feels pain, and under compulsion reveals what reward he has earned on the Lord's reckoning. He is therefore saying that not only is he not forced to declare that he was a lesser man, but that he had labored more than all of them.[2]

This did not please those who, out of misguided zeal for the law of their ancestors, rejected his preaching as being that of an enemy of Moses' teaching, because he said that the law was coming to an end and did not seem to them to be an apostle at all. Instead they preferred the other apostles because they were not so adamantly opposed to the law, and took a poor view of Paul in comparison with them.

[12]The signs of a true apostle were performed among you in all patience, with signs and wonders and mighty works.

Paul humbles himself only to rise to his true height. He talks about his patience because for a long time he put up with them as if they were sick people. His intention was to cure them of their errors by using the medicine of signs and wonders.

[13]For in what were you less favored than the rest of the churches, except that I myself did not burden you? Forgive me this wrong!

Paul is still recommending himself by using humility, for he is making it clear that the Corinthians had nothing less than what the other churches had, and indeed had more than they did. He preached the gospel to them for no payment, which was something not permitted to any of the churches, according to the Lord's saying: *The workman is deserving of his pay.*[3] So he says, *If I deserve wrong in return for my good deed, forgive me.* Every fool is an accuser of a good man. Paul asks forgiveness from them for a deed which in reality merits praise, in order to expose them for what they are.

[14]Here for the third time I am ready to come to you. And I will not be a burden, for I seek not what is yours but you; for children ought not to lay up for their parents, but parents for their children.

Paul says this perhaps to avoid being thought to have adopted this practice at the start as a way of commending himself to them, but later on to be willing to take payment from them for preaching the gospel. He is making it clear that he is steadfast in this resolve, out of fear that later on he might seem to be changing his behavior, and that then there would be some-

---

[1]Cf. Mk 1:2-11. [2]Cf. 1 Cor 15:10. [3]Lk 10:7.

thing for which he might be blamed by hostile critics.

Paul is making it clear that he did not want to accept money from them, because his aim was to win the Corinthians themselves. Once they understood that he attached more importance to them than to their money, they would come to appreciate his affection for them.

Paul means that he is their father, as he said in his first letter: *Through the gospel I begat you.*[1] It is parents in the physical sense who save money for their children, whereas spiritual fathers ought to receive payment for sustaining this present life. It is no great matter for those who teach spiritual things to receive material rewards in payment. But Paul is giving such strong confirmation of the fact that he is unwilling to take money that he metaphorically applies terms suitable to a physical father to one who is a spiritual father instead. Not only does he not want to receive anything from them—he wants to give them something! This accords with what he has already said above: *I robbed other churches, accepting support for my service to you.*[2] By saying this, he is giving them a prod so that they may understand what a great man he is and what they deserve for having failed to appreciate the wise provision made by such a great apostle.

[15]I will most gladly spend and be spent for your souls. If I love you the more, am I to be loved the less?

Now Paul is openly expressing the love and affection which he has for them, since he is prepared not only to spend lavishly on their behalf, but even to die for the salvation of their souls. Similarly, the apostle John also says that, following the example of the Savior, *we ought to lay down our lives.*[3]

Paul calls on the Corinthians to be loving because they ought to love him more, especially as he was the one through whom they had heard the way of salvation and by whom they were also won for God, being made believers instead of unbelievers and purified instead of defiled.

[16]But granting that I myself did not burden you, I was crafty, you say, and got the better of you by guile.

Paul makes explicit all the charges which an opponent might make against him in order to clear himself on all counts. For he did not deal deviously with the Corinthians but straightforwardly, with a single purpose where he himself was concerned and two purposes with regard to them. Where they were concerned, he wanted to make provision for them in the sight of God and not seek their wealth in this life. For himself, God's promise to him for the future would be enough. He might have been suspected of despising them because the sums which they offered him were too small, and that he thought he should be paid more, so that considering his merits, he was not rejecting money but regarding it with contempt because the [small] amount was unworthy of him.

[17]Did I take advantage of you through any of those whom I sent to you?

Paul is saying that the people whom he sent to them did not suggest that if they wanted the apostle to be well-disposed toward them they should offer him an amount [of money] commensurate with his personal standing. In that case they would have realized that a cunning plot had been devised by the apostle, and it would be demonstrated that Paul had acted not only out of contempt but out of greed.

[18]I urged Titus to go, and sent the brother with

---

[1] 1 Cor 4:15. [2] 2 Cor 11:8. [3] 1 Jn 3:16.

him. Did Titus take advantage of you? Did we not act in the same spirit? Did we not take the same steps?

It is obvious that since nothing like this was done by any of Paul's colleagues, the unanimous verdict on him was that he was of good character, with no trace of greed in him.

[19]*Have you been thinking all along that we have been defending ourselves before you? It is in the sight of God that we have been speaking in Christ, and all for your upbuilding, beloved.*

What Paul is saying is this: *You have been doubtful about this for a long time, thinking that we are not dealing with you straightforwardly.* They were being stirred up by the false apostles who wanted to rob them and so were claiming that the apostle was acting deceitfully, presumably because he wanted to get more out of them.

Paul is so eager for the Corinthians to have a true and good opinion of him that he is using reasoned argument and direct testimony to assure them that he is presenting himself in this way not in order to further his own advantage but to build them up. He thinks that in this way he may indeed encourage them to love him, without becoming a burden on their finances or compromising the authority of his power to rebuke their vices. There is no doubt that it is to the advantage of someone who is rebuked in order that he should mend his ways, if the person in charge of him refuses offerings in order to be free to rebuke.

[20]*For I fear that perhaps I may come and find you not what I wish, and that you may find me not what you wish; that perhaps there may be quarreling, jealousy, anger, selfishness, slander, gossip, conceit, and disorder.*

Since it has not yet happened that all those he has rebuked in the first letter have corrected the vices of which they were charged, Paul wishes, when he goes to them, to appear to do so as a man of authority, so that being frightened they might reform and he might find them as he wants them to be.

He says this with the aim that they may appear as they should be in the company of an apostle, and that both sides may take great delight in each other. A person finds someone else quite different from what he would wish if he makes himself so disposed as to be at odds with him.

Finally, he is referring to the errors which he rebukes in the previous letter, where they were in a state of internal dissension, denouncing individuals and asserting the priority of one man over another.

[21]*I fear that when I come again my God may humble me before you, and I may have to mourn over many of those who sinned before and have not repented of the impurity, immorality, and licentiousness which they have practiced.*

Paul is giving this warning in advance, so that he will not find them the same as they were long before, with their different vices which consisted of actions or particular charges— particular charges, because every action is blameless in itself, but the charge of disorder makes it wrong. Something becomes illicit when it is done in a way which is prohibited.

Paul is saying that he is being humbled by those sinners because, like a devoted father, he is starting to complain about the sins of his children. What father would not rejoice when his sons behave well? Thus it is inevitable that he should mourn once again if they behave badly. So he is giving a warning that if they have not repented of their previous acts of fornication or other uncleanness or unchastity, they should do it now, the way others have done (as he hints). If that happens, he will have nothing to be upset about when he comes.

When he says: *I may have to mourn over many of those who sinned before and have not repented*, Paul is saying that some have repented but others have not. This contradicts Novatian, who claims that fornicators cannot repent or be received back into communion. Paul is affirming that they have indeed repented, and because of this they have been received back into the peace of the church. He is affirming the existence of three types of sins when he mentions fornication, unchastity and uncleanness.

2 Corinthians 13

¹This is the third time I am coming to you. Any charge must be sustained by the evidence of two or three witnesses.

Paul has already said that he is prepared, now that he is about to come. He is here appealing to the law, according to which any person is to be acquitted or condemned by two or three witnesses. He is issuing a warning that when he comes, the Corinthians must also be acquitted in this way.

²I warned those who sinned before and all the others, and I warn them now while absent, as I did when present on my second visit, that if I come again I will not spare them—

Paul means that earlier, when he was with them, he had told them to mend their ways, so as not to be rebuked to their shame. Now again, he is affirming that in his absence he is saying the same thing, so that after the second rebuke, if they have not reformed, there may be no case for leniency toward them.

³since you desire proof that Christ is speaking in me. He is not weak in dealing with you, but is powerful in you.

The Corinthians are seeking proof that Christ

is speaking in the apostle when they do not obey his teachings, wanting to test him to see whether he will dare to exact retribution and thus be understood to be of reliable authority, so that he may be feared in the future. For someone who despises a teacher is looking to be corrected.

Christ is powerful among the Corinthians because they have seen the dead raised up in his name, demons put to flight, the paralyzed recovered, the deaf given hearing, speech restored to the dumb, the lame running and the blind seeing. These are all acts of power and not weakness. Finally, as a result of this they have been drawn to the faith.

⁴For he was crucified in weakness, but lives by the power of God. For we are weak in him, but in dealing with you we shall live with him by the power of God.

It is true that Christ was crucified because of our sins, so that by destroying death, he would free from death those who believed in him. He therefore allowed himself to be made weak on our behalf in order to conquer death for us. For by descending to the dead, he who knew no sin at all and had been killed as if he were a sinner abolished the sentence of Adam, so that for the rest of time those who die in his name would not be held captive by death, but would have the sure hope of going to heaven. Therefore, having been killed because of our weakness, he came to life again through the power of the Father, so as to prove to his disciples that his teachings were true, giving an example of them in his own person.

We are weak in him. Paul is referring here to the personal experience of the apostles, who were made weak by being treated badly, imprisoned and beaten. It is clear that if they were made weak by unbelievers, this weakness did not occur among believers, but rather success, because believers are made strong by being weak. Death inflicted by unbelievers is life as far as believers are concerned, for they will rise again through the power of God to live with Christ.

⁵Examine yourselves, to see whether you are holding to your faith. Test yourselves. Do you not realize that Jesus Christ is in you?—unless indeed you fail to meet the test!

Paul is teaching that the brothers should sort this matter out among themselves; they get more upset if they consult with one another. He therefore wanted this business of making proof to be understood as a trial, because all proving is a trial, though not every trial is a proving. If God is said to make trial that is a proving [of someone's worth], but if the devil is said to make trial, that is a temptation, because he is trying to overthrow someone. A man sometimes makes trial in order to prove someone's worth, but sometimes he does it to trap another person instead.

Paul is saying this because if we do not know how to put one another to the test, we do not know whether Christ is in us or not. To fail to meet the test is not to know the faith inherent in our religion or profession. A person who has a sense of faith in his heart knows that Jesus Christ is within him.

⁶I hope you will find out that we have not failed.

Paul is calling them to a knowledge of the faith and an upright life. Once they have recognized the authority of the apostle and his worth in God's sight, they will start to be concerned about themselves.

⁷But we pray God that you may not do wrong—not that we may appear to have met the test, but that you may do what is right, though we may seem to have failed.

Paul is praying for them with the same affection as always, that they may abstain from evil things, *not that we may appear to have met the test,* he says, that is, not that we may seem to have authority while you are sinning, *but that you may do what is right, though we may seem to have failed.* What is this? Is the apostle praying that he might seem to have failed? Surely not! Rather, what he is praying for is this, that he and his colleagues will be humbled, as it were, by seeing the Corinthians so well behaved that he will not dare rebuke them. If they are humbled in this way, they will appear to have failed, for it is when they judge sinners with the authority granted to them that they are seen to be approved as genuine by God. If then there are no people for them to judge, it looks as if they have failed through the lessening of their authority.

⁸For we cannot do anything against the truth, but only for the truth.

Paul is saying this because power is not given against the truth. They cannot reprove someone who is living a good life, but only someone who is an enemy of the law. This power will come to nothing if people have done what is good. Hence he says to the Romans: *Do you want not to fear power? Do good, and you will have praise from that power.*[1] Since therefore it is by doing good that a person does not fear power, power is made powerless in him. This is in a sense to have failed, because the factor by which he is approved as genuine comes to nothing.

⁹For we are glad when we are weak and you are strong. What we pray for is your improvement.

To be weak is not to exercise power. Paul wants the Corinthians to be strong so that by

---

[1] Rom 13:3.

good behavior they may overcome their vices and avoid being punished or rebuked. The petition in his prayer is that they should be made perfect in this and should not sin, since they have been brought to fulfillment in the power of a good life and in uncorrupted faith.

[10]I write this while I am away from you, in order that when I come I may not have to be severe in my use of the authority which the Lord has given me for building up and not for tearing down.

It is self-evident that he is giving a warning while absent, with the intention that he may find them behaving better, and so when he comes, he will not have to rebuke them shamefully, making the sinners blush in the assembly of the brethren.

[11]Finally, brethren, farewell. Mend your ways, heed my appeal, agree with one another, live in peace, and the God of love and peace will be with you.

The joy referred to here will come when the Corinthians mend their ways, after which it will be possible for perfection to come too. But before that there will be consolation, enabling them to abandon the pleasure of the present in favor of hope for things to come. He tells them to be of one mind because of their previous state of disagreement. They should all think alike, and if they are in agreement they will have peace. The God of peace is Christ, who said: *My peace I give you, my peace I leave you.*[1] He is also the God of love, because again he says: *I give you a new commandment, that you love one another*, and *In this everyone shall know that you are my disciples, if you have for one another the love with which I have loved you.*[2]

The peace of God is one thing, but the peace of the world is another. Even malign and foul people in the world have peace, but it works to their damnation. The peace of Christ is free from sins, because it flees faithlessness, spurns trickery and rejects evil deeds. This peace is pleasing and congenial to God and inimical to the devil. A person who has peace will also have love, and the God of both will protect him forever.

[12]Greet one another with a holy kiss. [13]All the saints greet you.

This is a church way of greeting. These kisses are spiritual, not carnal. Through bodily embracing they bring about a coupling of minds with a longing that does not belong to the flesh but to the spirit.

Paul is calling the Corinthians to holiness, so that they may be bold enough to return the greeting of the saints. For they are greeted by the saints with the intention that they should imitate them.

[14]The grace of the Lord Jesus Christ and the love of God and the fellowship of the Holy Spirit be with you all.

Here is the intertwining of the Trinity and the unity of power which brings all salvation to fulfillment. The love of God has sent us Jesus the Savior, by whose grace we have been saved. The fellowship of the Holy Spirit makes it possible for us to possess the grace of salvation, for he guards those who are loved by God and saved by the grace of Christ, so that the completeness of the Three may be the saving fulfillment of mankind.

---

[1]Jn 14:27. [2]Jn 13:34-35.

Scripture Index